W9-DDX-120

ISSUES IN INTERNET LAW
Society, Technology, and the Law

by Dr. Keith B. Darrell

Issues In Internet Law
By Dr. Keith B. Darrell
Amber Book Company
www.amberbookcompany.com
U.S.A.

Cover Photograph by Marc S. Sillman

Cover Concept & Design by Keith B. Darrell

Library of Congress Catalog Card Number: 2007939811
Issues In Internet Law / Keith B. Darrell

Inquiries regarding foreign rights and translation rights should be addressed to
info@AmberBookCompany.com.

ISBN: 978-0-9771611-4-0

Third Edition • December 2007

Dedicated to my grandmother, Muriel S. Patiteaux,
on her 97th birthday, January 17, 2008.

ACKNOWLEDGEMENTS

This book would not have been possible without the contributions of many individuals. Some contributed moral support and encouragement, some technical prowess and support, some graciously allowed the use of their documents, while others contributed by being active participants in the development of Internet law. The latter group, and those who chronicled their exploits before me, are acknowledged separately in the footnotes that accompany this volume.

Deep within the pages of this book lurks the profound influence of many teachers who made time to help me learn to read, listen, think, and write: Russell Brines, William J. Carney, Betty Owen, John Smolko, and Cindy J. Wilmer.

Several other colleagues carefully read portions of the manuscript in its later stages and offered excellent suggestions for revisions: Larry Brown, Scott Greenberg, Batton Lash, and Jeremy Pound.

Several individuals allowed me to publish their e-mails or contracts so that my readers could learn from them: Carol Moncrief, John Parker, Denise Schmeichler, and Dan Wallach.

Finally, there are those individuals whose very presence provided continual encouragement throughout this project: Rino diStefano, Hero Joy Nightingale, Alison Pestcoe, Adrienne Sillman, Marc Sillman, and of course, Amber.

PREFACE TO THE 3ʳᵈ EDITION

In the BBC TV series "*Black Adder*," Samuel Johnson presents his new book "the dictionary" to the prince regent, explaining that it has been his life's work for the past 40 years to write a book containing every word in the English language.[1] "How frabjupulous!" Rowan Atkinson, in the title role, snidely remarks. Johnson's face betrays an involuntary grimace as he realizes the word frabjupulous (made up on the spot by Black Adder) is not in his book. Black Adder continues to pepper his conversation with more imaginary words until the frustrated Johnson rips the pages from his book and tosses them into the fireplace, resigned to return to the drawing board. Like Johnson, I begin each new edition filled with pride borne of accomplishment, but as work begins on the subsequent edition, I too, feel the urge to rip out pages of the earlier edition and consign them to the fire pits of some nether region.

Law does not exist in a vacuum. Laws are a response to societal needs, often stimulated by technological change. Thousands of years ago, societies crafted laws to deal with false and malicious statements spread orally by their members (slander). With the advent of the printing press, such lies (libel) were able to be endowed with both permanence and the ability to travel unaided by human voice or physical accompaniment; indeed, one could anonymously post a flyer filled with lies and misrepresentations about another individual for all eyes in the kingdom to view. Another thousand year leap has turned that anonymous flyer on a tree into an Internet post that reaches all eyes worldwide and instantly achieves viral permanence.

While the Internet has created a new stage upon which for society to act, it is merely an extension of society itself. As one of the Internet's founding fathers, Vincent Cerf, stated, "Most of the content on the network is contributed by the users of the Internet. So what we're seeing on the net is a reflection of the society we live in."[2] He correctly points out that we do not need to fix the Internet with a slew of new laws but rather need to address those societal ills directly. "When you have a problem in the mirror you do not fix the mirror, you fix that which is reflected in the mirror." Or to paraphrase Walt Kelly, "We have met the Internet and it is us."

End Notes

[1] "Ink and Incapacity," Black Adder the Third, BBC television, original air date September 24, 1987.
[2] "Call to Regulate the Net Rejected," BBC News, August 29, 2007.
[3] *Ibid.*
[4] Walt Kelly, Pogo comic strip, 1970: "We have met the enemy and he is us."

PREFACE TO THE 2ⁿᵈ EDITION

Here we go again. A lot has happened in the short time since the first edition. But then, that's the point, isn't it? This book is about change. Change brought on by advances in technology and the effects on society and, in turn, how the law copes with those changes.

This is not meant to be a "law book" — at least not in the sense that you can turn to a page and immediately read a definitive answer as to what the state of the law is on any given topic. In the Internet Age, in a world where changes occur at light speed on a daily basis, the only state of the law (at least as it relates to technology) is the state of flux.

This book is written on three levels. The first focuses on explaining new advances in technology, albeit in a simplistic manner. It is assumed that the reader is not a computer geek (although many are) and merely knows how to boot up his or her computer. Technical phrases are defined along the way and there is also a glossary of technical terms in the back of the book. Just enough technical detail is provided so that the reader can visualize the situation. Those seeking a more detailed explanation of how things work should peruse the footnotes and read some of the source material in the citations.

The second level is a view through the prism of society and culture. Advances in technology have always changed societies, and there has never been as far-reaching and profound an advance as the Internet. By reaching across all borders into all societies and cultures, the Internet has created a single virtual world — a melting pot where each society's cultures, mores, and values are interchanged. Differing political, religious, and cultural ideas, practices and beliefs assail web visitors at each mouse click. From the comfort of your living room you can enter the website, *i.e.*, the world, of a Muslim boy in Afghanistan, a Russian girl in the Ukraine, a Japanese student, a Klansman in Alabama, a gay man in San Francisco, or a bedridden woman whose only contact with the outside world is the Internet. A woman in China learns what life is like for her counterpart in London; a Jewish boy reads the daily blog of an Arab teenager, while an evangelical preacher's son reads the online diary of a young man describing coming to grips with the realization of his own homosexuality. It would be impossible for the Internet not to change the very fabric of every society on earth.

Some nations want to block access to, or at least filter, content on the Internet. Marketers realize the Internet provides unsurpassed access to consumers, but such access may entail threats to privacy, manipulation of children, risk of fraud, and undesired annoyances such as spam. The Internet has become the world's largest, most pervasive soapbox where anyone and everyone can have his 15 minutes of fame. But the downside of such unlimited global access is that the megaphone of the Internet can be used to disseminate misinformation, libel, and hate speech. Laws are required to protect consumers, investors, children, and those who are defamed, or subjected to hate speech. But with hundreds of nations, each with its own jurisprudence, cultural and societal mores, philosophies, and legal systems, which laws will prevail and — even if every nation on earth shared the same jurisprudence — how could any single nation apply its laws to a technology that knows no boundaries? The Internet is like a giant snake slithering across every country — each nation focuses on the portion of the snake it sees (rather than the snake as a whole) and tries to apply its jurisprudence to that portion. The third level of this book looks at the attempts of nations to overlay their laws upon the Internet.

Once again, it is assumed the reader is not a lawyer (although many may be). While lawyers may find this book to be an excellent survey of legal issues arising from the Internet, it is written for the non-lawyer, and as such is not as in-depth as an attorney would most likely require; however, for the attorney or law student unfamiliar with the numerous issues in Internet law, this book does provide a basic foundation and a good starting point — for the journey on the information superhighway must begin with a first step.

PREFACE

Webster's Dictionary defines serendipity as "the faculty or phenomenon of finding valuable or agreeable things not sought for." The Fixx distilled the essence of serendipity even simpler in their song "One Thing Leads to Another." And therein lies the origin of this book you are now reading.

Serendipity. I had a small retail business when commercial websites were first beginning to appear on the Internet. I hired a local web design company to create a website for my business. Two months and $600 later, I had an unfinished website and they had abandoned their nearby office. I resolved to learn how to create my own website. It was quite possibly the best $600 I ever lost, because I so thoroughly enjoyed working with this new technology that I later started my own web design company. One thing leads to another.

Serendipity. Several years into my web design business, I decided to promote the business by teaching at local colleges and adult education programs. I approached the first school with three proposals — a web design class, an HTML class and, as a throw-away notion, an Internet law class. They informed me they already had instructors teaching web design and HTML and, as I dejectedly headed toward the door, I heard in a trailing voice, "but this Internet law proposal looks interesting…" One thing leads to another.

Serendipity. I scoured high and low searching for a suitable textbook on Internet law that I could assign to my students. Surprisingly, I found very few dealing with the subject and those that were available were geared toward law schools, *i.e.,* very expensive and extremely technical. Since my audience were probably not going to be lawyers and were unlikely to spend more than $100 on a textbook, my search came up empty-handed. Someone should really write a straight-forward and affordable book on Internet law for the average person, I thought. One thing leads to another.

INTRODUCTION

As the Internet continues its development from a nascent technology to an integral part of our daily personal and business lives, it will have a profound effect on the way we interact with others, both personally and professionally. Many legal issues familiar in the "offline" world will also arise in an "online" context. While legislative bodies struggle to understand the new medium and draft laws that will adequately address these new issues, it is more often than not left up to the courts to interpret and apply existing laws and court decisions to issues of Internet law. Many of these laws, including for example, the First Amendment to the U.S. Constitution drafted more than two centuries ago, were written by men who could not conceive of the new technologies (*e.g.,* telephones, fax machines, computers, and the Internet) to which their words would be applied today.

Both the legislatures and the courts must distill the fundamental legal concepts ingrained within the framework of those early cases and statutes and apply them to the issues arising from the 21st century application of new technologies. The Internet is an innovation that opens a Pandora's Box of legal issues to be painted upon a canvas of myriad nations, or as Canadian Justice Sharlow commented:[1]

> The issue of the proper balance in matters of copyright plays out against the much larger conundrum of trying to apply national laws to a fast-evolving technology that in essence respects no national boundaries. Thus in *Citron v. Zündel*,[2] the Canadian Human Rights Tribunal wrestled with jurisdiction over an alleged hate website supplied with content from Toronto but posted from a host server in California. In *Reference re Earth Future Lottery*,[3] the issue was whether sales of tickets from an Internet lottery in Prince Edward Island constituted gambling "in the province" when almost all of the targeted on-line purchasers resided elsewhere. The "cyber libel" cases multiply. In *Braintech, Inc. v. Kostiuk*,[4] the British Columbia Court of Appeal refused to enforce a Texas judgment for Internet defamation against a B.C. resident where the B.C. resident's only connection with Texas was "passive posting on an electronic bulletin board."[5] There was no proof that anyone in Texas had actually looked at it. On the other hand, in *Dow Jones & Co. v. Gutnick*,[6] the High Court of Australia accepted jurisdiction over a defamation action in respect of material uploaded onto the defendant's server in New Jersey and downloaded by end users in the State of Victoria. The issue of global forum shopping for actions for Internet torts has scarcely been addressed. The availability of child pornography on the Internet is a matter of serious concern. E-Commerce is growing. Internet liability is thus a vast field where the legal harvest is only beginning to ripen.

So who needs to know about Internet law? Perhaps you are about to make a website for yourself, or your company or organization. Or maybe you already have an online business. You may simply engage in e-commerce by buying things online. In short, just about anyone who comes in contact with the Internet can benefit from an understanding of the legal issues related to the

Internet. Such contact may come through surfing the World Wide Web, participating in a Usenet newsgroup or List Serv, or in a chat room or online forum, or by sending or receiving e-mail.

The contact may involve issues of commerce and contract law, or sexual harassment in the workplace, or freedom of speech, or invasion of privacy. Suppose you buy something online; was that online contract you clicked on really enforceable, even if you just scrolled down and did not read it? Does receiving pornography in the office e-mail from other employees constitute sexual harassment? Can someone insult you online and get away with it? Can they find information online to stalk you? What can you legally place on your website? And what are you not legally allowed to put on your website? Do you own your domain name? Can a public library censor your use of its Internet-linked computers? Can someone else read your e-mail? Is it legal to gamble online? How "private" is your private information after you disclose it to a website? Is a student exercising his First Amendment rights when he creates a hate website on a public school's Internet server? Do other countries address these issues differently from the U.S.? Which country's laws apply on the Internet? These are just some of the issues we will address in this book.

This book can be read by the average person to develop an awareness of issues in Internet law. It can also be used as a textbook. In the latter capacity, each chapter contains a quiz with answers in the Appendix. The Cases Section on the Issues in Internet Law website (www.IssuesinInternetLaw. com) contains a selection of court cases dealing with subjects that are referred to throughout the book. These cases have been edited and condensed from their original size because the casual reader would be unlikely to wade through the full-length decisions, especially since many decisions digress from the topic that the case is being used to illustrate. Thus, the edited cases presented on the website are illustrative, not inexhaustible; the interested reader is encouraged to seek out the full, unedited versions through either the case citations or the footnoted hyperlinks provided within the text.

To paraphrase Justice Shaw above, Internet law "is thus a vast field where the legal harvest is only beginning to ripen." With that in mind, the reader is urged to visit the www.IssuesInInternetLaw. com website regularly to view updates in the law which have occurred since this book's publication.

End Notes

[1] *Society of Composers, Authors & Music Publishers of Canada v. Canadian Ass'n. of Internet Providers*, 2004 SCC 45. This case is included in the Cases Section on the Issues in Internet Law website (www.IssuesinInternetLaw. com).

[2] (18 January 2002), T460/1596 (Can. H.R.Trib.).

[3] [2003] 1 S.C.R. 123, 2003 SCC 10.

[4] (1999), 171 D.L.R. (4th) 46 (CA) [leave denied [1999] S.C.C.A. No. 236].

[5] *Ibid*, (para. 66).

[6] (2002), 194 A.L.R. 433, 2002 HCA 56.

DISCLAIMER

There is a reason that this book is titled *"Issues* in Internet Law." This book is designed to serve as a red flag for issues in Internet law. A good lawyer does not know the law; he only knows where to find it. That is because the law is constantly changing and varies by jurisdiction. Even more so, in an area where a new technology is involved, such as the Internet, the law can change daily. This book cannot and does not attempt to state what "the law" is; it merely seeks to make the reader aware of legal issues surrounding the Internet; it is the responsibility of the reader to ascertain, on his own or through use of legal counsel, what the exact nature of the law is in his jurisdiction and how it may apply to his unique circumstances. This book is sold with the understanding that neither the publisher nor the author is engaged in rendering legal services. DO NOT RELY ON THIS BOOK FOR LEGAL ADVICE; if legal or other expertise is required, the reader is advised to seek the services of a competent attorney.

Every effort has been made to make this book as complete, accurate, and up-to-date as possible. However, there may be mistakes, both typographical or in content. Therefore, this book should be used only as a general guide and considered current only up to the date of publication. Readers are urged to submit corrections on the corrections form available on the **IssuesInInternetLaw.com** website and to check the "Updates" section of that website for post-publication changes in Internet law related issues.

The quizzes and their "answers" in this book are purely meant to be illustrative of emerging issues in Internet law. The answers are not definitive "right" answers; they merely serve as an analysis of the issues raised with speculation on how courts might rule, based on rationales of previous cases. They are presented to make the reader *think*; not to provide definitive answers to legal questions.

The purpose of this book is to educate and enlighten. Neither the author nor the publisher shall have any liability or responsibility to any person or entity with respect to any loss or damage caused, or alleged to have been caused, directly or indirectly, by the information contained in this book.

Note to Teachers & Librarians

Amber Book Company values your input in making each edition of *Issues In Internet Law: Society, Technology, and the Law* an improvement over the previous edition. The technology of the Internet is changing at warp speed every year, resulting in new legal and social consequences on a near daily basis. In order to stay current, Amber Book Company has released a new edition of *Issues In Internet Law: Society, Technology, and the Law* every year for the past three years.

Teachers can help by e-mailing us, at *info@AmberBookCompany.com*, and describing how they use the book in their classrooms, what they would like to see covered in future editions, and what, if any, errors they have found in this edition. As our way of thanking you for your assistance, Amber Book Company will send complimentary copies of future editions to selected instructors.

Librarians should plan to order each and every annual edition of *Issues In Internet Law: Society, Technology, and the Law,* as even a year-old edition will quickly be made obsolete by the rapid advances in technology and law.

While you may still order copies through your traditional vendors, or through online booksellers like Amazon.com, Amber Book Company does sell direct with volume discounts. And be sure to check out some of the other fine books offered by Amber Book Company, listed in the back of this book and on our website.

Order from www.AmberBookCompany.com

Amber Book
Company

Table of Contents

PART ONE: INTRODUCTION TO LAW

CHAPTER ONE: INTRODUCTION TO LAW

PART TWO: INTELLECTUAL PROPERTY

CHAPTER TWO: COPYRIGHT BASICS

CHAPTER THREE: COPYRIGHT INFRINGEMENT

PART THREE: UNINVITED GUESTS

CHAPTER SEVEN: SPAM

CHAPTER EIGHT: CYBER CRIMES

PART FOUR: PRIVACY

CHAPTER NINE: PRIVACY AT WORK

PART FIVE: 1st AMENDMENT FREE SPEECH /FREE PRESS

CHAPTER THIRTEEN: FREE SPEECH

CHAPTER FOURTEEN: FREE SPEECH: THE DARK SIDE OF THE WEB

PART SIX: WEB CONTRACTS

CHAPTER FIFTEEN: CONTRACTS

PART SEVEN: WEB 2.0 AND BEYOND

CHAPTER SIXTEEN: ISSUES ON THE HORIZON

APPENDIX

PART ONE

INTRODUCTION TO LAW

CHAPTER ONE

INTRODUCTION TO LAW

> This chapter provides an overview of the American legal system, with special attention paid to the concepts of federalism and jurisdiction. Also discussed is how to read and evaluate a court's written opinion.

WHEN THE U.S. CONSTITUTION was written, the drafters purposely set up a system of checks and balances to disburse power amongst three distinct branches of government. This separation of powers resulted in the creation of Congress (the legislative branch), the Presidency (the executive branch), and the Judiciary (the judicial branch). The legislative branch makes laws, the executive branch enforces laws, and the judicial branch interprets those laws. The state governments also follow the three-tier separation of powers model.

How Many Jurisdictions?

Jurisdiction is the limit or territory within which a court has the power, right, or authority to interpret and apply the law. Each state has its own jurisdiction, and both laws enacted by different state legislatures and interpretation of those laws by different state courts may vary.

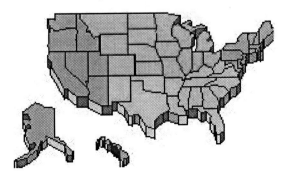

How many jurisdictions are there in the United States?

At first glance, you might guess 50, since there are 50 states. But the correct answer is 51! There are indeed 50 state jurisdictions, but the federal government also exercises jurisdiction in certain matters. This is due to the concept of *federalism*.

Federalism

Federalism is a system of government where a written constitution divides power between a centralized government and a number of regional governments. Each government is supreme within its proper sphere of authority, and both the centralized and regional governments act directly upon the people through their officials and laws. The powers of the federal government are enumerated by the U.S. Constitution. The 10th Amendment to the Constitution

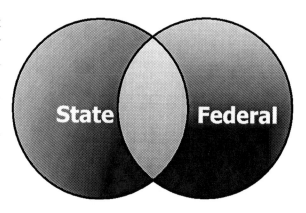

reserves to the states all powers not specifically granted to the federal government. At times, there may be overlapping areas where both the state and federal governments have an interest.

If a state law is contrary to either the U.S. Constitution or a valid federal law, then the U.S. Supreme Court can declare the state law unconstitutional. The U.S. Supreme Court can also declare laws passed by Congress unconstitutional.

American Court System Explained

• *The United States Supreme Court* consists of nine justices and is based in Washington, DC. It can hear appeals involving issues of federal law, regardless of whether the cases arise in state courts or federal courts. It may choose to accept or reject which cases it will hear; however, it must hear certain rare mandatory appeals and cases within its original jurisdiction (as specified by Article III of the U.S. Constitution).

• *The United States Court of Appeals* for the Federal Circuit (CAFC) reviews civil appeals from district courts dealing with minor claims against the U.S. government (non-tort monetary claims under $10,000),[1] appeals in patent right cases, and appeals of international trade disputes. It is unique in that it is the only one of the 13 federal circuit courts whose jurisdiction is based on subject matter rather than geography.

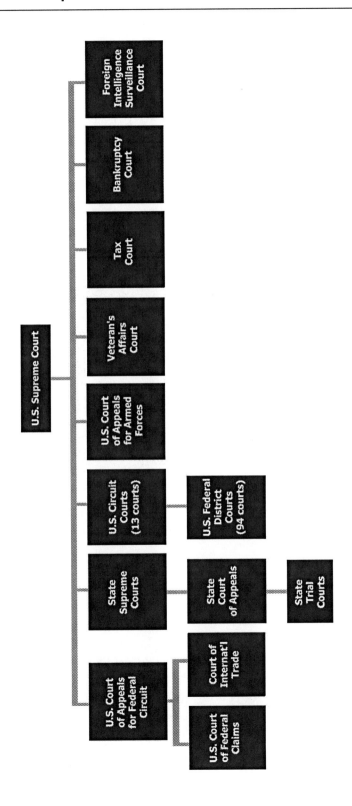

- *The United States Court of International Trade* specializes in (and its jurisdiction is limited to) cases that involve international trade and customs law. Appeals from this court go to the U.S. CAFC.

- *The United States Court of Federal Claims* (formerly the United States Claims Court) has limited jurisdiction in federal cases involving more than $10,000, conflicts from the Indian Claims Commission, and cases involving certain government contractors. Appeals from the U.S. Claims Court go to the U.S. CAFC.

- *United States Circuit Courts of Appeal* reviews cases from U.S. District Courts in their respective circuits. Each state and U.S. District Court is in one of 11 geographic circuits. Appeals from these courts go to the U.S. Supreme Court.

- *United States District Courts* consist of 94 federal district courts that handle criminal and civil cases involving federal statutes or the U.S. Constitution, admiralty and maritime cases, and civil cases between citizens from different states where the amount at stake is more than $75,000 (*i.e.*, "diversity jurisdiction").

- *The United States Tax Court* has jurisdiction involving disputes over federal income tax assessments. While other courts may also hear tax disputes, this is the only court in which taxpayers may litigate the dispute prior to paying the disputed tax amount.

- *The United States Bankruptcy Court* is a federal court that has subject matter jurisdiction over bankruptcy cases (state courts cannot hear bankruptcy cases). Each of the 94 federal judicial districts handles bankruptcy matters . Bankruptcy judges are appointed for a term of 14 years.

- *United States Court of Appeals for the Armed Forces* exercises worldwide appellate jurisdiction over U.S. military personnel on active duty and other persons subject to the Uniform Code of Military Justice. It is composed of five civilian judges appointed for 15-year terms by the president of the United States with the advice and consent of the Senate.

- *The United States Court of Appeals for Veterans Claims* hears appeals from the Board of Veterans Appeals, an administrative board that hears appeals from the Department of Veterans Affairs. Appeals from this court go to the U.S. CAFC. The court is composed of seven judges appointed for 15-year terms by the president of the United States with the advice and consent of the Senate.

- *The Foreign Intelligence Surveillance Court* has limited jurisdiction "to hear applications for and grant orders approving electronic surveillance anywhere within the United States under the procedures set forth in" the Foreign Intelligence Surveillance Act of 1978.[2] The court is composed of seven federal district court judges from different circuits, appointed by the Chief Justice for staggered terms. Individual judges review the Attorney General's applications for authorization of electronic surveillance aimed at obtaining foreign intelligence information.

- *State Supreme Courts*, called the State Supreme Court in almost all states, are the final court of appeal for all but a small number of state cases. However, if a case involves a right protected by the U.S. Constitution, then a party may appeal to the U.S. Circuit Court of Appeals.

- *State Trial Courts* are where almost all cases involving state civil and criminal laws are initially filed (typically called Municipal, County, District, Circuit, or Superior Courts). Appeals from state trial courts usually go to State Courts of Appeals.

Federal Circuit Courts

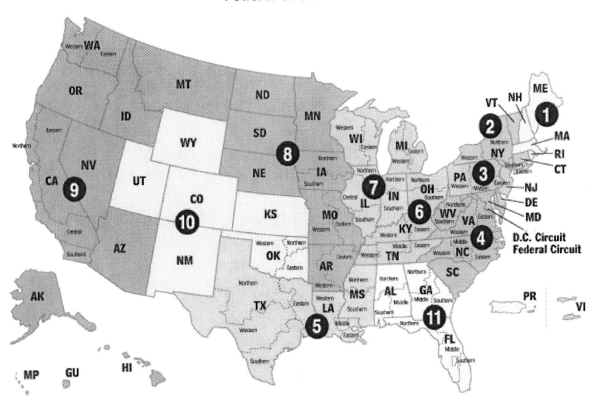

There are 13 Federal Circuits: one for the District of Columbia, the Federal Circuit (which covers the entire country) and 11 other circuits detailed below.

- 1st Circuit — Maine, Massachusetts, New Hampshire, Rhode Island, and Puerto Rico

- 2nd Circuit — Connecticut, New York, and Vermont

- 3rd Circuit — Delaware, New Jersey, Pennsylvania, and the Virgin Islands

- 4th Circuit — Maryland, North Carolina, South Carolina, Virginia, and West Virginia

- 5th Circuit — Louisiana, Mississippi, and Texas

- 6th Circuit — Kentucky, Michigan, Ohio, and Tennessee

- 7th Circuit — Illinois, Indiana, and Wisconsin

- 8th Circuit — Arkansas, Iowa, Minnesota, Missouri, Nebraska, North Dakota, and South Dakota

- 9th Circuit — Alaska, Arizona, California, Guam, Hawaii, Idaho, Montana, Nevada, Northern Mariana Islands, Oregon, and Washington

- 10th Circuit — Colorado, Kansas, New Mexico, Oklahoma, Utah, and Wyoming

- 11th Circuit — Alabama, Florida, and Georgia

- DC Circuit — District of Columbia

- Federal Circuit

Jurisdiction & Venue

As you can see, there are a lot of courts. In which court should a plaintiff (the person suing) file the lawsuit? Venue, *i.e.*, the proper location for trial of a lawsuit, is determined by whether the court has authority to hear the case. For example, venue in criminal cases is the judicial district or county where the crime was committed; and in civil cases, venue is usually the district or county where the defendant resides, where the contract was executed or is to be performed, or where the act occurred.

We said that jurisdiction involves the court's authority to hear the case. Upon review of the filed case, if the court determines that it lacks jurisdiction, it must dismiss the case. Note that by dismissing the case on the grounds of lack of jurisdiction, the court is not addressing — let alone deciding — the merits of the case; it is only deciding that it is not allowed to hear the case. To hear the case, the court must have jurisdiction over either the parties, the subject matter, or the thing in dispute. These three types of jurisdiction are known, respectively, as personal jurisdiction, subject matter jurisdiction, and *in rem* jurisdiction (Latin for "jurisdiction over the thing itself"). Since in rem jurisdiction arises relatively seldom, and since subject matter jurisdiction is relatively straightforward, most jurisdictional questions will turn on personal jurisdiction. But where is the proper place to file cyberspace lawsuits, where the dispute arises in an intangible location with parties potentially residing anywhere in the world? Before we can answer this question, we must first review the three forms of jurisdiction.

Personal Jurisdiction

Personal jurisdiction (also known as *in personam* jurisidiction, Latin for "jurisdiction over a person") asks, "Does the court have authority over the parties (*i.e.*, the defendant, the person being sued) in the dispute?" Note that the question is really does the court have authority over the defendant, since the plaintiff submits to jurisdiction simply by filing the lawsuit. There are several ways that the court may have personal jurisdiction:

- If the defendant resides or operates a business in the state

- If there is a meaningful connection or contact between the defendant and the state where the lawsuit is filed

- "Gotcha" Jurisdiction — where the defendant sets foot into the state

- If the defendant has caused an injury within the state

- "Minimum Contacts" — if a business regularly solicits business in the state, derives substantial revenue from goods or services sold in the state, or engages in some other persistent course of conduct there

- By consent, which can be through the appointment of a registered agent for service of process, or by contractual agreement, including an online click-wrap agreement

Subject Matter Jurisdiction

Subject matter jurisdiction asks, "Does the court have authority to hear the case?" As you will recall from our discussion of federalism and the 10th Amendment, all power not granted to the federal government resides with the states. Thus, state courts have *"general" jurisdiction* and can hear any type of case not exclusively delegated to federal courts. However, the federal courts have exclusive subject matter jurisdiction if the case arises under the U.S. Constitution or federal laws related to patent, bankruptcy, copyright, maritime, securities,[3] or aviation laws. In those cases, the lawsuit must be filed in federal court.

In Rem Jurisdiction

Some litigants will employ inventive means to allow their case to be tried in their desired forum. Harrods, the famous London department store ("Harrods UK"), wanted to sue its former affiliate in Buenos Aires, South America ("Harrods BA"). Harrods BA had registered 60 variations of Harrods' name with a domain name registrar in Virginia. Unable or unwilling to get jurisdiction over Harrods BA in the United Kingdom or Argentina, Harrods UK instead chose to file its trademark infringement and dilution case in Virginia, home of the registry of Internet domain names. The case, *Harrods Ltd. v. Sixty Internet Domain Names*,[4] was filed in federal court in Virginia as an *in rem* action against the 60 domain names themselves. An *action in rem* means that the plaintiff is proceeding against a "thing" as opposed to a "person" (*in personam*). The court found that in rem jurisdiction existed because the domain name registry was in Virginia. Thus the court regarded the domain name as a piece of property that can be sued in its own right. (The effect of a domain name being regarded as a property right versus a contract right is discussed at length in Chapter Five). Harrods U.K. would probably not have been able to avail itself of the tactic of seeking in rem jurisdiction against a domain name itself as a piece of property in a jurisdiction outside of the United States because most other countries view domain names as contractual, not property rights. The case illustrates an inventive method to obtain jurisdiction in a desired forum.

Jurisdiction in Cyberspace

Let us return to our question, *Where is the proper place to file cyberspace lawsuits, where the dispute arises in an intangible location with parties potentially residing anywhere in the world?* In the European Union, the answer is relatively straightforward; EU law looks to where the harm occurred and not to whether the defendant targeted a specific state. Unfortunately, the United States applies a more complex approach to finding personal jurisdiction. Rather than focusing on where the injury occurred, U.S. law looks at whether the defendant "purposefully availed" himself (or itself, in the case of a corporation) of the forum state. U.S. courts look for some action taken by the defendant to establish purposeful ties with its state; simply posting an advertisement on a website viewable in that state would not be enough to find jurisdiction, since anyone, anywhere could view the ad. (However, if the ad were targeted specifically to residents of that state, that might help the court conclude that a purposeful tie with the state had been established).

In addition to purposeful availment, the court will look to whether it was foreseeable that the defendant would be haled into court in that forum. Of course it is foreseeable that merely by establishing a website, a nonresident defendant's product or services might end up in the forum state; however, the key is whether the defendant's conduct and connection with the forum state would make it reasonable to anticipate that he would be haled into court there.[5]

Next, the court will consider fairness factors; these include the burden on the defendant, the interest of the plaintiff, and the forum state's interest (see the *Scarcella* case, below).

Finally, the court will determine if there has been sufficient minimum contact with the forum state to warrant a finding of personal jurisdiction. One method often employed is the concept of a "sliding scale of Internet activity."[6] At one end is the "active website" — here the defendant has transmitted files to the forum state or contracted with residents of the forum.[7] In the middle is the gray area of the level of "interactivity" and the commercial nature of any information exchanged.[8] At the opposite end of the spectrum is the "passive website" where only information has been posted or limited communication has occurred.[9] In the latter case, most courts would conclude that creating a website was not by itself an act purposefully directed toward the forum state. But if the defendant were to do something additional to serve or exploit the forum state (*e.g.,* directly targeting or encouraging residents of the forum state to use the website) then it might find jurisdiction.

Other factors the court might consider are: the location of the website's server, the location of the defendant's principal place of business, the defendant's state of residence, sales made by the defendant to the forum state, and solicitation of the forum state's residents by the defendant.

Jurisdictional Examples

Now let us examine some Internet jurisdiction cases. DontDateHimGirl.com was the brainchild of Miami writer Tasha C. Cunningham. Designed as the Internet equivalent of the bathroom wall, the Florida-based website invited disgruntled women to "tell all" about their bad ex-boyfriends. Todd Hollis, a Pennsylvania attorney, found himself described on the website as a herpes-ridden gay or bisexual who had passed on a sexually-transmitted disease and fathered multiple children with different women. Understandably upset, he sued Cunningham for defamation in a Pennsylvania court [10] (We will discuss the merits of this case further in Chapter 13 but it is relevent here for its procedural issues). Cunningham raised the Communications Decency Act (CDA) as a defense but the court never considered her defense or Hollis' defamation claim; instead, it dismissed the case for lack of personal jurisdiction over the defendant. The court found that Cunningham did not have sufficient minimum contacts with Pennsylvania for it to be able to exert jurisdiction over her. The website's server was in Florida, the defendant resided in Florida, and the website had solicited comments from all over and did not specifically solicit comments from Pennsylvania. Did this mean that the defendant bore no liability for the comments posted on her site, or that other sites could now engage in the same behavior with impunity? No, because the court never addressed the issues in the case; it simply said the Pennsylvania court was not the right venue to debate them. The plaintiff might find that Florida would be a more proper venue for his lawsuit against the Florida-based defendant. The Pennsylvania court might have found it had jurisdiction had Hollis sued only the Pennsylvanian residents who posted the comments about him, instead of suing the out-of-state website owner.

A New York man dissatisfied with a motor he had purchased on eBay sued the Missouri seller in a New York Court. The court held that the online auction process — consisting of a single transaction — did not rise to the level of purposeful conduct required to establish personal jurisdiction in a breach of contract action. The court ruled that a single sale, "without more, does not constitute sufficient purposeful availment to satisfy the minimum contacts necessary to justify summoning across state lines, to a New York court, the seller of an allegedly non-conforming good." [11]

In another New York case, Best Van Lines, a New York-based moving company sued [12] an Iowa resident for defamation in a New York federal court. The defendant created a gripe website (see Chapter 13 for a discussion of gripe websites), movingscam.com, soliciting posts from disgruntled customers of moving van companies. The site "provides consumer-related comments, most of them derogatory, about household movers in the United States." [13] The defendant had posted comments on the site claiming that Best Van Lines was operating without legal authorization and without the insurance required by law. Dismissing the case for lack of personal jurisdiction, the 2nd Circuit held that Best Van Lines failed to demonstrate personal jurisdiction under New York's "long-arm" statute[14] requirements because the defendant had not transacted business in New York nor had the lawsuit arisen from such transactions. Posting defamatory comments on a website accessible in New York was not enough; the requirements of the long-arm statute had to be met for a finding of personal jurisdiction.

In another case[15] involving the New York long-arm statute, a Manhattan attorney sued his aunt and uncle, Florida residents, for hacking his law firm's website and replacing his résumé with a photograph of the lawyer labeled "Pig of the Year," in which he leans back in a chair and appears to say, "I'm going to eat everything in site (sic)." The couple moved to dismiss the lawsuit claiming among other things that the court lacked personal jurisdiction. While the aunt and uncle did have certain minimum contacts with New York (both defendants had New York professional licenses although did not derive any business income from that state), the court held it did not have personal jurisdiction because the state long-arm statute set a stricter requirement for jurisdiction — while the physical presence of the defendant in New York is not required by the statute to find jurisdiction, the tortious[16] act must have been committed in New York. If, as in this case, the tortious act (*i.e.*, defamation) was committed in Florida, even if the damage from the act occurs in New York, the court will not find personal jurisdiction over the out-of-state defendants.

A U.S. district court in Virginia dismissed a lawsuit by America Online (AOL) accusing a group of Florida computer technicians of maintaining a computer network that bombarded AOL with spam, holding that simply sending e-mails through AOL's computers located in Virginia did not establish that Virginia had jurisdiction over the defendants. More than half of all worldwide Internet traffic passes through Virginia because it is home to AOL and 1,300 other Internet Service Providers (ISPs) or technology firms. The ruling would not prevent AOL from suing the defendants in Florida, where they resided. However, AOL probably chose to file suit in Virginia because it has the toughest anti-spam law in the country. In December 2003, the Virginia anti-spam statute was used to indict two North Carolina men, the first people in the U.S. to be charged with felonies for sending junk e-mail.[17] In April of 2004, a third person, the sister of one of the men, was also indicted, and a month later, a fourth person, this time from Texas, was indicted for violating Virginia's anti-spam laws. Each charge carried a sentence of one–to–five years in prison and a fine of up to $2,500. The Virginia statute targets spammers who intentionally alter an e-mail header or other routing information and try to send either 10,000 e-mails within a 24-hour period or 100,000 in a 30-day period.[18] A spammer can also be prosecuted if a specific transmission generates more than $1,000 in revenue, or if total transmissions generate $50,000. It is because of this tough anti-spam statute that ISPs such as AOL would prefer to litigate spam cases in Virginia.

Jurisdictional Balance

The Internet has changed the dynamics of legal jurisdiction. As Judge Warren Ferguson, of the 9th Circuit, wrote: [19]

> It is increasingly clear that modern businesses no longer require an actual physical presence in a state to engage in commercial activity there. Businesses may set up shop, so to speak, without ever actually setting foot in the state where they intend to sell their wares. Our conceptions of jurisdiction must be flexible enough to respond to the realities of the modern marketplace.

Companies doing business on the Internet now face the burden of having to defend against lawsuits in multiple jurisdictions anywhere, at anytime. In deciding jurisdictional questions, courts must balance the burden faced by the defendant with the legitimate interests of the plaintiff.

To avoid having to spend resources litigating all over the country, companies often place "choice of forum" clauses in their agreements with customers. AOL has such a clause in its online click-wrap agreement. However, in a recent case, AOL's "choice of forum" clause was held unenforceable. In _Scarcella v. America Online_, [20] Russell Scarcella filed a small claims action for $5,000 against AOL after an AOL technical support person told him to delete a specific folder, which he did, resulting in the loss of 1,500 e-mail addresses. Scarcella filed his claim in Manhattan's small claims court, despite the fact that the "choice of forum" clause stipulated that all claims be filed in Virginia. AOL responded by filing a motion for dismissal, arguing that the New York court lacked subject matter jurisdiction because of the "choice of forum" clause. The court denied AOL's motion to dismiss, finding the clause unenforceable on public policy grounds. "The general policy of giving effect to forum-selection clauses must yield to the scheme enacted by the legislature specifically to ensure that civil justice is meaningfully accessible to those seeking the adjudication of small claims," the court said. The court found that the public policy interest of providing an inexpensive and informal venue for small claims, _i.e._, the establishment of small claims courts, outweighed enforcement of the "choice of forum" clause. The court added, "The essential features of a small claims court are extremely low costs or none at all, no formal pleadings, no lawyers, and the direct examination of parties and witnesses without formality by a trained judge who knows and applies the substantive law," noting the expense the plaintiff would have to bear in traveling to and litigating in Virginia. AOL has appealed the decision and the decision has no effect on the enforceability of forum clauses in cases that fall outside of the requirements (_i.e.,_ dollar amounts) of small claims court.

Court Decision

Courts do not make laws. Only legislatures can enact laws. Courts interpret laws enacted by a legislative body and then apply that interpretation to a specific fact pattern.

A court's written opinion can be dissected into four parts. The first part is the *Fact Situation*; this is a description of the facts specific to the case at hand, *i.e.*, who are the players and what happened. The second part is the specific *Issue* of law raised by this fact situation; this is the issue that the court is being asked to decide. The third part is the *Holding*; this is the court's actual ruling, the answer to the question raised in the issue. This is the part that causes one side to leave the courtroom smiling while the other party displays less sanguine emotions. The holding (also called the decision or ruling) becomes a binding rule of law. The fourth part is the court's *Rationale*. This is the thought process used by the court in arriving at its decision. The rationale is extremely important because it gives observers valuable insight into how the court might apply the law in a similar circumstance, albeit with a somewhat different fact situation.

As we look at various issues in Internet law, we will encounter issues that have not been addressed yet by courts, and issues where courts in varying jurisdictions have decided the same issue in opposite ways. By studying the rationales of previous decisions, we can infer the direction a court might take on first addressing an issue or that an appellate court might take on resolving a split of opinion.

Once a court has issued its decision, its holding takes on the force of law. Courts are loath to overturn judicial rulings once they have been made, in part because doing so is a public admission of a previous mistake, but primarily because of the instability that would ensue from a constantly changing landscape of legal decisions continually being overruled. Thus the courts adhere to the concept of precedence, or *stare decisis* (Latin for "let the decision stand"). Courts will rarely overrule a previous decision, instead preferring to "*distinguish*" the fact situation of the current case from fact situation of the previous case, thus rationalizing a different result.

Court decisions are filed in the clerk's office of the courthouse and are available for the public to read or copy. A small percentage of these decisions are published in books called "*reporters*;" these reporters are published periodically and stocked by various law libraries. In this manner, an attorney in Delaware can read about a case that occurred in California. While a case from another jurisdiction has no precedential effect, the attorney may find the rationale useful in making a similar argument to his own court. Of course, if the case is from the same jurisdiction, then it can be cited as precedent.

Decisions that are not submitted to the reporters but remain filed away at the clerk's office are called "*unpublished decisions.*" Generally, unpublished decisions may not be cited as precedent; some courts do not allow unpublished decisions to be cited for any reason [21] and go so far as to sanction lawyers who cite them. [22] Published opinions differ from unpublished opinions in that they are written by judges rather than law clerks and they go through many drafts and much editing and revision before being released. It makes sense that a judge would spend more time crafting and dressing up an opinion that will be read by his peers and available worldwide than an opinion that will sit unnoticed in a file cabinet in the local courthouse. At least, that was the case until the technology of the Internet enabled unpublished decisions to be published in legal databases and on the World Wide Web. This caused a movement among some courts and lawyers pushing to allow citation of unpublished opinions. [23] Even U.S. Supreme Court Chief Justice John Roberts said "A lawyer ought to be able to tell a court what it has done." [24] The opposing view was expressed by 9th Circuit Judge Alex Kozinski, who said that because unpublished opinions are drafted by staff attorneys and law clerks instead of judges, "When the people making the sausage tell you it's not safe for human consumption, it seems strange indeed to have a committee in Washington tell people to go ahead and eat it anyway." [25] However, as Judge Richard Arnold of the 8th Circuit succinctly put it: [26]

> We do not have time to do a decent enough job, the argument runs, when put
> in plain language, to justify treating every opinion as a precedent. If this is true,
> the judicial system is indeed in serious trouble, but the remedy is not to create an
> underground body of law good for one place and time only.

In 2006, the U.S. Supreme Court adopted Rule 32.1 of the Federal Rules of Appellate Procedure requiring that federal courts allow citation of unpublished cases, effective January 1, 2007. Although the new rule allows lawyers to *cite* unpublished opinions in federal circuit courts (it does not apply to state courts), it leaves to the circuit courts' discretion the *precedential* value, if any, to be assigned to unpublished opinions. So the issue of precedence in unpublished opinions remains unresolved. To quote Judge Arnold again: [27]

> The question presented here is not whether opinions ought to be published, but
> whether they ought to have precedential effect, whether published or not. We
> point out, in addition, that "unpublished" in this context has never meant "secret."
> So far as we are aware, every opinion and every order of any court in this country,
> at least of any appellate court, is available to the public. You may have to walk into
> a clerk's office and pay a per-page fee, but you can get the opinion if you want it.

Summary

Jurisdiction, the court's authority to hear a case, is the limit or territory within which a court has the power, right, or authority to interpret and apply the law. Federalism is a system of government where a written constitution divides power between a centralized government and a number of regional governments. Venue is the proper location for trial of a lawsuit. A court must have either personal, subject matter, or *in rem* jurisdiction to hear a case. Courts must seek jurisdictional balance by weighing the burdens faced by a defendant against the legitimate interests of the plaintiff. Judicial opinions are comprised of four elements — the fact situation, the issue, the holding, and the rationale. Courts rely on precedence to reduce the instability that would result from a constantly changing landscape of legal decisions continually being overruled. Court decisions that are not submitted to the reporters but remain filed at the clerk's office are called "unpublished decisions." Generally, unpublished decisions may not be cited as precedent, although they are now widely available due to electronic databases and the Internet.

Chapter One Notes

[1] The "Little Tucker Act," 28 U.S.C. § 1346(a)(2), confers jurisdiction on district courts for claims of $10,000 or less. Appeals are taken to the Federal Circuit.

[2] The Foreign Intelligence Surveillance Act of 1978 (FISA), Pub. L. No. 95-511, 92 Stat. 1783 (codified as amended at 50 U.S.C. §§ 1801-1811, 1821-1829, 1841-1846, 1861-62).

[3] Some securities lawsuits may be brought under state fraud statutes.

[4] *Harrods, Ltd. v. Sixty Internet Domain Names*, 302 F.3d 214, 225 (4th Cir. 2002).

[5] "The foreseeability that is critical to due process analysis is not the mere likelihood that a product will find its way into the forum state. Rather, it is that the defendant's conduct and connection with the forum state are such that he should reasonably anticipate being haled into court there." *World-Wide Volkswagen Corp. v. Woodson*, 444 U.S. 286, 297, 100 S. Ct. 559 (1980). *See also, Asahi Metal Indus. Co. v. Superior Court*, 480 U.S. 102, 112, 107 S. Ct. 1026 (1987) (the "placement of a product in the stream of commerce, without more, is not an act the defendant purposefully directed toward the forum State.").

[6] *Zippo Mfg. Co. v. Zippo Dot Com*, 952 F.Supp. 119 (W.D. Pa. 1997).

[7] "…contracts with residents of the forum state that involve the knowing and repeated transmission of computer files over the Internet, personal jurisdiction is proper." *Zippo*, *ibid*. at 1124.

[8] "The exercise of jurisdiction is determined by the level of interactivity and commercial nature of the exchange of information that occurs on the website." *Ibid*. at 1124 (citing *Maritz, Inc. v. Cybergold, Inc.*, 947 F. Supp. 1328 (E.D. Mo. 1996).

[9] *Ibid*. at 1124.

[10] *Hollis v. Joseph*, Case No. GD06-012677 (Allegheny County Ct., Pa. Apr. 2007).

[11] *Sayeedi v. Walser*, 15 Misc. 3d 621 (N.Y.C. Civ. Ct. Feb. 27, 2007).

[12] *Best Van Lines v. Walker*, 2007 U.S. App. Lexis 15152 (2nd Cir. June 26, 2007).

[13] *Ibid*.

[14] A long-arm statute is a state law that gives the state court jurisdiction over an out-of-state defendant whose actions caused damage in that state or to one of its residents.

[15] *Davidoff v. Davidoff*, Case No. 101728/06, (Supreme Ct., New York County, May 10, 2006).

[16] A tort is a civil (non-criminal) wrongful act, whether negligent or intentional.

[17] Jeremy Jaynes and his sister Jessica DeGroot were convicted on November 3, 2004; the third defendant, Richard Rutkowski, was acquitted. All three defendants were North Carolina residents.

[18] Jaynes and DeGroot used fake Internet addresses to send more than 10,000 spam e-mails to AOL subscribers on three days in July 2003 — a volume that made the crime a felony under the Virginia statute.

[19] *Gator.com Corp. v. L.L. Bean, Inc.*, 341 F.3d 1072 (9th Cir. 2003), *vacated*, 366 F.3d 789 (9th Cir. 2004).

[20] *Scarcella v. America Online*, 2004 NY Slip Op 51021, (New York City Civ. Ct., Sept. 2004) (unpublished).

[21] The U.S. Courts of Appeals for the 2nd (based in New York City), 7th (based in Chicago), 9th (based in San Francisco), and federal circuits prohibit citation of unpublished opinions, while six other circuits discourage it. *See* Tony Mauro, "Supreme Court Votes to Allow Citation to Unpublished Opinions in Federal Courts," Legal Times, April 13, 2006.

[22] *Sorchini v. Covina*, Case No. 99-56257, D.C., No. CV-92-02825-CBM, (9th Cir. filed May 4, 2001), which states

in part: "Counsel represents that she violated the rule (against citing unpublished decisions)…we may bear part of the responsibility by issuing unpublished dispositions…and so tempt lawyers to cite them as precedent." The court then declined to sanction the attorney and ironically enough, in one of its only two footnotes to the opinion, cited _Bush v. Gore_, 121 S. Ct. 525 (2000), the case the U.S. Supreme Court insisted was "limited to the present circumstances" and could not be cited as precedent.

[23] Molly McDonough, "Door Slowly Opens For Unpublished Opinions," ABA Journal Report, April 21, 2006.

[24] Dennis Crouch, Patently O: Patent Law Blog, April 13, 2006, _available at_ www.patentlyo.com/patent/2006/04/unpublished_opi.html (accessed September 25, 2007).

[25] Tony Mauro, "Supreme Court Votes to Allow Citation to Unpublished Opinions in Federal Courts," Legal Times, April 13, 2006.

[26] _Anastasoff v. United States_, 223 F.3d 898 at 904 (8th Cir. 2000).

[27] _Ibid._

Chapter One Quiz

What are the challenges for legislators posed by the Internet?

What are the challenges for courts posed by the Internet?

Who can benefit from studying Internet law?

How many jurisdictions are there in the United States?

What is federalism?

Which court has jurisdiction to hear appeals in patent rights cases?

How many federal circuits are there?

What is venue?

Where is venue in criminal cases?

Where is venue in civil cases?

What question does subject matter jurisdiction ask?

What question does personal jurisdiction ask?

How can a person submit to a court's jurisdiction online?

What is the public policy justification for small claims court?

What is an action in rem?

What are the four parts of a court's written opinion?

What is the purpose of studying the rationales of previous decisions?

Why do courts adhere to the rule of precedence?

[Answers in Appendix]

PART TWO

INTELLECTUAL PROPERTY

CHAPTER TWO

COPYRIGHT BASICS

> This chapter discusses what a copyright is, how to obtain one, what it does and does not protect, and the concepts of "fair use" and "public domain." Also discussed is Creative Commons, an innovative alternative to traditional copyright.

COPYRIGHT IS ONE OF the four forms of intellectual property. The other three forms of intellectual property are trademarks, patents, and trade secrets. Certain things are not copyrightable: facts, ideas or concepts, procedures or methods of operation, U.S. government works, titles, names, short phrases and slogans, symbols, designs, and mere lists. However, while copyright might not apply, patent or trademark might be applicable.

Copyright law protects original works, which the Copyright Act of 1976[1] defines as:

- Literary works

- Musical works, including accompanying words

- Dramatic works, including accompanying music

- Pantomimes and choreographed works

- Pictorial, graphic, and sculptural works

- Motion pictures and other audiovisual works

- Sound recordings

- Architectural works

The Act also covers *compilations*, which means that the selection, ordering, and presentation of otherwise unprotectable facts may be protectable (*e.g.*, databases). Copyright law also protects written words on a website, software programs running on a website, photographs in JPG, GIF, and PNG digital formats, and music and sound recordings in MP3 format.

Exclusive Rights of the Copyright Owner

The Copyright Act grants certain exclusive rights to the copyright holder. These exclusive rights are:

- Reproduction

- Derivative Works

- Distribution

- Public Performance

- Display

- Audio/Video transmission

Filing A Copyright

To file a copyright, the person seeking the copyright must send an application form to the Copyright Office.[2] An application form may be downloaded online at the Copyright Office's website (www.copyright.gov/forms). Along with the application form, the Copyright Office requires (at the time of this book's publication) a $45 fee[3] and one copy of the unpublished work (two copies if published).

Filing an application is not necessary to create a copyright. Original works are automatically protected once they are *created and fixed in a tangible medium*. But there are reasons to file an application. Registration establishes a public record of claim and is also a prerequisite for an infringement suit. Registration also establishes prima facie evidence of the validity of the copyright if made within five years of publication. If registered within three months after publication or prior to infringement, the copyright holder can receive statutory damages and attorneys' fees; otherwise only actual damages and profits are recoverable.

The © Symbol

Registration is not required to use the © symbol, since a common-law copyright arises upon publication of the work. However, the copyright notice must be in valid form. A valid copyright notice consists of all of the following:

1. The © symbol, and the word "copyright" or abbreviation "Copr.;"

2. The year of *first* publication of the work (not necessarily the current year); and

3. The name of copyright owner.

"(c) 2008 My Company, Inc." is not a valid copyright notice; the letter "c" within parentheses is not legally sufficient to replace the actual © symbol.

Length of Protection

When the U.S. Constitution[4] was first drafted, copyrights had a life of 14 years, with one extension for a total life of 28 years. Since then, Congress has continually expanded the term of copyrights. The most recent extension was the Sonny Bono Copyright Term Extension Act (CTEA),[5] which extended the term of copyright protection by 20 years[6] for works copyrighted after January 1, 1923. As a result, copyrighted work, owned by an individual, created after January 1, 1978 now has a term of the life of the author plus 70 years. Copyrighted work, owned by two or more authors, now has a term of 70 years after the death of the last surviving author. "Work-Made-For-Hire" now has a term of 95 years from either the first publication or 120 years from the year of creation, whichever occurs first. The CTEA is both a prospective extension as well as a retroactive one. The result of the CTEA was to prevent a number of works, beginning with those published in 1923, from entering the public domain. Thousands of works due to enter the public domain were instead preserved under private ownership until at least the year 2019. The Supreme Court, in a 7–2 decision, has upheld the CTEA as constitutional.[7]

"Work-Made-For-Hire"

In a "Work-Made-For-Hire," the person who commissions the work is deemed to be the author of the work and owner of all of the rights, including all rights in copyright, throughout the world, for the duration of the copyright. Under this doctrine, the work's creator has no rights to his creation except whatever rights the contract itself may specify.

A work product may be considered "Work-Made-For-Hire" where the creator is an *employee* or an independent contractor. If the work was prepared by an employee within the *scope of his employment*, then the employer owns the copyright to the work. "Within the scope of employment" means that it was part of his job duties to create the work. Merely because an employee creates a work that is later acquired by his employer is not sufficient to make it "Work-Made-For-Hire."

If the work was *specially ordered or commissioned* (*i.e.*, prepared by an independent contractor) as part of a collective work and the parties agree in writing that it is "Work-Made-For-Hire," then the work is considered "Work-Made-For-Hire." This writing requirement has created a dilemma. Suppose an independent contractor (not an employee) is hired to write a book or a song, or design a website, or create any other sort of work of art. Now let us further suppose that based on the initial conversation, the independent contractor starts work on the project before a written contract is given to her. The contract arrives either halfway through the project or when she has finished her work and she signs it. Is the project "Work-Made-For-Hire?" The Circuit courts are split and the Supreme Court has yet to hear a case to resolve the conflict. The 2nd Circuit[8] held that the Copyright Act "requires parties agree *before* the creation of the work that it will be a "Work-Made-For-Hire," *but* the *actual writing memorializing* the agreement need not be executed before the creation of the work. However, the 7th Circuit[9] disagrees, requiring a writing prior to the creation of the work.

Note that there is no writing requirement for copyright, but absent a written agreement, *patent* rights will belong to the employee (rather than to the employer) who develops an invention within the scope of his employment.

"Fair Use" Doctrine

The "Fair Use" doctrine is an affirmative defense to a copyright infringement claim. It allows limited use of a copyrighted work for criticism, comment, news reporting, research, scholarship, or teaching. The "Fair Use" doctrine is not a simple test, but rather a delicate balancing of interests; only a court can determine if a particular use qualifies as a fair use.

To make that determination, the court looks at four factors. First, what is the purpose and character of the use? For example, is the use educational or commercial? Educational use tips the scales towards fair use. Second, what is the nature of the work? For example, is it factual or creative? Work of a factual nature tips the scales towards fair use. Third, how does the amount and substantiality of the portion of the work used relate to the entire work? For example, in _Kelly v. Arriba Soft,_ [10] the court held that an online image search engine website could use low resolution thumbnails of copyrighted photographs but not full-size images. And finally, fourth, what is the effect of the use on the potential market for, or value of, the work? A finding that the use would decrease the potential market for, or value of, the copyrighted work would militate against a finding of fair use.

These factors are not always easy to ascertain, even for the courts. In _Perfect 10 v. Google, Inc.,_ [11] a California federal court issued a preliminary injunction against Google for infringing on a pornographic website's copyright by indexing and displaying thumbnails of the site's images in its search results. The court distinguished this case from _Arriba_ on two grounds. First, applying the "use" test, it found that Google's use of the photographs was commercial in nature. In _Arriba_, clicking on the thumbnail took the user to the copyright holder's website; but here the users were taken to websites that were infringing on Perfect 10's copyright by displaying the photos without permission, and where Google would receive revenue if the infringing third-party website was also a Google Ad-Sense partner. In those instances, the court wrote, "Google's thumbnails lead users to sites that directly benefit Google's bottom line." [12] Second, applying the "effect of the use on the potential market for and value of the copyrighted work" test, the court found that Google's use of thumbnails likely did harm Perfect 10's efforts to sell small thumbnail-sized images to mobile phone users.

However, the 9th Circuit reversed the lower court's findings, reasoning that Google's use of the thumbnail images was "highly transformative" and that the public benefit of Google's search engine outweighed any potential commercial use of the thumbnails. [13] This case is a perfect example of courts attempting to balance the free flow of information online with the protection of copyright holders.

Quoting from unpublished materials exposes you to greater risk than quoting from published materials. Creative works receive more protection than fact-based works. Close paraphrasing may constitute copyright infringement if done extensively. Lack of attribution or credit, or improper credit, weighs against a finding of fair use. However, merely acknowledging the source of copyrighted material does not substitute for getting permission. So placing a copyrighted image on your website and simply adding the copyright holder's copyright information below the image does not protect you from an infringement suit. The court will weigh all of the above factors in determining whether fair use can be used as an affirmative defense.

Public Domain

Public domain refers to created materials that *either by law do not get copyright protection, or whose protection under the law has lapsed.* Since materials in public domain lack copyright protection, you do not need permission to use them. But keep in mind, whether materials are in public has no bearing on whether they fall into public domain. Do not erroneously assume that everything on the Internet is in public and therefore in public domain and freely usable without permission. Material is only in public domain if the copyright has expired or it was not copyrightable in the first place.

Felony Copyright Infringement

In addition to *civil* liability, copyright infringers may also face *criminal* liability for felony copyright infringement if the infringement is willful, and for commercial advantage or private financial gain, or by reproduction and distribution on a large scale (*i.e.*, 10 copies of a $2,500 work in an 80-day period).

The No Electronic Theft Act

Criminal liability for copyright infringement can also ensue from a 1997 federal law known as the *No Electronic Theft Act.* [14] The Act prohibits unauthorized distribution over a computer network of copyrighted material with a value greater than $2,500. Note that in the No Electronic Theft Act, Congress eliminated the felony copyright infringement requirement to show a profit motive — only distribution need be shown.

The Visual Artists Rights Act

In 1990, Congress passed the Visual Artists Rights Act (VARA), which protects the moral rights of artists who produce a "work of visual art." [15] Moral rights are defined as the ability of authors to control the eventual fate of their works. It is not about ownership of the work but rather about ensuring the work's integrity by preventing revision, alteration, or distortion of the work, regardless of who the ultimate owner may be.

VARA only protects the artist's moral rights in paintings, drawings, prints, sculptures, and photographs, existing in a single copy or a limited edition of 200 signed and numbered copies or fewer. [16] Additionally, the photographs must have been taken for exhibition purposes only.

The Act does not apply to posters, maps, globes, charts, technical drawings, diagrams, models, applied art, motion pictures or other audiovisual work, books, magazines, newspapers, periodicals, databases, electronic information services, electronic publications, merchandising items or advertising, or any promotional, descriptive, covering, or packaging material or container.[17] VARA also does not apply to Work-Made-For-Hire.[18]

Moral rights under VARA are not transferable and terminate with the life of the artist (or last surviving artist if there are co-creators), although they may be waived by the artist, usually by contract at the time of commission or purchase. VARA grants the artist the right of attribution and the right of integrity. The *right of attribution* entitles the artist to be properly credited for her work; or conversely, to demand that her name be removed from any work that has been distorted, mutilated, or modified; or to demand that her name be removed from any work she did not create.[19] The *right of integrity* precludes others from distorting, mutilating, or modifying her work; it also prevents the destruction of works of "recognized stature."[20]

Legal remedies for violation of VARA are damages, profits made by the infringer, injunctions, and/or impoundment or destruction of the work. Statutory damages range from 750–to–$30,000;[21] however, if the infringement was committed willfully, the court in its discretion may increase the statutory damages up to $150,000.[22] The court also has discretion to reduce the damages to $200 if the infringer was not aware and had no reason to believe that her acts constituted copyright infringement.[23] VARA does not preclude state law claims, such as Right of Publicity, misappropriation, trademark infringement, and defamation.

Creative Commons

Creative Commons, a methodology developed by Stanford law professor Lawrence Lessig, is a new approach to copyright that is gaining prominence on the web. His view is that the "all or none" copyright approach, where the creator either allows or prohibits use of his work, stifles artistic growth in the digital age. Lessig proffers what he terms "a more flexible approach," described on his Creative Commons website[24] as having "built upon the 'all rights reserved' of traditional copyright to create a voluntary 'some rights reserved' copyright."

Under Creative Commons, the creator offers a portion of rights but subject to certain conditions. There are 11 of these conditions, called Creative Commons licenses. They include "Attribution" (permission to publish if proper credit is given), "Non-Commercial" (permission to publish for non-commercial purposes), "No Derivative Works" (permission to publish the original but no works derived from the original), "Share Alike" (permission to distribute derivative works only under a license identical to the license that governs the creator's work), and "Sampling" (permission to take and transform pieces of the work for any purpose other than advertising). Creators can "mix and match" these licenses. As of this writing, more than 10 million works have been distributed through these licenses. Author Cory Doctorow sold 10,000 copies of his novel through bookstores but half a million copies were distributed online as free e-books under a Creative Commons license.[25] In effect, the name recognition that Doctorow may receive from those 500,000 non-paying readers may pay off greater than the royalties he might have received from them (assuming they all would have purchased his book) as he may now have a loyal readership willing to pay for future novels. Exposure for an unknown creator, rather than pecuniary gain, may be the greatest benefit offered to creators by Creative Commons.

Creative Commons may ultimately be embraced by the traditional media companies who currently see the Internet as the greatest threat to creator's rights. Indeed, the motion picture and music industries are decrying the downloading of films and music, much as they did the invention of the video tape recorder, and much as record companies feared radio. "At every turn in history we see this new model of distribution that people say is going to destroy art itself," Doctorow said, adding that such fears have been proven wrong time and time again.[26] Traditional media companies might be wise to embrace technologies such as file-sharing and digital copying and co-opt them, and Creative Commons may offer them one means to do so.

A work protected by a Creative Commons license may identify itself as such by use of a Creative Commons ⓒⓒ symbol (similar to the Copyright © symbol but with a double 'C') or it may be listed in the CreativeCommons.org searchable archives.[27] Also, both the Yahoo! search engine and the Firefox web browser allow people to search the web for works of art licensed by Creative Commons.

Justin Ho-Wee Wong used a Creative Commons license on his more than 11,000 photographs posted to his Yahoo Flickr photo sharing account. The particular license allowed any use, even commercial, as long as he was credited. Wong, a church youth counselor, photographed 15-year-old Alison Chang at a church-sponsored car wash in Dallas, Texas and posted the photo to his Flickr account. Apparently, an Australian ad agency decided that rather than hire a model for its new ad campaign, it would simply search through Flickr's collection of photos to find one it liked. They must have liked Alison's photo a lot, because her image was cropped out of the photo, flipped and blown up to appear on a billboard in Adelaide, Australia as part of a cell phone company Virgin Mobile's ad campaign. The billboard touts the double-entendre "virgin–to–virgin" text services beneath Alison's photo and above her photo, in large letters reads: "Dump Your Pen Friend."[28]

Change sued Virgin's American subsidiary, Virgin Mobile, USA, seeking damages under the Right of Publicity (see Chapter 10).[29] Wong is also a party to the suit, claiming that Virgin did not honor all the terms of the Creative Commons license. If the case is not dismissed (Virgin Mobile, USA claims it has nothing to do with its Australian counterpart Virgin Mobile Australia) it will be one of the first cases to deal with Creative Commons.

Summary

Copyright, one of the four forms of intellectual property, is governed by the Copyright Act of 1976, as amended. Copyright laws protect original works, but not ideas or facts. The Act grants the copyright holder exclusive rights of reproduction, derivative works, distribution, public performance, display, and audio/video transmission. A common law copyright arises upon publication. The copyright notice must be in valid form. The most recent extension of copyright terms was the Sonny Bono Copyright Term Extension Act; as a result, copyrighted work owned by an individual created after January 1, 1978 now has a term of the life of the author plus 70 years. In a "Work-Made-For-Hire," the person who commissions the work is deemed to be the copyright holder.

The "Fair Use" doctrine is an affirmative defense to a claim of copyright infringement that balances the free flow of information online with the protection of copyright holders. The court looks at (1) the purpose and character of the use; (2) the nature of the work; (3) how the amount and substantiality of the portion of the work used relates to the entire work; and (4) the effect of the use on the potential market for, or value of, the work.

Works that by law do not receive copyright protection or whose term has expired are said to be in the public domain. Material is only in public domain if the copyright has expired or it was not copyrightable in the first place. Liability for copyright infringement may be both civil and criminal.

The Visual Artists Rights Act protects the moral rights of artists who produce a "work of visual art." Moral rights are defined as the ability of authors to control the eventual fate of their works. It is not about ownership of the work but rather about ensuring the work's integrity by preventing revision, alteration, or distortion of the work, regardless of who the ultimate owner may be.

The new concept of Creative Commons offers a flexible approach to copyright issues, where the creator offers a portion of rights but subject to certain specified conditions, called Creative Commons licenses.

Chapter Two Notes

[1] Copyright Act of 1976, as Amended, 17 U.S.C. § 101 *et seq.*

[2] Copyright information is available online at Library of Congress, "U.S. Copyright Office," *available at* www.copyright.gov (accessed September 25, 2007).

[3] For current fees, visit the Copyright Office website, *available at* www.copyright.gov/docs/fees.html.

[4] Copyright and Patent Clause, U.S. Const., art. I, § 8, cl. 8.

[5] 17 U.S.C. § 302(a).

[6] Under the 1976 Copyright Act, copyright protection lasted from a work's creation until 50 years after the author's death.

[7] *Eldred v. Ashcroft*, 537 U.S. 186, 221, 123 S. Ct. 769, 790 (2003).

[8] *Playboy Enterprises, Inc. v. Dumas*, 53 F.3d 549 (2nd Cir. 1995) *cert. denied*, 116 S. Ct. 567 (1995).

[9] *Schiller & Schmidt, Inc. v. Nordisco Corp.*, 969 F.2d 410 (7th Cir. 1992).

[10] *Kelly v. Arriba Soft*, 280 F.3d 934 (9th Cir. Feb. 6, 2002) *withdrawn*, 311 F.3d 811 (9th Cir. July 3, 2003). This case is included in the Cases Section on the Issues in Internet Law website (www.IssuesinInternetLaw.com).

[11] *Perfect 10, Inc. v. Google, Inc.*, Case No. CV 04-9484 AHM (SHx) (C.D. Cal., Feb. 2006) *aff'd in part, rev'd in part, remanded* (9th Cir. May 16, 2007).

[12] *Ibid.*

[13] *Ibid.*

[14] 17 U.S.C. § 101.

[15] Visual Artists Rights Act of 1990 (VARA), 17 U.S.C. § 106A.

[16] Copyright Act of 1976, 17 U.S.C. § 101.

[17] *Ibid.*

[18] *Ibid.*

[19] 17 U.S.C. § 106A(a)(1) and (2).

[20] 17 U.S.C. § 106A(a)(3).

[21] 17 U.S.C. § 504(c)(1).

[22] 17 U.S.C. § 504(c)(2).

[23] *Ibid.*

[24] Creative Commons, *available at* http://creativecommons.org (accessed September 25, 2007).

[25] Creative Commons, "Interview with Cory Doctorow," *available at* http://creativecommons.org/getcontent/features/doctorow (accessed September 25, 2007).

[26] Ariana Eunjung Cha, "Creative Commons Is Rewriting Rules of Copyright," Washington Post, March 15, 2005, p. E01.

[27] Creative Commons website, fn. 24, *supra.*

[28] *Chang v. Virgin Mobile USA*, Case No. _____ (ND Tex. 2007).

[29] Noam Cohen, "Use My Photo? Not Without Permission," New York Times, October 1, 2007.

Chapter Two Quiz

Silly Sally has written an opera. She neglected to register her work with the copyright office. However, Sally did place "(c) 2008 Silly Sally" on the opera. Sally wrote the opera while she was working at Fred Flintstone's musical instrument repair shop. Fred claims he should be the copyright holder since it was a "Work-Made-For-Hire."

The ever-industrious Sally also invented a new type of guitar pick while she was working for Fred. Both Sally and Fred agree that the guitar pick was developed within the scope of Sally's employment.

Fred asked Betty Rubble to create a sales brochure for his business. Betty was not an employee of Fred's but had produced brochures for several local businesses including Slate's Rock & Gravel Co. Betty started work right away after speaking with Fred and she was almost finished a week later when the contract Fred had mailed arrived on her doorstep. Fred wants to know if the brochure is "Work-Made-For-Hire." Betty included in the brochure several photographs of the various types of musical instruments that "Flintstone's Fiddles" repairs. She used photographs from an educational book on musical instruments and believes this to be a "fair use." Betty also added the copyright holder's information below each photograph. Betty also used a photograph of a Stradivarius violin that she found online for the cover of the brochure. Betty told Fred that since the photograph was on the Internet in public, it was O.K. to use it since it was obviously in the public domain.

If you are using this book in a classroom, discuss the issues raised and the liability of all parties. Otherwise, try to list the issues involved and probable outcomes before turning to the answers in the Appendix.

[Answers in Appendix]

CHAPTER THREE

COPYRIGHT INFRINGEMENT

This chapter examines direct, contributory, and vicarious infringement of copyrighted content online, with a focus on linking, file-sharing, and the Digital Millennium Copyright Act.

Copyright Infringement

COPYRIGHT INFRINGEMENT OCCURS WHEN the infringer publishes or distributes copyrighted material without the permission of the copyright holder. That means there is no copyright infringement if:

- The material is not published or distributed. "Publish or distribute" includes posting online to a website, blog, or usenet group, e-mailing or sending as an attachment in chat or IM (Instant Messaging).

- The material must be copyrighted. If it is in the public domain (*e.g.*, the copyright period has expired or the material was produced by the government), then there can be no infringement.

- The copyright holder has given permission (*e.g.*, stated within the material, in a separate letter authorizing its use, or pursuant to a license, contract, or Creative Commons License). Note however that permission may be limited to specific uses, formats, or media.

There are three types of infringement: direct, contributory, and vicarious. A *direct infringer* commits the copyright infringement directly; most instances of direct infringement involve either placing copyrighted material on one's website or publishing a website to which one does not hold the copyright. A *contributory infringer* helps others to commit copyright infringement. A *vicarious infringer* has the right and ability to control an infringer's activity and receives a direct financial benefit from the infringement.

Direct Infringement of Website Content

When collating content to place on your website, there are certain caveats to bear in mind. For example, under U.S. copyright law[1] it is illegal to copy someone's text, artwork, music, or photographs without their permission and publish them on your website. You need to be sure that you either own the copyright to any materials you place on your website or have the copyright owner's permission to use such materials on your website.

If It Is Not Your Copyright, Do Not Publish It on Your Website

Take the case of *Playboy v. Sanfilippo.*[2] One can imagine Mr. Sanfilippo sitting in his room staring at stacks of his lifetime collection of Playboy magazine and a beat-up copy of a "Create Your Own Website" book when the epiphany hit him — why not set up an adult website where visitors could pay to see his collection of 7,500 photographs of naked women — all scanned from copies of Playboy magazine. Playboy, however, was not very happy about this and promptly sued Mr. Sanfilippo for copyright infringement. Playboy prevailed because it showed the *necessary elements of an infringement claim*: (1) it had a valid copyright and (2) the defendant violated the copyright owner's exclusive rights as listed in the Copyright Act.

Notice that intent, knowledge, injury, or damage are ***not*** required elements of a copyright infringement action. At the time of the lawsuit, the statutory damages ranged from $500–to–$100,000 per infringement (*i.e.*, per photo) — Playboy asked for damages of $285,420,000! However, the court awarded Playboy a more reasonable $3,737,500. Still, stop and think how elated you would be to win $3.7 million in the lottery. Now picture how Mr. Sanfilippo must have felt having to write a check for that amount to Playboy! So remember, it is illegal to copy someone's photos and put them on your website!

An interesting case arose when USA Next, a conservative group, published an advertisement on the Internet criticizing the American Association of Retired Persons (AARP).[3] The ad contained a photograph of a soldier with a red "X" over him and two men kissing and the caption "The REAL AARP Agenda." The gay couple in the photograph sued the ad's producer for $25 million for libel and invasion of privacy, contending that they "did not consent to serve as models for a homophobic and mean-spirited campaign for a political group with whose views they strongly disagree."[4] USA Next said that the ad was meant to show that the AARP is out of touch with "mainstream America," while the plaintiffs argued that the ad portrayed them in a false light as unpatriotic during wartime. Ironically, the defendants countered that they did not need permission from the two men pictured in the photograph, since the photograph was taken by a Portland newspaper and they had posed for the photograph (taken to accompany a story on the issuance of marriage licenses to same-sex couples). However, the defendants admitted that USA Next's consultant had taken the photograph from the Portland Tribune's website without the newspaper's permission. Thus it would appear that the newspaper might have a valid cause of action for copyright infringement against USA Next, regardless of the outcome of this lawsuit.

Be Sure It Is Really Yours!

Say the local newspaper just published a very favorable story about your business, or a review of the restaurant you own, or a complimentary article detailing your years of community service and, in any of these scenarios, you wish to publish the article on your website. After all, the article is all about you, or your business. However, since the article was already published elsewhere, it is a copyrighted work, and you will be infringing on the copyright holder's exclusive rights of reproduction and distribution if you publish it on your website!

Suppose you want to place your company brochure online on your website. The brochure has a beautiful copyrighted photograph on its cover, but you paid the copyright holder for a license to use it on your brochure. Can you post the brochure, with the licensed photo, on the Internet? The answer is probably not, unless it is a broad license that would include republication in other media like the Internet. This is an example of permission being limited to specific uses, formats, or media. So when negotiating licenses, the licensee should keep in mind that he will want as broad a license as possible to accommodate future uses, while the licensor should be mindful of losing potential future revenue by agreeing to too broad a license.

Direct Infringement of the Website Itself

Many websites are designed by professional web designers for clients, who then use the websites for personal or business use. The copyrightable elements of a website include the "*look and feel*" of the overall website, software applications, scripts, graphics (photographs and artwork), and text. Who owns the copyright to a website created for a client by a web designer?

Recall from the previous chapter that the creator of the work is the copyright holder; by default, the web designer becomes the copyright owner unless the website development agreement (*i.e.*, a contract between the website designer and his client) states otherwise.

The contract may define "developer content" and "company content" and assign rights to each. It may grant the client a license to use a copyrighted work, while the actual copyright is still held by the designer. Note that a license to use a copyrighted work does not grant the right to create a derivative work (recall again from the previous chapter that derivative works are an exclusive right of the copyright owner). Therefore, if the web designer retains the copyright and grants only a license to the client, should the client later choose to publish an updated version of the website, the new version may be a derivative work and thus an infringement of the web designer's copyright.

In a case illustrating copyright ownership of a website absence a written agreement,[5] Vyne, a web designer, was hired by a magazine to create a website. He began work based on an oral agreement, creating files, code, graphics, and the site design. While the contract was being drafted, a dispute arose. The contract had not been signed but the parties had both performed according to their prior understandings under the contract. Vyne claimed ownership of the files, code, programming, and graphics for the website, and threatened to shut it down unless additional fees were paid. The issue raised by the case was who owned the copyright to the website, since there was no written agreement regarding copyright ownership or license rights. The court held that *absent a signed contract, the web designer had granted an implied non-exclusive license to the client* to use copyrighted software and files on the website by virtue of the parties' course of dealings and industry custom, and for which the designer had been paid. Therefore, the client did not violate the designer's copyright, since its use was under a lawful license. However, the court added that the implied license was revocable absent proper consideration (*i.e.*, payment), but where there was proper consideration, the non-exclusive license would remain irrevocable. The non-exclusive license does not have to be in writing. The court noted that the Statute of Frauds, which bars oral contracts, was not applicable because the license is implied from the conduct of the parties (this was not the first website the designer had made for the client). The court declined to rule on whether the website was a "Work-Made For-Hire."

Contributory Infringement of Website Content

If third parties are allowed to publish material on your website, you may incur liability for what they post.[6] While not a direct infringer (since you did not post the infringing material) you might be a contributory infringer by providing the means for the infringement to occur. They might post material that is copyrighted, thereby infringing on the copyright holder's valid copyright, or they might post libelous or defamatory comments,[7] or profanity (what this author calls the "Graffiti Factor"). Some likely places where third parties might be able to publish on your website include discussion forums and message boards, chat rooms, guest books, and blogs. While the federal Communications Decency Act (CDA, discussed at length in Chapter 14) broadly protects ISPs and other "publishers" from liability for content posted by others, it is not a license to infringe copyrights, defame others, or violate trade secrets.

Copyright infringement is not the only risk from third-party postings, as they may also contain *defamation* (see Chapter 13) or publication of *trade secrets* (see Chapter 6). One blogger was sued for both defamation and publication of trade secrets after the content in question was posted by readers in the comments section of his blog. The blogger maintained a blog on search engine optimization (*i.e.*, how to make one's website rank higher in search engine results), and a maker of search engine optimization software objected to negative comments posted by the blogger's readers about its optimization tools and marketing practices.[8] The case was dismissed for lack of personal jurisdiction by the Nevada federal court, leaving open the question of possible liability of a blogger for third-party comments posted on his blog.

Newspapers' websites have recently experienced the "Graffiti Factor." In an effort to introduce interactivity with their online readers, some newspaper websites have set up message boards adjacent to news articles inviting comments from readers. Here, however, the old axiom "be careful what you wish for because you might just get it" applies in full force. Many of the newspapers ended up eliminating the message boards after a deluge of profanity and racist comments were posted by their readers.[9] The newspapers cited lack of staff needed to monitor the forum 24 hours per day as a reason for eliminating the message boards. In one case, the Washington Post closed one of its blogs to readers' comments after a wave of reader postings that included personal attacks, profanity, and hate mail directed at the paper's ombudsman.[10] Several months prior to that, the Los Angeles Times pulled the plug on its editorial page wiki just two days after inaugurating the forum because visitors were posting pornographic material.[11]

Sometimes the "Graffiti Factor" can result from a well-intentioned source. The Ventura County (California) Star published a story about a man who killed four people before committing suicide in a Wal-Mart. The Star was uncertain of the man's identity but a reader posted her guess as to the killer's identity on a comment section of the Star's website.[12] While her guess turned out to be correct, the newspaper had not confirmed the man's identity and had refrained from publishing its own unconfirmed reports. As one commentator put it, "unbound by traditional journalism rules like making sure she was right, she posted the name."[13] The newspaper's staff debated whether to remove the woman's posting, fearing the consequences if her guess was incorrect—an innocent person defamed as a murderer. Ultimately, it chose to leave the posting untouched.

So what can you do to protect yourself from liability? Obviously, one way would be to not allow third parties to post on your website. However, that may not be feasible given the nature or purpose of your website. So if you are going to host discussion forums, message boards, and blogs on your website, make sure you have a moderator responsible for policing and cleaning up third-party postings. Chat room software often comes with filters that can block certain words and phrases, including profanity. Instead of using a guest book that automatically posts user comments to the website, have the guest book form use a "mailto: form" to send the comments directly to you for review before posting them to the website.

Remember, the court does not need to find that you intended to infringe upon another's copyright, or even that you knew the third-party had posted the material on your website, to hold you liable for copyright infringement. However, lack of intent to infringe or lack of knowledge of infringement may reduce the amount of statutory damages awarded.

Contributory Infringement Through Linking

The World Wide Web is so-named because every web page contains hypertext links to other web pages, analogous to navigating one's way through a spider's web. There are three types of links to other web pages: a simple hypertext link, inlining, and deep-linking.

Hypertext Linking Issues

A *hypertext link* is a word or phrase (usually underlined) which, when clicked, will take the user to a new web page. For example, a website could contain a sentence that reads "My bicycle is a <u>Schwinn</u>," where Schwinn is a hyperlink which, when clicked on, takes the user to the Schwinn website. But does the website need permission from Schwinn to link to its website? What if Schwinn does not want to be associated with the referring website? Does a simple hypertext link require permission from the website to which you wish to link?

Accounting firm KPGM apparently believed so, when in 2001, it sent an e-mail[14] to a young man in Great Britain, advising him to remove the link to its website from his web page, stating: "Please be aware such links require that a formal agreement exist between our two parties, as mandated by our organization's Web Link Policy."

This immediately brings to mind two issues: (1) Can a website unilaterally enforce provisions or restriction in its online policy statements on others, and (2) how could it actually follow through on such enforcement? To quote President Andrew Jackson, when faced with a Supreme Court ruling he did not like: "The court has made its decision; now let them enforce it,"[15] a quip referring to the fact that the judicial branch lacks any enforcement power.

None of this was lost on the savvy 22-year-old web consultant, who shot back a letter of his own to the company, saying that "my own organization's Web Link Policy requires no such formal agreement."[16] He summed up the matter in a comment on his own web blog, stating the obvious problem with KPMG's policy: "If every hyperlink used on the web required parties at both sides of the link to enter into a formal agreement, I sincerely doubt that the web would be in existence today."

While no American court has yet ruled on this issue, it would probably be a good idea to obtain permission before linking to another website. While links from a referring website tend to improve a website's ranking in search engines, a website might not always want to be associated with the referring page. For example, a hate group might place a link on its website to the target of its hatred. A neo-Nazi website might have an article on "Jewish Control of the Media" and link to a Jewish celebrity's website. Then, search engine queries for that celebrity would yield the neo-Nazi website among the results. In such a case, the Jewish celebrity might object to being linked to the neo-Nazi website.

From a copyright standpoint, merely placing a text link is equivalent to telling someone where to find the source of the information. Most likely, a text hyperlink would not be considered an infringement. However, there may be some circumstance where even hyperlinking might be considered a form of contributory infringement.

In the previous chapter, we discussed the _Perfect 10 v. Google, Inc.,_[17] case, where Google was sued by a pornographic website for displaying thumbnail photos from that website in its search engine results. While the court ruled that the public benefit of Google's transformative use of the photos outweighed protecting the copyrighted material, it added a surprising comment that could reshape American law on linking. In addition to displaying thumbnail photos in its search results, Google also displays a hyperlink to the full size image and a hyperlink to the referring page. Some of these referring pages were not the Perfect 10 website but other pornographic websites that were illegally posting Perfect 10's copyrighted photos. The court stated that these hyperlinks could make Google a contributory infringer since it was providing access to the infringing websites:[18]

> There is no dispute that Google substantially assists websites to distribute their infringing copies to a worldwide market and assists a worldwide audience of users to access infringing materials. * * * Google could be held contributorily liable if it had knowledge that infringing Perfect 10 images were available using its search engine, could take simple measures to prevent further damage to Perfect 10's copyrighted works, and failed to take such steps.

The case was remanded to the lower court to determine if, based on the facts, Google had failed to take steps to prevent harm to Perfect 10's copyrighted material. Unfortunately, the court did not elaborate on what "simple measures" would be appropriate, so we may expect more litigation in this area.

Australian courts have applied the concept of contributory infringement to include website owners who hyperlink to infringing websites.[19] In Australia, where copyright infringement is a crime punishable by fine and/or imprisonment, an 18-year-old was arrested and prosecuted for linking to a website that may have offered infringing downloads.[20] This case is notable because the man (who was a minor at the time he placed the link) had no relation to the infringing website and subsequently faced criminal, not civil penalties.

In another Australian case,[21] the court found both the website operator and the ISP guilty of contributory infringement. A retired policeman set up a website, mp3s4free.net, that linked to music files on websites that he did not own; the copyright owners (several large music companies) then sued for infringement. In ruling that linking without permission to copyright music posted elsewhere online was illegal, the three-judge panel at the Federal Court of Australia relied on the Australian Copyright Act, which lists the following three factors as relevant to determining whether a person has authorized infringement of copyrighted sound recording:

- The extent (if any) of the person's power to prevent the copyright infringement

- The nature of any relationship existing between the person and the person who infringed copyright, and

- Whether the person took any other reasonable steps to prevent or avoid the copyright infringement, including whether the person complied with any relevant codes of practice

Based on *Perfect 10 v. Google, Inc.*, it appears that U.S. courts may be headed toward a similar analysis (although the Australian court[22] based its analysis on a test contained within its own statute). However, the Australian court held that both the website linking to an infringing website offering copyrighted MP3 files and its ISP were liable as contributory infringers, even though neither defendant offered or hosted the files. This is much further than any American or European court has stretched the definition of contributory infringement. In fact, in the United States, the CDA § 230 would most likely preclude a finding of ISP liability on the basis that the ISPs lack control over content hosted on their systems by their customers.[23]

When dealing with hyperlinks, the safest course for a website owner would be to get either *express consent* from the other website or *implied consent*, as through the use of *reciprocal links.* Generally, mere hyperlinks to other pages should not be problematic unless the pages contain infringing copyrighted material (*i.e.*, a link to a site illegally displaying another's copyrighted material). However, before using graphic links comprised of trademarks from the linked website, express consent should be obtained to avoid a trademark infringement claim. It is also advisable to use a *linking disclaimer*, such as: *"Our website does not guarantee, approve, or endorse the information or products available at these websites, nor does a link indicate any association with or endorsement by the linked website."*

Conversely, what if one wishes to link from a third-party's website? In *LiveUniverse, Inc. v. MySpace, Inc.*, a U.S. district court addressed whether a social networking site can prevent its users from posting certain links.[24] MySpace had deactivated links from competitor Vidilife.com (owned by LiveUniverse). MySpace claimed it does not prevent anyone from visiting competitors' sites, but had "no responsibility to build a moving walkway to a competitor's store."[25] The court agreed, dismissing the case.

Inline Linking Issues

Inline linking, or "inlining," is the process of displaying a graphic file on one website that originates at another. It is also known as *hotlinking* by those who participate in the practice and as *bandwidth theft* by those who are victimized by it.

Forum and message board software often allow users to use graphic avatars in each of their postings. Frequently users will selected an image (usually copyrighted) that they have found on the web and hotlink to that image so that every time they post a message in the forum, the forum server downloads the graphic from the original website's server, thus increasing the bandwidth usage and cost for the original website owner. Not only does the original posting count toward the original website's bandwidth usage allocation, but so does each instance of someone loading the forum page containing the graphic.

In one situation, a fan of the Dilbert comic strip placed an inline link to the strip on his website. He did not copy the graphic to his server; it remained on the copyright holder's server. However, when his page loaded, the strip appeared on his page because of an inline link to the image file on the copyright holder's server.

The fan received a cease and desist e-mail[26] from the copyright holder's attorney, explaining that the strip was copyrighted material and insisting that he remove the link. The fan replied that he had very carefully created the website so as to avoid copyright problems in that he *"pulled images from the copyright owner's server"* but did not store any copyrighted images on his server.

(One might argue, before even examining the technical details, that "pulling images from the copyright owner's server" just has the sound of taking something that does not belong to you).

The attorney replied that since the Copyright Act[27] prohibits the unauthorized *display* of a copyrighted work, inlining of the Dilbert comic strip was a violation. This mooted the issue of whether the images had been "copied or reproduced" onto his server, because the Act also protects the copyright holder's exclusive right of display.[28] He pointed out that under the Act, statutory damages for infringements after notice is given to the infringer could be as high as $100,000 per infringement. Since the fan's website was coded to link to each day's comic strip, that would be $100,000 per day! The website was quickly removed.

The attorney also explained that his client was in the business of selling intellectual property rights; indeed, its only product was selling to others the right to copy and display those rights (the comic strip characters). If others were allowed to use those rights without paying, his client would lose its ability to make money. The copyright holder would lose control over the context in which the property is displayed were inline linking allowed. He cited as an example, inlining the Dilbert comic strip to the Ku Klux Klan's web page which could "erode the value of the property in a way that will be very difficult to measure." Ironically, the exchange ended with the fan being granted the right to display a single Dilbert comic strip on his website, albeit in reduced form.

The legal status of inline linking has still not been completely resolved. Proponents argue that in inline linking, there is no copy being made by the alleged infringer. Rather, the object inline linked is pulled directly from the host server with no intermediate copy being made by the accused infringer. However, as we have seen above, this does not address the fact that the work is still *displayed*, even if not copied. Opponents argue that the copyrighted work is effectively appearing as part of a web page belonging to someone other than the copyright holder. Inlining is more likely than hypertext linking to violate copyright as it creates a potential for creating a derivative work and could cause confusion as to the association, if any, between the two websites.

Deep-linking Issues

Deep-linking refers to a hypertext link that bypasses a website's home page and takes the user directly to an internal page. There are no U.S. laws prohibiting deep-linking but recent U.S. court decisions have called into question the legality of the practice. There has been a great deal of controversy over whether the practice constitutes an infringement on copyright.

Opponents argue that the Copyright Act protects the creative process, which includes the decision of how much of a work to display and in what order in which to display it.

Control over these factors is important because deep-linking can cause websites to lose income, as their revenues are often tied to the number of viewers who pass through their home page; if visitors bypass the ads on the home page by coming into the website through a back-door via a deep-link, then the ads are never seen. Also, it may erroneously create an impression that the two linked websites are associated or endorse each other.

Proponents argue that the Internet was created to promote fast and easy dissemination of information. Direct links to a website's interior pages enhance usability since, unlike generic links, they specifically relate to users' goals. An e-commerce usability study[29] showed that more than a quarter of purchase failures were due to difficulty getting from the home page to the correct product page; preventing deep-linking would eliminate a quarter of potential sales from visitors coming from search engines. In _Ticketmaster v. Microsoft_,[30] Microsoft's "Sidewalk" events web guide offered users a deep-link to Ticketmaster's ticket purchase page. Although Microsoft was actually promoting Ticketmaster sales and sending it thousands of customers, Ticketmaster was upset despite the increased business traffic because the link took users directly to the event page, bypassing its advertisers on its home page. (The case was settled out-of-court in early 1999).

With the rise in popularity of video sharing websites such as YouTube, the practice of deep-linking to podcasts or videos with infringing content on such websites has buttressed the contributory infringement argument.

Sometimes deep-linking may present a case for direct infringement, rather than contributory infringement. In a recent Texas case,[31] a federal district court held that providing an unauthorized deep link to a live audio webcast infringed on the holder's copyright. SFX Motor Sports produces "Supercross" motorcycle racing events and streams live audio of the events on its website, where sponsors have paid for ads (usually consisting of sponsor logos). By deep-linking to the audio webcasts, the defendant enabled web visitors to bypass the SFX site — and hence its advertisers — thus causing economic harm to SFX. Note that in this case, since the linked content was on the copyright holder's own website, the defendant was not contributing to an existing infringement; he was committing the infringement. Thus, he was not a contributory infringer but rather a direct infringer.

Framing Issues

Framing is the process of allowing a user to view the contents of a second website while it is framed by information from the first website. It is actually taking deep-linking one step further. The problem with framing is that it could cause possible confusion about, or be used intentionally to misrepresent, an affiliation or endorsement by the framer of the framed website. The framed website loses control over the content surrounding it; for example, a pornographic website could open up a framed window on its website deep-linked to the yearbook page of a Catholic girl's school, under the title "Up and Cummers." Many of the arguments for and against deep-linking also apply to framing, but the combination of display of copyrighted material and juxtaposition of the material with the framer's own material in a manner that could cause confusion or be misleading would most likely be a strong factor toward a finding of infringement.

A website may expressly prohibit inline linking or framing of its website in its published "Terms of Use." But as discussed above, the enforceability of "Terms of Use" is questionable. In _Ticketmaster v. Tickets.com_,[32] the court held that a contract is not created simply by use of a website; there must be affirmative assent, such as clicking on a click-through agreement. The concept is that there cannot be a unilateral agreement on terms of website usage imposed on the visitor. There must be mutually expressed agreement. There is an inherent Catch-22[33] in conditioning a visitor's use of a website on terms in a page he may not even see until he has completed his use or perusal of the website. Visitors often can view an entire website before stumbling onto the "Terms of Use" page if at all.

The Digital Millennium Copyright Act

The Digital Millennium Copyright Act (DMCA)[34] is actually a 1998 amendment to the U.S. Copyright Act of 1976. Title I of the Act provides for criminal prosecution with up to 10 years imprisonment for circumventing technical measures that protect copyrighted works. The first time the law was applied was in the case of an individual who developed software to override the manufacturers' copyguard on DVDs so that copyrighted DVDs could be freely copied.

Title II of the Act, known as the Online Copyright Infringement Liability Limitation Act (OCILA) establishes protection (_safe harbor_) for Online Service Providers (OSPs) whose customers commit online copyright infringement. An OSP might be an Internet Service Provider (ISP) who provides access to the Internet (_e.g.,_ AOL or a dial-up ISP) or a website that provides an online service (_e.g.,_ a search engine, a bulletin board system [BBS] operator, or a website like YouTube.com or ebay.com).[35] Under the DMCA, the OSP does not have to monitor its service for infringements; the burden rests on the copyright holder. To qualify for the safe harbor provision, the online service provider must:

- Implement, and notify users of, a policy to terminate infringers;

- Designate a "copyright agent" to receive infringement complaints;

- Provide means for notice to the OSP to delete the infringement (or hotlink);

- Not have been aware of the infringement (*i.e.*, no turning a "blind eye" toward infringements by its customers);

- Not gain any financial benefit attributable to the infringing material; and

- Upon notification of claimed infringement, "respond expeditiously to remove, or disable access to, the material."

The safe harbor provisions provide protection from liability for copyrighted content illegally posted by users, so long as the OSP removes such content "expeditiously" upon being notified of the infringement; so far, no court has defined what amount of time qualifies as "expeditiously."

Notification of the alleged infringement is referred to as a "*takedown notice.*" There is no requirement for the OSP to determine if the content is copyrighted by someone other than the poster and posted without permission; in fact, any delay in responding to the takedown notice to make such a determination could subject the OSP to liability, since a delay might be considered counter to the statute's "expeditiously" language. As a practical matter, most OSPs are likely to respond to takedown notices by immediately removing the material without an independent investigation of whether it was indeed a copyright infringement.

Such a situation happened in 2007 on the website YouTube.com when Viacom, Inc. sent a takedown notice to YouTube,[36] complaining that a parody of its Comedy Central TV show "*The Colbert Report*" had infringed on its copyright. As you will see in Chapter Four, it is permissible to reference a copyrighted work for the purpose of parody. If the material in question was a true legal parody then it would not have been an infringement and should not have been removed.

Under the DMCA, the right of redress to wrongfully removed content is not against the OSP who removed it but rather against the sender of the takedown notice. The alleged infringer may file a *counter notification* to the OSP; the OSP then has 10 business days to provide the takedown notice filer with a copy of the counter notification and replace the material within 10–to–14 business days following receipt of the counter notification, unless the filer notifies the OSP that it has filed a restraining order against the subscriber to prohibit the infringment

In the Viacom case, the Electronic Frontier Foundation and Stanford Law School's Center for Internet and Society filed a lawsuit against Viacom (The suit was dropped a month later after Viacom agreed to establish a website and e-mail "hotline," and promised to review any complaint within one business day and reinstate content erroneously taken down.).

There is a tendency for some content producers to engage in "takedown fever" (Viacom alone sent YouTube more than 100,000 takedown notices) with results that border on insanity. When Christopher Knight, an independent film-maker, launched his campaign for his local school board, he naturally turned to promoting his candidacy through a homemade video clip uploaded to YouTube. A Viacom-owned TV show, *Web Junk 2.0*, broadcasted Knight's entire video clip (without obtaining his permission) as part of a segment on web videos (Hey Viacom, broadcasting someone else's work without permission is known as copyright infringement!). Knight then posted a clip of the Viacom show spotlighting his own clip on YouTube. Shortly thereafter, Viacom, charging that Knight was infringing on its content, sent YouTube a takedown notice and Knight was notified by YouTube that if he repeated such copyright infringement then his YouTube account would be cancelled. [37] The adage about people living in glass houses not throwing stones comes to mind.

The Effect of the DMCA — Before and After

Prior to passage of the DMCA, the Supreme Court was faced with one of the most far-reaching copyright decisions of the 20th Century. Sony Electronics had begun commercially marketing a video tape recorder that allowed users to copy TV programs onto a video tape cassette. The motion picture industry cried fowl and sued Sony as a contributory infringer, since its video tape recorder enabled others to commit copyright infringement. However, in 1984 in <u>Sony v. Universal City Studios</u>, [38] the Supreme Court found that while the Sony Betamax video tape recorder could obviously be used to copy movies and TV shows it also had "*commercially significant non-infringing uses*," (*e.g.,* "time-shifting"—recording TV shows for later viewing and for viewing home movies). Thus, the Supreme Court created the *Betamax Test*: Is the technology capable of commercially significant non-infringing uses?

Two years after passage of the DMCA, in 2000, the motion picture industry once again tried to block a new technology that would allow users to copy movies, this time from DVDs. The defendant offered, for download on his website, software to copy DVDs protected by the Content Scramble System. The Supreme Court ruled that this was a copyright infringement that violated the DMCA. [39] Had the DMCA existed 20 years earlier, the home video recording industry might never have gotten off the ground.

Peer–2–Peer Networking

Peer–2–Peer (P2P) networking enables direct communication or sharing of information between individual users through their computers. In a traditional computer network, traffic travels to the server and then back to each node in a highly centralized system where all of the activity centers around the server. A *true P2P network* is a decentralized model of computer networking where traffic travels between two users' computers and not through a central server.

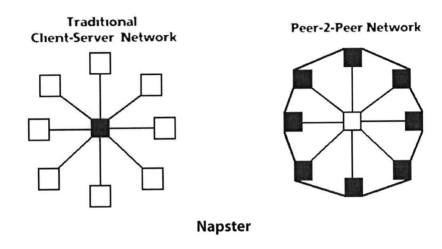

Napster

P2P networking became a (if not *the*) major issue in online copyright infringement with the launch of Napster and its progeny in 1999. Devised by college student Shawn Fanning, Napster was a software program that let millions of users link their computers and share their favorite songs in a common pool of downloadable free music. People interested in specific music tracks reviewed the online catalogs and directly downloaded the music file from other members' computers. Napster was a *centralized* file-sharing P2P service. Users connected to the central Napster server and told it what files they had; Napster's central server indexed all the available files of all users and cross-referenced this index with incoming user requests for specific files. When it found a match, the two users connected to each other to transfer the file. Thus Napster was a *modified P2P network* with its server performing an indexing function, while the actual music files remained on the users' computers.

Contributory Infringer

From our discussion of linking earlier in this chapter, you already know that a direct infringer is one who makes and shares copies, and that a contributory infringer is one who knows or has reason to know of the infringement and induces, causes, or materially contributes to infringing conduct of another. Napster was not a direct infringer because it did not make or distribute the copyrighted works. But in 2001, the

9th Circuit held that Napster was a contributory infringer.[40] The court applied a two-part test: The contributory infringer must (1) *"know or have reason to know"* of a direct infringement, and (2) *materially contribute* to the infringing activity. Since Napster was a centralized file-sharing P2P service it was materially contributing to the infringement.

Likewise, in <u>In re Aimster</u>,[41] the court ruled that Aimster, another P2P network, was a contributory infringer because it (1) offered no evidence that its P2P software had any non-infringing use, and (2) had clear knowledge of infringement. The court focused on the fact that Aimster's software tutorial gave only one example of file-sharing: the sharing of copyrighted music, which showed knowledge of the infringing activity and a material contribution to it. Aimster failed to use Betamax Defense; *i.e.*, showing that the technology is capable of commercially significant non-infringing uses.

A Defeat For the Recording Industry

In 2003, a California federal district court ruled against several movie and recording studios in a copyright infringement suit against P2P companies Grokster and StreamCast (maker of the Morpheus P2P software).[42] This was the first victory by P2P developers over the powerful recording industry. The court found that the P2P companies were not guilty of contributory infringement because of the Betamax Defense, citing non-infringing uses such as the circulation of e-books, promotional videos and demo games on their P2P networks. The court made a significant distinction between centralized and decentralized file-sharing services. Grokster and StreamCast escaped liability because they were *decentralized* — they did not actively facilitate and could not stop their users' infringing activity.

The 9th Circuit upheld the federal district court's decision on appeal in 2004, ruling[43] that P2P networks were legal and that makers of decentralized P2P software should not be held responsible for their users' actions. In a major defeat for the motion picture industry, the court reaffirmed the Betamax Rationale: While sometimes used to download copyrighted material, P2P software is also used in a number of non-infringing ways. (In fact, P2P software has been used by computer programmers to exchange code, by scholars to share treatises, and by political organizations to exchange ideas. During the 2004 election campaign, the political group MoveOn.org used P2P networks to distribute political ads. Another political website, <u>OutragedModerates.org</u>, disseminated government documents via P2P networks.)

The court went on to rebuke the motion picture industry, saying it is unwise to alter copyright law in a way that could stifle innovation just to suit well-established players in a market, given the ways in which technology often changes the market for the better in the long run. The case was appealed to the U.S. Supreme Court and that decision is discussed below, but first we must discuss the concepts of vicarious infringement and inducement, and review the situational context of file sharing at the time the courts were deciding these issues.

Vicarious Infringement

Vicarious infringement is liability for the infringing acts of another. The theory of vicarious infringement holds that if you control the infringer and make money from his infringements, you can be held liable in his place. Vicarious infringement occurs when a party has the right and ability to control an infringer's activity and receives a direct financial benefit from the infringement.

A California federal court ruled in 2004, that *credit card companies cannot be held liable for copyright infringements committed by their customers.* In that case, [44] Perfect 10, a website offering its subscribers photographs of naked women, sued Visa and MasterCard, under the theory of vicarious infringement. Perfect 10 claimed that by completing transactions at websites that sold stolen Perfect 10 images, the credit card companies were vicarious infringers. The court, however, disagreed: [45]

> The ability to process credit cards does not directly assist the allegedly infringing websites in copying plaintiff's works. * * * Defendants do not provide the means for distributing those works to others, nor do they provide bandwidth or storage space with which to transfer or store the works.

The decision was upheld on appeal by the 9th Circuit in 2007. [46] In a similar case, [47] after a media conglomerate bought Napster, record companies sought to hold *investors* liable for vicarious infringement of copyrighted songs, by suing the shareholders on the basis that by financing Napster while infringement was occurring, they were enabling it, although the court sidestepped that issue in deciding the case.

Illegal Music File-Sharing

In June 2003, the Recording Industry Association of America (RIAA) announced that it would file lawsuits against individuals, and by 2007 it had sued 30,000 individuals. [48] The tactic scared many people away from file-sharing and resulted in quick settlements with many defendants. The recording industry's scare tactic has brought it hostility from music-sharing fans and embarrassment from the nature of some of the defendants it has named in its lawsuits. One early defendant was a 12-year-old New York honor student who ultimately settled with the multi-million dollar recording industry by paying $2,000 (copyright infringements by law can cost between $750–to–$150,000 per song).[49] A 66-year-old Boston woman was sued by the RIAA, who charged that she had illegally shared more than 2,000 songs through Kazaa (a file-sharing P2P network) and sought up to $150,000 for each song.[50] However, the fact that the woman owned a Macintosh computer (Kazaa runs only on Windows-based computers) led the RIAA to drop the lawsuit although it reserved "the right to refile the complaint if and when circumstances warrant." Or, as summed up sarcastically by one observer, "just in case she buys a PC, installs Kazaa, acquires a taste for hip-hop, and decides to start sharing files."[51] Other defendants included a grandmother accused of downloading music by a band called "Incubus"[52] and a dead woman. The deceased 83-year-old defendant was charged by the RIAA with uploading more than 700 pop, rock, and rap songs to the Internet under the screen name "smittenedkitten." Her daughter claimed that her mother hated computers and would not allow one in her house, and the RIAA has since admitted that it is unlikely that the deceased woman was actually "smittenedkitten."[53] However, this merely emphasizes the problems and inaccuracies replete in the RIAA's lawsuits.[54]

So far, only one RIAA case has gone all the way through a jury trial, mainly because most defendants choose to accept the RIAA settlement offer rather then the more expensive option of fighting a prolonged legal battle.[55] One article noted that innocent defendants often find themselves "bullied into accepting a carefully chosen sum that is substantially smaller than the legal fees required to fight the accusations."[56] But that may change after the decision in _Capitol Records v. Foster_,[57] where an innocent defendant turned the tables on the record company that sued her and recovered $70,000 in attorneys fees. The RIAA sued Deborah Foster in November 2004, after claiming it had evidence that an IP address associated with her ISP account was engaged in illegal file sharing. The Oklahoma woman denied that she was file sharing and the following year the RIAA added her adult daughter to its complaint (the RIAA won a default judgment against the daughter). The RIAA's fallback position was its claim that Foster — if not a direct infringer — was nonetheless a vicarious infringer as she provided the account that her daughter allegedly used to commit the infringement. However, rather than pursue this course, the RIAA chose to drop its claim, as the court explained:[58]

> The plaintiffs assert that had the case continued, they would have proved their secondary liability claims. Specifically, they contend they would have been able to show that the defendant knew or "should have known" that her Internet account was being used by a member of her household to infringe the plaintiffs' copyrights. That may be so. The plaintiffs, however, chose not to pursue the claim.

The Court finds disingenuous the plaintiffs' assertion that "had they been given an opportunity, they would have been able to prove vicarious infringement." The plaintiffs were in no way deprived of an opportunity to prove their allegations. They moved, voluntarily, to dismiss their claims after the defendant had already made a substantial investment toward defending against those claims.

And once the claim was dismissed, the defendant then filed a motion to recover her legal costs. As this was the first file sharing case in which the RIAA has been required to pay attorney's fees, it sets an important precedent for wrongfully-sued defendants to recover their legal costs and might encourage more defendants to stand up to the powerful organization.

It would seem that the RIAA follows a poker approach to its litigation: bluff strongly, then fold if the stakes start to look too high.

Tanya Andersen was a disabled, single mother of a 7-year-old daughter, living on Social Security in Oregon[59] when, in 2005, she received a letter from a Los Angeles law firm accusing her of downloading gangsta rap music under the name "gotenkito@kazaa.com" at 4:20 a.m. The letter claimed that she had downloaded 1,300 files, that she owed hundreds of thousands of dollars for copyright infringement, and directed her to contact Settlement Support Center, LLC. That firm has been described as a "debt collection company…formed by the record companies for the sole purpose of coercing payments from people who had been identified as targets in the anonymous information farming suits."[60] Andersen denied the accusations and offered to let the RIAA inspect her computer; she also Googled the alias the RIAA claimed she used and found that the same name on a MySpace page of a young man who admitted that he downloaded music illegally.[61] Andersen turned this information over to the RIAA, who responded by suing her.

According to a subsequent lawsuit filed by Andersen, the RIAA attempted to interrogate her 10-year-old daughter, claiming that the child had illegally downloaded music three years earlier at the age of seven. To this end, the lawsuit alleged, an RIAA agent engaged in pretexting, claiming to be her daughter's grandmother called the child's former elementary school inquiring about her attendance.[62] The RIAA continued to insist on a face-to-face interrogation of the child, despite Andersen's attempts to limit depositions of the then 10-year-old to telephone or video-conferences.

Andersen's lawsuit revealed that "the record company plaintiffs employed MediaSentry as their agent to break into Ms. Andersen's personal computer (and those of tens of thousands of other people) to secretly spy on and steal information or remove files."[63] Finally, Tanya filed a motion to force the RIAA to prove that she illegally downloaded music; literally hours before the deadline to respond to the motion, the RIAA dropped its case. In poker terminology, Andersen called the RIAA's bluff and they folded.

But Andersen was not about to let it end there, after two years of significant legal expenses, emotional distress, and humiliation. She filed a class action lawsuit against the RIAA, claiming "negligence, fraud, negligent misrepresentation, federal and state RICO, abuse of process, malicious prosecution, intentional infliction of emotional distress, violation of the Computer Fraud and Abuse Act, trespass, invasion of privacy, libel and slander, deceptive business practices, misuse of copyright law, and civil conspiracy."[64] (RICO is the Racketeer Influenced and Corrupt Organizations Act, which provided treble damages in lawsuits). In poker terms, this is called "you can't fold, I call and raise you." The outcome of this case may determine the future of RIAA cases.

In another example of the RIAA folding its hand as the stakes increased, Paul Wilke considered himself a victim of RIAA inaccuracies like the ones described earlier, when he was sued by the RIAA for allegedly sharing music over a P2P network.[65] Wilke fought back by filing a motion for summary judgment, arguing that it was a case of mistaken identity, based solely on his name, an IP address, and a list of songs flagged by file-sharing software. The RIAA responded with a motion for expedited discovery to give it the opportunity to find enough evidence to prevent the case from being dismissed, which on its face appears an admission that the three factors it typically uses to bring cases might not withstand a motion for summary judgment, let alone prove infringement. The RIAA quickly dropped the case against Wilke, amidst speculation amongst bloggers of the potential damage a loss in such a case would have to future RIAA lawsuits.

The U.S. Court of Appeals for the District of Columbia held that the RIAA could not use the subpoena process under the DMCA to obtain the name of a Verizon Internet Services customer suspected of sharing 800 audio files.[66] As the RIAA's lawsuits relied on the DMCA's subpoena process, this ruling makes it more difficult for the RIAA to identify prospective defendants. Since most file-sharers remain essentially anonymous by using screen names, the RIAA has resorted to using IP addresses to track down file-sharing ISP accounts, a method rife with inaccuracies like those recounted above. Even so, most individuals named as defendants choose a quick settlement over a prolonged and expensive trial. Indeed, as of October 2006, no RIAA lawsuit had gone to trial, with most of the cases either being settled or dropped by the RIAA.[67]

Some courts have provided limited protection to ISP customers. In 2004, a U.S. district court in Pennsylvania held that ISPs served with subpoenas demanding names of file-sharers must first provide their customers with detailed notice of their rights before complying with the subpoena. Such notice must not only inform the customer of the music industry's attorneys' pending subpoena but also provide information on challenging it, including a list of attorneys and information on jurisdiction. The notice reads, in part: "To maintain a lawsuit against you in the District Court in Philadelphia, the record companies must establish jurisdiction over you in Pennsylvania. If you do not live or work in Pennsylvania, or visit the state regularly, you may be able to challenge the Pennsylvania court's jurisdiction over you." This may affect those ISP customers who live in neighboring states. While the decision only applies to the Eastern District of Pennsylvania, it represents another step in the evolution of the law in this area as courts move to protect the privacy and due process rights of file-sharers accused of copyright infringement.[68]

In contrast however, at the same time in the United Kingdom, the British High Court ruled that ISPs when subpoenaed must reveal the names and addresses of Britons accused of file-sharing copyrighted songs.[69] The British Phonographic Industry (BPI) and the International Federation of the Phonographic Industry sought the ruling after announcing that they would begin suing British music fans who download copyrighted songs from file-sharing networks. Upon obtaining the information from the ISP, the BPI would notify the file-sharers of the charges and offer them the opportunity to settle the case.

The U.S. government cracked down on felony criminal copyright infringement with the Justice Department's launch of "Operation Digital Gridlock," the first federal enforcement action against copyright infringement on P2P networks.[70] It targeted illegal distribution of copyright-protected movies, software, games, and music on *private* sharing networks that use the NeoModus' Direct Connect technology, rather than going after *public* P2Ps like Kazaa or e-Donkey. The enforcement action by the Justice Department's Computer Crime and Intellectual Property Section resulted in two convictions for conspiracy to commit felony criminal copyright infringement.[71]

States have also begun to crack down on criminal copyright infringement. In 2005, Arizona prosecuted a University of Arizona student for uploading digital copies of recently released movies and music.[72] The student, charged with possession of unauthorized copies of intellectual property, a felony, was sentenced to three months in jail, deferred with three years probation, community service and a $5,400 fine. Unlike many downloaders who download copyrighted files for their personal use or to trade, this student was selling the files he had downloaded.

However, both the states and the U.S. federal government are powerless to stop copyright infringement of U.S. copyright holders by foreign entities. While treaties such as the Berne Convention or the World Intellectual Property Organization (WIPO) Copyright Treaty may enable the United States to lodge a complaint with a foreign government, enforcement of alleged infringement remains in the hands of the foreign government, whose laws or definitions of infringement may differ from the United States, and not all nations are signatories to the treaties. For example, until recently Moscow prosecutors refused to press criminal charges against AllofMP3.com, a popular Russian website that sold copyrighted American songs for mere pennies and entire albums for a dollar.[73]

Meanwhile, legal, fee-based online music services have evolved and prospered, with Apple's popular iTunes (totaling 82% of legal downloads in 2005[74]) and Roxio's revamped version of Napster finding a large legitimate market.

The INDUCE Act

The Inducing of Copyright Infringement Act of 2004 (the INDUCE Act) was a proposed bill that would have eliminated the Betamax Standard used over last two decades to determine liability in infringement cases. Recall that the Betamax Standard states that if the technology is capable of commercially significant non-infringing uses, then it does not violate the law. Under the bill, it would have made no difference if the technology has substantial non-infringing uses; makers of devices with multiple uses, (*e.g.*, computers and copy machines), could be liable for inducing infringement. Any device that could be used to store or play illegally obtained files could be targeted in a lawsuit — the result of which could ban file-sharing networks, P2P networks, Tivo, and even VCRs.

The proposed law was extremely favorable to the music and motion picture industries. The bill's sponsor, Republican Senator Orrin Hatch of Utah, is a conservative who co-authored the controversial DMCA and has received $158,000 in campaign contributions from TV, movie, and music industries.[75] In 2003, he proposed that copyright holders be allowed to destroy remotely computers used by people who download copyrighted songs. Titled as the INDUCE Act — "Inducement Devolves into Unlawful Child Exploitation Act" — the bill was labeled as anti-child pornography but it was really a back-door way to eliminate P2P file-sharing.

Although the INDUCE Act was deleted from the Family Entertainment and Copyright Act of 2004 submitted to the U.S. House of Representatives in December 2004 it — or similar legislation — could resurface in a future session of Congress.

A Victory for the Recording Industry

The recording industry won the next round in the copyright battle when the U.S. Supreme Court handed down its decision in *MGM v. Grokster*[76] in June 2005. In the unanimous decision, the court overturned the 9th Circuit's ruling that makers of decentralized P2P software should not be held responsible for their users' actions but it did not go so far as to rule the technology, *i.e.*, P2P networks, illegal. The Supreme Court did not address the issue of whether the technology itself was legal. The recording industry had hoped for just such a pronouncement, but instead, the Supreme Court focused on how Grokster and StreamCast marketed and promoted themselves to potential customers and whether they encouraged the illegal use of their technology. Justice David Souter wrote in the majority opinion:[77]

> We hold that one who distributes a device with the object of promoting its use to infringe copyright … is liable for the resulting acts of infringement by third parties.

That issue has been commonly referred to as "inducement," *i.e.*, actively encouraging users to engage in infringing activities. Thus the Supreme Court, in effect, has adopted the rationale of the Induce Act (discussed above) that would have punished companies that induced customers to violate copyright law.[78] The Induce Act had been proposed in response to the 9th Circuit's earlier decision in favor of Grokster and StreamCast. Souter called Grokster and StreamCast's unlawful intent "unmistakable," stating that there was "substantial evidence" that Streamcast had "induced" people to use its software to share copyrighted files illegally. (However, the Supreme Court sent the case back to the lower court for a trial on the issue of whether Grokster and StreamCast did induce copyright infringement. In September 2006, the same federal judge who, in 2003, ruled that file-sharing firms could not be held liable for the actions of the users of their software held that the distributor of the Morpheus online file-sharing software had induced file-sharing of copyrighted music, stating "evidence of StreamCast's unlawful intent is overwhelming.").[79]

The decision applied a standard of vicarious liability upon manufacturers of technology for the illegal uses of their technology by their customers, *e.g.*, file-sharing companies are to blame for what users do with their software. However, makers of other technology, such as photocopiers, cameras, i-Pods, and even computers could be liable under the standard of vicarious liability enunciated in *MGM v. Grokster*. The test appears to be whether they actively and knowingly encourage the illegal use, such as copyright infringement. The recording industry had argued in this case that the defendants had control over their end-users because the software companies could have modified the software to prevent users from sharing copyrighted files. This "control" would impute vicarious liability, they argued.

Recall that the 9th Circuit had ruled that P2P networks could not be held liable for copyright infringement because they could be used for legitimate purposes as well (the Betamax Standard). The Supreme Court said that the Betamax Standard was still valid but that the 9th Circuit had interpreted the Sony decision too broadly. But the court did not elaborate because it itself was split on whether Grokster and StreamCast had violated *Sony*. So the Supreme Court appears to have upheld the Betamax Standard and the apparent legality of the underlying technology while subjecting the manufacturers to vicarious liability for illegal uses of that technology if the manufacturer actively promoted and marketed such illegal uses.

On the one hand, the decision will have a chilling effect on companies that produce digital media products, as they will now have to guard against lawsuits for contributing to, or inadvertently encouraging, copyright infringement. On the other hand, one could interpret this case as a road map laid out by the court for other P2P companies to abide by to avoid infringement lawsuits. The inference of the court's opinion appears to be that liability will turn on whether the defendant's actions (*i.e.*, marketing and promotion) reveal an intent to contribute (indirectly or vicariously) to copyright infringement. Companies that avoid the appearance of such intent may be able to avoid liability.

While the Supreme Court has not yet addressed the issue of whether the underlying P2P technology itself is legal, there is the possibility that Congress could declare the technology illegal. In 2007, Congress held hearings at which several congressmen charged that P2P networks posed a "national security threat" by virtue of enabling federal government employees unintentionally to share sensitive or classified documents from their computers. [80] One example cited was that of a Department of Transportation worker whose daughter installed the P2P file-sharing program Limewire on her home computer, exposing certain government documents to the network. This begs the questions "Why did a government employee have sensitive or classified files on a home computer?" and "Why would a government employee allow a child access to a computer containing sensitive or classified files?" The solution to any perceived threat to national security is not to prohibit a technology that enables communication among its users (an action that would probably be in direct violation of First Amendment freedom of speech rights) but rather to regulate and control those in the government who handle sensitive or classified files. Government should require written authorization for installation of P2P programs on its computers and properly train its employees. There already exist laws against leaking classified documents. Any perceived "national security threat" emanates not from the technology itself, but rather from the way individuals use that technology.

Ownership Rights of Downloaded Music

The ability to download music raises some interesting questions. Can a legally downloaded song be resold? You can buy a music CD at the music store and legally sell it to your friend or on eBay. What if you legally purchased a downloaded song and burned it to a single CD and sold it to the same friend or on eBay? Is there a difference? What if you burned the song to multiple CDs and sold them all? Would it make a difference, or be infringement, if you burned the song to multiple CDs for personal use?

In 1908, the U.S. Supreme Court established the "First Sale" doctrine, holding that the buyer of a copyrighted work can sell or give away that work without the permission of the copyright owner.[81] In that case, Macy's Department Store sold a book for 89¢, even though the publisher had inserted a notice in the book stating that any retail sale under a dollar would be considered copyright infringement. Although the 1908 court decision (and its subsequent codification in the 1909 Copyright Act) applied to copies that had been sold, the Copyright Act of 1976 codified the doctrine to apply to any "owner" of a lawfully made copy, eliminating the requirement of a sale.[82]

In 2007, Universal Music Group (UMG) filed a copyright infringement suit against a man whose livelihood consisted of buying collectible albums at used record stores and then selling them on eBay.[83] UMG claimed that because the CDs were promotional CDs given by record companies to radio stations and music publications that the "First Sale" doctrine did not apply. Interestingly, UMG does not appear to have sued any used record stores for selling promotional (or other) records. Section 109 of the Copyright Act would seem to refute UMG's position, although the case was still pending at the time of this book's publication.

In the realm of software, publishers contend that the "First Sale" doctrine does not apply because software is licensed, not sold, under the terms of an End User License Agreement (EULA). Many retailers have complained about online resales of their product on eBay but none have yet gone so far as to claim copyright infringement.[84]

Summary

There are three types of infringement: direct infringement, contributory infringement, and vicarious infringement. A direct infringer is one who commits the copyright infringement directly. A contributory infringer is one who helps others to commit copyright infringement. A vicarious infringer is one who has the right and ability to control an infringer's activity and receives a direct financial benefit from the infringement.

All content placed on a website should be original or used with permission of its creator. Webmasters must put in place mechanisms to prevent others from posting copyrighted material to their websites. Websites can connect to other websites through hypertext links, inline linking, deep-linking, or framing. A hypertext link is a word or phrase that when clicked takes the user to a new web page. Inline linking, or "inlining," is the process of displaying a graphic file on one website that originates at another. Deep-linking refers to a hypertext link that bypasses a website's home page and takes the user directly to an internal page. Framing is the process of allowing a user to view the contents of a second website while it is framed by information from the first website. Certain forms of linking may confer liability for contributory copyright infringement.

The Digital Millennium Copyright Act makes it a crime to circumvent technical measures designed to protect copyrighted works. Title II of the Act, known as the Online Copyright Infringement Liability Limitation Act (OCILA) establishes protection (safe harbor) for Online Service providers (OSPs) whose customers commit online copyright infringement. An OSP might be an Internet Service Provider (ISP) who provides access to the Internet or a website that provides an online service. Notification of the alleged infringement is referred to as a "takedown notice." There is no requirement for the OSP to determine if the content is copyrighted by someone other than the poster and posted without permission. The alleged infringer may file a counter notification to the OSP.

The Betamax Test asks "Is the technology capable of commercially significant non-infringing uses?" Peer-2-Peer (P2P) networking enables direct communication or sharing of information between individual users through their computers. The concept of "inducement" refers to actively encouraging users to engage in infringing activities. The Supreme Court has enunciated a standard of vicarious liability on technology manufacturers for the illegal uses of their products by their customers who actively and knowingly induce or encourage the illegal use.

Chapter Three Notes

[1] Copyright Act of 1976, as amended, 17 U.S.C. § 101 *et seq.*

[2] *Playboy Enters., Inc. v. Sanfilippo*, 46 U.S.P.Q.2d 1350 (S.D. Cal. 1998). This case is included in the Cases Section on the Issues in Internet Law website (www.IssuesinInternetLaw.com).

[3] "Gay Couple Sues Conservative Group Over Use of Their Photo in Internet Ad," Associated Press wire report, March 11, 2005.

[4] According to the complaint filed in the case.

[5] *Holtzbrinck Publ'g Holdings, L.P. v. Vyne Communic'ns., Inc.*, Case No. 97 Civ. 1082, 2000 U.S. Dist. LEXIS 5444 (S.D.N.Y. Apr. 25, 2000).

[6] As discussed in Chapter 13, *infra*, there may be some circumstances where the website owner (or ISP) may be shielded from liability for third-party postings by § 230 of the Communications Decency Act (CDA).

[7] Defamation online is discussed at length in Chapter 13, *infra*.

[8] *Software Development & Investment of Nevada d/b/a Traffic Power.com v. Aaron Wall, d/b/a SEO Book.com*, Case No. 05-A-508400-C (8th Judicial District, Clark County, Nevada, Aug. 2005); *Software Development & Investment of Nevada d/b/a Traffic-Power.com v. Wall d/b/a Seobook.com*, Case No. 2:05-cv-01109-RLH-LRL (D. Nev. motion to dismiss granted Feb. 13, 2006).

[9] "Paper Cuts Off Website Forum," Los Angeles Times, May 21, 2005. Many newspapers have instituted a policy of banning comments during major news events. The Roanoke (VA) Times closed a message board it had set up to discuss the killing spree at Virginia Tech in April 2007. Some newspapers, like the Sacramento (CA) Bee, ban anonymous comments and require readers to use their real names in posts. *See* Janet Kornblum "Rudeness, Threats Make the Web a Cruel World," USA Today, July 30, 2007.

[10] Steve Outing, "When User Comments Become Community Journalism," E-Media Tidbits, June 2, 2005, *available at* www.poynter.org/column.asp?id=31&aid=83324 (accessed September 25, 2007).

[11] Katharine Q. Seelye, "Paper Closes Reader Comments on Blog, Citing Vitriol," New York Times, January 20 2006.

[12] *Ibid.*

[13] Steve Outing, fn. 10, *supra.*

[14] E-mail posted on Chris Raettig's website, *available at* http://chris.raettig.org/email/jnl00036.html (accessed September 25, 2007).

[15] In 1832, the Cherokee Indians lived on land guaranteed them by a treaty with the U.S. government. After gold was discovered on the land, the state of Georgia attempted to seize the land. The Cherokees sued and in *Worcester v. Georgia*, 31 U.S. 515 (1832), the Supreme Court ruled their favor. Georgia refused to obey the court. President Andrew Jackson said, "(Chief Justice) John Marshall has made his decision; now let him enforce it." Jackson sent federal troops to evict the Cherokees, who were forced to travel the "Trail of Tears" to Oklahoma, with thousands dying enroute.

[16] Chris Raettig's website, fn. 14, *supra.*

[17] *Perfect 10, Inc. v. Google, Inc.*, Case No. CV 04-9484 AHM (SHx) (C.D. Cal., Feb. 2006) *aff'd. in part, rev'd in part, remanded* (9th Cir., May 16, 2007).

[18] *Ibid.*

[19] Chris Jenkins, "ISP Liable in 'MP3s4free' Case," Australian IT, July 15, 2005.

[20] Simon Hayes, "Man Charged in Copyright Case," Australian IT, June 7, 2005.

[21] *Cooper v. Universal Music Australia Pty. Ltd.,* [2006] FCAFC 187 (December 18, 2006).

[22] In June 2007, the High Court of Australia refused to grant leave to hear an appeal, upholding the decisions of the trial judge and Full Federal Court that the defendant had authorized copyright infringement.

[23] *See* further discussion on the CDA and publisher liability in Chapter 13.

[24] *LiveUniverse, Inc. v. MySpace, Inc.,* Case No. 2:06-cv-06994-AHM-RZ (CD Cal. June 5, 2007).

[25] Kellie Schmitt, "Judge Lets MySpace Block Links to Its Competition," The Recorder, July 25, 2007.

[26] E-mails on Dan Wallach's website, *available at* www.cs.rice.edu/~dwallach/dilbert/um_letters.html (accessed September 25, 2007).

[27] Copyright Act of 1976, as amended, 17 U.S.C. § 101 *et seq.*

[28] *See* Chapter Two.

[29] Jakob Nielsen's Alertbox, "Deep Linking Is Good," March 3, 2002, *available at* www.useit.com/alertbox/20020303.html (accessed September 25, 2007).

[30] *Ticketmaster v. Microsoft*, Civil Action No. 97-3055 DDP (C.D. Cal. Apr. 28, 1997); case settled in January 1999, Microsoft agreed not to deep-link into Ticketmaster's website.

[31] *Live Nation Motor Sports, Inc. v. Davis*, Case No. 3:06-CV-276-L (N.D. Tex. Dec. 12, 2006).

[32] *Ticketmaster v. Tickets.com*, 2000 U.S. Dist. Lexis 4553, 54 U.S.P.Q.2d (BNA) 1344 (C.D. Cal Mar. 27, 2000).

[33] The phrase "Catch-22," derived from the 1961 novel of the same name by Joseph Heller about the madness of war, has evolved into common use to mean a cyclical conundrum.

[34] Digital Millennium Copyright Act, 17 U.S.C. § 512.

[35] The issue of whether P2P networks also qualify for safe harbor protection under § 512 of the Digital Millennium Copyright Act was left unsettled by the court in *A & M Records v. Napster*, fn. 40 *infra*, when it chose not to extend the safe harbor provisions to the Napster software program and service.

[36] Actually, it was one of more than 100,000 takedown notices sent by Viacom to YouTube. *See* Nate Anderson, "DMCA Takedown Backlash: EFF Sues Viacom Over Colbert Parody Clip," Arstechnica.com, March 22, 2007.

[37] Christopher Knight, "Viacom Hits Me with Copyright Infringement for Posting on YouTube A Video That Viacom Made by Infringing on My Own Copyright!," The Knight Shift blog, August 29, 2007, *available at* http://theknightshift.blogspot.com/2007/08/viacom-hits-me-with-copyright.html (accessed September 25, 2007).

[38] *Sony v. Universal City Studios*, 464 U.S. 417 (1984).

[39] *Universal City Studios v. Reimerdes*, 111 F. Supp. 2d 294 (S.D.N.Y. 2000). This case is included in the Cases Section on the Issues in Internet Law website (www.IssuesinInternetLaw.com).

[40] *A & M Records v. Napster*, 239 F.3d 1004 (9th Cir. 2001). This case is included in the Cases Section on the Issues in Internet Law website (www.IssuesinInternetLaw.com).

[41] *In re Aimster*, 334 F.3d 643 (7th Cir. 2003).

[42] *MGM v. Grokster*, 259 F. Supp.2d 1029 (C.D. Cal. 2003).

[43] *MGM v. Grokster*, Nos. 03-55894, 03-55901, 03-56236, 2004 WL 1853717 (9th Cir. Aug. 19, 2004) (slip op.).

[44] *Perfect 10, Inc. v. Visa Int"l. Servs. Ass'n.*, 71 U.S.P.Q.2d 1914 (N.D. Cal. 2004).

[45] *Ibid.*

[46] *Perfect 10, Inc. v. Visa Int'l. Servs. Ass'n.*, Case No. 05-15170 (9th Cir. July 3, 2007).

[47] *UMG Recordings, Inc. v. Bertelsmann AG*, 222 F.R.D. 408 (N.D. Cal. 2004).

[48] Jeff Leeds, "Labels Win Suit Against Song Sharer," New York Times, October 5, 2007.

[49] Jefferson Graham, "RIAA Lawsuits Bring Consternation, Chaos," USA Today, September 10, 2003.

[50] Chris Gaither, "Recording Industry Withdraws Suit," Boston Globe, September 24, 2003.

[51] Eric Bangeman, "Et Cetera: Bullet for Bullet," September 24, 2003, Ars Technica.com, *available at* http://arstechnica.com/news.ars/post/20030924-2868.html (accessed September 25, 2007).

[52] Jefferson Graham, fn. 49, *supra.*

[53] Nate Mook, "RIAA Sues Deceased Grandmother," BetaNews, February 4, 2005, *available at* www.betanews.com/article/RIAA_Sues_Deceased_Grandmother/1107532260 (accessed September 25, 2007).

[54] Bruce Gain, "RIAA Takes Shotgun to Traders," Wired News, October 4, 2005.

[55] As this book went to press, the RIAA won its first jury verdict in a file-sharing case. In *Capitol Records v. Thomas* (formerly *Virgin Records America, Inc. v. Thomas*), Case No. 06-CV-01497 (D.C. Minn. Oct. 5, 2007), the RIAA convinced a jury that Jaimmie Thomas had used Kazaa P2P file-sharing network to download songs. Thomas was ordered to pay $9,250 per song for 24 songs, totalling $220,000. The jury instructions left open grounds for appeal: Instruction No. 14 stated that the mere act of downloading constituted infringement and Instruction No. 15 stated that making copyrighted sound recordings *available* for electronic distribution on a P2P network constituted infringement *regardless of whether actual distribution has been shown.* Thomas may have downloaded the songs to a folder on her computer that was accessible to other Kazaa users, but there was no evidence at trial that Kazaa users actually downloaded songs from Thomas' computer. Is there infringement absent distribution? Is downloading alone, without distribution, theft and not infringement? While the verdict might not survive an appeal, it is uncertain whether the defendant has the financial means to appeal or whether the RIAA might offer a reduced settlement amount in exchange for her agreement not to appeal.

[56] Eliot Van Buskirk, "Scoop: Label Must Pay P2P Defendant's Legal Fees," Wired Listening Post, February 7, 2007.

[57] *Capitol Records, Inc. v. Foster,* Case No. Civ. 04-1569-W, (W.D. Okla. Feb. 6, 2007).

[58] *Ibid.*

[59] Florin Tibu, "Atlantic Records Sues 7-Year-Old Girl," Softpedia, March 27, 2007, *available at* http://news.softpedia.com/news/Atlantic-Records-Sues-7-yo-Girl-50342.shtml (accessed September 25, 2007).

[60] *Andersen v. Atlantic Recording Corp.,* Case No. 3:2007cv00934, (D.C. Or. filed June 22, 2007).

[61] Ashbel S. Green, "Woman: I'm No Music Pirate," The Oregonian, June 27, 2007.

[62] *Ibid.*

[63] *Andersen v. Atlantic Recording Corp.,* fn. 60, *supra.*

[64] Eliot Van Buskirk, "Tanya Anderson Files Class Action Suit Against the RIAA," Wired blog, August 16, 2007.

[65] *Elektra v. Wilke,* Case No.06-CV2717 (N.D. Ill. *dismissed,* Oct. 13, 2006).

[66] *Recording Indus. Ass'n of America, Inc. v. Verizon Internet Servs., Inc.,* 351 F.3d 1229 (D.C. Cir. 2003).

[67] Eric Bangeman, "RIAA Drops File Sharing Case," Ars Technica.com, *available at* http://arstechnica.com/news.ars/post/20061015-7990.html, October 15, 2006 (accessed September 25, 2007).

[68] Katie Dean, "File Sharers Win More Protection," Wired News, October 28, 2004.

[69] Matthew Caron, "Good To Be An American," Copyfutures blog, October 16, 2004, *available at* http://lsolum.typepad.com/copyfutures/2004/10/good_to_be_an_a.html (accessed September 25, 2007).

[70] Joris Evers, IDG News Service, "Feds Bust File-Sharing Sites," PCWorld.com, August 25, 2004.

[71] Grant Gross, IDG News Service, "P-to-P Operators Plead Guilty," PCWorld.com, January 19, 2005.

[72] Associated Press wire report, March 8, 2005.

[73] John Borland, "Legal Reprieve for Russian MP3 Site?," CNET News.com, March 7, 2005. In 2005, the Moscow City Prosecutor's office ruled that Russian copyright laws do not cover online distribution of creative works but in May 2006 it reversed its position and began a criminal probe against AllofMP3.com. In October 2006, Visa stopped processing credit card transactions for AllofMP3.com and the Bush administration warned that allowing AllofMP3.com to continue could jeopardize Russia's entry into the World Trade Organization (W.T.O.). *See* Greg Sandoval, "Visa Halts Its Service for allofmp3.com," CNET News.com, October 18, 2006. In June 2007, AllofMP3.com was shut down but a nearly identical new site, mp3Sparks.com, was set up by the same owner. In August 2007, the site owner was acquitted of copyright infringement by a Russian court, after the defendant argued that he had paid royalties to the Russian Multimedia and Internet Society (however many Western firms refuse to recognize this organization or accept its offers of payments). The website said it would resume business, but as part of Russia's entry into the W.T.O., the United States and Russia agreed in principle "on the objective of shutting down websites that permit illegal distribution of music and other copyright works," and listed AllofMP3.com as an example. *See* "Russia Throws Out Net Piracy Case," BBC News, August 15, 2007.

[74] Charles Duhig, "Digital Music Sales Soar; Industry Hopes Downloads Eventually Offset CDs' Decline," Los Angeles Times, October 4, 2005.

[75] "INDUCE Act Will Ban P2P Networks and Apple iPod, Critics Say," Legal News Watch, June 22, 2004; *see also* Joanna Glasner, "File-Trading Bill Stokes Fury," Wired News, June 24, 2004.

[76] *MGM v. Grokster*, 545 U.S. 913 (2005).

[77] *Ibid.* Several weeks after the *Grokster* decision, the Bush administration, through White House spokesman Scott McClellan, stated "The president believes that the manufacturer of a legal product should not be held liable for the criminal misuse of that product by others. We look at it from a standpoint of stopping lawsuit abuse." Ironically, he was referring to proposed legislation before Congress to protect gun manufacturers and dealers from lawsuits over gun crimes, not to P2P software.

[78] Lawrence Lessig has written an interesting op-ed article wherein he contends that the Supreme Court in *Grokster* has usurped Congress' copyright-making policy, noting that historically the court had previously deferred to Congress to define the scope of copyright, as in *Sony v. Universal City Studios, fn. 38, supra.* He argues that the *Grokster* court expanded the Copyright Act "to cover a form of liability it had never before recognized in the context of copyright — the wrong of providing technology that induces copyright infringement." Lawrence Lessig, "Make Way for Copyright Chaos," New York Times, March 18, 2007.

[79] Associated Press wire report, September 27, 2006. Kazaa and Grokster settled out-of-court.

[80] Anne Broache, "Congress: P2P Networks Harm National Security," CNET News.com, July 24, 2007.

[81] *Bobbs-Merrill Co. v. Straus*, 210 U.S. 339 (1908).

[82] Copyright Act of 1976, 17 U.S.C. § 109.

[83] *Universal Recordings, Inc. v. Troy Augusto*, Case No. 2:07-cv-3106 SJO (AJWx), (C.D. Cal. filed May 2007).

[84] *See* Elaine Hughes, "Online Resales Worry Retailers," USA Today, August 1, 2007.

Chapter Three Quiz

Fred Flintstone hires web designer Barney Rubble to create a website for Flintstone's Fiddles Repair Shop. Barney asks Fred for a photograph of Fred to use on the website and Fred gives Barney a copy of a magazine that has a very flattering photograph of Fred accompanying an article on Flintstone's Fiddles. He tells Barney to use that photograph and to copy the text of the article onto the website's "About Us" page. Fred also gives Barney an old Flintstone's Fiddles brochure with a cover photograph of famous violinist Rock Granite. Fred assures Barney that the photo was licensed and paid for to use in the brochure so they can use it on the website.

Barney has included a message board and guest book on the website. Fred is concerned because visitors have been posting product reviews from music magazines on the message board and Slate's Rock & Gravel Co. has been filling the guest book with spam. Barney has cleverly designed the website with frames so that on one page the eBay website auction listings for musical instruments appears framed within Fred's website. On the home page Barney has used an inline link to cause a copyrighted photograph of Clay Limestone, a famous musician, to appear on the page. Barney assures Fred that there is no copyright concern here because the photograph is still hosted on the original server and has not been "copied" to Fred's server.

Meanwhile, Pebbles and Bamm-Bamm have been downloading music from Quartzaa, a decentralized P2P file-sharing network. The Bedrock United Record Producers (BURP) is suing Mr. Quarry, owner of Quartzaa, as a contributory infringer. What defenses can Mr. Quarry use? BURP has subpoenaed Rocklink, the ISP, to discover the identity of the downloaders. What issues does this raise for both Rocklink and Pebbles and Bamm-Bamm?

Noticing Pebbles and Bamm-Bamm's growing interest in music, Fred has an epiphany and decides to expand his business to include music lessons to schoolchildren. So with the help of a good HTML book, a six-pack of Shale beer and a long weekend, Fred completely revamps the Flintstone's Fiddles website. A short time later, Barney files a copyright infringement lawsuit against Fred. Fred tells Barney that he cannot sue him for making modifications to his own website. Is Fred right?

If you are using this book in a classroom, discuss the issues raised and the liability of all parties. Otherwise, try to list the issues involved and probable outcomes before turning to the answers in the Appendix.

[Answers in Appendix]

CHAPTER FOUR

TRADEMARK BASICS

> This chapter discusses the Lanham Act, international trademarks, the Madrid System, the U.S. Anti-Dilution Act, and the concepts of direct and contributory infringement, dilution, blurring, tarnishment, and parody.

The Lanham Act

TRADEMARKS ARE THE SECOND of the four forms of intellectual property that we will examine in this section. Trademark law in the United States falls under the purview of the Lanham Act,[1] passed by Congress in 1945. The Act expanded the concept of infringement, permitted registration of service marks, provided incontestability status for marks in continuous use for five years, and provided that federal registration of a trademark would constitute "constructive notice of the registrant's claim of ownership thereof." *Trademarks* identify goods, while *service marks* identify services. The Act defines a trademark as:

> any word, name, symbol, or device, or any combination thereof used by a person…to identify and distinguish his or her goods, including a unique product, from those manufactured and sold by others and to indicate the source of the goods, even if the source is unknown.

Filing A Trademark

In the United States, *trademarks arise from use, not registration*, so it is not necessary to register a trademark. There are, however, compelling reasons to register with the U.S. Patent and Trademark Office (U.S.P.T.O.).[2] Registration establishes a public record of claim (*i.e.*, "constructive notice") and evidence of ownership. Trademark registration with the federal government means that federal court jurisdiction may be invoked if a dispute arises. Another advantage is that U.S. registration can serve as the basis for securing registration in foreign countries. Also, once filed with U.S. Customs, registration can help the trademark owner stop imports of infringing foreign goods from entering the country. So while it is not required to register a trademark, there are strong reasons to do so.

Trademark Search

The trademark registration process begins with a search by the applicant to determine if anyone else has filed an application for the same trademark. Searches can be conducted online using TESS (the Trademark Electronic Search System) at http://tess2.uspto.gov. Often the patent attorney will conduct the search. The first place to look is in the *U.S.P.T.O. Trademark Database*. However, the database is not all-inclusive, as it is limited to text marks, does not contain alternate spellings, is not current, and does not include state trademarks, common-law trademarks, foreign trademarks, or domain names — only federal trademarks.

Another good place to search, especially if one plans to use a trademark as part of the domain name, is *WHO IS*,[3] a domain name database maintained by domain name registrars. Then there is *AllWhoIs*,[4] a mega search engine website that searches WHO IS databases at multiple domain name registries. Finally, trademarks can be searched internationally through the *International Archives* from all of the Madrid Protocol countries.

Trademark Registration

To register a trademark in the United States, one must file an application consisting of:

- The name of the applicant

- The name and address for correspondence

- A clear drawing of the trademark

- A listing of the goods or services

- Five specimens showing the trademark as it is actually used

- The required filing fee for at least one class of goods or services

Applications may be filed by mail (to Commissioner for Trademarks, Box-New App-Fee, 2900 Crystal Drive, Arlington, VA 22202-3513) or online using TEAS (the Trademark Electronic Application System) at www.uspto.gov/teas. Registration of a trademark is not immediate; it may take more than a year from the time that the application is filed, if it is approved. The approval process begins with the U.S.P.T.O. comparing the trademark and the goods and services described in the application against those already registered. If the proposed trademark passes the examination, it is then published in the Official Gazette of the Patent and Trademark Office, affording an opportunity for objections by anyone who feels they may be harmed by registration of the trademark.

The U.S.P.T.O. may issue an "*office action*," *i.e.*, a non-final rejection of the application, because of the existence of "*identical or similar marks*" or if it believes the mark is "generic or descriptive." As this is a very complex area of law, one should always use a *patent attorney*, *i.e.*, a specialized attorney with knowledge and experience in patent law who has passed a special exam and is registered to practice before the U.S.P.T.O. The U.S.P.T.O. also registers non-lawyers who act as "*patent agents*" and can prepare patent applications but cannot practice law (*e.g.*, litigate patent matters or write contracts related to patents).

Once obtained, trademark protection can last indefinitely, but it must be renewed every 10 years and the trademark must be maintained or it will be deemed lost. Failure to use the trademark will result in the abandonment of the trademark (although an abandoned trademark may be re-registered). If the trademarked term becomes a part of the common usage (*i.e.*, genericized), the phrase will fall into the public domain, so it is important that trademark owners educate businesses and consumers on appropriate trademark use by visibly and actively promoting use of their trademarks as adjectives and not as nouns.

These trademarks began as names for specific products but gradually became so common that they became generic names and the trademark owners lost their trademarks: Allen Wrench, Aspirin, Cellophane, Celluloid, Corn Flakes, Dry Ice, Escalator, Granola, Heroin, Jungle Gym, Kerosine, Kitty Litter, Lanolin, Linoleum, Mimeograph, Nylon, Photostat, Plasterboard, Raisin Bran, Shredded Wheat, Thermos, Trampoline, Webster's Dictionary, Yo-Yo, Zeppelin, and Zipper.

These trademarked names are still valid but are often misused to refer to a generic product: *Astroturf* (artificial grass), *Baggies* (food bags), *BAND-AID* (self-adhesive bandage), *Bic* (ball point pen), *Breathalyzer* (breath alcohol analyzer), *Bubble Wrap* (air-filled plastic packing material), *Chap Stick* (lip balm), *Crock-Pot* (slow cooker), *Dictaphone* (dictation recorder), *Dixie cups* (disposable bathroom cups), *Dumpster* (large trash can), *Fiberglass* (glass fiber), *Frisbee* (flying disc), *Formica* (laminated plastic surface), *Go-Kart* (mini racing cars), *Hoover* (vacuum cleaner), *Hula Hoop* (dancing ring), *Jacuzzi* (whirlpool bath), *Jeep* (army vehicle), *Jell-O* (gelatin dessert), *Kleenex* (tissue), *Laundromat* (self-service laundry), *Magic Marker* (felt-tip marker), *Muzak* (background music), PhotoShop (a software program), *Plexiglas* (clear plastic sheets), *Post-It* (self-adhering notepaper), *Polaroid* (instant photograph), *Popsicle* (frozen confection), *Q-tip* (cotton swab), *Realtor* (real estate agent), *Rolodex* (rotary card file), *Saran wrap* (transparent plastic wrap), *Scotch tape* (transparent adhesive tape), *Speedo* (tight-fitting swimsuit), *Styrofoam* (polystyrene filler), *Tabasco* (hot spicy sauce), *Teflon* (non-stick surface), *Tupperware* (food storage ware), *Vaseline* (petroleum jelly), *Velcro* (re-usable fastening tape), and *Xerox* (photocopy).

International Trademarks

The Internet has opened new avenues to international commerce. A lone individual can create a website and begin marketing and distributing goods and services around the world. Therefore, it is more important than ever to protect one's trademarks worldwide, especially in any country where revenue is derived. Nike learned this the hard way during the 1990 Olympics in Barcelona, Spain, when the firm had to make its sponsored athletes cover the Nike name because a Spanish firm had been granted a Spanish trademark for sportswear under the Nike trademark.

European Registration

In 1992, 12 European nations created the European Common Market. Shortly thereafter, the European Community Trademark Registry was created. The registry allows a single trademark application to be valid in all member nations, rather than having to file separately in each country. Registration only applies to the member nations; applicants must still file separately in other non-member countries.

Registration of a trademark in the registry provides the ability to prevent others from using the trademark within the European Community and the ability to bring a cause of action concerning use of the trademark within the member states by using the Community trademark law and courts. At the time of this book's publication, the Community Trademark Registry included 27 member states. Trademarks registered with the Community Trademark Registry are permitted to use the ® symbol in all member states.

The Madrid System

The Madrid System is an international clearinghouse for registration of trademarks in multiple jurisdictions worldwide. The System is administered by the International Bureau of the World Intellectual Property Organization (WIPO) in Geneva, Switzerland. The Madrid System is comprised of two treaties drafted nearly a century apart: the Madrid Agreement Concerning the International Registration of Marks (1891) and the Madrid Protocol (1989). The Madrid Agreement and the Madrid Protocol are collateral but independent of each other.

The Madrid System provides a trademark owner with the possibility of protecting his trademark in multiple countries by simply filing one application directly with his own national or regional trademark office. It it a convenient and cost-effective way of filing and maintaining trademark rights in foreign countries. Under the Madrid System, after a trademark owner has either applied for registration or registered a trademark in his home country (and paid the domestic filing fee), he need only file a single additional application in one language (either English, French or Spanish) and pay a fee in the local currency, rather than file multiple applications separately in each trademark office of each member country. The Madrid System provides a process of international registration, not a single international trademark — trademark applicants get a bundle of national rights, not a single international right.

The Madrid Protocol,[5] a treaty for the international registration of trademarks, was adopted in Madrid, Spain, on June 27, 1989 and took effect in the United States in November 2003. The Protocol applies only to signatories of the treaty. Canada and Mexico are not signatories but the United States has signed the treaty (however, the United States is not a signatory to the Madrid Agreement). The treaty provides that a single application is valid for 10 years, and renewable for further 10-year terms. The Madrid Protocol signatories are: Albania, Antigua and Barbuda, Armenia, Australia, Austria, Belarus, Benelux (Belgium, Netherlands, and Luxembourg), Bhutan, Bulgaria, China, Croatia, Cuba, Cyprus, the Czech Republic, Denmark, Estonia, Finland, France, Georgia, Germany, Greece, Hungary, Iceland, Iran, Ireland, Italy, Japan, Kenya, North Korea, South Korea, Kyrgyzstan, Latvia, Lesotho, Liechtenstein, Lithuania, Macedonia, Moldova, Monaco, Mongolia, Morocco, Mozambique, Namibia, Norway, Poland, Portugal, Romania, the Russian Federation, Serbia and Montenegro, Sierra Leone, Singapore, the Slovak Republic, Slovenia, Spain, Swaziland, Sweden, Switzerland, Turkey, Turkmenistan, Ukraine, the United Kingdom, the United States, and Zambia.

The ® Symbol

The ® registered trademark symbol identifies a trademark as registered with the U.S.P.T.O. A valid registration notice consists of the ® symbol, and/or "Registered in the U.S. Patent and Trademark Office" or the abbreviation "Reg. U.S. Pat. and Tm. Off."

Failure to use the notice does not affect the validity of the trademark. However, if used, the trademark owner does not need to prove that the defendant had actual notice of registration in order to recover damages and profits, since registration serves as constructive notice to the world. The ® symbol should not be used if the trademark is not registered with the U.S.P.T.O. Instead, the ™ symbol should be used to designate trademarks not protected by federal registration (*i.e.*, state or common law marks). In the case of a service mark, the ᔆᴹ symbol is used.

Trademark Infringement and Dilution

Trademarks are protected by law from both infringement and dilution. In determining *infringement*, the court looks at whether the similarity between the trademarks is "likely to cause confusion" in the minds of consumers.[6] The stated objective of the law is to protect consumers. However, a court may find *dilution* of a trademark even if there is no likelihood of confusion. The test for dilution is: "*would the strong association the public has between the famous trademark and the plaintiff be diluted?*"

Under the Lanham Act, as amended,[7] to prove trademark dilution, the plaintiff must show that:

1. The plaintiff is the owner of a trademark that qualifies as a "distinctive and famous" trademark as measured by the totality of the eight factors listed in the Lanham Act § 43(c)(1),

2. The defendant is making commercial use,

3. In interstate commerce,

4. Of a trademark or trade name,

5. And the defendant's use began after the plaintiff's trademark became famous,

6. And the defendant's use causes dilution by lessening the capacity of the plaintiff's trademark to identify and distinguish goods or services.

To be considered as "distinctive and famous," the Lanham Act provides that the following factors may be weighed:

1. The degree of inherent or acquired distinctiveness of the trademark,

2. The duration and extent of use of the trademark in connection with the goods or services with which the trademark is used,

3. The duration and extent of advertising and publicity of the trademark,

4. The geographical extent of the trading area in which the trademark is used,

5. The channels of trade for the goods or services with which the trademark is used,

6. The degree of recognition of the trademark in the trading areas and channels of trade used by the trademark's owner and the person against whom the injunction is sought,

7. The nature and extent of use of the same or similar trademarks by third parties, and

8. Whether the trademark was registered under the Act of March 3, 1881, or the Act of February 20, 1905, or on the principal register.

The court weighs several factors to determine if a trademark has been infringed upon, including the strength of the trademark, the similarity of parties' service, the evidence of actual confusion, the degree of care likely to be exercised by consumer; and in domain name disputes, the similarity of trademark to the domain name and the domain name registrant's intent in choosing the name.

The U.S. Anti-Dilution Act

In 1996, Congress passed the U.S. Anti-Dilution Act as an amendment to the Lanham Act.[8] Prior to that date, trademark owners had to rely on state anti-dilution laws to pursue remedies for dilution as no federal anti-dilution laws existed. This Act is sometimes more useful to the trademark owner than an infringement claim because the Act does not require a showing of a "likelihood of confusion." Instead, the test is a *commercial use in commerce* of a *"famous mark"* if the use *"causes dilution of the distinctive quality of the famous mark."* Note that the Act only applies to "famous" trademarks. While Congress did not define "famous" within the Act, it did list eight factors[8] for a court to consider in determining whether a trademark is indeed "famous." Courts make this determination on a case-by-case basis.

Under the Act, dilution can occur even when a famous trademark is used by another on non-competing goods, *e.g.*, "Maytag cameras" or "Smith & Wesson washing machines." This would be an example of *"blurring,"* where consumers see the trademark used by another to identify a non-competing good, thereby diluting the unique and distinctive significance of the mark.

A second type of dilution is *tarnishment*, when the other party's use of the mark tarnishes, degrades, or brings ridicule to the distinctive quality of the mark. For example, when a website with the domain name AdultsRUs.com was launched, ToysRUs sued under the U.S. Anti-Dilution Act with little difficulty persuading the court of the dilution of its famous trademark by tarnishment.[9] By contrast, Hormel, maker of Spam (the meat product, not the junk e-mail) tried unsuccessfully to convince the 2nd Circuit Court of Appeals that a forthcoming Muppets movie character had tarnished its trademark.[10] The upcoming film "Muppet Treasure Island" introduced a new Muppet character, Spa'am, the high priest of a tribe of wild boars that worships Miss Piggy as its Queen. Hormel feared tarnishment of its trademark, as the court explained:[11]

> Hormel also expresses concern that even comic association with an unclean "grotesque" boar will call into question the purity and high quality of its meat product. But the district court found no evidence that Spa'am was unhygienic. At worst, he might be described as "untidy." * * * Moreover, by now Hormel should be inured to any such ridicule. Although SPAM is in fact made from pork shoulder and ham meat, and the name itself supposedly is a portmanteau word for spiced ham, countless jokes have played off the public's unfounded suspicion that SPAM is a product of less than savory ingredients. For example, in one episode of the television cartoon "Duckman," Duckman is shown discovering "the secret ingredient to SPAM" as he looks on at "Murray's Incontinent Camel Farm." In a recent newspaper column it was noted that "In one little can, Spam contains the five major food groups: Snouts. Ears. Feet. Tails. Brains." * * * In view of the more or less humorous takeoffs such as these, one might think Hormel would welcome the association with a genuine source of pork. Nevertheless, on July 25, 1995, Hormel filed this suit alleging both trademark infringement and dilution.

The court went on to note that while a trademark may be tarnished when its likeness is placed in the context of sexual activity, obscenity, or illegal activity, in this case there was no negative association through its use:[12]

> The *sine qua non* of tarnishment is a finding that plaintiff's mark will suffer negative associations through defendant's use. Hormel claims that linking its luncheon meat with a wild boar will adversely color consumers' impressions of SPAM. However, the district court found that Spa'am, a likeable, positive character, will not generate any negative associations. Moreover, contrary to Hormel's contentions, the district court also found no evidence that Spa'am is unhygienic or that his character places Hormel's mark in an unsavory context. Indeed, many of Henson's own plans involve placing the Spa'am likeness on food products. In addition, the court also noted that a simple humorous reference to the fact that SPAM is made from pork is unlikely to tarnish Hormel's mark. Absent any showing that Henson's use will create negative associations with the SPAM mark, there was little likelihood of dilution.

The U.S. Anti-Dilution Act has been used heavily in domain name disputes to force cybersquatters to relinquish domain names to the trademark owner. The theory used is that dilution occurs when web visitors give up searching for the trademark holder's goods online in frustration after countless encounters with the cybersquatters' sites instead of the true trademark holder's website. However, the Act is only applicable where a "famous" trademark is at issue. Holders of non-famous trademarks in such situations must seek recourse through the Anti-cybersquatting Consumer Protection Act. Domain name disputes and cybersquatting are discussed at length in the next chapter.

Trademark Infringement or Parody?

It is permissible to reference a copyrighted work or trademark for the purpose of *parody*. The courts have accepted the dictionary definition of parody as "literary or artistic work that imitates the characteristic style of an author or work for comic effect or ridicule."[13] A legal parody involves the conveyance of two *simultaneous* but contradictory messages — it must target the work but be apparent that it is not the original.

PETA, People for the Ethical Treatment of Animals, filed a trademark infringement lawsuit against a man who had registered the domain name PETA.org.[14] The defendant had registered the domain name and set up a website at that URL titled "People Eating Tasty Animals." The website contained links to meat, fur, hunting, leather, and animal research, all of course opposed by PETA. The court held that the website was not a legal parody because the domain name alone did not convey the second message (*i.e.*, parody). The defendant argued that the second message was in the content of the website itself, but court rejected that view, stating that it was not conveyed *simultaneously*.

Search engine firm Google charged Booble.com, which marketed itself as an adult search engine, with trademark infringement. Google alleged that Booble copied its distinctive look with similar logo design and page layout. Google sent Booble a standard cease and desist letter which evoked a detailed and well-written response from Bobble's attorneys raising the defense that the Booble website was a parody of Google. The letter stated, in part, "Our client's website is in fact a successful parody, which simultaneously brings to mind the original, while also conveying that it is not the original." The letter then attempted to show that Booble had not met the necessary element of confusion in the minds of consumers for a finding of trademark infringement, by stating that the domain names were entirely different, that Booble only searched the web for adult content, and that the Booble mark differed from Google's in that it "features a woman's chest...uses the phrase, 'The Adult Search Engine'...posts a warning that the website contains explicit content...and...disclaims any association with Google.com."[15] The letter ended by tweaking the Google lawyers by pointing out that the sole case they referenced in their cease and desist letter was a copyright case, not a trademark case, and that "although some analytic similarities exist between copyright and trademark parody cases, Google neither claims copyright infringement in its letter, nor is any relevant portion of its website copyrightable."[16] Ouch!

The owners of the two websites eventually reached an agreement and Booble.com modified the design of its page.[17] Ironically, upon revamping the design and abandoning any attempt at parody, Booble's owner reported that the website he started as a joke had begun generating significant traffic as a serious adult search engine.[18]

Direct and Contributory Infringement

The concepts of direct and contributory infringement, which were discussed as they applied to copyright in the previous chapter, can also be applied to trademarks.

Upscale jeweler Tiffany's sued eBay for trademark infringement, claiming that nearly three-quarters of the items labeled as "Tiffany's" on the Internet auction website were fakes.[19] Tiffany's charged that while eBay did not directly sell counterfeit Tiffany's products — and thus was not a *direct infringer* — it was a *contributory infringer* by facilitating and promoting the sale of thousands of pieces of counterfeit Tiffany jewelry. The issue of whether eBay was a contributory infringer would turn on *whether the auctioneer or the trademark owner should monitor goods sold on Internet auction websites for counterfeits.* eBay argued that it had anti-fraud mechanisms in place, such as its "feedback" system where buyers and sellers rate each other publicly, the fact that it allowed firms to shut down sellers who they claimed violated their intellectual property rights,[20] and its willingness to remove auction listings in "obvious violation" of intellectual property laws.

Tiffany's buttressed its argument that eBay was a contributory infringer by pointing out that the amount of fake goods sold on eBay was so substantial that eBay profited significantly from the trade and promoted it. Unlike the business model of a newspaper publishing classified ads, eBay collects part of the sale price, in effect sharing in the profits of each transaction. However, while a contributory infringement claim might arise by allowing counterfeits to be sold on its website, eBay must have "knowingly facilitated" the counterfeiting to be deemed a contributory infringer. Tiffany's also claimed direct infringement, because eBay bought advertising links on Yahoo! and Google. A search for "Tiffany" or "Tiffany's" with these search engines results in eBay's links appearing atop the page. Tiffany argued that these links lead to sellers who offer counterfeit goods on eBay's website and that by advertising them eBay was infringing upon Tiffany's trademark.

Summary

The Lanham Act governs U.S. trademark law. A trademark can consist of any word, name, symbol, device, or combination that identifies and distinguishes the holder's goods from another's. Trademarks identify goods, while service marks identify services. Trademarks arise from use, not registration, but registration has many advantages. The trademark registration process begins with a search by the applicant to determine if anyone else has filed an application for the same trademark. Trademark applications are filed with the U.S. Patent and Trademark Office. Once obtained, trademark protection can last indefinitely, but the trademark must be renewed every 10 years and maintained or it will be deemed lost. If the trademarked term becomes a part of the common usage, the phrase will fall into the public domain.

The Madrid System provides a trademark owner with the possibility of protecting his trademark in multiple countries by simply filing one application directly with his own national or regional trademark office. The Madrid System is comprised of two treaties drafted nearly a century apart: the Madrid Agreement Concerning the International Registration of Marks (1891) and the Madrid Protocol (1989). The Madrid Agreement and the Madrid Protocol are collateral but independent of each other. The Madrid System provides a process of international registration, not a single international trademark

The ® symbol designates a registered trademark and the ™ symbol designates a trademark not protected by federal registration but rather by state registration or common law.

Trademarks can be subjected to infringement or dilution. In determining infringement, the court looks at whether the similarity between the trademarks is "likely to cause confusion" in the minds of consumers. The test for dilution is: "would the strong association the public has between the famous trademark and the plaintiff be diluted?" The U.S. Anti-Dilution Act does not require a showing of a "likelihood of confusion." Instead, the test is a "commercial use in commerce" of a "famous mark" if the use "causes dilution of the distinctive quality of the famous mark." The Act has been used heavily in domain name disputes to force cybersquatters to relinquish domain names to the trademark owner.

A parody that targets a trademark while simultaneously being apparent that it is not the original trademark is not an infringement.

Chapter Four Notes ▭▭▭▭▭▭▭▭▭▭▭▭▭▭▭▭

[1] Lanham Act, 15 U.S.C. § 1125.

[2] U.S. Patent and Trademark Office, *available at* www.uspto.gov (accessed September 25, 2007).

[3] WhoIs website, *available at* www.whois.com (accessed September 25, 2007).

[4] AllWhoIs, *available at* www.allwhois.com (accessed September 25, 2007).

[5] Madrid Protocol, *available at* www.wipo.int/madrid/en (accessed September 25, 2007).

[6] *See Hormel Foods Corp. v. Jim Henson Prods., Inc.*, 73 F.3d. 497, 37 U.S.P.Q.2d 1516 (1996), where the court found that an "unclean grotesque boar" porcine Muppet named "Spa'am" would not cause confusion in the minds of consumers with plaintiff's pork product, "Spam." This case is included in the Cases Section on the Issues in Internet Law website (www.IssuesinInternetLaw.com).

[7] Lanham Act, fn. 1, *supra*. The U.S. Anti-Dilution Act, § 43(c)(1) of the Lanham Act, was amended in 2006 to eliminate the requirement of a showing of actual economic harm to the famous mark's economic value, in response to the U.S. Supreme Court decision in *Moseley v. V Secret Catalogue*, 537 U.S. 418 (2003), as well as the split decisions amongst the federal circuits. Under the new standard, a party is entitled to an injunction against the user of a trademark that is "likely to cause dilution," Trademark Dilution Revision Act of 2006, 15 U.S.C. § 1125(c)(1).

[8] 1996 U.S. Anti-Dilution Act, Lanham Act § 43(c)(1).

[9] *Toys 'R' Us, Inc. v. Akkaoui*, 40 USPQ 2d 1836, 1836-39 (N.D. Cal. 1996).

[10] *Hormel Foods Corp. v. Jim Henson Prods., Inc.*, fn. 6, *supra*. The case was files under New York's anti-dilution statute, N.Y. Gen. Bus. Law § 368-d (McKinney 1984), not under the federal Anti-Dilution Act which was not signed into law until 1996.

[11] *Ibid.*

[12] *Ibid.*

[13] *Campbell v. Acuff-Rose Music, Inc.*, 510 U.S. 569, 582 (1994).

[14] *PETA, Inc. v. Doughney*, 113 F. Supp.2d 915 (E.D. Va 2000). This case is included in the Cases Section on the Issues in Internet Law website (www.IssuesinInternetLaw.com).

[15] Garrett French, "Booble Responds To Google: Read Letter," WebProNews, *available at* www.webpronews.com/ebusiness/seo/wpn-4-20040129BoobleRespondsToGoogleReadLetter.html (accessed September 25, 2007).

[16] *Ibid.*

[17] Gretchen Gallen, "Booble Tests Mainstream Ad Blitz," XBiz News, November 12, 2004.

[18] *Ibid.*

[19] *Tiffany (NJ), Inc. v. eBay, Inc.*, Case No. 04-CV-4607 (S.D.N.Y. 2004).

[20] eBay's VeRO (Verified Rights Owner) program allows participants (mostly software, media or fashion trademark owners) to notify eBay of fakes, request removal of infringing eBay listings, and request personal information about alleged infringers.

Chapter Four Quiz

Silly Sally has decided to name her new guitar pick the "Noise Pick." Sally advertises her new product in a music industry magazine as the "Noise Pick®." Mr. Slate files an infringement and dilution lawsuit against Sally claiming her trademark is likely to cause confusion with his own trademark, the "Rockpick®." The Rockpick is a large mechanical machine used to smash boulders.

Meanwhile, Dusty Grit has setup a website for his fictional product, a guitar pick that doubles as a nasal implement, which he calls the "Nose Pick™." The website goes into great detail describing the guitar pick that doubles as a nose pick. Sally, believing that the similarity will confuse her potential customers, files an infringement lawsuit against Dusty. Does Sally have a good legal argument? What defenses might Dusty raise?

Dusty also has a message board on his website where visitors can "buy and sell picks of any kind." Some of the message board participants have been offering fake "Noise picks" on the message board.

If you are using this book in a classroom, discuss the issues raised and the liability of all parties. Otherwise, try to list the issues involved and probable outcomes before turning to the answers in the Appendix.

[Answers in Appendix]

CHAPTER FIVE

TRADEMARK AND DOMAIN NAMES

This chapter explores trademarks and domain names, the Truth in Domain Names Act, the Anti-cybersquatting Consumer Protection Act, the Uniform Domain Name Dispute Resolution Policy, meta tags, and keyword search advertising.

Are Domain Names Property?

THERE ARE TWO CONTRASTING views regarding the legal status of Internet domain names. One view holds that domain names are *intellectual property rights*, while the other holds that domain names are licenses, thus *contractual rights*. The distinction is important because property rights offer more protections than do contract rights. Also, a property right lasts indefinitely until it is conveyed, whereas a contract right is limited to an express (*i.e.*, defined) term upon which it will expire. Another way of looking at the domain name issue is, do you *lease* it or do you *own* it?

The 9th Circuit has accepted the view that a domain name is "property." Sometimes the "property" can be very valuable. Stephen Cohen stole Gary Kremen's[1] domain name, sex.com, simply by submitting a fake transfer letter with a forged signature to Network Solutions, the domain registrar. Cohen went on to make at least $40 million from the website. Kremen subsequently won a $65 million judgment against Cohen, who promptly transferred his assets overseas and fled to Tijuana, Mexico.[2] The court ruled in *Kremen v. Cohen*[3] that Network Solutions should be held liable for giving the name to someone else without properly informing its rightful owner, under the theory that Kremen had a property right in the domain name sex.com,[4] and Network Solutions committed the tort of conversion by giving it away to Cohen (reversing that portion of the lower court's decision).[5] In finding a property right, the court compared registering a domain name to staking a claim to a plot of land at the title office.

That is an apt analogy, as the rush for domain names is reminiscent of the 19th Century Gold Rush, when prospectors descended upon claims offices to file their land claims for what they perceived as valuable property. While not every claim turned into a small fortune, some did. The same is true today with Internet real estate. The purchase and sale of domain names is an estimated $2 billion industry and is projected to double by 2010.[7] Domain names are registered at a rate of 90,000 per day![8] In 2006, sex.com sold for $12 million and creditcheck.com sold for $3 million.[9]

However, there are federal cases that expressly have found that a domain name is *not* tangible real property. One state supreme court even held that domain names should be considered services rather than property. (The lower court holding in *Kremen,* subsequently reversed, also had considered a domain name not as property but rather as a service, likening it to a telephone number. A better analogy might be to view the numeric IP address underlying the domain name as akin to a telephone number, whereas the domain name itself is more like a trademark.). The counterview to the domain name being a property right is the view that the domain name is merely a *contract* that the owner has with the domain name registrar. In fact, Network Solutions describes a domain name in terms of a *contractual license between itself and the registrant.* Lawyers from most countries outside of the United States agree that a domain name is a contract right from a domain registry.

If considered a property right, then the *scope* of a property interest in a domain name may vary widely in the United States, *since states create and define property interests, not federal courts.* Property rights are established through either a state's supreme court decisions under common law or through statutes approved by state legislators. So even if domain names are property interests, the state will define the scope of such property rights.

Fraudulent domain name transfers like the one in *Kremen* continue to occur. In 2004, a 19-year-old German faced computer sabotage charges after hijacking the German eBay website domain eBay.de, redirecting website visitors to a different domain name server (DNS). The teen said he had requested DNS transfers for several websites, including Google.de, Web.de, Amazon.de and eBay.de "just for fun," after discovering how to do a DNS transfer online.[9] The other requests were denied but the eBay transfer went through, although no explanation was given for how the domain could have been transferred without the owner's consent . (In 2007, Google.de, the German Google domain, was hijacked the same way).[10] The domain was transferred back to eBay.

Four months later, a New York ISP discovered that its domain had been hijacked.[11] Officials at Panix.com, which provides Internet access and e-mail services to New York City, Long Island,

Westchester, Rockland County, and New Jersey, discovered that ownership of its domain had been moved during the night to a company in Australia, the DNS records had been moved to the United Kingdom, and the company's e-mail had been redirected to a company in Canada! As improbable as it may seem, fraudulent transfers of domain names without the owner's consent continue to occur, affecting even major companies. New rules governing the transfer of domain name ownership that went into effect in November 2004 have only exacerbated the problem. These new ICANN rules automatically approve inter-registry transfer requests after five days unless countermanded by the domain owner; previously domain ownership and nameservers were unchanged until the owner had replied affirmatively to the transfer request.

Domain Name Tricks

Domain Misspellings

Typosquatting is a form of cybersquatting (discussed later in this chapter) where the typosquatter registers a misspelled version of a prominent trademarked domain name in the hope that visitors will reach the website by accidentally mistyping the trademarked URL. The aim of the typosquatter is to drive traffic to his website, where visitors click on advertising links that in turn generate revenue for the typosquatter (often the landing page is a domain parking website with no real content other than hyperlinks based on keywords similar to the misspelled word in the domain name). Courts will find trademark infringement where the trademark owner's name has been intentionally misspelled in a bad faith attempt to divert visitors away from the targeted website to the violator's website. In addition to landing on pay-per-click websites, visitors are frequently routed to a competitor's website or to a pornographic website. Upon landing on the pornographic website, visitors frequently find themselves "mouse-trapped."

"Mouse-Trapping"

Mouse-trapping occurs when a website visitor cannot leave a website without clicking on a succession of pop-up windows. Usually the visitor's web browser's back button is disabled. Each pop-up window contains another ad for a pornographic website, and the website owner is usually paid between 10¢ and 25¢ per click by the advertisers. One defendant admitted earning between $800,000-to-$1 million per year through mouse-trapping.[12] Mouse-trapping may be considered a "deceptive practice" under the Federal Trade Commission Act.

Pagejacking

Pagejacking occurs where the offender steals the contents of a website by copying some of its pages, putting them on a website that appears to be the real website, and then inviting people to the fake website through deceptive means. By moving enough of a website's content and page description information within each page, pagejackers can submit the fake website to major search engines to be indexed. Search engine users then receive results from both the real and the fake websites and may be easily misled into clicking on the wrong one, being redirected to a pornographic or equally undesired website. As an additional annoyance, visitors subjected to pagejacking may also encounter mouse-trapping. Pagejacking is prohibited as a "deceptive practice" under the Federal Trade Commission Act.

Pagejacking is also used in phishing schemes, where the fake page is set up to procure account numbers and passwords or other personal data from the visitor. Phishing is discussed in greater detail in the cyber crimes section (Chapter Eight) of this book.

The Truth in Domain Names Act

Enacted by Congress in 2003 as part of the PROTECT Act,[13] the Truth in Domain Names Act[14] makes it illegal to use a "misleading domain name" with the intent to deceive a person into viewing obscenity or to deceive a minor into viewing "material that is harmful to minors." The Act may be vulnerable to a First Amendment challenge however, because the terms "misleading," "obscenity" and "harmful to minors" are inherently vague.

The Truth in Domain Names Act was used to arrest an infamous cybersquatter[15] who for years had made millions of dollars by linking pornographic websites to domain names similar to popular trademarks, before being arrested in 2003.[16] Taking advantage of children who type domain names incorrectly, the typosquatter had registered 3,000 domain names that included "Teltubbies.com," "Bobthebiulder.com," "Dinseyland.com" and 41 variations on teen pop idol Britney Spears' name that directed web visitors to a pornographic website.

Personal Names as Domain Names

Can using another person's name as your domain name be misleading?[17] Likewise, do you have a property interest in your own name? A father registered the domain name "Veronica.org" and filled the website with photographs of his two-year-old daughter Veronica. The man was shocked when Archie Comics fired off a letter from its attorney accusing him of trademark infringement and demanding that he turn over the domain name to the comic book publisher, known for publishing stories about a group of teenagers named Archie, Jughead, Reggie, Betty and *Veronica*. The father replied that he had purchased the domain name for his daughter Veronica, that it was a non-commercial ".org" domain, and that the website made no reference to Archie Comics, its trademarks, or its products. He assured Archie Comics that it would be a few years before his two-year-old daughter would have the necessary skills even to attempt to design a logo that could be confused with Archie's logo.[18] The following news report shows the risk of negative publicity and ridicule corporations take when attempting to pursue such specious claims:[19]

> Archie Comic Publications has been forced to slink away with its tail between its legs after the public relations debacle that followed its threats against two-year-old Veronica Sams of Los Angeles. Lawyers for Archie Comics apparently were worried that the public might confuse pictures of little Veronica sitting in her bathtub with the teenage cartoon character named Veronica that graces the pages of Archie Comics.

In a similar situation, computer manufacturer Dell (named after company founder Michael Dell) took umbrage with the URL of Spanish web designer Paul Dell (no relation to Michael), www.dellwebsites.com. Dell's trademark infringement claim cited a "risk of confusion between the web designer's website and its own[20] and demanded that Paul Dell sign over the domain name to the PC manufacturer at his own expense. One news report sarcastically cited that the amount of confusion caused by Paul Dell's web design website had not seemed to have had a noticeable effect on Dell Computer's revenue, which during that period had increased by 20% to $23 billion.[21]

In another case, Penguin Books published "Katie.com" — a book by Katie Tarbox, a teenage victim of an online predator. Tarbox expanded the "Katie.com" book into a TV show and a school curriculum to teach children about online safety. But there was a slight problem — the actual domain name Katie.com was owned by a completely different "Katie" — Katie Jones. Jones, who had purchased her domain name four years earlier, complained of massive undesired e-mail and heavy website traffic resulting from the book's publication. After the book "Katie.com" appeared on bookshelves Jones, queasy about keeping her child's photographs on a website marketed as part of a book about pedophiles, revamped it into a public protest[22] against Penguin. She charged Penguin co-opted her domain name knowing, when it titled the book, that she owned Katie.com (Tarbox, the author, had her own website at Katiet.com). Penguin continued to promote Katie.com, pausing only to print this small addition to the copyright notice in the 2001 paperback edition: *"the publishers wish to make clear the author of Katie.*

com and events described in *Katie.com* have no connection whatsoever with the website found at domain name address www.katie.com, or with e-mail address katie@katie.com." After Tarbox hit the TV talk shows, Jones claimed that Tarbox and Penguin (rather than offering to buy the domain name) had suggested she "donate" it to them, since she would be unable to sell it, as it was now inexorably linked with their media marketing campaign (Tarbox stated on her website [23] that neither she nor her publisher ever attempted to buy the domain name from Jones). Jones compared it to publishing a book with her home phone number or address as the title. Ironically, the book is about the abuse of the Internet to disrupt an innocent girl's life. Eventually Penguin relented and renamed Katie.com *"A Girl's Life Online."*

Uzi Nissan, an Israeli, came to America in 1976 and started several business with his family name — "Nissan Foreign Car Mobile Repair Service" in 1980, "Nissan International, Ltd.," an import-export firm, in 1987, and "Nissan Computer Corp." in 1991. As he explains on his website,[24] Nissan is proud of the long heritage of his family name, which is also the biblical word for the seventh month in the Hebrew calendar. In 1994, he registered the domain name Nissan.com to promote his computer business. The following year, he registered a service mark for Nissan and his logo with the state of North Carolina. Nearly five years after that,[25] Nissan Motors Ltd., a automobile manufacturer founded in Japan in 1933,[26] sued Uzi Nissan to enjoin him from using his family name for business purposes on the Internet and $10 million in damages.[27] The district court stated:[28]

> Although there is no absolute right to use one's name as a trademark, the Ninth Circuit has recognized a "judicial reluctance to enjoin use of a personal name." *E. & J. Gallo Winery v. Gallo Cattle Co.*, 967 F.2d 1280, 1288 (9th Cir. 1992) * * * An injunction limiting the use of an infringing personal name should be 'carefully tailored to balance the interest in using one's name against the interest in avoiding public confusion.' *E. & J. Gallo Winery*, 967 F.2d at 1288.

The district court found that automobile-related advertising on Uzi Nissan's website infringed on the plaintiff's trademark, but that the non-automobile advertising was non-infringing. It proceeded to issue an injunction requiring the defendant to post a disclaimer on his website stating that he was not affiliated with Nissan Motor Co. and displaying a link to the plaintiff's website, and refraining from displaying automobile-related information, advertisements, promotions, or Internet links on the website.[29]

On appeal, the court remanded the case to the district court to determine the issue of trademark dilution.[30] It also held that the lower court's injunction prohibiting the defendant from displaying links to disparaging comments about Nissan Motor Co.

was an unconstitutional content-based restriction that violated First Amendment free speech rights. The appellate court upheld the lower court's finding that the automobile-related advertising on the website infringed on the plaintiff's trademark, but that the non-automobile advertising was non-infringing. The U.S. Supreme Court affirmed that Uzi Nissan's <u>Nissan.net</u> and <u>Nissan.com</u> websites did not violate Nissan Motors' trademark[31] (although the case was sent back to the Los Angeles district court to resolve other issues).

The previous cases involved individuals and/or corporations each claiming a right to a name in which each had some legitimate interest. Archie Comics had a character named Veronica and David Sams had a daughter with that name. Michael Dell and Paul Dell were both born with the Dell surname and each had a legitimate interest in using his surname to describe his business. Likewise, both Katie Tarbox and Katie Jones were born with the name "Katie." And Uzi Nissan was also born with his surname and had a legitimate interest in using his own surname in his business. But what about the case where an individual usurps another's name?

Such was the case when a paid political consultant to a Democratic candidate launched a disparaging website with the URL named after the Republican opponent, Robin Ficker. The federal court ruled[32] that the website owner's First Amendment rights outweighed the protections offered by the Anti-cybersquatting Consumer Protection Act. Astoundingly, the court found "no irreparable harm" to the plaintiff by the attack website in the plaintiff's name, <u>robinficker.com</u>, launched days before the election. The court attempted to rationalize its decision by stating, "by entering public arena he invited comments and critiques."

Since the election ended shortly thereafter, appealing the case was a moot point for the plaintiff, Robin Ficker. However, had the case been appealed, a more rational court might have swiftly overturned this court's decision. First, the court did not consider the plaintiff's Right of Publicity (*i.e.*, an individual's right to control and profit from commercial use of his name, likeness, and persona).[33] Obviously, the plaintiff had no control over this unauthorized appropriation of his identity, although arguably the context of a political campaign may not be a commercial use. Second, the court stated there was no irreparable harm, despite the obvious harm given that the intent of the website was to sully the reputation of a candidate days before an election; voters would come to <u>Robin.Ficker.com</u>, read the disparaging articles posted by his opponent's political consultant and presumably then vote for the opponent. Third, the court borrowed the "public figure" standard from defamation law, *i.e.*, that public figures, because they choose to thrust themselves into the public limelight to influence the resolution of the issues in a particular public controversy,[34] must meet a higher burden of proof to show libel or defamation.[35] But this misplaced analogy ignores the fact that even public figures still retain rights, including, no matter how diminished, the Right of Privacy and the Right of Publicity (if recognized in that state). And fourth, the court said that the potential damage to the defendant's First Amendment free speech rights outweighed any damage to the plaintiff; this ludicrous statement completely ignores the fact that the defendant's First Amendment freedom of expression could have been accomplished with a different domain name that was not misleading as the one he had chosen.

A more recent political domain name dispute occurred in the 2008 presidential election campaign when the Barack Obama campaign sought to take over a website created by an ardent supporter. Joe Anthony began a MySpace fan page — myspace.com/barackobama — for Senator Barack Obama after listening to the senator give the keynote address at the 2004 Democratic convention. As Obama became a presidential candidate, Anthony's MySpace fan page gained 160,000 "friends." [36] Initially, Anthony collaborated informally with the campaign on the MySpace site. As the site grew in popularity, Anthony asked the campaign for monetary compensation, citing the time involved in maintaining the site. The campaign balked at the amount he wanted ($39,000) and raised concerns over having someone not on the campaign staff — indeed someone they had never met — controlling what had become a valuable campaign asset. The Obama campaign then asked MySpace to transfer the URL myspace.com/barackobama to the campaign, claiming the candidate should have the right to control his own MySpace domain name. MySpace resolved the conflict with a brilliant solution: it gave the name to the Obama campaign but agreed to transfer the 160,000 "friends" to Anthony's replacement site. [37] MySpace executive Jeff Berman explained the company's reasoning: [38]

> We felt under the circumstances that Senator Obama had the right to the URL containing his name and to the official campaign content that was provided, but that the user should retain the basic elements of the profile, including the friends who had been accumulated.

Cybersquatting

A "cybersquatter" is one who deliberately and in bad faith registers domain names in violation of the rights of the trademark owners. Cybersquatters' motives include extorting payment from the trademark owner, hoarding names to resell to the highest bidder, diverting visitors to pornographic websites, diverting consumers to a competitor's website, and defrauding consumers.

Anti-cybersquatting Consumer Protection Act

To prevail in an infringement suit, trademark law required that there be a *"use in commerce"* of the infringing trademark. Cybersquatters got around the "use in commerce" requirement by refusing to sell the domain name (*i.e.*, no offer of sale, thus no commerce) or by registering a name but not creating a website at the URL, since if there was no web page, there could be no "use in commerce." Not creating a web page also effectively eliminated any claim of *"consumer confusion."* And if they did have a web page on the domain name URL, the cybersquatters could reduce "consumer confusion" by posting on the website a disclaimer to the effect that the website was not related to the trademark holder's mark.

The Anti-cybersquatting Consumer Protection Act (ACPA)[39] closed these loopholes in the existing trademark laws. The ACPA does not require actual "use" in commerce. The test is "registers, traffics in, or uses a domain name," which means mere registration will suffice. However, the plaintiff must show both that the domain name registrant had a *"bad faith intent* to profit from" a trademark and that the registrant *registered, trafficked in, or used a domain name identically or confusingly similar to the trademark.*

A federal appeals court ruled in 2004 that an anti-abortion activist violated trademark law by registering multiple domain names (including drinkcoke.org, mycoca-cola.com, mymcdonalds.com, mypepsi.org, and my-washingtonpost.com) and using them to point visitors to his anti-abortion websites with pictures of aborted and dismembered fetuses.[40] By registering "WPNI.org," which is similar to WPNI.com, the domain name for Post-Newsweek employees e-mail addresses, anti-abortion activist Bill Purdy was able to intercept e-mails to reporters. The 8th Circuit Court held that the names that Purdy had registered were "confusingly similar" to the trademarked ones and thus violated the ACPA. The court upheld a preliminary injunction ordering Purdy to relinquish the domain names. Purdy contended that he was exercising his First Amendment right to criticize companies that he claimed promoted abortion and not using the domain names for commercial profit, and thus lacked the "bad faith intent to profit" required by the Act. But since Purdy had included some commercial messages on his websites, the court did not have to decide if the outcome would be the same on a "non-commercial" website. It ruled that while Purdy had the right to express his message online, the First Amendment would not protect misappropriation of trademarks to do so, citing the confusion that would be created in the minds of consumers.

Cyber Poachers

Cyber poachers grab domain names when a domain name that a company had *previously registered* becomes available for any of a number of reasons; *e.g.,* if the company let the registration expire by mistake, or through domain name registrar error, or through fraud.

Shared Domain Name

It is possible for two trademark owners to coexist amicably using the same trademark with different products/services, or regions. One method used by some companies is to register the common trademark as a domain name and then, on the home page at the URL, provide a split screen for each trademark. For example, Pez Candy split its web page in half.[41] Clicking on the left half takes the visitor to the website of the Pez subsidiary for North and South America, while clicking on the right half takes the visitor to the website of the Pez subsidiary for Europe, Asia, Oceania, and Africa.

Uniform Domain Name Dispute Resolution Policy

The Internet Corporation for Assigned Names and Numbers (ICANN),[42] the organization responsible for domain name registration oversight, has set up an administrative (*i.e.,* non-judicial) process to help resolve domain name disputes. *The Uniform Domain Name Dispute Resolution Policy* (UDRP) is a quick and cost-effective alternative to a lawsuit, as the arbitration process is usually settled within a few months from the first filing.[43] There is no appeal process in the UDRP, but the parties can still go to court if they wish. Although the UDRP frequently sides with trademark owners, surprises occur since, unlike the U.S. court system, there is no reliance on precedence.

The UDRP applies to *all* Global Top Level Domains (.com, .net, .org, .aero, .biz, .coop, .info, .museum, .name, .pro); and *some* Country Top Level Domains (.nu, .tv, .ws); but not to .gov, .mil, or .int. domains. Most domain name registrars inform anyone registering a new domain name that the registration is subject to the UDRP.

A complainant must meet all three UDRP threshold requirements to be entitled to transfer or cancellation of the domain name registration — if even one is not established, then the entire complaint fails. The complainant must prove that:

1. The domain names are *identical or confusingly similar*, and

2. The registrant has *no legitimate interest* in the name, and

3. The domain name was *registered and used in bad faith.*

To start the process, the complainant must either sue the domain-name holder or submit a complaint to an approved dispute resolution service provider. The current approved dispute resolution service providers[44] are: the Asian Domain Name Dispute Resolution Centre, CPR Institute for Dispute Resolution, the National Arbitration Forum (NAF), and the World Intellectual Property Organization (WIPO). The latter two organizations, WIPO and the NAF, deal with most of the dispute arbitration cases.[45]

Search Terms & Infringement

Meta Tags

Meta tags are relevant key words used by search engines to index pages, allowing web surfers to find tagged pages in searches. Since meta tags are placed in the HTML document, they are entirely within the web designer's control. So if a website owner places someone else's trademark in his meta tags, has he committed trademark infringement? The answer depends on why he placed the trademarked terms in his meta tags. If his purpose was to divert traffic from the trademark owner's website to his own website, then he may have infringed on the owner's trademark rights. However, if he was merely using the trademarked terms to describe his content in a factual manner, it would be considered "*fair use.*"

In <u>*Niton Corporation v. Radiation Monitoring Devices*</u>,[46] a rival x-ray manufacturing firm copied Niton's meta tags on to its website, including phrases like "The Home Page of Niton Corporation, makers of the finest lead, radon, and multi-element detectors."[47] This blatant and willful meta tag infringement was sufficient for the court to grant a preliminary injunction against the defendant's use of the meta tags.

However, in <u>*Playboy v. Terri Welles*</u>,[48] Terri Wells, a former Playboy "Playmate of the Year," used the trademarked phrases "Playboy" and "Playmate" in her website's meta tags. The court held that her use of the trademarks was a fair use because it accurately described and identified her.[49] Her website made no effort to trick or confuse consumers into believing it was somehow related to Playboy; in fact, her website included a disclaimer stating it was not. (Of course, search engine robots and spiders could also index the disclaimer, causing people searching for those terms to end up on her website).

Keyword Search Advertising

Keyword advertising is the practice of search engines responding to a query for one company's products with information about those of another manufacturer. About 98 percent of the search engine firm Google's revenues come from keyword advertising.[50] Google lets advertisers bid for placement in "sponsored" areas of search-result listings, pairing ads with listings generated by relevant keywords. Since web searches are the primary way people find products and services online, keyword advertising is highly effective for marketers — enabling them to reach web searchers but pay only when searchers click on their links — and a big moneymaker for search engines like Google. However, many of these ads are linked to branded or trademarked names of products and services. Thus the question arises if when entering, for example, the phrase "Adidas sneakers" into a search engine a banner ad for competitor Nike appears does this violate Adidas' trademark?

In other words, when does the use of keyword search ads become abuse? How do you say you repair Volkswagens without using the trademarked term "Volkswagen?"[51] Following the logic of _Welles_, that would seem to be a fair use. But some marketers bid for their rivals' keywords to garner their traffic. In 1999, Playboy lost a lawsuit to prevent two portals (Netscape and Excite) from generating hardcore sex ads when visitors searched for its trademarked terms "Playboy" and "Playmate."[52] But the 9th Circuit reversed the case in 2004, ruling that Playboy's trademark terms "_Playboy_" and "_Playmate_" should be protected even in Internet searches that prompt pop-up ads.[53]

Google has had limited success in this area domestically but has not fared well overseas. U.S. federal trademark laws protect a trademark against a "use in commerce," but courts are split over whether using a competitor's trademark as a keyword to trigger ads in search results is a "use in commerce" under the statute. Google and other search engines have been fierce critics of Utah's 2007 Trademark Protection Act, which lets firms register their trademarks as "electronic registration marks" and prohibits use of trademarks registered under the Act to trigger online ads.[54] At the time of this book's publication, there was some question as to whether the Utah law could withstand a constitutional challenge. But while courts are split over the issue and many commentators have assailed the new Utah law, cases such as _Buying for the Home v. Humble Abode_[55] — where a New Jersey court denied a motion for summary judgment holding that search engine keyword-triggered advertising had satisfied the "use" requirement of the Lanham Act — continue to call the issue into question.

Overseas, in 2005, Google settled a lawsuit with GEICO over the automobile insurer's claim that Google's policy of selling ads tied to searches for the keywords "GEICO" and "GEICO Direct" to GEICO's competitors infringed on its trademark; and in the same year a federal court dismissed a case against Google by a computer repair firm over its practice of letting businesses purchase keyword ads to be displayed when users typed in a competitor's name, holding that selling keyword advertising is not a trademark use in commerce.[56] A French court, in 2004, ruled that Google's French subsidiary could not link competitors' ads to the trademarks of a European resort hotel.[57] The resort had sued Google because Google charged competitors of Le Meridien Hotels and Resorts to have their ads pop up in search results containing Le Meridien's trademarked terms. Google has stated its intention to appeal the decision. Google's subsidiary also lost an appeal to the Court of Appeals in Versailles to overturn a decision ordering it not to display keyword ads next to search results for a French travel agent's trademarks.[58] Just a month earlier, Louis Vuitton SA won a similar case against Google. Under French law, the practice of keyword advertising is considered a trademark violation in most cases.

U.S. law is unclear about the responsibility, if any, of search engines to police trademarks in paid searches. Google says advertisers are responsible for the keywords and ad text they use, but that on request, Google will perform a limited investigation. The law is also unclear about the responsibility, if any, of search engines to give trademark holders visibility in search results based on keywords related to their trademarked terms (*i.e.*, the term may appear as a buried link in a long list of results). Trademark owners seek to assert their rights to trademarked keyword ads because, as discussed in the previous chapter, by law they risk losing their trademarks if the terms become a part of the common usage and they cannot show that they have tried to contest it. That is what happened to Sony in Austria, where Sony lost the right to its "Walkman" trademark in 1994. Sony had sued Austrian company Time Tron Corporation for describing its range of portable cassette players as Walkmans in a sales catalog, effectively using the trademarked term generically to mean any portable cassette player. The court found that Sony had not taken sufficient steps to prevent the generic use of its trademark after failing to seek a retraction when it appeared listed as a noun in a 1994 German dictionary.[59]

Of course, sometimes keyword advertising can backfire. An Associated Press wire story entitled "Fatal Fire Caused By Candle, Official Says" describing how a Philadelphia firefighter was killed in a fire caused by "an unattended fragrance candle" automatically pulled up along side the news article ads for fire department uniforms, and immediately below the article an ad from a fragrance candle manufacturer, complete with a picture of one of its products, a lit candle. And when a television station ran the headline "Man Gets 6 Months For Putting Urine In Co-Workers' Coffee" accompanying the story was a generated keyword ad that read "Tempt Your Taste Buds With Our Recipes."

Summary

Domain names have been viewed as either intellectual property rights or contract rights. The distinction is important because property rights offer more protections than do contract rights. Also, a property right lasts indefinitely until it is conveyed, whereas a contract right is limited to an express (*i.e.*, defined) term upon which it will expire. The purchase and sale of domain names is an estimated $2 billion industry and is projected to double by 2010. Domain names are registered at a rate of 90,000 per day!

Domain misspellings, mouse-trapping, and pagejacking are methods used to mislead web surfers into viewing web pages. Courts will find trademark infringement where the trademark owner's name has been intentionally misspelled in a bad faith attempt to divert visitors away from the targeted website to the violator's website (typosquatting). Mouse-trapping occurs when a website visitor cannot leave a website without clicking on a succession of pop-up windows. Pagejacking occurs where the offender steals the contents of a website by copying some of its pages, putting them on a website that appears to be the real website, and then inviting people to the fake website through deceptive means.

The Truth in Domain Names Act was a response to misleading domain names. It makes it illegal to use a "misleading domain name" with the intent to deceive a person into viewing obscenity or to deceive a minor into viewing "material that is harmful to minors." The Act may be vulnerable to a First Amendment challenge however, because the terms "misleading," "obscenity" and "harmful to minors" are inherently vague.

A cybersquatter is one who deliberately and in bad faith registers a domain name that infringes on a trademark. The Anti-cybersquatting Consumer Protection Act closed loopholes in the existing trademark laws that had been used by cybersquatters. It does not require actual "use in commerce;" the test is "registers, traffics in, or uses a domain name," (*i.e.*, mere registration will suffice) but there must be a "bad faith intent."

The Uniform Domain Name Dispute Resolution Policy was established by the Internet Corporation for Assigned Names and Numbers, as a quick and cost-effective alternative to a lawsuit, to resolve domain name disputes.

Meta tags are relevant key words used by search engines to index web pages. Placing a trademark in a meta tag may be an infringement if the purpose is to divert traffic from the trademark holder's website. Courts are split over whether trademarks used in keyword advertising may be infringements.

Chapter Five Notes ▰▰▰▰▰▰▰▰

[1] Gary Kremen is also the founder of <u>Match.com</u>, the Internet's largest dating website.

[2] Cohen was finally captured by Mexican police in 2005 after six years as a fugitive and returned to the U.S.

[3] *Kremen v. Cohen*, 337 F.3d 1024 (9ᵗʰ Cir. 2003). This case is included in the Cases Section on the Issues in Internet Law website (<u>www.IssuesinInternetLaw.com</u>).

[4] The domain name <u>sex.com</u> was sold in 2006 to Escom LLC for an estimated $14 million. "Sex.com Sold," CNET News.com, January 19, 2006.

[5] *Kremen v. Cohen*, 99 F. Supp. 2d 1168 (N.D. Cal. 2000).

[6] *Ibid.*

[7] Adam Goldman, "Internet Domains Snagging Huge Amounts of Money," Associated Press wire report, July 16, 2007.

[8] *Ibid.*

[9] Martin Fiutak, "Teenager Admits eBay Domain Hijack," CNET News.com, September 8, 2004. Many teens commit computer crimes, but their motivation is mostly "curiosity and a hunger for excitement rather than wanting to cause trouble," according to psychologist Shirley McGuire of the University of San Francisco, who conducted an anonymous survey of 4,800 San Diego high school students. She reported that only 10% surveyed said they committed computer crimes "to cause trouble or make money." *See* Marilyn Elias, "Most Teen Hackers More Curious Than Criminal," USA Today, August 19, 2007.

[10] John Blau, "Google.de Domain Gets Kidnapped," IDG News Service, January 23, 2007.

[11] Steven Musil, "ISP Suffers Apparent Domain Hijacking," CNET News.com, January 16, 2005.

[12] John Zuccarini, discussed at fn. 15, *infra*. Associated Press wire report, May 24, 2002.

[13] PROTECT Act of 2003 (Pub. L. No. 108-21).

[14] Truth in Domain Names Act, 18 U.S.C. § 2252B.

[15] John Zuccarini, *FTC v. Zuccarini*, 01-CV-4854, (E.D. Pa 2002).

[16] Associated Press wire report, "Man Sentenced for Registering Misleading Web Site Names," USA Today, February 27, 2004.

[17] Anti-cybersquatting Consumer Protection Act, 15 U.S.C. § 1125(D)(1)(A) protects "the owner of a mark, including a personal name which is protected as a mark" but does not apply to individuals whose names are not trademarked.

[18] Beth Lipton Krigel, "Archie Comics Fights Parent for Domain," CNET News.com, January 15, 1999.

[19] David Loundy and Blake Bell, "E-Law Updates: Domain Name Disputes (Big Company vs. Little Baby)," March 1999.

[20] Kieren McCarthy, "Dell Joins Domain Name Hall of Shame (Again)," The Register, January 26, 2005.

[21] *Ibid.*

[22] Katie Jones website, *available at* <u>www.katie.com</u> (accessed September 25, 2007).

[23] Katie Tarbox website, "Important Statement Regarding Katie.com and Katie Jones" *available at* <u>www.katiet.com/message1.htm</u> (accessed September 25, 2007).

[24] Uzi Nissan website, "The Story," *available at* <u>www.ncchelp.org/The_Story/the_story.htm</u> (accessed September 25, 2007).

[25] Nissan attorney Leland Dutcher claims that in 1994 "there wasn't an understanding of the power of the Internet as a marketing tool" but that five years later the company "became concerned that a very large number of [customers] were going looking for us at a website at nissan.com that we didn't have," Stephen Cass, Spectrum Careers website, "Nissan v. Nissan," *available at* www.spectrum.ieee.org/careers/careerstemplate.jsp?ArticleId=i100302 (accessed September 25, 2007). This raises the interesting question of whether a corporation that was not sharp enough to register its own name as a URL deserves the right to usurp the name from a more prescient registrant bearing the same name. Taken at face value, Dutcher's comments would appear he is suggesting that Nissan Motor Co.'s admitted shortsightedness and lack of vision justify a court ordering the transfer of the domain name to it.

[26] Nissan Motor Co. first registered its trademark in the U.S. in 1959. *Nissan Motor Co., Ltd. v. Nissan Computer Corp.*, 89 F. Supp. 2d 1154, (C.D. Cal. Mar. 23, 2000), although the Nissan trademark was not used in the United States until 1983; before that, Nissan Motor Co. marketed its cars under the Datsun brand name. (Uzi Nissan's name was first registered on his birth certificate in 1951), Uzi Nissan website, fn. 24, *supra*.

[27] *Nissan Motor Co., Ltd. v. Nissan Computer Corp.*, fn. 26, *supra*. The California District Court admitted that the defendant was not located in, and did not sell any products or services in, California but nonetheless found jurisdiction based on the fact that the defendant placed advertising on his website through contracts with five California-based companies — Asimba, Inc., Ask Jeeves, Inc., CNET, Inc., GoTo.com, Inc., and RemarQ Communities, Inc.

[28] *Ibid.*

[29] *Ibid.*

[30] *Nissan Motor Co., Ltd. v. Nissan Computer Corp.*, Case No. 02-57148 *et al.*, D.C. No. CV-99-12980-DDP (9th Cir. 2004).

[31] "Nissan's Appeal Over Website Rejected," Los Angeles Times, April 19, 2005.

[32] *Ficker v. Tuohy*, 305 F.Supp.2d 569, (D. Md. 2004). This case is included in the Cases Section on the Issues in Internet Law website (www.IssuesinInternetLaw.com).

[33] The Right of Publicity is a common law right, the applicability of which varies from state to state. See the discussion in Chapter 10.

[34] *Time, Inc. v. Firestone*, 424 U.S. 448 (1976).

[35] *New York Times v. Sullivan*, 376 U.S. 254 (1964).

[36] MySpace is a social network and a "friend" is one who joins the user's social network.

[37] Micah L. Sifry, "The Battle to Control Obama's MySpace," TechPresident.com, May 1, 2007.

[38] *Ibid.*

[39] Anti-cybersquatting Consumer Protection Act, 15 U.S.C. § 1125(d).

[40] *Coca-Cola Co. v. Purdy*, 382 F.3d 774 (8th Cir. 2004).

[41] Pez website, *available at* www.pez.com (accessed September 25, 2007).

[42] Internet Corporation For Assigned Names and Numbers, *available at* www.icann.org/ (accessed September 25, 2007).

[43] Sheri Qualters, "Arbitration Is Weapon of Choice in Growing Number of Domain Name Disputes," National Law Journal, October 9, 2006.

[44] *Available at* www.icann.org/udrp/approved-providers.htm (accessed September 25, 2007).

[45] Sheri Qualters, fn. 42, *supra*.

[46] *Niton Corp. v. Radiation Monitoring Devices, Inc.*, 27 F. Supp. 2d 102, 105 (D. Mass. 1998).

[47] *Ibid* at 104.

[48] _Playboy Enters., Inc. v. Welles_, 7 F.Supp. 2d 1098 (S.D. Cal. 1998). This case is included in the Cases Section on the Issues in Internet Law website (www.IssuesinInternetLaw.com).

[49] In a similar case currently being litigated at the time of this book's publication, Half Price Books sued BarnesandNoble.com in November 2002, claiming that it violated and diluted its trademark by advertising sale books in a subtitle "Half-Price Books & Special Values" on a menu tab. Following the rationale of _Welles_, this might be considered a permissible truthful description by a competitor of the price of their books. _See_ Stefanie Olsen, "BarnesandNoble.com Loses Round in Trademark Case," CNET News.com, November 29, 2004. On a motion for summary judgment, the court ruled against BarnesandNoble.com, allowing the case to go forward. _Half Price Books, Records, Magazines, Inc. v. BarnesandNoble.com, LLC_, 2004 U.S. Dist. LEXIS 223691 (N.D. Tex. Nov. 22, 2004).

[50] Stefanie Olsen, "Google Loses Trademark Dispute in France," CNET News.com, January 20, 2005.

[51] In _Volkswagenwerk Aktiengesellschaft v. Church_, 411 F.2d 350, 352 (9th Cir. 1969), the 9th Circuit held that the defendant was able to advertise that he repaired Volkswagen vehicles as long as he did not do so in a manner "which is likely to suggest to his prospective customers that he is part of Volkswagen's organization of franchised dealers and repairmen." And likewise, in _Bijur Lubricating Corp. v. Devco Corp._, 332 F.Supp.2d 722 (D. NJ Aug. 26, 2004), Bijur manufactured and sold Bijur lubrication systems; Devco was in the business of selling replacement parts for the Bijur system on its website, where Devco placed the trademarked name "Bijur" in its meta tags. The court held that Devco's use of its competitor's trademark in its meta tags did not constitute infringement or dilution in violation of the Lanham Act.

[52] _Playboy Enters., Inc. v. Netscape and Excite_, 55 F. Supp. 2d 1070 (C.D. Cal. 1999).

[53] _Playboy Enters., Inc. v. Netscape Communications Corp._, 354 F.3d 1020 (9th Cir. Jan. 14, 2004).

[54] (Utah) Trademark Protection Act (SB 236, Chapter Law 365 (2007).

[55] _Buying for the Home, LLC v. Humble Abode LLC_, 459 F.Supp.2d 310 (D.N.J. Oct. 19, 2006).

[56] _Rescuecom Corp. v. Google, Inc._, 456 F. Supp. 2d 393 (N.D.N.Y. Sept. 28, 2006). Since this was a district court holding it does not set a binding precedent, however other courts may be persuaded by its reasoning and agree that search engines are not infringing on trademarks by selling keyword advertising.

[57] "Google Loses French AdWords Case," Outlaw.com, January 24, 2005.

[58] Peter Sayer, IDG News Service, "Google France Loses Appeal in AdWords Trademark Dispute," PCWorld.com, March 18, 2005.

[59] _Sony Europe v. Time Tron Corporation_, (Austria 1994).

Chapter Five Quiz

Barney Rubble registers his domain name, Barney.com. Barney plans to post photographs of his little boy Bamm-Bamm lifting the family car and playing with his friend Pebbles. However, the creators of the children's icon "Barney the Brontosaurus," an anthropomorphic orange brontosaurus, have filed a trademark infringement lawsuit against Barney Rubble claiming that his Barney.com website is infringing on their registered "Barney" trademark. They point to the fact that Barney has placed the phrases "Barney" and "orange brontosaurus" in his website meta tags.

The creators of Barney the Brontosaurus have also filed suit against Sy B. Squatter, who has registered the domain names Barnie.com and BarnieTheBrontosaurus.com. When children mistakenly type in the misspelling of Barney's name at those websites they are taken to a pornographic website, MutantTeenageLesbianTurtles.com and every attempt to exit the website results in the appearance of a succession of pop-up ads for more sex websites.

Are either of the Barney creators' lawsuits likely to succeed? Why or why not?

If you are using this book in a classroom, discuss the issues raised and the liability of all parties. Otherwise, try to list the issues involved and probable outcomes before turning to the answers in the Appendix.

[Answers in Appendix]

CHAPTER SIX

PATENTS AND
TRADE SECRETS

> This chapter examines patents and trade secrets, as well as the Paris Convention of 1883, the Patent Cooperation Treaty of 1970, and the Convention on the Grant of European Patents of 1973.

Patents

PATENTS ARE THE THIRD of the four forms of intellectual property that we will examine in this section. Several Internet companies have availed themselves of patents to procure monopoly rights in certain inventions. The concept of being awarded a monopoly for a new invention is not an idea borne of the Internet Age, but rather dates back to the Founding Fathers, who included that right within the U.S. Constitution.[1] Just as trademarks fall under the purview of the Lanham Act, patents are governed by the Patent Act.[3]

A patent is a *government-issued grant* that confers on the inventor the right to *exclude* others from making, *using, offering for sale, or selling* the invention for a period of *20 years,*[3] measured from the *filing date*[4] of the patent application. "Any new and useful process, machine, manufacture, or composition of matter, or any new and useful improvement thereof"[5] may be patented. The term "process" is defined as "process, art or method," and includes a new use of a known process, machine, manufacture, composition of matter, or material.

Patents are similar to copyrights in that one cannot copyright or patent an idea. Copyright law prevents the copying of the expression of ideas, but does not protect the ideas themselves; likewise, patent law protects inventions, but not mere ideas. In both cases, there must be some identifiable embodiment of the idea before there can be intellectual property protection. Patents are in one respect the opposite of trade secrets, another form of intellectual property discussed later in this chapter. The inventor must make a full disclosure of the invention, *i.e.*, not hold back any secrets, to obtain a patent; in exchange for patent rights, the patent (*i.e.*, how the invention works) becomes public information. Thus, a patent is the opposite of a trade secret, (*e.g.*, the formula for Coca-Cola), which by its very nature is secret, whereas a patent is open and public.

Patent rights are *exclusionary*; the holder does not necessarily have the right to use the invention. The patent holder has the right to *exclude* others from making, using, selling, or offering to sell the invention. He can *stop* others from using it; or he can *license* his patent in exchange for royalties. The true value of a patent comes from licensing revenue or from preventing a competitor's use. A license can be one of three types:

- An *exclusive license* to a single licensee

- A *non-exclusive license* to multiple licensees, or

- A *license within a limited field* of use

There are three types of patents. The *utility patent*, which applies to inventions that have a use and protects functionality, is the most common. *Design patents* protect the appearance of an object. *Plant patents* protect the appearance and color of plants. Most patents expire after 20 years (an exception is design patents, which expire after 14 years). U.S. patents are enforceable only in the United States and its territories; separate patent systems exist in most countries.

To obtain a patent, the invention must be:

- *Novel* — not known or used by others in the United States, or patented or described in a printed publication here or abroad, or in public use or on sale in the United States more than one year prior to the application for patent

  ◊ Telling friends and family about the invention may toll the one-year grace period

  ◊ The inventor must file for patent protection on his new invention within the one-year grace period or lose all rights to patent protection

  ◊ While the United States has a one-year grace period, most other countries do not, so it is advisable for inventors to file an application before any public disclosure. Otherwise such public disclosure might preclude the filing of international applications

- *Non-obvious* — not obvious to a person having ordinary skill in the pertinent art as it existed when the invention was made. The patent examiner will compare the invention with *prior art* (*i.e.,* everything publicly known before the invention as shown in earlier patents and other published material), and judge whether any differences between the prior art and the invention would have been "obvious to a person having ordinary skill in the pertinent art as it existed when the invention was made"

  ◊ A change in size or substitution of one material for another would probably be considered obvious and hence not patentable

- *Useful* — it must have current, significant, beneficial use as a process, machine, manufacture, composition of matter or improvements to one of these. ("Composition of matter" relates to chemical compositions and may include mixtures of ingredients as well as new chemical compounds). If it is a machine, it must also perform its intended purpose to be patentable, otherwise it is not considered useful. For example, a perpetual motion machine would not be patentable because it would not work (the concept violates the laws of physics)

Abstract ideas, laws of nature, and physical phenomena are not patentable.

Filing the Application

Before filing a patent application, a search for prior art must be made. Prior art is important because the most common ground to invalidate a patent is that the invention is not novel or obvious in light of prior art (*i.e.,* what already exists anywhere in the world).

Once the prior art search has been completed, a patent application must be filed with the U.S. Patent and Trademark Office (U.S.P.T.O.).[6] Filing *is* necessary — *patents do not arise from use*, as do copyrights and trademarks. Since this is a very technical area of law, a *patent attorney*, licensed to practice before the Patent Office, should be retained to assist with the application. Once filed, the application is reviewed by a patent examiner. The review, which may take from nine–to–18 months, is similar to that of the trademark application process in that the examiner will issue an "office action" which cites the review findings, often resulting in a denial of the application. The patent attorney then responds either by arguing the points raised or amending the application. Applicants should be aware that obtaining a patent can be *expensive* and *time-consuming*. There are both filing fees and issue fees (if the patent is granted) and in some cases periodic maintenance fees. Note that the U.S.P.T.O. does not enforce patents or deal with infringements claims; those matters are handled by the federal courts. The U.S.P.T.O. merely processes patent applications.

The Patent Application

The patent application has several parts:

- The *petition* — the formal request for a patent

- The *abstract* — a short technical summary of the invention that includes a statement of the use of the invention

- The *specification* — a detailed description of the features of the invention, including how to make and use the invention

- The *claims* section — a brief statement in precise legal language of what is being patented, written primarily to show the examiner how the invention differs from prior art (the claims section is the most important part of the application)

- The *drawings* section — a graphical representation of the invention (or in the case of software or chemicals, a flowchart)

As stated earlier, the grace period is very strict. Failure to file a timely patent application can result in effective donation of patent rights to the public domain. The patent application *must* be filed within *one year* of the occurrence of any one of the following:

- Description of the invention in a publication

- Public use of the invention

- Patenting of the invention by another

- An offer to sell the invention

Who Is the Patent Holder?

The United States has a "first to invent" patent system as opposed to most other countries that have a "first to file" system. If two U.S. inventors attempt to patent the same invention, the one who can prove that he conceived the invention first will get the patent. If two inventors worked together jointly on the invention then they should file as joint inventors. However, one who is merely a financial backer of the invention may not file as a joint inventor. If the inventor is deceased, then his or her legal representatives may file the application. Likewise, if the inventor has been declared legally insane, then his guardian may file the patent application.

In the United States, patents are filed in the name of *inventor*, unlike the rest of world which allows companies to file for ownership of patents. Therefore, smart companies should require a written contract obligating the employee or independent contractor to transfer ownership of the patent to the company. In fact, most companies routinely include a clause requiring assignment of patent rights in their employment contracts. There are three scenarios where an employer might become the patent owner:

- Employment Agreement — Prior to creating the invention, the inventor signed an employment contract requiring assignment of all patent rights to the employer. A few states restrict the scope of these assignment clauses [7]

- "Hired to Invent" — the employee was specifically hired for the purpose of inventing the item or solving a stated problem

- Shop Right — a common law right granting a non-exclusive and non-transferable license to the employer allowing use of an invention created during the course of employment by its employee. [8] The non-exclusive nature of this right means that the employee could simultaneously license the invention to a competitor of his employer. The shop right normally arises only where the employee has used the employer's resources (*e.g.*, time, money, supplies, labor) to create the invention

Patents and the Internet

On the Internet, patents protect software (which is also protected by copyright) and business methodology.

One example of a *software patent* is the GIF patent, the source of a patent infringement case that could have affected many of the images on the Internet. In 1987, CompuServe, a major ISP at the time, created GIF, an efficient image file format, using the LZW file compression scheme. Seven years later Unisys announced that it had filed for, and received in 1985, a patent on the LZW algorithm. (Thus this was a "submarine" patent, *i.e.*, submerged unseen until it surfaces to fire at its target). While Unisys had owned the patent since 1985, it had only pursued hardware, not software licenses. Unisys sued CompuServe for infringement. The case was settled and the developers had to pay Unisys royalties. Meanwhile, other developers, concerned that they could no longer use GIFs on the Internet without paying royalties, created PNG as a royalty-free graphic format alternative to GIF. [9]

Some examples of *business methodology patents* granted to Internet firms are the Priceline.com "Reverse Auction" and the Amazon.com "One-Click." Priceline.com's "Reverse Auction" business methodology is simply a service whereby consumers name the price that they are willing to pay and Priceline finds sellers willing to meet the buyers' stated needs and price. Amazon.com's One-Click Patent is described as a business methodology for placing an order whereby in response to a single act (a mouse click) an item may be ordered from an e-commerce website. Through the use of cookies, additional information needed to complete the order will have been previously obtained and stored on Amazon's database, so the order can be processed with only one mouse click. Many critics object to the notion of patenting business methodologies, on the basis that methodologies like Priceline.com's and Amazon.com's are neither novel nor non-obvious.

Amazon.com demonstrated its use of its exclusionary rights as a patent holder in December 1999, just before the busy online holiday shopping season, by obtaining an injunction against online competitor Barnes and Noble (www.bn.com), forcing it to replace its own one-click ordering system with a slightly more complicated ordering system. [10]

There have now been many *web-related patent filings*, including one-click online shopping, online shopping carts, the hyperlink, video streaming, internationalizing domain names, pop-up windows, targeted banner ads, paying with a credit card online, framed browsing, and affiliate linking.

Some of the patents can involve innovative uses of existing technology. In June 2004, the U.S.P.T.O. granted Digital Envoy a patent for its IP Intelligence technology, which pinpoints the physical location of web surfers down to the city level, based on their Internet Protocol (IP) address. [11] Google then licensed the patent from Digital Envoy to deliver geo-targeted ads on its website. Google later applied the technology to deliver geo-targeted ads to its Google AdSense partners on their websites, prompting Digital Envoy to sue Google for allegedly exceeding the patent license by allowing the technology's use on third-party websites. [12]

Patent Infringement

As discussed above, the "claims" section of the patent application contains a set of claims that define what the inventor seeks to protect with his patent. Infringement is determined by comparing the language of the claims with the actual product. For the patent to be infringed upon, the product must match the definition given in at least one claim. To infringe, each and every element of that claim must be present in the infringing product. If even a single element is missing, then the product does not infringe.

Since a patent examiner has examined it, a patent is presumed by the court to be valid. The burden of proof is therefore on the accused infringer to prove that the patent is invalid and should not have been granted, due to any one of the following:

- Prior art not previously considered

- Insufficient disclosure of the invention

- Fraud

Because the federal government grants patents, federal courts have jurisdiction in patent infringement cases. If the trial court finds that there has been infringement, the patent holder may ask the court for either an injunction (to prevent further infringement) or for monetary damages. As shown in Chapter One, all appeals in patent cases go to the U.S. Court of Appeals for the Federal Circuit, in Washington, DC (established in 1982), with further appeal possible to the U.S. Supreme Court.

International Patents

Patent protection for a U.S. patent extends *only* throughout the United States and its territories and possessions. A U.S. patent alone will not give an inventor the right to exclude those in foreign countries from making or using the invention. Instead, patent protection usually *must be sought in each individual country* in which protection is desired. Many countries have a requirement that the patented product be manufactured in that country within a specified time frame (often three years). This is known as the "*working requirement.*" Failure to meet the working requirement will void the patent in some countries, but others will simply grant compulsory licenses to anyone who applies.

The *Paris Convention of 1883* deals with the protection of industrial property (*i.e.*, patents, utility models, industrial designs, trademarks, service marks, trade names, and repression of unfair competition).[13] It is one of the most important treaties in intellectual property law. It provides that citizens in signatory nations are treated equally to citizens in the countries in which they seek patent protection; *i.e.*, the signatory nation will grant the same rights in patent and trademark matters to citizens of other signatory nations as it gives to its own citizens. The Convention provides that if the inventor subsequently files patent applications for the same invention in other member countries within one year after filing the first one, the later applications receive a fictional filing date equal to the filing date of the first patent application. This is known as "convention priority." The Paris Convention is supervised by the World Intellectual Property Organization (WIPO).

The *Patent Cooperation Treaty of 1970* enables the inventor to seek patent protection simultaneously in each of a large number of countries by filing a single "international" patent application.[14] There are 137 signatories to the treaty, including United States, most of the European Community, and Japan. The process begins with the filing of an international patent application in one country's "receiving office." An international patent search is conducted for prior art, and an opinion regarding patentability is issued, along with an "International Search Report." Eventually both the report and the application are published.

The *Convention on the Grant of European Patents of 1973* (European Patent Convention or EPC), set up the European Patent Organization and a legal framework by which European patents are granted.[15] The contracting nations are: Belgium, Germany France, Luxembourg, the Netherlands, Switzerland, the United Kingdom, Sweden, Italy, Austria, Liechtenstein, Greece, Spain, Denmark, Monaco, Portugal, Ireland, Finland, Cyprus, Turkey, Bulgaria, the Czech Republic, Estonia, Slovakia, Slovenia, Hungary, Romania, Poland, Iceland, Lithuania, Latvia, and Malta (with Norway expected to join in 2008). Once granted, a European patent has the same force and effect as a national patent in each of the contracting nations.

Trade Secrets

Trade secrets are the fourth of the four types of intellectual property that we will examine in this section. Trade secrets are confidential practices, methods, processes, designs, or other information used by a company to compete with other businesses. The elements of a trade secret are:

- Information that is not generally publicly known

- Information that confers on its holder an economic benefit derived from its secrecy

- Information that is the subject of reasonable efforts to maintain that secrecy

Trade secrets, like copyrights, trademarks, and patents, are a form of intellectual property. In one respect, a trade secret is the opposite of a patent. Recall from earlier in this chapter that in exchange for patent rights, the patent (*i.e.*, how the invention works) becomes public information. Thus a trade secret is by its very nature secret, whereas a patent is open and public.

With one exception noted below, trade secrets are subject to state, not federal law, so the law on trade secrets will vary by jurisdiction. However, about 45 states have adopted a model statute known as the *Uniform Trade Secrets Act* (UTSA).[16] The UTSA defines trade secrets as "information, including a formula, pattern, compilation, program, device, method, technique, or process that derives independent economic value from not being generally known and not being readily ascertainable and is subject to reasonable efforts to maintain secrecy."[17]

Inventions, formulas, recipes, designs, software designs, manufacturing processes, instructional methods, document tracking processes, and customer or supplier lists can comprise trade secrets. One does not file a trade secret, as is the case with other intellectual property; trade secret protection attaches automatically when information of value to the owner is kept secret by the owner. Simply locking the information in a file cabinet marked "Confidential" is sufficient. However, trade secret protection may be lost if the owner fails to take reasonable measures to protect it. Unlike copyrights and patents, trade secrets do not expire within a set period.

Misappropriation of Trade Secrets

Trade secrets are subject to misappropriation usually by either corporate espionage or breach of a confidentiality agreement. However, discovery of protected information by independent research or reverse engineering is not misappropriation. For example, if a soft drink scientist stumbles across the exact formula for Coca Cola in his laboratory, he has not misappropriated a trade secret. Remedies for misappropriation include monetary damages, recovered profits, reasonable royalties, and injunctive relief.

The Economic Espionage Act of 1996 makes the misappropriation or theft of trade secrets a federal offense. The first part of the Act deals with theft of trade secrets to benefit foreign governments, but the second part of the Act focuses on theft or misappropriation in the corporate environment. Section 1832, entitled "Theft of Trade Secrets," applies to products produced for, or placed in, interstate or foreign commerce. Penalties include fines (up to $5 million for an organization found guilty) and imprisonment (up to 10 years). The Act applies not only to one who steals the trade secrets but also to one who "receives, buys, or possesses such information, knowing the same to have been stolen or appropriated, obtained, or converted without authorization." [19]

In a recent case, Apple Computer sued a student for disclosing trade secrets on his website. A 13-year-old boy from New Woodstock, New York built a website in 1998 and under the alias "Nick dePlume" [20] began publishing insider news and rumors about Apple Computer. His website, as the first to break the news that Apple would launch a G4 version of the PowerBook laptop series, quickly became a leading source for Apple insider news among Apple fans, bringing him millions of monthly page views. Despite warnings from Apple to cease publishing proprietary information, Nicholas Ciarelli continued to do so, and in December 2004, after another revelation by his website, Apple sued him for illegally misappropriating trade secrets. [21] Although Ciarelli did not have a direct relationship with the company, Apple's lawsuit alleged that his website induced tipsters to break non-disclosure agreements. The website contained a phone number for tips and a link to an e-mail form labeled *Got Dirt?*, which added that he "appreciates your news tips and insider information." Third parties are prohibited by the UTSA from exposing information knowingly obtained from sources bound by confidentiality agreements. Ciarelli, a 19-year-old Harvard University student at the time of the lawsuit, claimed that he was a "journalist" protected by the First Amendment. [22] (See the discussion of news blogs in Chapter 13). However, critics argued that his website also has a commercial component, [23] as it featured paid ads from technology companies. Ciarelli countered that his website benefited Apple by creating valuable "buzz" about forthcoming products. The lawsuit has the potential to backfire on Apple, as it may antagonize many Apple fans to see one of their own attacked by the computer giant. [24] Indeed, one blogger commented that Apple should hire Ciarelli, not sue him.

Summary

Several Internet companies have availed themselves of patents to procure monopoly rights in certain inventions. Patent law is governed by the Patent Act; patent applications are processed by the U.S. Patent and Trademark Office; and infringement claims are decided by the federal courts. A patent is a government-issued grant that confers on the inventor the right to exclude others from making, using, offering for sale, or selling the invention. A patent is an exclusionary right. Patents are similar to copyrights in that one cannot copyright or patent an idea. Copyright law prevents the copying of the expression of ideas, but does not protect the ideas themselves; likewise, patent law protects inventions, but not mere ideas. In both cases, there must be some identifiable embodiment of the idea before there can be intellectual property protection.

The true value of a patent comes from licensing revenue or from preventing a competitor's use. Most patents expire after 20 years (design patents expire after 14 years). To obtain a patent, an invention must be useful, novel, and non-obvious. A patent application requires a search for prior art. Prior art is important because the most common ground to invalidate a patent is that the invention is not novel or obvious in light of prior art (*i.e.*, what already exists anywhere in the world).

Filing is necessary; patents do not arise from use. The patent application consists of the Petition, Abstract, Specification, Claims, and Drawings. The patent application must be filed within one year of description of the invention in a publication, public use of the invention, patenting of the invention by another, or an offer to sell the invention. In the United States, patents are filed in the name of *inventor*, unlike the rest of world which allows companies to file for ownership of patents. Patents protect software and business methodologies. A patent is presumed by the court to be valid; the burden of proof is on the accused infringer to prove it is invalid and should not have been granted.

International patent protection is governed by three treaties. The Paris Convention of 1883 is one of the most important treaties in intellectual property law. It provides that citizens in signatory nations are treated equally to citizens in the countries in which they seek patent protection. The Patent Cooperation Treaty of 1970 enables the inventor to seek patent protection simultaneously in each of a large number of countries by filing a single "international" patent application. The Convention on the Grant of European Patents of 1973 provides a legal framework by which European patents are granted.

Trade secrets are confidential practices, methods, processes, designs, or other information used by a company to compete with other businesses. The elements of a trade secret are information that is not generally publicly known, confers on its holder an economic benefit derived from its secrecy, and is the subject of reasonable efforts to maintain that secrecy. About 45 states have adopted a model statute known as the Uniform Trade Secrets Act.

Inventions, formulas, recipes, designs, manufacturing processes, instructional methods, document tracking processes, and customer or supplier lists can comprise trade secrets. One does not file a trade secret, as is the case with other intellectual property; protection attaches automatically when information of value to the owner is kept secret by the owner. Protection may be lost if the owner fails to take reasonable measures to protect it.

Trade secrets are subject to misappropriation by corporate espionage or breach of a confidentiality agreement. However, discovery of protected information by independent research or reverse engineering is not misappropriation. The Economic Espionage Act of 1996 makes the misappropriation or theft of trade secrets a federal offense.

Chapter Six Notes ▰▰▰▰▰▰▰▰▰▰▰▰▰▰▰▰▰▰▰▰▰

[1] U.S. Const., Art. I, § 8: "Congress shall have power ... to promote the progress of science and useful arts, by securing for limited times to authors and inventors the exclusive right to their respective writings and discoveries."

[2] Patent Act, 35 U.S.C. § 101. "Inventions patentable: Whoever invents or discovers any new and useful process, machine, manufacture, or composition of matter, or any new and useful improvement thereof, may obtain a patent therefor, subject to the conditions and requirements of this title."

[3] Most patents expire after 20 years (an exception is design patents, which expire after 14 years).

[4] However, patents are not enforceable until the day of issuance.

[5] Patent Act, fn.2, *supra*.

[6] U.S. Patent and Trademark Office, *available at* www.uspto.gov (accessed September 25, 2007).

[7] California, Delaware, Illinois, Kansas, Minnesota, North Carolina, Utah, and Washington all have statutes imposing limited restrictions on the scope of assignment clauses in employer contracts.

[8] *See Gill v. U.S.*, 160 U.S. 426 (1896), establishing an estoppel principle that if an employee acquiesces and participates in the use of the invention in the employer's business, he is estopped from preventing the employer's use of the invention or requiring that the employer pay royalties.

[9] In June 2003, Unisys' U.S. patent on LZW expired, but the patent remained valid in Europe and Japan until June 2004 and in Canada until July 2004. A patent that IBM had filed on the same algorithm expired in August 2006.

[10] *Amazon.com v. BarnesandNoble.com*, 73 F.Supp.2d 500 (W.D. Wash. Dec. 1, 1999) *vacated and remanded* 239 F.3d 1343 (Fed. Cir., Feb. 14, 2001).

[11] Digital Envoy press release, June 29, 2004, *available at* www.digitalenvoy.net/news/press_releases/2004/pr_062904.html (accessed September 25, 2007).

[12] Jonathan Skillings and Stefanie Olsen, "Google Hit with 'Geo-location' Lawsuit," CNETNews.com, March 30, 2004. Digital Envoy lost the case.

[13] Paris Convention of 1893, *available at* www.wipo.int/treaties/en/ip/paris/trtdocs_wo020.html (accessed September 25, 2007).

[14] Patent Cooperation Treaty of 1970, *available at* www.wipo.int/pct/en/texts/articles/atoc.htm (accessed September 25, 2007).

[15] Convention on the Grant of European Patents of 1973, *available at* www.wipo.int/clea/docs_new/pdf/en/ep/ep001en.pdf (accessed September 25, 2007).

[16] The text of the Uniform Trade Secrets Act is included in the Cases Section on the Issues in Internet Law website (www.IssuesinInternetLaw.com).

[17] *Ibid.*

[18] Economic Espionage Act of 1996 , 18 U.S.C. § 1831, *et. seq.*

[19] *Ibid*, § 1832(a)(3).

[20] A "nom de plume" is a French phrase meaning "pen name" or pseudonym.

[21] *Apple Computer, Inc. v. DePlume*, No. 05-CV-33341 (Cal. Super. Ct., Santa Clara County filed Jan. 4, 2005); *see also* Jonathan Finer, "Teen Web Editor Drives Apple to Court Action," Washington Post, p. A01, January 14, 2005.

[22] While this raises the interesting issue of "What is a journalist?," or more precisely, "Who may be considered a journalist?," the First Amendment was not written merely to protect journalists; the First Amendment is a broad restriction on government prohibiting it from restricting speech by its citizens.

[23] The U.S. Supreme Court has ruled that the First Amendment protects commercial speech, but to a lesser degree than non-commercial speech. However, even newspapers, which contain paid advertising, do not forfeit their First Amendment protection by doing so.

[24] See the discussion on company lawsuits against cyber gripers and the risk of negative publicity, in Chapter 13.

Chapter Six Quiz

Wilma Flintstone is not your ordinary housewife. Wilma has invented a revolutionary new house cleaning apparatus, which she has named the "Wonder Broom." The Wonder Broom squirts a cleaning solution onto the floor that is specially formulated to lift up the dirt so that the broom can easily sweep it up. Wilma unveiled her invention two years ago in a two-page spread in *"Good Housekeeping"* magazine. Last week Wilma filed a patent application, however she did not reveal the formula for her special cleaning solution, either in the article or in her patent application, claiming it is a trade secret. Today she received an office action letter from the U.S. Patent & Trademark Office informing her that her patent application had been rejected. On what basis could the U.S.P.T.O. reject Wilma's application?

If you are using this book in a classroom, discuss the issues raised and the liability of all parties. Otherwise, try to list the issues involved and probable outcomes before turning to the answers in the Appendix.

[Answers in Appendix]

PART THREE

UNINVITED GUESTS

CHAPTER SEVEN

SPAM

> This chapter discusses spam — what it is, where it comes from, and how to avoid it. Attention is focused on state and federal anti-spam laws, including the CAN-SPAM Act.

SPAM, NOT TO BE confused with the Hormel product, is *unsolicited e-mail*, usually fraudulent business schemes, chain letters, and political or offensive sexual messages. Most Internet users consider spam to be a major annoyance. It clogs e-mailboxes and causes users to waste time sorting out the legitimate e-mail from the junk e-mail. Spammers might well consider the potential *negative backlash* from consumers from their mass e-mail campaigns, as the very act of spamming may alienate the prospective customer.

Why then do spammers spam? Quite simply, because it works. Spam is a cheap, highly effective method of marketing. Marketing is a numbers game and spam allows the spammer to reach huge numbers of people at minimal cost. If only a fraction respond favorably, the spammer will have made back the cost of the mass mailing many times over his initial investment. Twenty percent of U.S. residents say they buy products from spammers, according to a May 2004 Yahoo! Mail survey.[1] As some consumers welcomes spam, it is proliferating, congesting blogs, cell phones, and instant messages. Spam is estimated to account for 80%-to-90% of all U.S. e-mail.[2]

Where Does Spam Come From?

How do spammers find you? It seems that you have more e-mail from spammers than friends filling your mailbox each day, but how did they learn your e-mail address?

They may *buy* your e-mail address — 1.5 million e-mail addresses can be purchased for less than $15. Or they may get your e-mail address by using software programs known as "*harvesters*" that pluck names from websites, newsgroups, or other services where users display their e-mail address. Not only do spammers clog e-mail accounts with unsolicited mass mailings; now the spammers have also turned to instant messages, pop-up ads, blogs, and website guest books. But there are some steps you can take to limit your exposure to spam.

Streetwise Tips to Avoid Spam

- *"NOBODY'S HOME!"*   **Do Not Reply to Spam!**

Sure, they promise to remove your name from their list if you reply to their e-mail, but they are lying! What the spammers really want is to confirm that they have a valid e-mail address. By replying, all you are doing is confirming that they have a "good" e-mail address; you will have just made your e-mail address infinitely more valuable to the spammer, who will also sell your address to every other spammer, meaning you will soon be inundated with even more spam. Replying to spam is the technological equivalent of the hobo mark[3] of old.

- *"NO SHOUT-OUTS!"*   **Do Not Post Your E-Mail Address on Your Website!**

It may seem like a good idea at the time, but by posting your e-mail address on your personal home page you are merely rolling out the welcome mat to spammers. Spammers, as discussed earlier, use software to "harvest" e-mail addresses from websites. This software crawls through the Internet looking for text strings that resemble "you@yoursite.com." Once found, your e-mail address joins thousands of other harvested addresses in the spammer's database. An alternative to posting your e-mail address on your website is to use a query form instead of an e-mail link — the sender can send you a message without your e-mail address being displayed. Of course, this approach will only work on your own website, so you still need to use discretion when posting your e-mail on a third-party's website, such as on a guest book or blog. Also, check to see who else may be posting your e-mail address online (*e.g.*, do a Google search for you own e-mail address). Check the organizations to which you belong; opt out of member directories that may place your e-mail address on their website.

- *"'ANONY MOUSE' IS IN THE HOUSE"*   Use an Alias E-Mail Address in Newsgroups!

Newsgroups are an e-mail address goldmine for spammers, since most display the poster's e-mail address on each message posted as well as in the message header. If you post to a newsgroup, you are going to get spam. Most newsgroup-related spam is sent to the address in the message header, even if other e-mail addresses are included in the text of the posting. But you can still participate in the newsgroup discussion without being subjected to a flood of spam by using a different e-mail address from the one you normally use for friends or business. Have a "public" address for newsgroups and a "private" address for friends or business (similar to having an unlisted phone number). You can set up a free Hotmail or Gmail e-mail address just for use on news groups.

- *"WHAT YOU TALKIN' ABOUT, WILLIS?"*   **Do Not Reveal Your E-Mail Address Unless You Know How It Will Be Used!**

If a website requests your e-mail address, then it obviously wants to use it for some purpose; be sure you know what that purpose is. Read the "Terms of Use" and "Privacy Statement" of any website before supplying your e-mail address. Inquire if they intend to share or sell your e-mail address. Do you really want further e-mails from this website?

- *"TALK TO THE HAND!"*   **Use a Spam Filter!**

While there is no such thing as a perfect spam filter, e-mail filtering software can help keep spam at a manageable level, and also reduce the risk of exposure to e-mail borne viruses. Spam filters are available both from ISPs and from commercial software companies.

- *"DO NOT FEED THE BEARS"*   **Never Buy Anything Advertised in Spam!**

There is a reason why parks have signs that say "Do Not Feed the Bears!" If you feed them once, they will keep coming back! Do not encourage the spammers! The reason that marketers spam is because they make money convincing people to buy a product. If no one buys the products advertised in spam, then there will be no benefit for companies to spam. In short, do not reward the spammers!

The CAN-SPAM Act

After years of trying, Congress finally passed an anti-spam bill. The CAN-SPAM Act of 2003 (Controlling Assault of Non-Solicited Pornography and Marketing Act)[4] pre-empted more than 30 state laws and brought uniformity to the legal effort to fight spam. But the Act is less restrictive than some state laws and, because of First Amendment free speech concerns, it *does not ban sending spam*. The Act does not preempt state laws that prohibit "falsity and deception" in commercial e-mails, and states may retain certain portions of their existing anti-spam laws, or enact new laws. The Act is enforced by the Federal Trade Commission (F.T.C.).

The CAN-SPAM Act:

- Requires the use of accurate headers in e-mail messages — a valid return address must be used to deter "spoofing"

- Requires procedures for recipients to opt out of future e-mails, *i.e.*, "unsubscribing"

- Requires clear labeling of commercial e-mail as advertising

- Requires listing a valid physical address within the e-mail

- Forbids e-mail address harvesting

- Mandates a feasibility study of setting up a "do-not-e-mail" registry, similar to the popular "do not call" registry

Since the introduction of the CAN-SPAM Act, the F.T.C. has required sexually-oriented spam to be labelled "SEXUALLY EXPLICIT" in the subject line and has concluded that the proposed "do-not-e-mail" registry would be impossible to implement.

Enforcement under the Act falls to the F.T.C., state attorneys general, and ISPs — the Act does not create a private right of action for individuals to sue spammers for violation of the Act.

In April 2004, the U.S. Department of Justice charged four Illinois men under the Act[5], and three months later Massachusetts used the Act to charge a Florida man suspected of spamming thousands of consumers. In November, 2005, timeshare spammer Peter Moshou was sentenced to a year in prison under the Act.[6] The first trial conviction under the CAN-SPAM Act occurred in January 2007, when a California man was convicted of e-mailing thousands of AOL subscribers pretending to represent the AOL billing department and requesting credit card information.[7] (This kind of "phishing" attempt is discussed in detail in Chapter Eight, the cyber crimes chapter of this book). A New York teenager gained the dubious distinction of the first conviction under the CAN-SPAM Act for sending spam through instant messaging (known as "*spim*"). Not only did the teen spam the MySpace IM system with 1.5 million messages, but he allegedly attempted a not-so-brilliant extortion scheme, threatening the social network with further spim attacks unless MySpace hired him as a consultant; he was arrested by local police and U.S. Secret Service officials while enroute to his pre-arranged meeting with MySpace executives.[8]

One federal court ruled that while the CAN-SPAM Act does not impose strict liability for violations by agents of an entity, it does impose vicarious liability if the entity had knowledge of the violation and control over its agents.[9] In that case, an online pornographic company hired affiliates to promote its website. The affiliates spammed in violation of the CAN-SPAM Act and the F.T.C. sought to hold the company strictly liable for the actions of its affiliates. The court ruled that the Act did not impose a strict liability standard, but that if it were found that the company knew its affiliates were violating the Act and had failed to exercise sufficient control over its agents, then it could be vicariously liable.[10]

As mentioned above, the CAN-SPAM Act does not outlaw spamming and one spammer actually argued that the Act should prevent an organization from blocking its spam if the spammer complied with the Act. White Buffalo Ventures set up a dating website, LonghornSingles.com, and targeted University of Texas students by obtaining their e-mail addresses through a Freedom of Information request. The University responded by blocking White Buffalo Ventures' IP address. White Buffalo Ventures sued, charging that the University was violating its First Amendment rights and that the CAN-SPAM Act precluded the school from blocking its IP address. A federal Texas trial court disagreed and a 5th Circuit three-judge panel upheld that decision, adding that the CAN-SPAM Act wasn't intended to prevent ISPs from filtering out spam. In 2006 the U.S. Supreme Court declined to hear White Buffalo Ventures' appeal, which effectively means that the 5th Circuit decision stands as the law on the issue.[11]

The latest trend for spammers is to send image-based spam in an attempt to slip the spam past spam filters. Most image spam is used in "pump and dump" stock-scam e-mails that tout a stock to raise its value, so the spammer can then quickly sell the stock at a profit.[12]

While the CAN-SPAM Act appears to have had limited effect against the onslaught of spam, and there have been no other federal anti-spam laws passed yet, various state anti-spam laws do exist.

State Spam Laws

Since e-mails travel across state lines, in drafting anti-spam laws the question invariably arises, is the spammer subject to the laws of the state from which the spam was sent or to the laws of every state to which in which it was received? Presumably, states would choose the second view, since each state drafts its laws with the intent of protecting its own citizens. But to accept the latter view would mean that for every e-mail address in his possession, the spammer would need to know the geographic location of every recipient! Alternatively, the spammer would need to determine if his e-mail campaign violated any state's laws, *i.e.*, a least common denominator approach, targeting his campaign to the most restrictive states' laws. Such confusion has led some courts to hold such laws based on that view unenforceable.

Many states require a label at the beginning of the subject line of certain types of unsolicited commercial e-mail messages.[13] Arizona, Colorado, Illinois, Indiana, Kansas, Michigan, Minnesota, Nevada, New Mexico, North Dakota, Oklahoma, South Dakota, Tennessee, Texas, and Utah require that the unsolicited e-mails contain a label ("ADV:") in the subject line and an opt-out mechanism in the body. California and Delaware have an *opt-in rule* for e-mail advertising, where the recipient must have agreed in advance to receive the e-mail, *e.g.*, by signing up for an e-mail list. Some states require that unsolicited bulk commercial e-mail messages must include an e-mail address for opt-out requests and requires senders to honor opt-out requests; Arizona, Arkansas, Colorado, Idaho, Illinois, Indiana, Iowa, Kansas, Maine, Michigan, Minnesota, Nevada, New Mexico, North Dakota, Oklahoma, Pennsylvania, Rhode Island, Tennessee, and Texas are among these states.

States that have laws that make it illegal to send unsolicited bulk e-mail containing falsified routing information include Connecticut, Delaware, Idaho, Illinois, Indiana, Iowa, Kansas, Louisiana, Maine, Maryland, Michigan, Minnesota, Nevada, North Carolina, North Dakota, Oklahoma, Pennsylvania, Rhode Island, South Dakota, Tennessee, Texas, Utah, Virginia, Washington, West Virginia, and Wyoming.

Three states have regulated unsolicited e-mails from attorneys. *Florida* has not enacted spam legislation, although a Florida Bar rule[14] requires that attorneys who advertise via unsolicited e-mail place "legal advertisement" in the subject line. *Kentucky* requires attorneys who advertise via written, recorded, or electronic communication targeted at potential clients to include the words "THIS IS AN ADVERTISEMENT" prominently in each communication. *Louisiana* requires attorneys who advertise via unsolicited e-mail targeted at potential clients to use a subject line that states, "This is an advertisement for legal services."

Virginia has the toughest anti-spam law in the country. In December 2003, the statute was used to indict two North Carolina men, the first people in the U.S. to be charged with felonies for sending junk e-mail.[15] One of the men was sentenced to nine years imprisonment. Five months later, his sister was indicted for violating Virginia's anti-spam laws, as was a Texan in May of 2004. Each charge carried a sentence of one–to–five years in prison and a fine of up to $2,500. The Virginia statute targets spammers who intentionally alter an e-mail header or other routing information and try to send either 10,000 e-mails within a 24-hour period or 100,000 in a 30-day period.[16] A spammer can also be prosecuted under the statute if a specific transmission generates more than $1,000 in revenue or if total transmissions generate $50,000.[17]

Foreign Spam Laws

Some countries have *"opt-in" laws* on e-mail forbidding unsolicited e-mail unless the recipients have previously indicated a willingness to receive it. Of course, the question remains, how would the foreign country be able to *enforce* that law against an American spammer?

Using Existing U.S. Laws to Fight Spam

As discussed at the beginning of this chapter, spammers run the risk of receiving negative feedback from the unhappy recipients of their unsolicited e-mails. They may be willing to send out a million e-mails at once, but they do not want to receive a million complaints in their e-mail in-box the next morning. Therefore most spammers use false headers to avoid negative feedback following a large scale unsolicited e-mailing. *Trademark and unfair competition laws* have been used against spammers who identify their messages as coming from someone else. The F.T.C. has promulgated stringent advertising laws. Truth in advertising laws apply to e-mail marketing, so spam containing misleading or false statements can subject the spammer to purview of the F.T.C.

Most states have laws already on their books that can be adapted for use in the fight against spam. For example, a federal court in Iowa awarded an ISP in excess of a billion dollars against a spammer using the Iowa Ongoing Criminal Conduct Act in combination with the federal Racketeer Influenced and Corrupt Organizations Act (RICO) which allows for treble damages.[18]

Sometimes there may be both criminal and civil remedies to spam. In 2003, a man accused by Earthlink, a major ISP, of using 343 e-mail accounts to send 825 million spam messages for products like herbal sexual stimulants was sentenced to three years in prison.[19] In a separate civil action, Earthlink won a $16 million judgment against him.[20] ISPs not only fight spam by expressly prohibiting their users from spamming in their "Terms of Use" agreements; many ISPs and e-mail providers now offer free spam-blocking tools. Many commercial spam-blocking tools are publicly available also.

One unique weapon against spam is the civil lawsuit. There are at least two cases where recipients of spam have sued the product's manufacturer for failing to live up to its advertised claims. In one case, a New Jersey man sued a Florida company for false advertising, alleging that the company's herbal penis enlargement pills did not work.[21] In the second case,[22] responding to an unsolicited e-mail, a California man paid Leading Edge Marketing $160 for its "VigRx Oil." When the penis enlargement herbal supplements failed to work, the man sued the British Columbian company for fraud, theft, and money-laundering.

Murking

A *Murkogram* is spam that includes a *disclaimer* stating that the message cannot be considered spam because it is in compliance with Bill S.1618 Title III, known as the Inbox Privacy Act.[23] That alone should be a tip-off, as the astute reader knows that only statutes, *i.e.*, laws enacted by the legislature, have the force of law. Bills are merely proposed laws that only become law when passed by the legislature (state legislature or Congress) and signed into law by the chief executive (governor or president). In 1999, U.S. Senator Frank Murkowski, for whom the Murkogram is dubiously named, proposed a law requiring that spam include the sender's correct name, physical address, IP address, phone number, and an option for recipients to remove themselves from the sender's list (an opt-out option). The proposal was not enacted because of objections from ISPs that the requirements would present too heavy an administrative burden. But many spammers cite the proposed law as a way of legitimizing their spam. A typical boilerplate statement in the e-mail suggests that (1) the e-mail, even though not requested, was in conformance with the (actually non-existent) law since it identified the sender, and (2) the recipient had no grounds for taking action against the sender. Such spammers are said to be "Murking."

Mail Bombs

Every e-mail account is allocated a certain amount of disk space. Disk space on all e-mail servers is a finite, limited resource that must be shared among all accounts on that server. A huge amount of mail may fill recipient's disk space on the server or may be too much for the server to handle, causing the server to stop functioning. A mail bomb is a massive amount of e-mail sent to a specific person or computer network with the intention of disrupting service to all mail server customers. Mail bombs are a form of denial of service attack. Internet users who have been spammed or flamed (*i.e.*, publicly attacked) in a newsgroup often retaliate with mail bombs attacks, although the practice is illegal.

Permission-Based Marketing

Not all bulk e-mail is spam. Only unsolicited bulk e-mail is considered to be spam. Some bulk e-mail is permission-based, meaning that the recipient has asked to receive it. This occurs when a website visitor voluntarily agrees to receive a newsletter or other e-mail, known as "opt-in e-mail."

Summary

Spam, unsolicited e-mail, is estimated to account for 80%-to-90% of all U.S. e-mail. Spammers may buy e-mail addresses or use software programs known as *"harvesters"* that pluck names from websites, newsgroups, or other services where users display their e-mail address. Spam clogs e-mail accounts, instant messages, pop-up ads, blogs, and website guest books.

The CAN-SPAM Act brought uniformity to state efforts to regulate spam but does not prohibit spam. The Act is less restrictive than some state laws but does not preempt state laws that prohibit "falsity and deception" in commercial e-mails, and states may retain certain portions of their existing anti-spam laws, or enact new laws. The Act is enforced by the Federal Trade Commission (F.T.C.). The CAN-SPAM Act requires the use of accurate headers in e-mail messages, procedures for recipients to opt out of future e-mails, clear labeling of commercial e-mail as advertising, and listing a valid physical address within the e-mail. It also forbids e-mail address harvesting and mandates a feasibility study of setting up a "do-not-e-mail" registry.

Enforcement under the Act falls to the F.T.C., state attorneys general, and ISPs — the Act does not create a private right of action for individuals to sue spammers for violation of the Act. A federal court has ruled that while the CAN-SPAM Act does not impose strict liability for violations by agents of an entity, it does impose vicarious liability if the entity had knowledge of the violation and control over its agents. Compliance with the Act by a spammer does not preclude an ISP from filtering out spam or blocking a spammer's IP address.

Many states have laws regulating spam, including opt-in and opt-out provisions, labeling requirements, and prohibitions against false headers. Trademark and unfair competition laws have been used against spammers who identify their messages as coming from someone else. Spam containing misleading or false statements can trigger F.T.C. review under the truth in advertising laws. There may be both criminal and civil remedies to spam. Commercial spam-blocking tools are also available to combat spam.

A mail bomb is a massive amount of e-mail sent to a specific person or computer network with the intention of disrupting service to all mail server customers. Mail bombs are a form of denial of service attack.

Chapter Seven Notes ▰▰▰▰▰▰▰▰▰▰▰▰▰▰▰▰▰▰▰▰▰▰▰▰

[1] Jon Swartz, "Poll Shows Some Look Forward to Reading Spam," USA Today, July 27, 2004.

[2] Bob Sullivan, "Now, Two-thirds of All E-mail is Spam, and in the U.S., Spam Tops 80 Percent Mark," MSNBC.com, May 22, 2004, *available at* www.msnbc.msn.com/id/5032714/ (accessed September 25, 2007); *see also* Sharon Gaudin, "90% Of E-mail Will Be Spam By Year's End," InformationWeek, February 22, 2007.

[3] During the Great Depression, hobos would leave a mark on the door of a home where they had received a handout as a sign to other hobos that the home was a "soft touch."

[4] CAN-SPAM Act of 2003, 15 U.S.C. § 7701-7713.

[5] The defendants — Daniel J. Lin, James J. Lin, Mark M. Sadek and Christopher Chung, and a company (Phoenix Avatar) — were charged with sending hundreds of thousands of spam e-mails for fake diet and hormone products.

[6] *United States v. Moshou*, Case No. _____ (D. Fla. 2005).

[7] *United States v. Goodin*, Case No. 06-110 (C.D. Cal. Jan. 2007).

[8] *United States v. Greco* (C.D. Cal. Mar. 22, 2005). *See also*, John Leyden, "NY Teen Charged Over IM Spam Attack," The Register, February 22, 2005.

[9] *United States v. Cyberheat, Inc.*, CV-05-457-TUC-DCB (D. Ariz. Mar. 2, 2007).

[10] Strict liability, in criminal law, is liability for which defendants will be convicted even if they were ignorant of one or more factors that made their acts or omissions criminal. Vicarious liability is liability imputed to one for the actions of another. Agency law is based on the doctrine of respondeat superior, whereby an employer is liable for the actions of his employee.

[11] Anne Broache, "Supreme Court Won't Hear Spam Appeal," CNET News.com, January 9, 2006.

[12] Eric B. Parizo, "Image Spam Paints A Troubling Picture," SearchSecurity.com, July 26, 2006.

[13] Alaska, Arkansas, Illinois, Indiana, Kansas, Louisiana, Maine, Minnesota, North Dakota, Oklahoma, Pennsylvania, South Dakota, Tennessee, Texas, Utah, and Wisconsin had required a label ("ADV: ADLT") at the beginning of the subject line of any sexually explicit unsolicited commercial e-mail message, if the sender knew the recipient was a resident of that state; however, the F.T.C.'s 2004 labeling requirement that all sexually-oriented spam to be labelled "SEXUALLY EXPLICIT" in the subject line has now superseded the states' requirements.

[14] Fla. R.P.C. 4-7.6(c)(3).

[15] *Jaynes v. Virginia*, 48 Va. App. 673 (Sept. 5, 2006). Jeremy Jaynes and his sister Jessica DeGroot were convicted on November 3, 2004. Jaynes was sentenced to nine years imprisonment (upheld on appeal); DeGroot did not receive a prison sentence and the third defendant, Richard Rutkowski, was acquitted. All three defendants were North Carolina residents.

[16] Jaynes and DeGroot used fake Internet addresses to send more than 10 million spam e-mails a day to AOL subscribers on three days in July 2003 — a volume that made the crime a felony under the Virginia statute; Associated Press wire report, "Trial Shows How Spammers Operate," USA Today, November 14, 2004.

[17] Jaynes' spamming yielded him as much as $750,000 per month, even though he only averaged one response for every 30,000 e-mails, at $40 per response; *ibid.*

[18] Associated Press wire report, December 18, 2004. The Iowa law allowed plaintiffs damages of $10 per spam

e-mail and RICO tripled that amount. The defendants failed to appear in court and the plaintiffs were granted a default judgment, although it is unlikely to be collected since the whereabouts of the defendants is unknown. The ISP's inbound mail servers had received up to 10 million spam e-mails a day in 2000.

[19] Howard Carmack of Buffalo, New York, also known as the "Buffalo Spammer." *See* Julia Angwin, "How Ruthless Youngblood Cracked An Elusive Spammer, Wall Street Journal, May 13, 2003.

[20] Paul Roberts, "Buffalo Spammer Gets 3.5 to 7 Years," IDG News Service, May 27, 2004.

[21] Lester Haines, "Man Sues Bigger Penis Pill Company," The Register, February 16, 2005.

[22] John Leyden, "Californian Sues Penis Pill Spammers For Fraud," The Register, February 9, 2004.

[23] Inbox Privacy Act of 1999, *available at* www.spamlaws.com/federal/106s759.shtml (accessed September 25, 2007).

Chapter Seven Quiz

Eddie Haskell has started a new online mail order business selling penis enlargers. Eddie invested $50 in harvesting software to "harvest" e-mail addresses from newsgroups and websites. He then sent a mass e-mailing to two million addresses advertising his "Eddie Haskell Penis Enlarger." He assured recipients of his e-mail that this was not "spam" because the message was in compliance with Bill S.1618 Title III, as the mailing contained the sender's valid e-mail address and a provision to opt out of future mailings.

Wally Cleaver was one of the recipients of Eddie Haskell's e-mail and, angered at all the recent spam he had been receiving, Wally retaliated by sending a mail bomb to Eddie.

Wally's younger brother Beaver also received Eddie's e-mail and had a marketing epiphany: he set up a website called "Beaver Sex Enhancement Products" where visitors could sign up for his weekly e-mail newsletter showcasing the latest sex toys.

If you are using this book in a classroom, discuss the issues raised and the liability of all parties. Otherwise, try to list the issues involved and probable outcomes before turning to the answers in the Appendix.

[Answers in Appendix]

CHAPTER EIGHT

CYBER CRIMES

This chapter discusses cyber crimes —e-mail spoofing, phishing, pharming, identity theft, illegal uploads & downloads, and cyberstalking. It also looks at federal statutes that criminalize certain online activity, including the Securities Act, the Securities & Exchange Act, the Fair Housing Act, the USA PATRIOT Act, and the Wire Wager Act.

THE INTERNET HAS PROVIDED unimaginable opportunities for individuals, regardless of the distance separating them, to connect and interact with each other. And the onset of such opportunities has attracted a multitude of unscrupulous people, like mice to cheese. At best they may be after your money; at worst, your life! Crimes of the Information Age include e-mail spoofing, phishing, identity theft, invasion of privacy,[1] fraud, gambling, cyberstalking, and terrorism.

E-Mail Spoofing

E-mail spoofing is the *forgery of an e-mail header* so that the message looks like it came from someone other than the true sender (*i.e.*, the spammer). Spammers spoof with the hope that the recipient will open the e-mail and possibly even respond, while hiding their own e-mail address to avoid a negative backlash from recipients. Such an unscrupulous spammer could send someone spoofed e-mail that appears to be from you with a message that you did not write. E-mail spoofing is illegal under the CAN-SPAM Act. Spammers spoof because:

- They wish to avoid identification and subsequent liability under anti-spam laws

- They want to hide their true identity because the e-mail contains content that violates state or federal law (*e.g.*, obscenity, child pornography, offers of prostitution or illegal drugs, threats, or harassment)

- They want to trick you into opening an e-mail that appears to come from someone you know in order to infect your computer with a contains a virus or Trojan Horse[2] (discussed below)

- It may be a phishing attempt (discussed below)

- It may be a "social engineering" attack to trick the recipient into divulging confidential information (*e.g.*, a spoofed e-mail claiming to be from someone in a position of authority, asking for sensitive data, such as passwords, credit card numbers, or other personal information — any of which can then be used for a variety of criminal purposes.

Phishing

Phishing (pronounced "fishing") is an Internet scam in which unsuspecting users receive official-looking e-mails that attempt to trick them into disclosing online passwords, user names, and personal information. The scam victims are usually tricked into clicking a link that takes them to a "spoofed" (*i.e.*, fake) version of the real organization's website. The visitor is then tricked into revealing account numbers, credit card numbers, social security numbers, and passwords. (Such pagejacking,[3] where the fake page is set up to procure account numbers and passwords or other personal data from the visitor, is also discussed in Chapter Five, the Trademark and Domain Names section of this book.) One form of pagejacking attack modifies the victim's browser by replacing the address bar with a Java applet allowing the scammer to take victim to any website while still displaying the address of the true organization's website in the browser's window. So when the user clicks on the link in the phishing e-mail, he is taken to a phony website set up by the scammer, although the page will look authentic, at times even down to the URL displayed in the browser's address bar.[4]

Phishing (an obvious allusion to fishing for information) is one form of social engineering to trick the recipient into revealing confidential information. The unfortunate effect of phishing is that it undermines consumer confidence in web-based transactions. Even if a familiar website that you do business with (*e.g.*, your bank or credit card company) sends you an e-mail stating that you need to verify or update your account information, instead of clicking on the URL in the e-mail, you should go directly to their website and then verify it; do not click the e-mailed link! Reputable financial institutions will not ask their customers to update confidential information through e-mail. And if the e-mail contains a phone number to call, contact the institution first to ensure that the listed phone number is legitimate and not a direct line to an identity thief. As of 2007, the latest versions of Microsoft's Internet Explorer browser,

Mozilla's Firefox browser, and Opera's browser all contained anti-phishing software that offered some protection by alerting users to suspicious websites that might be spoofed phishing sites.

According to one e-mail security firm, the number of "phishing" e-mails circulating on the web increased from 279 to 215,643 over a six-month period ending April 2004.[5] By 2007, it was estimated that there were 6.1 billion phishing attacks each day![6] The average amount lost by U.S. Internet users to phishing scams was $1,200 in 2003; presumably that amount would be exponentially higher today.[7] Phishing e-mails often claim to be sent from trusted sources, such as eBay, PayPal, banks, and even the U.S. Internal Revenue Service. Can you tell the difference between a legitimate e-mail and a phishing scam? Take an online phishing quiz at: www.sonicwall.com/phishing.

Personalized phishing is a targeted variation of phishing, where the victim receives an e-mail already containing personalized accurate account information that the phisher has previously obtained from other sources of misappropriated consumer data. Using the victim's name and accurate account information, the phisher then ask the victim for even more sensitive information, which he in turn can sell to identity thieves and other scammers at a premium.

A more targeted variation, known as *spear-phishing,* occurs when the spear-phisher poses as a high-level executive in the targeted corporation and demands confidential information from one of the employees. Once the spear-phisher has obtained passwords, he can install Trojan horses or other malware to access company data. Spear-phishers are normally not random hackers but sophisticated criminals seeking financial gain, trade secrets or military information.[8] Spear-phishing has been particularly effective in military settings, where soldiers have been trained to follow orders from a superior without questions. For example, at the U.S. Military Academy at West Point, N.Y., 500 cadets received an e-mail from Col. Robert Melville informing them of a grading error and ordering them to click a hyperlink to correct their grades. More than 80% of the cadets clicked the enclosed link, as ordered. But there was no such officer as Col. Robert Melville; he was an invention of a National Security Agency computer security analyst offering the cadets a real-life training exercise in spear-phishing.[9]

The latest trend in phishing is the use of instant messaging instead of e-mail. The victim receives an IM (Instant Message), either from a friend's IM signature or from a spam message (known as "spim" when spam is sent as an IM). The IM contains a link to a website where the victim must first enter a user name and password to view the page. Of course, the page contains code to e-mail the victim's information to the phisher. For example, with the victim's Yahoo! user name and password, the phisher could easily read the victim's e-mail, access his Yahoo! wallet account, view his stock portfolio on his Yahoo! home page, impersonate him on Yahoo! Chat, and trade or sell any of this information. And since the phisher now has access to the victim's buddy list, he can send the same phishing lure in an IM to everyone on the victim's list, making it appear that they are receiving a message from a friend as well. The moral is to always be cautious before clicking on links in IMs or e-mails.

Similar to phishing is a scam referred to as *pharming*, where the web surfer attempting to reach a legitimate commercial website is unknowingly misdirected to a fake website. Pharming is a malicious web redirect that exploits the Domain Name System (DNS) used to translate a website's address into a numerical code for Internet routing. It is a combination of domain spoofing and DNS hijacking or DNS poisoning. One method of pharming attacks the host file on a individual's computer, usually by a virus or Trojan. (The host file converts standard URLs into the numeric strings that a computer understands). The second method of pharming is DNS poisoning, which attacks the equivalent of a host file on the domain name server itself, with the potential to misdirect large groups of users to the spoofed website.

You may recall two pharming attacks from Chapter Five, where someone fraudulently changed the DNS address for a New York ISP's domain panix.com and a German youth hijacked the domain for eBay.de. Pharming attacks can be hard to detect, since the fake website will look identical to the real one and appear to have the proper URL shown in the address bar. However, pharming spoofs can be avoided if the user only accesses the institution's website by HTTPS (Hypertext Transfer Protocol over Secure Socket Layer, or HTTP over SSL, *i.e.*, a secured URL) and not by ordinary HTTP Hypertext Transfer Protocol, *i.e.*, with no SSL protection), or if the user follows browser warnings about websites with invalid server certificates (*i.e.*, when a dialogue box asks the user if he wishes to trust the certificate because the name on the certificate does not match the website he is trying to reach).

Most phishing scams rely on the victim being duped into revealing personal information to the phisher. However, one phishing variant known as *keystroke phishing* attempts to retrieve the personal information without the victim's knowledge. In this variant, instead of directing the victim to a fake website that asks for personal information, the e-mail installs a Trojan program onto the victim's computer. The Trojan is a keystroke logger that records the keystrokes typed on the keyboard and writes the information to a text log file. The log file is then sent back through the Internet to the phisher, who hopes to receive the victim's login user ID and passwords for online bank accounts.

Identity Theft

Identity theft is a crime in which an imposter obtains key pieces of personal information (*e.g.*, Social Security number or driver's license number), to impersonate the victim to get credit, merchandise, or services in the victim's name or to provide the thief with false credentials. The imposter might run up debt in victim's name, or give the false identity to the police, creating a criminal record or outstanding arrest warrants for the unsuspecting victim. The imposter can obtain information by *phishing, database cracking, or social engineering (e.g.,* survey). Using an innocent survey with innocuous questions about the victim's mother's maiden name, the names of his children and pets, or his birth date can yield a surprising number of passwords and user names, which taken together with any other known information about the victim can be used to access accounts and obtain even more personal data.

Once a phisher has your credit card number, what does he do with it? A Russian phisher accumulated hundreds of credit card numbers and distributed them amongst his American "cashers" — young men who would then encode the numbers onto plastic cards and use them to withdraw money from ATMs. The cashers would then wire the funds — less their percentage — back to the Russian phisher.[10] Such cashers can make hundreds of thousands of dollars, according to postal inspectors.[11]

There are even websites set up for identity thieves to exchange stolen information internationally. In October 2004, law enforcement authorities arrested 28 people running websites designed to steal, sell, and forge credit cards and identification documents. The websites were hosted on servers outside the United States, in countries including Belarus, Canada, Sweden, and Ukraine. Suspects sold and exchanged stolen information and counterfeit documents such as credit cards, driver's licenses, birth certificates, and foreign and domestic passports. About 1.7 million stolen credit card numbers were bought or sold through these websites, as detailed in this excerpt from the U.S. Department of Justice press release:[12]

> …individuals from across the United States and in several foreign countries conspired with others to operate "Shadowcrew," a website with approximately 4,000 members that was dedicated to facilitating malicious computer hacking and the dissemination of stolen credit card, debit card and bank account numbers and counterfeit identification documents, such as drivers' licenses, passports and Social Security cards. The indictment alleges a conspiracy to commit activity often referred to as "carding" — the use of account numbers and counterfeit identity documents to complete identity theft and defraud banks and retailers.

Scammers can buy someone else's identity — date of birth, Social Security number, bank account number and online passwords, and even mother's maiden name — for between $14-to-$18 on underground online forums.[13] A credit card number alone could be purchased for as little as a dollar.[14] About 5,000 credit cards were traded or sold on the online black market in the second half of 2006.[15]

Identity theft may be spreading to the Internet, but it is not new. According to the F. T.C., in 2001 only three percent of people who reported identity fraud cited misuse of their Internet accounts as the cause.[16] That means 97% of identity theft occurred through offline causes! Despite the risks inherent online, which we will discuss further in this chapter, it is still safer to give out your credit card number on a secured web page than to hand your card in person to an unknown waiter or salesperson.

Social Security Numbers

The Social Security Administration reports misuse of Social Security numbers jumped from 11,000 instances in 1998 to 65,000 in 2001.[17] The identity theft crisis can be traced to the fact that the Social Security number has become Americans' *de facto national identifier*. But the Social Security number was never meant to be a national identity number. So how did it reach this point?

The Social Security Act of 1935[18] did not even mention Social Security numbers, but merely authorized the creation of some type of record-keeping scheme to track employee contributions to Social Security. Thus, Social Security numbers were originally created in 1936 solely for tracking workers' Social Security earnings records.[19] Unlike many European countries, the United States did not have, or desire, a national identity card.[20] By executive order, President Franklin Roosevelt required all federal agencies to use the Social Security number "exclusively" to identify individuals.[21] In 1961, the Civil Service Commission adopted the Social Security number as an official federal employee identifier and in that same year the Internal Revenue Code was amended to require taxpayers to use it on their tax returns.[22] In 1964, the Treasury Department required savings bond purchasers to disclose their Social Security numbers as a precondition of purchasing the bonds. With the creation of Medicare in 1965, individuals over age 65 were required to obtain a Social Security number.[23] The following year, the Veterans Administration began using the Social Security number as the hospital admissions number and for patient record keeping. In 1967, during the Vietnam War, the Defense Department substituted the Social Security number in place of the military service number for identifying Armed Forces personnel. Then in 1970, the Bank Records and Foreign Transactions Act required that all banks, savings and loan associations, credit unions, and brokers/dealers in securities obtain the Social Security numbers of all of their customers.[24]

In 1972, the Social Security Act was amended to mandate that the Social Security Administration issue numbers to all legally-admitted aliens (including foreign workers with visas) and anyone receiving or applying for any benefit paid for by federal funds.[25] It also authorized the Social Security Administration to begin issuing numbers to school children. The Tax Reform Act of 1976 let states use Social Security numbers in the administration of taxes, general public assistance, and driver's license or motor vehicle registration so individuals were then required to provide their Social Security numbers to the states for these purposes.[26] The Food Stamp Act of 1977[27] mandated disclosure of Social Security numbers of all household members as a condition of eligibility for the food stamp program and in 1981 such disclosure became necessary for participation in the school lunch program.[28] That same year, potential inductees were required to disclosure their Social Security numbers to the Selective Service System upon draft registration.[29] The following year, all federal loan applicants had to disclose their Social Security numbers to the lender.[30] In 1988, disclosure of an applicant's Social Security number was made a condition of eligibility for HUD housing.[31] And in 1994, Congress authorized the use of Social Security numbers for jury selection.[32]

As Congress continually expanded the use of the Social Security number over the years, it steadfastly proclaimed (through various studies and committee reports) that the Social Security number should not be used as a national identifier; but in fact, that was what it was becoming. Since its introduction, the Social Security number has been used by many institutions, including hospitals, banks, and brokerage firms, as a means of customer identification. The problem with this is that when multiple databases and record systems are all indexed to the same identifier and meant to be easily accessible to selected users, it is difficult to permit access to only some of the information about a person while restricting other topics. That is why the Social Security number is so valuable to identity thieves; it truly is the key to a person's identity.

No federal law governs — or even limits — the use or disclosure of Social Security numbers among *private* entities. This leaves private companies free to deny credit, services, or membership to anyone refusing to divulge his Social Security number. But there are laws placing limits on public and publicly funded entities. Chief among them is the Privacy Act of 1974. Also known as the *Family Educational Rights and Privacy Act (FERPA) of 1974*, the Privacy Act requires all government agencies (federal, state, and local) requesting Social Security numbers to provide a disclosure statement on the request form explaining if the Social Security number disclosure is mandatory or optional, how the Social Security number will be used, and under what statutory authority the it is being requested.[33] The Act prohibits denial of government benefits or services if a individual refuses to disclose his Social Security number, unless disclosure is required by federal law or is to an agency that has been using Social Security numbers prior to January 1975 (when FERPA went into effect).

The *Buckley Amendment* to FERPA *permits the federal government to cut funding to public schools that violate the privacy of student records. It applies to state colleges, universities, and technical schools that receive federal funding.*[34] Its purpose is to *protect the privacy of students* and give students access to their records to assure the accuracy of the contents of those records.

School officials may not disclose personally identifiable information (including Social Security numbers) about students nor permit inspection of their records without the written permission of the student, except in certain situations permitted by the Act. However, while the Act creates a federal restriction on the actions of these institutions, *it does not create a right of private suit.* In <u>Gonzaga University v. Doe</u>, a recent college graduate sued his school, claiming that a university employee had revealed personal information without the student's consent, thereby damaging his chance to get a job.[35] The Supreme Court held that the graduate could not bring a private cause of action under § 1983[36] (a federal statute often used to sue to enforce one's rights in federal court) to enforce his rights under FERPA. The court stated that FERPA does not grant individuals the right to sue in their own right in court; instead, the individual must file a complaint with the institution or with the Secretary of Education, the latter then being required to investigate, review, order compliance and if necessary terminate federal funding if the school does not comply.

Safeguard Your ID Information

There are many ways in which an identity thief can acquire an individual's personal identification information. It can be stolen over the phone (*e.g.,* by someone posing as a bank, credit card company, phone or electric company, or other service provider to confirm or update the victim's information), from the victim's mailbox or garbage can (*e.g.,* credit card offers, account statements, and bill payments), online (*i.e.,* if the victim enters information on an insecure website), or from stores in which the victim shops (*e.g.,* dishonest clerks). There are several ways to safeguard personal identification information to prevent identity theft:

- Cross-shred (not just tear) documents containing personal identification information

- Order and review a copy of your credit report at least twice a year (You are entitled to one free copy annually). The websites for the three credit bureaus are www.equifax.com, www.experian.com, and www.transunion.com

- Call the Credit Card Industry's Opt-Out Hotline at (888) 567-8688 [*888-5OptOut*] to stop receiving pre-approved credit card offers by mail. The toll-free number was enacted as a requirement of a 1996 amendment to the Fair Credit Reporting Act. You can also opt out online at www.optoutprescreen.com

- Be aware of monthly billing cycles and protect your mail from theft. If planning an extended trip, call the U.S. Postal Service at (800) 275-8777 [*800-ASK-USPS*] to request a "vacation hold" on mail delivery service. Choose "delivery service" at the voice prompt. You can also request a vacation hold online at the U.S. Postal Service website, www.usps.com

- *Do not reveal your Social Security number unless absolutely necessary.* Remember, when you give someone your Social Security number, you are giving away the key to your personal identification!

- Do not carry seldom-used credit cards or any unnecessary identification (*e.g.,* voter registration card)

- Identity thieves are not always strangers; sometimes they turn out to be people from work, casual acquaintances, close friend, ex-lovers, or even relatives

- Do not give out personal information over the phone, through the mail, or through posts on the Internet

- Overwrite data on, and reformat, old hard drives

One often overlooked source of personal information for identity thieves is discarded hard drives. When a computer is disposed of, if the hard drive is not wiped clean then the data still remain on the drive and may be easily retrieved. Even files that are placed in the Windows Recycle Bin and deleted may often be recovered through the use of special file recovery software.[37] This is because the Windows command to delete files does not actually delete the data from your hard drive; it merely deletes the computer's own record of the fact that the disk space the data resides on is unavailable to other uses. The only method of irretrievably destroying data (other than physically destroying the hard drive with a hammer), is to use software that wipes or overwrites data on the disk through multiple passes. The U.S. Department of Defense uses DOD 5220.22-M, a standard generates and records random characters across the entire hard drive surface, destroying all of the data and resetting file sizes to zero.

Computers at schools, businesses, and doctor's offices all contain highly personal information ranging from financial data to medical histories, all of which often remain on the hard drives when the computers are donated or placed on eBay. In fact, confidential or personal data was left on 113 of 200 hard drives purchased on eBay in one study.[38] State agencies in Montana neglected to remove private information before retiring outdated state computers, which were subsequently donated to schools. An audit discovered that eight of the donated computers still contained 386 Social Security numbers, financial records for 182 people, 84 business files, and job applicant information.[39] And computers belonging to individuals may contain everything from passwords and bank account numbers to e-mailed love letters and personal diaries.

The problem is not limited to computers owned by individuals or business; many businesses lease computers. What happens when the leased computer is returned? Unless it has been "wiped" as described above, the data will remain on the computer, available to anyone at the leasing organization or to subsequent lessees. And it is not only hard drives in desktop and laptop computers that are at risk — PDAs, Pocket PCs, multimedia players, and certain cell phones have drives that may also contain sensitive data. While some nations have laws, such as the U.K.'s Data Protection Act, mandating that organizations delete personal data before disposing of hard drives, many do not comply with the law, making discarded drives a treasure trove for identity thieves.[40]

The Identity Theft Penalty Enhancement Act

The Identity Theft Penalty Enhancement Act, enacted in 2004, provides *mandatory* prison sentences for anyone possessing another person's identity-related information with the intent to commit a crime.[41] The Act adds two years for individuals who "knowingly transfer, possess, or use another's identity to commit a felony," and five years for "terror-related crimes." Unfortunately, the Act is simply a knee-jerk reaction to the realization of the growing problem of identity theft, merely updating existing penalties. It is unlikely that the minimum two-year sentence will deter someone intent on committing a crime that, under current law, can already lead to a 15-year prison sentence. Of course, the problem was not that there were not laws in place, but that the government must identify and capture the lawbreaker before those laws can be applied, in order to make a dent in the growing problem of identity theft. A more practical solution might be to pass laws that hold information handlers more accountable for the security of the data they collect and store. On the positive side, the Act is the first step toward centralizing enforcement at the federal level, to solve the problem of inadequate enforcement by the states (*e.g.*, as in cases where more than one state is involved and the states bounce a case back and forth).

Cookie Poisoning

Cookies are data placed on the user's computer by a specific website to enable the site to personalize the user's visit (*e.g.*, on e-commerce sites this may entail pulling up a previously completed customer profile), speed up transactions, and monitor the user's behavior (see the discussion of behavioral marketing in Chapter 11). *Cookie poisoning* is the *modification of a cookie* (*i.e.*, personal information stored in the user's computer) *by an attacker to gain unauthorized information about the user* for purposes such as identity theft. Cookies are "poisoned" when any of the stored values (*e.g.*, user IDs, passwords, account numbers and session keys) are altered. The cookie then follows the user from one part of the website to another. If hackers get on a website and steal a user's cookie, then they have access to that user's session. Websites should protect cookies (*e.g.*, through encryption of the stored values) before they are sent to the user's computer to prevent cookie poisoning.

Uploads & Downloads

Adware vs. Spyware

Adware is software that displays ads as the program runs. Software developers justify placing advertising in their product to recover programming development costs, thereby lowering the overall user cost. Adware is legal and often an alternative "full cost" version of the software without ads is available.

Spyware is software that accesses and uses an Internet connection in the background without the user's knowledge or explicit permission. It often includes programming code that tracks the user's personal information and forwards it to third parties, again without the user's knowledge or authorization. Spyware can get into a computer either as a software *virus* or when a user *installs a new software program* (by download or CD).

Spyware and adware both may contain data collecting programs, but the main difference is in *spyware* the data collecting program is installed for *malevolent purposes without the user's knowledge or consent*, whereas in *adware*, it is installed for *commercial purposes with the user's knowledge and consent,* (although the disclosure may have been buried in a long click-wrap agreement [42] and the consent may only have been given when the user clicked on it while downloading other programs).

Some online advertisers and P2P networks have placed programs on users' computers to monitor their activity or to use their computers' processors for other activities. Many users are frequently unaware that they are being monitored. Spyware can crash computers or slow performance and is often difficult to find and remove. However, software programs like Spybot, Spy Sweeper, and Ad-Aware can evict these unwanted guests from your computer. Undisclosed spyware may violate communications and computer trespass laws.

In 2004, the F.T.C. filed the first spyware case in the United States, against a group of software companies accused of infecting computers with spyware when users downloaded screensavers and P2P software and then trying to sell their victims software to remove it. [43] The companies would infect computers with unsolicited software that then displayed pop-up ads offering to remove the spyware for $30. One individual owned all three companies involved in the case and the F.T.C. settlement reached in 2006 imposed a $1.86 million fine. [44]

Not only are spyware firms subject to liability, but so are their customers. In another case, both a spyware developer and his customers were charged violating federal computer privacy laws. The software was marketed to spouses who suspected infidelity. The "Loverspy" program was disguised as an e-mailed electronic greeting card, with flowers and puppies as well as hidden spyware that recorded out-going e-mails and websites visited. Although more than 1,000 copies of Loverspy were sold, only four purchasers so far have been indicted, charged with "illegal computer hacking, through utilization of Loverspy, in furtherance of other criminal activity and with illegally intercepting the electronic communications of their victims," [45] each facing up to five years in prison and a maximum fine of $250,000. The spyware creator, Carlos Enrique Perez-Melara, was indicted on 35 counts of manufacturing, sending and advertising a surreptitious interception device (the Loverspy spyware), unlawfully intercepting electronic communications, disclosing unlawfully intercepted electronic communications, and obtaining unauthorized access to protected computers for financial gain. An arrest warrant was issued for the fugitive, who faced up to 175 years in prison if caught and convicted. [46]

Spyware can also be used to rob people. American investors have 10 million online brokerage accounts and approximately one quarter of all retail U.S. stock transactions are made through the Internet. [47] Thieves place spyware on the computer and using keystroke loggers capture the investor's account user name and password. With that information they can then access the investor's account and either sell off the account's portfolio and keep the proceeds or use the account for "pump and dump" schemes [48] to manipulate stock prices for profit. While spyware can easily be uploaded to a personal computer through opening an e-mail attachment or by a drive-by download, computers in publics places, such as brokerage office lobbies, libraries, hotel rooms, and Internet cafés, are most likely the preferred targets since they get a high volume of multiple users. The best protection against falling victim to such spyware would include frequently changing passwords and avoiding public computers to conduct transactions that require entering an account number or password. If you must do so, then at least empty the browser cache so that subsequent users of the same computer will not have access to your user name and password.

Drive-by Download

A *drive-by download* is a program *automatically downloaded* to a user's computer, often *without the user's knowledge or consent*. Unlike a *pop-up download*, which *asks for consent* (although usually in a way calculated to lead the user to respond affirmatively), a drive-by download occurs invisibly to user. It can be initiated by simply visiting a website, or viewing an HTML e-mail message, where code in the HTML uses ActiveX controls (a plug-in for Microsoft's Internet Explorer web browser) to install the software in the background. The code is often hidden in parts of the website not designed or controlled by its owner, *e.g.*, banner ads and widgets (third-party programs that can be embedded into an HTML page). Often, a drive-by download is installed invisibly along with another application. Drive-by downloads are used to infect a computer or steal sensitive data. Some merely change bookmarks, install unwanted toolbars or substitute a new browser home page, but others install Trojan keyloggers. An in-depth study of 4.5 million web pages by Google revealed that 10% contained malicious code that could infect a user's computer through drive-by downloads.[49] The best defense against drive-by downloads is for users to set their browser settings to the highest security level and to use up-to-date security software. Drive-by downloads are illegal and fall under the crime of *computer trespass*.

Malware

Malware (short for "malicious software") is any programming or file developed for the purpose of doing harm. Malware includes computer viruses, worms, and Trojan horses. A *worm* is a self-replicating virus that does not alter files but resides in the computer's active memory and duplicates itself. A *Trojan horse* is a program in which malicious or harmful code is hidden inside an apparently harmless program or data to later gain control and cause damage. The phrase comes from Homer's *Iliad*; during the Trojan War, the Greeks presented the citizens of Troy with a large wooden horse in which they had secretly hidden their warriors. At night, the warriors emerged from the wooden horse and overran and conquered Troy.

Wardriving, Piggy-backing, and Telecommunications Theft

"Wardriving" is the practice of driving with a Wi-Fi enabled laptop computer, mapping houses and businesses that have wireless access points. *Piggy-backing* is the use of a wireless Internet connection without permission. The theft of Internet access or bandwidth is actually the crime of *telecommunications theft*. People who use wireless access to the Internet at home or business are often unaware that their wireless signals can be transmitted 500 feet or further. These

signals can then be intercepted if the user has not encrypted the signal, allowing the interceptor to "piggyback" on the signal and log on to the Internet on a Wi-Fi equipped laptop computer.

A Florida man caught wardriving in his SUV with a laptop was charged with unauthorized access to a computer network, a third degree felony in that state,[50] while across the pond in the United Kingdom, in a case of first impression, a man caught with a laptop computer in front of a residential neighborhood building, using a homeowner's wireless network was fined £500 and sentenced to 12 months conditional discharge.[51]

An infamous 2003 case of wardriving occurred when Toronto, Canada police noticed a man driving the wrong way on a one-way street. Pulling the car over, they discovered that he was naked from the waist down, with his laptop computer downloading child pornography from the Wi-Fi connection of a nearby home.[52]

Wardriving situations like that case raise the specter of other potential problems. As Jeff Beard wrote in his LawTechGuru blog, "Now imagine that it was your Wi-Fi connection he hijacked, except that the authorities didn't catch the wardriver, but instead tracked the downloads back to your network from your ISP's logs. Talk about some explaining to do."[53] The possibility exists that Wi-Fi owners who negligently fail to secure their networks might be liable for the acts of wardrivers and other unauthorized users of their networks. Unauthorized access to a wireless network can not only be used for downloading but for uploading as well; spam, viruses, and Trojans could all be uploaded, potentially harming third parties.

Wardriving — driving with a Wi-Fi enabled laptop computer, mapping houses and businesses that have wireless access points — is not by itself a crime. It is the unauthorized use of a wireless Internet connection — the telecommunications theft — that makes the act illegal. If a business offers patrons the use of its Wi-Fi signals (as many do), then the users are not making unauthorized use of a wireless Internet connection. However, that scenario does raise the issue of what liability, if any, the business might have for any illegal acts committed by authorized users of its wireless Internet connection. Suppose a patron at a popular coffee house avails himself of its free Wi-Fi and downloads child pornography as he sips his Java. Or perhaps he uploads a Trojan to steal data from a business rival. Does the coffee house, as the provider of the Wi-Fi access, bear any liability? Might a court then go so far as to label the coffee house an Online Service Provider protected by the CDA? What if the patron sends out a spam mailing with an unauthorized copyrighted image; would the coffee house be considered a contributory infringer, since it enabled the copyright infringement by making the technology available? These are issues that have yet to reach the courts.

Several incidents of cyber crime involving unauthorized use of open Wi-Fi access points have been documented by the F.B.I., including an attempt to steal credit card transaction data from a Michigan department store in November 2003, an attempt to extort $17 million from a patent company through the use of unsecured wireless access points, and a phishing scheme in Georgia that used open wireless access points to send e-mail designed to trick recipients into revealing their credit card and banking information.[54] In the Michigan case, dubbed by the press as the first criminal conviction for wardriving, a man pled guilty to a federal misdemeanor of unauthorized access to a protected computer.[55] Paul Timmins and his roommate Adam Botbyl came across an unsecured network at Lowe's department store as Timmins was wardriving. He used the private corporate network to check his e-mail and his roommate returned six months later with a friend, Brian Salcedo, a young man still on probation for a juvenile computer crime conviction. In the Lowe's parking lot, the two men accessed the Lowe's network again, connecting to the local networks of Lowe's branches in Kansas, North Carolina, Kentucky, South Dakota, Florida, and California. Once inside, they changed the store's proprietary credit card software to enable them to retrieve customer credit cards numbers. Salcedo and Botbyl both pled guilty to computer intrusions, damage and fraud.[56] The 21-year-old Salcedo was sentenced to nine years in prison for hacking into the Lowe's computer system, the longest prison sentence to date for computer hacking.[57] Ironically, Salcedo's sentence was significantly greater than the 32-month sentence given to one of the leaders of the Shadowcrew scam discussed earlier in this chapter. Botbyl received a 26-month prison sentence.[58]

Pod Slurping

Apparently, not even the seemingly innocuous iPod is without its dark side. It is not just for music. High school students, hiding their iPods and other digital media players beneath their clothes, have been caught playing back voice-recorded test answers during school exams (cell phone texting of test answers being "so '90s."). Schools in Idaho, Washington, Ontario, and even Australia have banned digital media players once the non-tech generation of teachers and administrators got wise to the dual use of such devices.[59]

There have been reported instances of "pod slurping," *i.e.*, data thieves hooking iPods or other portable media players into corporate computers and networks to use them as portable hard drives to steal information.[60] Relatively inexpensive, easily concealable, prosaic in appearance, and with hard drives holding up to 160 gigabytes[61] of memory, portable media players are understandably a data thief's best friend. A keyboard is not even necessary; the data thief merely plugs the device into an open USB port and begins downloading data. To casual observers, he would appear merely to be listening to music on his iPod. Portable media players can store more than music files; they can also store other files, such as documents and spreadsheets. A typical word-processing file averages 25k–to–30k in file size, meaning that the average 60 gigabyte portable media player is capable of storing more than 2.25 million documents! Slurp!

Of course, data transfer works both ways. A corporate spy or disgruntled employee could use a portable data device deliberately to inject viruses and spyware into the corporate network (pod burping?).[62] Data thieves can also simply walk away with data already stored on disks or USB flash drives. According to computer security firm Symantec, 54 percent of all identity theft-related data breaches were attributable to lost or stolen data storage media.[63]

Cyberstalking

Cyberstalking is crime in which the attacker harasses the victim using electronic communication, such as e-mail, instant messaging, or messages posted to a website, chat room, or a discussion group. Cyberstalkers may also incite others against their victims by impersonating the victim, *e.g.*, sending offensive e-mails to employers, posting inflammatory messages on message boards (*i.e.*, "flaming"), or simultaneously offending dozens of chat room participants while disguised as the victim. The hapless victim is then banned from message boards, accused of improper conduct, and flooded with threatening messages from offended participants.

Cyberstalkers rely on the *anonymity* of the Internet to stalk their victims without being detected. Cyberstalking may develop from a real-world stalking incident and continue over the Internet, as in the Amy Boyer incident discussed in Chapter 10, or cyberstalking may begin online and also be followed by stalking in the physical world.

The online organization Working to Halt Online Abuse reported in 2002 that 52% of cyberstalkers were male and 35% female (in 13% of the cases gender was unreported).[64] Interestingly, the number of female cyberstalkers has been increasing as the number of male cyberstalkers has declined. In 2001, the male-to-female ratio was 5.8:3.2 but in 2000 it was 6.8:2.7.[65] Nearly half of the victims of cyberstalking were between ages 18 and 30, not necessarily surprising since this age group is the most Internet/computer savvy. Nearly half were unmarried, and between ⅔ and ¾ were Caucasian. About 40% knew the cyberstalker offline, and of those, 28% had met online, 27% were from former intimate relationships, 16% were friends and 9% were co-workers. Forty-two percent of the incidents reported stemmed from e-mail, 13% from chat rooms, 12% from message boards, 10% from instant messages, 7% from websites, and 4% from newsgroups.[66]

Incidents of *corporate cyberstalking* usually involve an organization stalking an individual. Although often initiated by a high-ranking company official with a grudge, any employee in an organization may conduct corporate cyberstalking. For example, someone within the corporation may target a former customer or employee who has sued the corporation. Less frequently, corporate cyberstalking may involve an individual stalking a corporation.

Despite the multi-jurisdictional nature of cyberstalking, no federal law exists to protect victims or define OSP responsibilities and liabilities. However, federal law does impose a $1,000 fine or five years imprisonment for anyone transmitting in interstate commerce any threat to kidnap or injure someone. State laws offer varying definitions, protections, and penalties when it comes to cyberstalking. Forty-one states expressly prohibit harassing conduct through the Internet, e-mail, or other electronic means. (Online harassment is discussed in detail in Chapter 14). When does harassment rise to the level of stalking? State cyberstalking laws vary widely in their requirements to find that cyberstalking has occurred. Some states consider a threat against the *victim's family* to qualify as cyberstalking while other states say that the threat must be directed against the individual. Certain state statutes require a showing of intent to cause "*imminent fear*" on the part of the stalker, whereas other states look to the victim requiring that he have knowledge that stalker is causing fear. Some statutes require a *direct* communication with the victim, whereas others would find cyberstalking has occurred if the stalker sent a message that the victim was *likely* to receive, even if not actually received. Some states will accept the threat of *injury to the victim's reputation* as meeting the definition of cyberstalking, while others require the threat of *physical injury*. Certain states have very low thresholds to find that cyberstalking has occurred: Arizona's statute simply requires that the victim be "seriously alarmed" or "annoyed." Four states (Idaho, Nebraska, New Jersey, and Utah) and the District of Columbia do not have any cyberstalking statutes.

Federal Statutes

The Securities Act of 1933 and the Securities and Exchange Act of 1934

Securities fraud is another offline crime that has entered the Internet Age. A defrauder will often use Internet message boards and chat rooms dedicated to the stock market to hype various stocks. By making wrongful posts in an attempt to manipulate securities prices, stating false "facts," "rumors," and alleged "inside information" or by mass e-mailing a barrage of bullish announcements about the subject company, the defrauder tries to "pump up" highly volatile share prices in small companies and then sell his own shares in those companies into the false demand that he has created. These "*pump and dump*" schemes are illegal and violate both state and federal securities laws. Often the defrauder will create a "sock puppet," *i.e.*, a false online identity to deceive others or promote a product or company.[67] Whole Foods Market C.E.O. John Mackey used a sock puppet on Yahoo! message boards from 1999 to 2006 to promote his company's stock (including making stock price predictions) and attack its competitors; the S.E.C. was examining Mackey's blog posts to determine if they violated securities laws.[68]

The chat rooms and e-mails of the Internet Age have replaced the boiler rooms and cold calls of the penny stock boom, as a faster and cheaper alternative for stock promoters.[69] The S.E.C. estimated that 100 million stock spam messages are e-mailed weekly, spiking share prices and trading volume, and contributing to investor losses.[70]

Sales of securities are subject, on the state level, to state securities laws and state common law fraud statutes, and on the federal level, to the Securities Act of 1933[71] and the Securities and Exchange Act of 1934.[72] Both the federal government and the states have watchdog agencies to administer the laws and guard against securities fraud, *i.e.*, respectively, the U.S. Securities and Exchange Commission (S.E.C.) and state securities administrators and divisions.

The Fair Housing Act

In January 2004, the U.S. Justice Department filed the first federal lawsuit against a website.[73] Filed in federal court on behalf of New Jersey, it claimed that Spyder Web Enterprises had published notices and online ads on its websites that discriminated on the basis of race, gender, family status, religion, and national origin, in violation of the *Fair Housing Act* (FHA).[74] The Justice Department argued that since the Internet was becoming an increasing source of housing information for home buyers, it was important that websites that post listings online follow federal anti-discrimination laws. However, no binding legal precedent was established by the case, since it was settled by *consent decree*, *i.e.*, the defendant agreed to abide by the law.

Had the case gone to trial, it would have raised an interesting issue. As you will see in Chapter 13, courts have held that § 230 of the Communications Decency Act of 1996 (CDA) protects websites from liability for most third-party postings. As the FHA prohibits discrimination on the basis of race, gender, family status, religion, and national origin, here we have a situation where two federal statutes come in conflict. Should a third-party post a discriminatory ad on a housing website, which federal statute would prevail? Both the interest in prohibiting discrimination and the interest in not placing an impossible oversight burden on websites are legitimate concerns. Furthermore, the advertiser could argue a First Amendment freedom of association right when it comes to placing an ad, such as for a home that is "close to synagogues" or for stating a preference in roommates. While it might be offensive to read an ad that states "no (fill in the blank)" an ad stating "lesbian preferred" might be helpful to both the advertiser and the prospective roommate. Two subsequent cases have recently addressed these issues.

In 2006, a public interest legal group sued Craigslist, an online version of a generic newspaper classifieds section, charging violation of the FHA, because of third-party posts containing discriminatory language on Craigslist's Chicago website with language such as "no minorities."[75] The plaintiff alleged more than 200 instances of what it considered discriminatory language, although Craigslist's CEO called any discriminatory language "rare" in the context of the 10 million housing ads the company receives each month.[76] The plaintiff argued that Craigslist should be held to the same standards as newspapers and other publication (rather than fall under the safe harbor of the CDA § 230). But Congress enacted § 230 because unlike newspapers, websites are often composed of content submitted by visitors without any intervention by an editor. The safe harbor provisions of § 230 have shielded such websites from traditional libel or copyright infringement liability provided they remove offending posts when notified. Craigslist informed users on every housing listing page that discriminatory posts are illegal under federal law and asked readers to contact the website if they saw offending posts, which would then be immediately removed. Craigslist's CEO has stated that discriminatory ads are "unacceptable" on Craigslist and that Craigslist users are strongly encouraged to report possible violations to Craigslist.[77]

The lawsuit against Craigslist was dismissed by the Chicago U.S. District Court in November 2006, based on Craigslist's compliance with the safe harbor provisions of the CDA § 230. However, the court took a circuitous path to reach what many observers thought would be the obvious result. Steering away from a growing body of case law that finds that the CDA § 230 confers a broad immunity upon OSPs, the court held that such immunity only exists where the OSP has not altered third-party content and caused injury. Drawing on the distinction (discussed at length in Chapter 13) between a "conduit of information" and a "publisher," the court held that OSPs are immune from lawsuits for information they transmitted but did not create. It remains to be seen other courts will adopt this reasoning and narrower interpretation of the breadth of the CDA § 230.

The 9th Circuit decision by a three-judge panel in _Fair Housing Council of San Fernando Valley v. Roommates.com,_ [78] would seem to follow the narrower interpretation. In that case, the website Roommates.com had users fill out a roommate preferences form that asked them to select preferences by gender, sexual orientation, or families (_i.e.,_ children).

On a practical level, the form makes perfect sense. Individuals not only have a legitimate interest in who they choose to share (or not share) an apartment or even a bedroom, but also a legal right under the First Amendment to choose with whom they wish to associate. For example, does it not make more sense for a single woman to state up front that she wishes to share her one bedroom Manhattan apartment with another woman, rather than have to fend off hundreds of responses from single men? Unfortunately, in a valiant but perhaps misplaced effort to prevent discrimination, the FHA precludes such forthrightness in advertising. Two points should be noted here. First, the FHA prohibits housing discrimination on the basis of race, gender, family status, religion, and national origin — note that sexual orientation is not included in that list as a protected class. Second, there is an exception in the FHA that allows discrimination by roommates in shared-housing situations — although *advertising* those discriminatory preferences is not allowed. This would seem to put an incredible burden on roommate seeker, who must follow up on every advertisement without the ability to weed out the unsuitable ones.

Roommates.com argued that even though legally the form ran counter to the FHA, it was protected by the CDA § 230, and the trial court agreed, granting the defendant summary judgment. However, the 9th Circuit reversed the lower court's decision stating that it was improper to grant summary judgment (meaning there were no genuine issues of material fact) because it believed there was an issue of fact as to the applicability of the CDA § 230 safe harbor.

The court focused on the facts that both the search menu and the roommate selection form used drop down menus that specified gender, sexual orientation, and children options; and that the site e-mailed users listings based on those same selected profile preferences. The court appeared to between unsure of whether the website was a "conduit of information" or a "publisher," because it created a drop down menu of choices which were then selected by the user. Was it merely transmitting the information or, by shaping it, actually creating it? That would be a question of fact for the lower court to decide, as the appellate court remanded the case.

One issue of debate by the appellate panel was whether the "additional comments" portion of the form in which users could type in free form remarks in their own words (as opposed to drop down menu choices) would be qualified for § 230 immunity. Two of the judges said it would, since the website was merely transmitting the language created by the user; however, the third judge disagreed, arguing that this was where the most objectionable comments appeared and that the site should be judged as a whole.

It will be interesting to see if, and how, other courts respond to these two decisions. For more on the CDA, turn to Chapter 13.

The USA PATRIOT Act

The *USA PATRIOT Act* ("Uniting and Strengthening America by Providing Appropriate Tools Required to Intercept and Obstruct Terrorism Act of 2001") was enacted by

Congress on October 26, 2001 in response to the September 11th terrorist attacks.[79] The Act is a very comprehensive piece of legislation and it is beyond the scope of this book to do any more than give a brief overview of the Act and how it applies to the Internet.

Introduced on the heels on the September 11th attacks, the bill was rushed through Congress and passed into law with exceptional speed. Normally a bill would be debated in Congress; the House and Senate would draft different versions; the two versions would then be meshed into a unified bill by a committee; and a legislative history of commentary from that committee and legal commentators would be created and serve as a resource for courts to look to so as to infer the intent of the bill's drafters. In this case, the 342 page bill amending multiple federal statutes was enacted into law in a mere five weeks, due to the prevailing public anxiety. America had been attacked on its own soil, the first attack on the continental United States since the War of 1812; more than 3,000 civilians had been killed in attacks on the two most important cities in the country, New York City and Washington, D.C. The Pentagon itself had been attacked and letters containing deadly anthrax were circulating through the U.S. postal system. The mood of the country was one of intense fear, and Americans turned to their government demanding protection and security. Congress and the president responded with the USA PATRIOT Act.

In times of such intense public fear, civil liberties are often not even a consideration, and simplistic knee-jerk responses that would never be seriously contemplated suddenly become established reality. If a democracy like the United States were to be attacked by a foreign country or culture, one simplistic and knee-jerk response might be to round up everyone in the United States from that foreign country or culture (even if they were now U.S. citizens) and put them in concentration camps (with no hearings, no judicial process, and no habeas corpus[80] rights). It would be effective, of course, but so offensive to the notions of civil liberties, freedom, and democracy upon which the United States is based that it would never happen. Except it did. With the stroke of a pen, President Franklin Roosevelt signed Executive Order 9066, and more than 110,000 people of Japanese ancestry on the Pacific Coast of the United States were physically removed from their home and placed behind barbed wire in "War Relocation Centers."

This is not to say that the USA PATRIOT Act was not necessary or that it is a bad law. It simply was rushed into law so quickly and under such an extreme public atmosphere that it lacked the necessary protection of civil liberties inherent in other legislation.

The USA PATRIOT Act amended many federal statutes, including:

- The Bank Secrecy Act of 1970 (BSA)[81]

- The Computer Fraud and Abuse Act of 1986 (CFAA) [82]

- The Electronic Communications Privacy Act (ECPA) [83]

- The Fair Credit Reporting Act (FCRA) [84]

- The Family Educational Rights and Privacy Act (FERPA) [85]

- The Foreign Intelligence Surveillance Act (FISA) [86]

- The Immigration and Nationality Act (INA) [87]

- The Money Laundering Act (MLA) [88]

- The Money Laundering Control Act (MLCA) [89]

- The Pen Register and Trap and Trace Statute (PRTTS) [90]

- The Right to Financial Privacy Act (RFPA) [91]

- The Federal Wiretap Statute [92]

Among its provisions, the Act lessened the standard by which the federal government may intercept electronic messages. The federal government is now allowed to intercept all messages "relevant to an ongoing criminal investigation" — the previous standard required that a crime first had to have been committed before messages could be intercepted. Additionally, the USA PATRIOT Act guidelines apply to all surveillance cases, not just those of suspected terrorists.

The Act lowered the legal bar by which the government can obtain Internet routing information. [93] The problem, from a civil liberties viewpoint, is that since content and routing information tend to be tied together, the government would have the ability to exceed its stated purpose and intrude deeper into the individual's privacy. For example, the data packet containing a sought after e-mail header also contains the rest of the e-mail; would it not be naive to think that government investigators would, after obtaining the header, not read the content? Or with Internet browsing, the website routing will automatically reveal what websites the individual has visited and what he did while on those sites. Some of the methods used to obtain routing information also include information about other customers of the same ISP; thus not only are the privacy rights of the investigation's target compromised, but so are those of individuals unrelated to the investigation.

The Act amended the law to allow the government to subpoena customer credit card numbers and bank account numbers from ISPs, in addition to the information it was previously allowed to subpoena (*i.e.*, customer's name, address, length of service, and method of payment).[94]

The Act also allowed ISPs to disclose voluntarily customer records and content of electronic transmissions to the government, "if the provider reasonably believes that an emergency involving immediate danger of death or serious physical injury to any person justifies disclosure of the information."[95] This makes sense in a situation where the ISP has reason to believe a customer intends to harm himself (*e.g.*, posting a suicide note online) or others (*e.g.*, see the Amy Boyer cyberstalking case in Chapter 10); however, in a broad reading it can be construed to apply to harm from any potential terrorist — terrorism by its very nature implies a constant state of emergency involving immediate danger of death or serious physical injury. So in effect, by labelling a suspect a terror suspect, the government could conceivably request ISP customer records and e-mails without a subpoena (of course, the ISPs could refuse the request).[96]

The USA PATRIOT ACT also introduced the "sneak and peek" search warrant, where the government executes a warrant without notice or with delayed notice. The Fourth Amendment to the U.S. Constitution guarantees citizens protection from unreasonable searches and seizures. The U.S. Supreme Court has ruled that law enforcement officials must obtain a search warrant and provide notice to any party whose property is to be searched before the search is conducted. Section 213 of the Act has eliminated this notice requirement in situations where "the investigation will be jeopardized" by giving notice. Once again, a broad reading of the phrase "jeopardized" would make this a very expansive search power.

Section 505 of the Act allowed the F.B.I., the U.S. Department of Defense, and other government agencies, secretly to demand information from ISPs without a court order by issuing secret "National Security Letters" (NSLs). These NSLs typically demand information about subscribers, including home addresses, phone calls placed, e-mail subject lines, and logs of websites visited. The ECPA restricted the F.B.I. from sending NSLs to telecommunications firms except in relation to an investigation of "an agent of a foreign power."[97] That once-strict standard was relaxed, first in 1993, and again with the USA PATRIOT Act. Prior to the USA PATRIOT Act, NSLs could only be used in investigations of suspected terrorists and spies. But the Act changed the law, so now the FBI need only say that an NSL may be "relevant" to a terrorist-related investigation and no court approval is required.

The F.B.I. issues more than 30,000 NSLs annually,[98] and not just to ISPs.[99] Librarians have been served with NSLs demanding that they turn over "all subscriber information, billing information and access logs" of patrons who used library computers.[100] Unlike subpoenas, NSLs do not require approval by a judge, grand jury, or prosecutor, but are instead issued by F.B.I. field supervisors.

A federal court in 2004 declared that provision of the USA PATRIOT Act unconstitutional, holding that NSLs violated both the First and Fourth Amendments. The USA PATRIOT Act forbids the recipient of an NSL from ever disclosing its existence "to any person." The court held that the mandatory gag order amounted to an "unconstitutional prior restraint of speech in violation of the First Amendment." (Prior restraint is discussed in detail in Chapter 14). Ironically, the American Civil Liberties Union, which brought the lawsuit, was unable to disclose information about the case, so as to avoid penalties for violating the USA PATRIOT Act's broad gag provision.

In _Doe v. Ashcroft_,[101] the ACLU filed a complaint on behalf of an ISP challenging the constitutionality of one of the statutes that had been amended by the USA PATRIOT ACT.[102] The statute, as amended, required ISPs to comply with F.B.I. requests for subscriber information (specifically name, address and length of service of the subscriber) and forbid the recipient from disclosing the order to anyone. The ISP had received an NSL, the terms of which prohibited disclosing its receipt to any person, and was requested to provide the requested records to the F.B.I. in person. The court wrote:[103]

> Because neither the statute, nor an NSL, nor the FBI agents dealing with the recipient say as much, all but the most mettlesome and undaunted NSL recipients would consider themselves effectively barred from consulting an attorney or anyone else who might advise them otherwise, as well as bound to absolute silence about the very existence of the NSL.

The court went on to address the overbreadth of the statute:[104]

> The evidence on the record now before this Court demonstrates that the information available through a § 2709 NSL served upon an ISP could easily be used to disclose vast amounts of anonymous speech and associational activity. For instance, § 2709 imposes a duty to provide "electronic communication transactional records," a phrase which, though undefined in the statute, certainly encompasses a log of email addresses with whom a subscriber has corresponded and the web pages that a subscriber visits. Those transactional records can reveal, among other things, the anonymous message boards to which a person logs on or posts, the electronic newsletters to which he subscribes, and the advocacy websites he visits. Moreover, § 2709 imposes a duty on ISPs to provide the names and addresses of subscribers, thus enabling the Government to specifically identify someone who has written anonymously on the internet.

A federal court in Connecticut subsequently enjoined the government from enforcing the gag order in the same statute where an NSL had been served on a library.[105] The two cases were combined in _Doe v. Gonzales._ [106] While the appeals were pending, and despite objections by civil libertarians over the sweeping powers that the USA PATRIOT Act granted to the federal government, the Act was renewed with minor changes by Congress in March 2006. [107] In light of the changes to the statute, the 2nd Circuit then remanded first case to the lower court and dismissed the second case as moot. In September 2007, the lower court held that, despite the revisions to the Act, the gag order provision of the NSL violated First Amendment freedom of speech rights, as both a prior restraint on speech and a content based ban. Even after the decision, F.B.I. agents can still use other means to obtain information from ISPs, including a subpoena, warrant, or court order.

Until 2005, the federal government intercepted e-mail messages through its _Carnivore_ program, the Internet surveillance system developed by the F.B.I. to monitor electronic transmissions of criminal suspects. Carnivore (later renamed the DCS-1000) could capture all e-mail messages to and from a specific user's account and capture all of the network traffic to and from a specific user or IP address. It could also capture all of the e-mail headers (including e-mail addresses) going to and from an e-mail account, but not the actual contents or subject line. Carnivore could also list all the servers that the suspect accessed, track everyone who accessed a specific web page or FTP file (_i.e._, uploaded or downloaded files) and track all web pages or FTP files that a suspect accessed. Critics charged that Carnivore did not include proper safeguards to prevent misuse and may violate individual constitutional rights. In January 2005, the F.B.I. announced that it was replacing Carnivore with commercial software to eavesdrop on computer traffic, reported to be less expensive and more effective. [108] The price tag for Carnivore has been estimated at between $6 and $15 million. [109]

The Wire Wager Act and Online Gambling

Online gambling reached $12 billion in 2006 and is projected to reach $25 billion by 2010 with half of that revenue coming from U.S. gamblers. [110] The ability to participate in gambling online has raised questions about the legality of the practice. Most states prohibit or regulate most or all forms of gambling. However, the Internet, with its ability to reach across state lines, once again raises the issue of how states can enforce their own regulations and prohibitions on this new technology. Although gambling websites may be based in countries where taking bets is legal, it is not necessarily legal for U.S. citizens to place bets through such websites. Eight states have laws against Internet gambling: Illinois, Indiana, Louisiana, Nevada, Oregon, South Dakota, Michigan, and Washington. Federal prosecutors contend that it is illegal for online gambling operators to solicit or accept bets from U.S. citizens, even if their operations are not in the U.S. [111] In two separate instances in 2006, two British online gambling executives were arrested when they touched U.S. soil. [112] In one case, Peter Dicks, chairman of London-based Sportingbet PLC, was arrested on a layover at a New York airport on a criminal warrant issued by the state of Louisiana; in the other case, David Carruthers, chief executive of BetOnSports.com, was flying from Costa Rica back to Great Britain when he was arrested on a layover at Dallas – Ft. Worth Airport on federal charges including racketeering and mail fraud. While Carruthers was charged with violating federal laws, Dicks was charged with violating state laws — a Louisiana law prohibiting computer gambling that carries a maximum sentence of five years in prison and a $25,000 fine. [113]

The primary concern raised by online gambling is the increased accessibility to gambling for *minors* and *pathological gamblers*. A United Kingdom study found 30 U.K. gambling websites that registered children as young as 11 years old to gamble online. [114] Gambling websites use credit cards and debit cards for age verification, but in the U.K. "Solo" debit cards are available to customers over age 11 and certain banks gives debit cards to any account holder over age 16. Some observers place the burden of responsibility on banks "*because issuing these cards to minors gives them access to all types of adult services, including porn sites.*" [115] Others argue that the banks should not be viewed as the gatekeepers to the realm of moral turpitude and that the responsibility lies with the online gambling industry to devise better ways to verify the age of its customers.

There are two basic types of online gambling. In *casino-style gambling*, the user has access to a wide variety of games (*e.g.*, blackjack, poker, roulette, and slot machines) with colorful graphics and background music. The user can pay by credit card or debit card, money transfers, or other electronic payment. The main concern about casino-style gambling from the gambler's viewpoint is whether the games are fair or rigged. The other form of online gambling, *sports gambling* websites, typically are not interactive and software-intensive (like casino-style websites), and are therefore cheaper to run. With these types of websites, gamblers have no concern over results tampering, since the outcome of sporting events is public knowledge. Gambling websites are usually offshore operations, based in island nations and Australia, Austria, Belgium, Germany, and South Africa.

The U.S. government has made several unsuccessful attempts to ban online gambling. In April 2000, the Internet Gambling Prohibition Act failed to pass Congress by 25 votes. Internationally, the U.S. ban on Americans gambling over the Internet led Antigua and Barbuda to file a trade complaint with the World Trade Organization (W.T.O.) against the United States. In 2004, a W.T.O. panel sided with Antigua and Barbuda, ruling that the United States' ban on Internet gambling violated global trade rules. The ruling was upheld twice by the W.T.O's appellate body and in March 2007 it declared the United States out of compliance with its rules. [116] To comply with the W.T.O. decision, the United States would have to allow U.S. citizens to gamble online or impose a total ban on all forms of Internet gambling (including buying lottery tickets online).

Likewise, the W.T.O. faced a Hobson's choice, as backing down would undermine its credibility, while sanctioning the United States risks a political backlash from its most powerful backer.

Lacking an existing federal law to outlaw online gambling, prosecutors, as with most legal issues involving the Internet, have tried to tailor existing laws to deal with emerging legal issues. In this case, prosecutors have turned to the Wire Wager Act, a 1961 law prohibiting use of "wire communication facilities for transmission in interstate or foreign commerce of bets or wagers or information assisting in placing of bets or wagers on any sporting event or contest."[117] In August 2000, the first defendant in an Internet offshore sports betting case was tried; the co-owner of an (Antigua) Internet gambling website was convicted under the Wire Wager Act, fined $5,000 and sentenced to 21 months in prison. Until a law specifically outlawing Internet gambling is passed, prosecutions of Internet offshore sports betting websites will be limited to the Wire Wager Act.

Under the Wire Wager Act, the government must prove that the defendant:

1. Was engaged in the *business of betting* or wagering, (*i.e.*, the defendant must have derived all or much of his income from the business of gambling; the law is *mainly enforced against bookmakers, not casual bettors*), and

2. *Transmitted, in interstate or foreign commerce*: (a) bets or wagers, (b) information assisting in the placement of bets or wagers, or (c) communication that entitled the recipient to receive money or credit as a result of a bet or wager, and

3. Used a "*wire communication facility*" to transmit these materials, and

4. Acted "*knowingly*," *i.e.*, knowingly, and not by accident or mistake, used a wire communications facility to engage in any prohibited forms of transmissions.

Congress next focused on going after the money instead of the players. In 2006, the Unlawful Internet Gambling Enforcement Act was signed into law.[118] This act makes it illegal for banks, credit card companies, and online payment systems to process payment to online gambling firms (with the exception of "fantasy" sports, online lotteries, horse racing and harness racing). The passage of the act caught the online gambling industry by surprise, as it was attached to the Safe Port Act bill shortly before Congress recessed. Since U.S. citizens account for more than half of industry-wide revenue, the impact of this new law was immediately felt by the online gaming industry, with the likelihood that online gambling firms would either have to concentrate on growing their non-American markets or go out of business. However, there remains the possibility that U.S. citizens might still be able to place online bets through non-U.S. payment processors, effectively emaciating the new law.

Summary

Cyber crimes include e-mail spoofing, phishing, identity theft, invasion of privacy, fraud, gambling, cyberstalking, and terrorism. E-mail spoofing is the forgery of an e-mail header so that the message appears to have originated from another source. Social engineering is aimed at tricking an individual into divulging confidential information. Phishing (pronounced "fishing") is an Internet scam in which unsuspecting users receive official-looking e-mails that attempt to trick them into disclosing online passwords, user names, and personal information. Personalized phishing is a targeted variation where the victim receives an e-mail with personalized account information previously obtained by the phisher. Spear-phishers poses as a high-level executive in the targeted corporation and demand confidential information from its employees.

Identity theft is a crime in which an imposter obtains key pieces of personal information to impersonate the victim to get credit, merchandise, or services in the victim's name or to provide the thief with false credentials. Only three percent of identity theft victims cited misuse of Internet accounts as the cause. The identity theft crisis stems from use of the Social Security number as the de facto national identifier. No federal law governs, or even limits, use or disclosure of Social Security numbers among private entities, but there are laws, such as the Privacy Act of 1974 and the Buckley Amendment, that place limits on public and publicly funded entities. One often overlooked source of personal information for identity thieves is discarded hard drives; if the drive is not wiped clean then the data still remain on it and may be easily retrieved. The Identity Theft Penalty Enhancement Act provides mandatory prison sentences for anyone possessing another person's identity-related information with the intent to commit a crime. Cookie poisoning is the modification of a cookie by an attacker to gain unauthorized information about the user for purposes such as identity theft.

Software threats may be posed from spyware, adware, and malware. With spyware, a data collecting program is installed for malevolent purposes without the user's knowledge or consent, whereas with adware, it is installed for commercial purposes with the user's knowledge and consent (although the disclosure may be buried in a long click-wrap agreement and the consent may only have been given when the user clicked on it while downloading other programs). A drive-by download is a program that is automatically downloaded to a user's computer, often without the user's knowledge or consent. Malware includes computer viruses, worms, and Trojan horses.

Wi-Fi networks are subject to unlawful intrusions. Wardriving is the practice of driving with a Wi-Fi enabled laptop mapping houses and businesses that have wireless access points. Piggy-backing is the use of a wireless Internet connection without permission. The theft of Internet access or bandwidth is the crime of telecommunications theft. By pod slurping, data thieves hook iPods or other portable media players into corporate computers and networks to use as portable hard drives to steal information.

Cyberstalking is crime in which the attacker harasses the victim using electronic communication, such as e-mail, instant messaging, or messages posted to a website, chat room or discussion group. Cyberstalkers rely on the anonymity of the Internet to stalk their victims without being detected.

Several federal laws apply to crimes on the Internet. "Pump and Dump" schemes that use the Internet to attempt to manipulate securities prices are illegal and violate both state and federal securities laws. A sock puppet is a false online identity to deceive others or promote a product or company. The federal Fair Housing Act may apply to real estate websites. An exception in the Act allows discrimination by roommates in shared-housing situations, although advertising those discriminatory preferences is not allowed. The USA PATRIOT Act, which amended many federal statutes, was rushed into law in a mere five weeks, due to prevailing public anxiety. It lacked the necessary protection of civil liberties inherent in other legislation. The Act allows the federal government to intercept all electronic messages "relevant to an ongoing criminal investigation." Use of National Security Letters by the F.B.I. secretly to demand information from ISPs without a court order has been held unconstitutionally by a federal court.

Federal prosecutors contend that it is illegal for online gambling operators to solicit or accept bets from U.S. citizens, even if their operations are not in the U.S. Without a federal law specifically outlawing Internet gambling, prosecutions of Internet offshore sports betting websites are limited to federal racketeering and mail fraud laws, the Wire Wager Act, and state laws. The Unlawful Internet Gambling Enforcement Act makes it illegal for banks, credit card companies, and online payment systems to process payment to online gambling firms.

Chapter Eight Notes

[1] Invasion of Privacy is a tort with civil penalties, however some jurisdictions, in response to Internet or high tech invasion of privacy, have drafted Invasion of Privacy criminal statutes (*e.g.,* criminal invasion of computer privacy or video voyeurism). Criminal invasion of computer privacy statutes usually involve unauthorized use of a computer to view confidential information about someone. For example, the Virginia Computer Crimes Act, Va. Code 18.2-152.1 *et seq.,* provides"

> A person is guilty of the crime of computer invasion of privacy when he uses a computer or computer network and intentionally examines without authority any employment, salary, credit or any other financial or personal information relating to any other person. "Examination" under this section requires the offender to review the information relating to any other person after the time at which the offender knows or should know that he is without authority to view the information displayed.

See also, Plasters v. Virginia, Case No. 1870993 (Va. Ct. App. June 27, 2000)(Unpublished). Note that this statute is concerned with *viewing* the private information. *Downloading* the information might fall under a state's computer theft statutes, while *republication* of the information might run afoul of copyright laws.

Video voyeurism statutes typically criminalize non-consensual photographic or video recording of individual in a state of undress or nudity in places where one has a reasonable expectation of privacy. Photos and videos of people in department store changing rooms, locker rooms, and even in one case, their own home (a video voyeurism law was passed in New York after a woman discovered her landlord had placed hidden video cameras in her apartment) have appeared on the Internet. The Video Voyeurism Prevention Act of 2004, 18 U.S.C.A. § 180, is limited to acts occurring on federal property, but most states have some sort of video voyeurism statutes:

Alabama (criminal surveillance, Ala. Code § 13A-11-32)

Alaska (indecent viewing or photography, Alaska Stat. § 11.61.123)

Arizona (surreptitious photographing, videotaping, filming, or digitally recording, Ariz. Rev. Stat. § 13-3019)

Arkansas (crime of video voyeurism, Ark. Code Ann. § 5-16-101)

California (disorderly conduct, Cal. Penal Code § 647(k))

Colorado (criminal invasion of privacy, Colo. Rev. Stat. Ann. § 18-7-801)

Connecticut (voyeurism, Conn. Gen. Stat. § 53a-189a)

Delaware (violation of privacy, Del. Code Ann. tit. 11 § 1335(a)(6)-(7))

Florida (video voyeurism, Fla. Stat. Ann. § 810.145, (1st degree misdemeanor; if a repeat offender it is a 3rd degree felony)

Georgia (unlawful eavesdropping or surveillance, Ga. Code Ann. 16-11-62)

Hawaii (violation of privacy in the 1st degree, Haw. Rev. Stat. § 711-1110.9 prohibits installation or use of a recording device in a private place used to record persons in a state of undress or engaged in sexual conduct; violation of privacy in the 2nd degree, Haw. Rev. Stat. § 711-1111, prohibits surreptitiously recording body and/or undergarments; sexual assault in the 4th degree, Haw. Rev. Stat. § 707-733(c) prohibits knowingly trespassing on property for the purpose of subjecting another person to surreptitious surveillance for the sexual gratification of the actor)

Idaho (crime of video voyeurism, Idaho Code § 18-6609)

Illinois (unauthorized videotaping, 720 Ill. Comp. Stat. 5/26-4; recording is a misdemeanor; distribution of images is a felony)

Indiana (voyeurism, Ind. Code Ann. § 35-45-4-5)

Kansas (eavesdropping, Kan. Stat. Ann. § 21-4001)

Kentucky (voyeurism, Ky. Rev. Stat. Ann. § 531.090)

Louisiana (video voyeurism, La. Rev. Stat. Ann. § 14:283)

Maine (violation of privacy, Me. Rev. Stat. Ann. tit. 17-A § 511(d))

Maryland (visual surveillance with prurient intent, Md. Code Ann., Crim. Law § 3-902)

Massachusetts (photographing, videotaping or electronically surveilling, Mass. Gen. Law. Ann. ch. 272, § 104(2); recording penalty is 2½ years; enhanced penalty for distribution of images is 5 years)

Michigan (installation, placement, use, of recording or transmitting device in private place, Mich. Comp. Laws § 750.539d)

Minnesota (interference with privacy, Minn. Stat. § 609.746; gross misdemeanor; repeat offenses or recording of a minor is a felony)

Mississippi (photographing, taping, or filming of a person in violation of an expectation of privacy, Miss. Code Ann. § 97-29-63)

Missouri (invasion of privacy, 1st degree, Mo. Ann. Stat. § 565.252 prohibits recording or photographing an individual without consent in a state of nudity while the person is located in a place where privacy is reasonably expected; invasion of privacy, 2nd degree, Mo. Ann. Stat.§ 565.253; specifically prohibits the use of a concealed recording device to photograph or video an individual's body or undergarments without consent.)

Montana (surreptitious visual observation or recordation, Mont. Code. Ann. § 45-5-223: recording within a residence – 6 month penalty; recording an adult in public – 6 month penalty; recording a minor in public – 2 year penalty)

Nebraska (unlawful intrusion, Neb. Rev. Stat. § 28-311.08)

New Hampshire (violation of privacy, N.H. Rev. Stat. Ann. § 644:9)

New Jersey (observation of sexual contact; reproduction or disclosure of images of sexual contact; dressing rooms, N.J. Stat. Ann. 2C:14-9; recording an individual is a 4th degree crime; distribution of images is a 3rd degree crime, subject to fine up to $30,000)

New York (unlawful surveillance 2nd degree, N.Y. Penal Law § 250.45; unlawful surveillance 1st degree, N.Y. Penal Law § 250.50, increased penalty for repeat convictions within a 10-year period; dissemination of unlawful surveillance, N.Y. Penal Law § 250.55 and § 250.60, misdemeanor for distribution, felony for sale or publication)

North Carolina (secretly peeping into room occupied by another person, N.C. Gen. Stat. § 14-202(e)-(f))

North Dakota (surreptitious intrusion, N.D. Cent. Code 12.1-20-12.2)

Ohio (voyeurism, Ohio Rev. Code Ann. § 2907.08(e))

Oklahoma (peeping Tom, Okla. Stat. tit. 21 § 1171)

Oregon (invasion of personal privacy, Or. Rev. Stat. § 163.700)

Pennsylvania (invasion of privacy, 18 Pa. Con. Stat. Ann. § 7507.1)

Rhode Island (video voyeurism, R.I. Gen. Laws § 11-64-2; penalty of three year imprisonment and/or fine)

South Carolina (eavesdropping, peeping, voyeurism, S.C. Code Ann. § 16-17-470; recording is a misdemeanor; distribution or multiple convictions is a felony)

South Dakota (taking pictures without consent, S.D. Codified Laws § 22-21-4)

Tennessee (unlawful photographing in violation of privacy, Tenn. Code Ann. § 39-13-605; recording is a misdemeanor; distribution of images is a felony)

Texas (improper photography or visual recording, Tex. Penal Code Ann. § 21.15)

Utah (voyeurism offense, Utah Code Ann. § 76-9-702.7; misdemeanor; if a minor under 14 or distribution is a 3rd degree felony)

Vermont (voyeurism, Vt. Stat. Ann. tit. 13 § 2638; recording penalty of up to 2 years imprisonment and/or $1,000 fine; distribution of images penalty of up to 5 years imprisonment and/or $5,000 fine)

Virginia (unlawful filming, videotaping or photographing of another, Va. Code Ann. § 18.2-386.1; misdemeanor; if a minor it is a felony)

Washington (voyeurism, Wash. Rev. Code § 9A.44.115)

West Virginia (criminal invasion of privacy, W.Va. Code § 61-8-28; recording or dissemination is a misdemeanor; repeated offense is a felony)

Wisconsin (invasion of privacy, Wis. Stat, § 942.08)

Wyoming (voyeurism, Wyo. Stat. Ann. § 6-4-304)

Some states criminalize invasion of privacy through forms of online harassment, *e.g.*, posting nude photos or sex tapes on the Internet for revenge or to embarrass an ex-boyfriend or girlfriend. *See* the discussion of online harassment in Chapter 14.

[2] A Trojan program is a malicious software program uploaded to the victim's computer without his knowledge, usually installed while the victim is downloading a different file. The name is derived from the Trojan horse from Homer's *Iliad*; during the Trojan War, the Greeks presented the citizens of Troy with a large wooden horse in which they had secretly hidden their warriors. At night, the warriors emerged from the wooden horse and overran and conquered Troy.

[3] Pagejacking is the theft of a website's contents by copying some of its pages, placing them on another website that appears to be the legitimate website, and then inviting people to the illegal website through deceptive means.

[4] "Phishing Con Hijacks Browser Bar," BBC News, April 8, 2004, *available at* http://news.bbc.co.uk/1/hi/technology/3608943.stm (accessed September 25, 2007).

[5] E-mail security company MessageLabs, *available at* www.messagelabs.com/default.aspx (accessed September 25, 2007).

[6] Dan Grabham, "10 Years of Phishing Attacks," tech.co.uk, March 26, 2007, *available at* www.tech.co.uk/computing/internet-and-broadband/news/10-years-of-phishing-attacks?articleid=1864041047, (accessed September 25, 2007).

[7] According to a 2003 survey by Gartner Research, a Connecticut information technology consulting firm. *See* www.gartner.com/5_about/press_releases/asset_89228_11.jsp (accessed September 25, 2007).

[8] Timothy L. O'Brien, "Gone Spear-Phishin'," New York Times, December 4, 2005.

[9] David Bank, "'Spear Phishing' Tests Educate People About Online Scams," Wall Street Journal, August 17, 2005.

[10] Kim Zetter, "Confessions of a Cybermule," Wired News, July 28, 2006.

[11] *Ibid.*

[12] U.S. Department of Justice press release, "Shadowcrew Organization Called 'One-Stop Online Marketplace for Identity Theft,'" October 28, 2004, *available at* www.cybercrime.gov/mantovaniIndict.htm (accessed September 25, 2007).

[13] Symantec Press Release, March 19, 2007, *available at* www.symantec.com/about/news/release/article.jsp?prid=20070319_01 (accessed September 25, 2007). *See also*, "Online Crooks Getting More Professional," Associated Press wire report, September 17, 2007. A Symantec report for the first half of 2007 stated that the United States was host to 64 percent of "underground economy" servers; Germany was second and Sweden

ranked third. China had one-third the world's computers taken over by bots (web robots that spam without the computer owner's knowledge or consent).

[14] *Ibid.*

[15] *Ibid.*

[16] Declan McCullagh, "Season Over for 'Phishing'?" CNET News.com, July 15, 2004.

[17] Statement by Senator Strom Thurmond before the U.S. Senate Judiciary Subcommittee on Technology, Terrorism, and Government Information regarding identity theft, July 9, 2002.

[18] Social Security Act of 1935 (Pub. L. No. 74-271).

[19] Pursuant to Treasury Decision 4704.

[20] However, in the post-9/11 world, Congress has shown an inclination toward creation of a national identity card, most recently with the passage of the Real I.D. Act of 2005 (Pub. L. No. 109-13).

[21] Exec. Order No. 9397 (3 CFR (1943-1948 Comp.) 283-284).

[22] Internal Revenue Code Amendments (Pub. L. No. 87-397).

[23] Internal Revenue Code Amendments (Pub. L. No. 89-384).

[24] Bank Records and Foreign Transactions Act (Pub. L. No. 91-508).

[25] Social Security Amendments of 1972 (Pub. L. No. 92-603).

[26] Tax Reform Act of 1976 (Pub. L. No. 94-455).

[27] Food Stamp Act of 1977 (Pub. L. No. 96-58).

[28] Omnibus Budget Reconciliation Act of 1981 (Pub. L. No. 97-35).

[29] Department of Defense Authorization Act (Pub. L. No. 97-86).

[30] Debt Collection Act (Pub. L. No. 97-365).

[31] Housing and Community Development Act of 1987 (Pub. L. No. 100-242).

[32] Social Security Independence and Program Improvements Act of 1994 (Pub. L. No. 103-296).

[33] Family Privacy Act of 1974, 5 U.S.C. § 552a.

[34] Buckley Amendment, 20 U.S.C. § 1232(g).

[35] *Gonzaga Univ. v. Doe*, 536 U.S. 273 (2002). This case is included in the Cases Section on the Issues in Internet Law website (www.IssuesinInternetLaw.com).

[36] 42 U.S.C. § 1983. Civil Action for Deprivation of Rights:

> Every person who, under color of any statute, ordinance, regulation, custom, or usage, of any State or Territory or the District of Columbia, subjects, or causes to be subjected, any citizen of the United States or other person within the jurisdiction thereof to the deprivation of any rights, privileges, or immunities secured by the Constitution and laws, shall be liable to the party injured in an action at law, suit in equity, or other proper proceeding for redress, except that in any action brought against a judicial officer for an act or omission taken in such officer's judicial capacity, injunctive relief shall not be granted unless a declaratory decree was violated or declaratory relief was unavailable. For the purposes of this section, any Act of Congress applicable exclusively to the District of Columbia shall be considered to be a statute of the District of Columbia.

[37] There is even a National Association for Information Destruction, *available at* www.naidonline.org/index. html (accessed September 25, 2007).

[38] Joris Evers, "Dumped Hard Drives Tell All," CNET news.com, May 31, 2005.

[39] "Agencies Left Private Information on Discarded Computers, Audit Shows," Associated Press wire report, May 25, 2005.

[40] Lucy Sherriff, "Investigators Uncover Dismal Data Disposal," The Register, February 17, 2005.

[41] Identity Theft Penalty Enhancement Act (Public Law 108-275).

[42] Click-wrap Agreements are discussed further in Chapter 15, *infra*.

[43] *F.T.C. v. Seismic Entm't. Prods., Inc.*, Civ. No. 04-377-JD (D.N.H. 2004); Stipulated Final Order for Permanent Injunction (Nov. 21, 2006).

[44] Roy Mark, "Spyware Operators Settles With F.T.C.," InternetNewsBureau.com, November 22, 2006, *available at* www.internetnews.com/bus-news/article.php/3645466 (accessed September 25, 2007).

[45] "Creator and Four Users of Loverspy Spyware Program Indicted," U.S. Department of Justice press release, August 26, 2005.

[46] "Jealous Lovers: No Web Snooping," Associated Press wire report, August 27, 2005, *available at* www.wired.com/news/privacy/0,1848,68674,00.html (accessed September 25, 2007).

[47] "Online Brokerage Account Scams Worry S.E.C.," Reuters wire report, October 13, 2006.

[48] Discussed *infra* in this chapter.

[49] "Google Searches Web's Dark Side," BBC News, May 11, 2007.

[50] "Florida Man Charged With Stealing Wi-Fi Signal," Associated Press wire report , July 18, 2005.

[51] Dan Ilett, "Wireless Network Hijacker Found Guilty," Silicon.com, July 22, 2005.

[52] Richard Shim, "Wi-Fi Arrest Highlights Security Dangers," CNET News.com, November 28, 2003.

[53] Jeff Beard, "Wi-Fi Hacker Arrest Raises Security & Liability Concerns," Law Tech Guru Blog, *available at* www.lawtechguru.com./archives/2003/12/02 wifi hacker arrest raises security liability concerns.html (accessed September 25, 2007).

[54] Twenty-one year old Brian Salcedo was sentenced to nine years in prison for hacking into the computer system of Lowe's Department Store, the longest prison sentence to date for computer hacking. U.S. Department of Justice Press Release, *available at* www.usdoj.gov/criminal/cybercrime/salcedoSent.htm (accessed September 25, 2007).

[55] Kevin Poulsen, "Wardriving Guilty Plea in Lowe's Wi-Fi Case," SecurityFocus.com, August 5, 2004, *available at* http://www.securityfocus.com/news/9281 (accessed September 25, 2007).

[56] *Ibid.*

[57] *See* fn. 53, *supra*.

[58] Kevin Poulsen, "Crazy-Long Hacker Sentence Upheld," Wired.com, July 11, 2006.

[59] "Some Schools Banning iPods to Stop Cheating," Associated Press wire report, April 27, 2007.

[60] Even Apple Computer discovered that its employees had used their iPods to smuggle corporate secrets out of the building. Hiawatha Bray, "iPod Can Be Music to a Data Thief's Ear," Boston Globe, June 6, 2005.

[61] The Archos 605 WiFi portable media player, introduced in June 2007, has a 160 GB drive.

[62] The author hereby humbly coins the phrase "pod burping" to refer to in use of a portable media device to inject viruses or malicious code into a corporate network.

[63] Symantec Press Release, March 19, 2007, *available at* www.symantec.com/about/news/release/article.jsp?prid=20070319_01 (accessed September 25, 2007).

[64] Working to Halt Online Abuse website, *available at* www.haltabuse.org/resources/stats (accessed September 25, 2007).

[65] *Ibid.*

[66] *Ibid.*

[67] Sock puppets have also been used by individuals to alter Wikipedia entries (either in self-promotion in their own entries or to detract from others in their entries) and to praise (their own) books on Amazon.com.

[68] The Wall Street Journal reported that the S.E.C. was examining Mackey's blog posts to determine if they violated securities laws. Mackey's sock puppet was exposed in an F.T.C. court filing in an antitrust case to prevent Whole Foods' acquisition of its competitor Wild Oats. *See* David Kesmodel and Jonathan Eig, "A Grocer's Brash Style Takes Unhealthy Turn," Wall Street Journal, July 20, 2007. *See also* Brad Stone and Matt Richtel, "The Hand That Controls the Sock Puppet Could Get Slapped," New York Times, July 16, 2007.

[69] Kit R. Roane, "Taking Penny Stocks Out of the Boiler Room," U.S. News & World Report, June 4, 2007, pp. 55-56.

[70] Karey Wutkowski, "SEC Cracks Down on Spam-driven Stocks," Reuters wire report, March 8, 2007.

[71] Securities Act of 1933, 15 U.S.C. § 77a *et seq.*

[72] Securities and Exchange Act of 1934, 15 U.S.C. § 78 *et seq.*

[73] *United States v. Spyder Web Enterprises*, Civil Action No. 03-1509 DMC (D. NJ Jan. 18, 2004).

[74] Fair Housing Act, 42 U.S.C. § 3601, *et seq.*

[75] John Borland, "Suit Against Craigslist Claims Discriminatory Ads," CNET News.com, February 8, 2006.

[76] Rebecca Carr, "Web Sites Carry Discriminatory Ads, Civil Liberties Groups Say," Cox News Service, July 16, 2006.

[77] *Ibid.*

[78] *Fair Housing Council of San Fernando Valley v. Roommates.com, LLC*, No. 04-56916, slip op. 5709 (9th Circuit May 2007).

[79] USA PATRIOT Act, (Pub. L. No. 107-56).

[80] Habeas corpus (Latin for "you have the body") is a writ directed to one holding an individual in custody or detention commanding that the detained individual be brought before a court to determine the legality of his detention. Its purpose is to ensure that individuals are not unlawfully detained. The writ of habeas corpus dates back to 13th century England and was adopted by the United States.

[81] Bank Secrecy Act of 1970, 31 U.S.C. §§ 5311-5355.

[82] Computer Fraud and Abuse Act of 1986, 18 U.S.C. § 1030.

[83] Electronic Communications Privacy Act, 18 U.S.C. § 2510, *et seq.*

[84] Fair Credit Reporting Act (FCRA), 15 U.S.C. § 1681.

[85] Family Educational Rights and Privacy Act (FERPA), 20 U.S.C. § 1232g.

[86] Foreign Intelligence Surveillance Act (FISA), 50 U.S.C. §§ 1801 *et seq.*

[87] Immigration and Nationality Act (INA), 12 U.S.C. § 1101.

[88] Money Laundering Act (MLA), 31 U.S.C. § 5318(h).

[89] Money Laundering Control Act (MLCA), 18 U.S.C. §§ 1956-57.

[90] Pen Register and Trap and Trace Statute (PRTTS), 18 U.S.C. §§ 3121-27.

[91] Right to Financial Privacy Act (RFPA), 12 U.S.C. § 3401 *et seq.*

[92] Federal Wiretap Statute, 18 U.S.C. §§ 2510-22.

[93] USA PATRIOT Act § 216.

[94] USA PATRIOT Act § 210.

[95] USA PATRIOT Act § 212.

[96] Google even refused to comply with a government subpoena requesting user search information. *See* Andrew Orlowski, "US Gov Demands Google Search Records," The Register, January 19, 2006.

[97] Electronic Communications Privacy Act, fn. 83, *supra*.

[98] NSLs can also be issued by the U.S. Department of Defense and other agencies.

[99] Barton Gellman, "The FBI's Secret Scrutiny: In Hunt for Terrorists Bureau Examines Records of Ordinary Americans," Washington Post, November 6, 2005, p. A01.

[100] *Ibid.*

[101] *Doe v. Ashcroft*, 334 F. Supp. 2d 471 (S.D.N.Y. Sept. 28, 2004).

[102] 18 U.S.C. § 2709. Counterintelligence Access to Telephone Toll and Transactional Record.

[103] *Doe v. Ashcroft*, fn. 101, *supra*.

[104] *Ibid.*

[105] *Doe v. Gonzales*, 386 F. Supp. 2d 66, 82 (D. Conn. 2005).

[106] *Doe v. Gonzales*, Case No. 05-CV-1256 (2nd Circuit Sept. 9, 2005).

[107] USA PATRIOT Improvement and Reauthorization Act of 2005, Pub. L. No. 109-177, 120 Stat. 192. (March 9, 2006).

[108] "FBI Tosses Carnivore to the Dogs," Associated Press wire report, January 18, 2005.

[109] *Ibid.*

[110] Michael A. Hiltzik, "Latest Arrest Chips Away at Online Betting," Los Angeles Time, September 8, 2006).

[111] *Ibid.*

[112] *Ibid.*

[113] Dicks was later released after New York's governor declined to sign a warrant extraditing him to Louisiana. "N.Y. Judge Declines To Hold Former British Online Gambling Exec," Associated Press wire report, September 29, 2006.

[114] Melissa Kite, "Government to Crack Down on Online Gambling by Children," telegraph.co.uk (daily online U.K. newspaper), August 1, 2004, *available at* www.telegraph.co.uk/news/main.jhtml?xml=/news/2004/08/01/ ngamb01.xml&sSheet=/news/2004/08/01/ixhome.html (accessed September 25, 2007).

[115] David Hood, spokesman for bookmaker William Hill, *see* Sarah Womack, "Gambling Websites Let Punters as Young as 11 Set Up Accounts," telegraph.co.uk (daily online U.K. newspaper), July 27, 2004, *available at* www.portal. telegraph.co.uk/news/main.jhtml?xml=/news/2004/07/27/ngamb27.xml (accessed September 25, 2007); "Children Able to Gamble on Net," BBC News, July 27, 2004, *available at* http://news.bbc.co.uk/1/hi/uk/3927645.stm (accessed September 25, 2007).

[116] Gary Rivlin, "Gambling Dispute With a Tiny Country Puts U.S. in a Bind," New York Times, August 23, 2007.

[117] Wire Wager Act, 18 U.S.C. § 1084: (a) Whoever being engaged in the business of betting or wagering knowingly uses a wire communication facility for the transmission in interstate or foreign commerce of bets or wagers or information assisting in the placing of bets or wagers on any sporting event or contest, or for the transmission of a wire communication which entitles the recipient to receive money or credit as a result of bets or wagers, or for information assisting in the placing of bets or wagers, shall be fined under this title or imprisoned not more than two years, or both. (b) Nothing in this section shall be construed to prevent the transmission in interstate or foreign commerce of information for use in news reporting of sporting events or contests, or for the

transmission of information assisting in the placing of bets or wagers on a sporting event or contest from a state or foreign country where betting on that sporting event or contest is legal into a state or foreign country in which such betting is legal.

[118] Unlawful Internet Gambling Enforcement Act of 2006, 31 U.S.C. §§ 5361-5367.

Chapter Eight Quiz

Gilligan received an e-mail notifying him that his bank account would be closed in 24 hours unless he confirmed his account information by clicking on a link in the e-mail and entering his account information on the bank web page. Gilligan later discovered that his bank account had been emptied. What happened and what crimes were committed?

Mary Ann visited a quilt-knitting website and now her computer is running very sluggishly. The Professor scanned her computer and discovered a spyware program on her hard drive was sending information from Mary Ann's computer to the quilt-knitting website. What happened and what crime were committed?

The Professor drove around the island with his WIFI-enabled laptop until he found a wireless signal coming from Mr. Howell's hut. The Professor intercepted the signal and logged onto the Internet to download an X-rated movie Ginger had starred in. What crimes were committed?

The Professor, noting a sign reading "Free WiFi for All Patrons," stopped for lunch at Mrs. Howell's Cyber Café Hut. The Professor sends unsolicited e-mail containing a copyrighted photo of the S.S. Minnow to advertise his new business, "Ship Shape Computing." He launches a mail bomb at a rival's server on the mainland, uploads a Trojan horse to Mr. Howell's computer to seek out and relay Mr. Howell's stock tips and transactions to him, and then downloads some images from lolitas4u.ru, a Russian child porn website. Should Mrs. Howell face any liability for the Professor's actions?

Mr. Howell has been using a sock puppet in several investment chat rooms and on several message boards touting the stock of Howell Industries, revealing tantalizing insider information and watching the share price rise 500%, whereupon he quickly e-mailed his broker with instructions to sell all his shares in Howell Industries. What crimes were committed?

Ginger, meanwhile, is frightened by the harassing e-mails that she has been receiving and the threatening messages she has been subjected to in the "Famous Actresses: Where Are They Now?" chat room. She seeks out the Skipper, who is online with 17-year-old Gilligan gambling on the HighSeasHighStakes.com casino website. What issues have been raised?

Gilligan finds a shipwrecked house boat in the lagoon and dutifully repairs it to seaworthiness. He then creates a website offering both day cruises and permanent housing on his house boat. Ginger complains that Mary Ann has posted a roommate notice on his website expressly stating that she does not want to room with lesbians. She enlists the aid of the Island Civil Liberties Union to file a lawsuit against Gilligan, claiming violation of the Fair Housing Act. Is she likely to prevail?

Mary Ann also sues Gilligan, claiming that Ginger's online roommate notice stating "women only" is in violation of the Fair Housing Act. Is she likely to prevail?

If you are using this book in a classroom, discuss the issues raised and the liability of all parties. Otherwise, try to list the issues involved and probable outcomes before turning to the answers in the Appendix.

[Answers in Appendix]

PART FOUR

PRIVACY

CHAPTER NINE

PRIVACY AT WORK

> This chapter examines privacy at work, including e-mail privacy, employer monitoring, ISP monitoring, the Electronic Communications Privacy Act, and the 2006 amendments to the Federal Rules of Civil Procedure affecting electronic discovery. Intrusion of one's private life into the workplace is also discussed.

MOST EMPLOYEES NOW INTERACT through e-mail, IMs, or intranets; nearly 90 million U.S. workers send 1.5 billion e-mails daily. The Internet has become a office fixture and computers are the 21ˢᵗ century filing cabinets — 90% of business documents are not printed and filed, but instead stored electronically.[1] But employers must be mindful that e-mail can provide evidence for employees claiming discrimination, harassment, or retaliation, and for customers seeking to sue the firm. At brokerage firm Merrill Lynch, e-mails from its investment analyst Henry Blodget were revealed to contain words such as "junk," "disaster," and "crap" to describe stocks that the firm was publicly recommending to its clients.[2] Such intra-office e-mails can be subpoenaed through the discovery process in a lawsuit.[3] In fact, under recent amendments to the Federal Rules of Civil Procedure (FRCP) discussed below, such electronic data must be disclosed "without awaiting a discovery request."[4]

Employees often think of e-mail as private correspondence that ends after the message is sent, but this is not really true. E-mails, and back-ups of e-mails, may exist on computer workstations, company servers, and ISP servers indefinitely. Employees' e-mail can reside indefinitely in backup tapes of corporate computer systems. Many businesses do not regularly purge old backups, and such archived e-mail can be a treasure trove for attorneys suing the company. Courts do not consider the destruction of e-mail and records according to a fair and consistent business policy to be destruction of evidence, and the amended FRCP provide a safe harbor that protects companies from sanctions for deleting e-mail as part of "routine, good-faith operation."[5]

Who Can Read Your E-Mail?

So you think your e-mail is private? What happens in Vegas may stay in Vegas, but what happens in your e-mail may travel around. You think that only the person that you send it to can read it? Consider who else, besides the intended recipient, might be perusing your e-mail — employers, hackers, mistaken recipients, ISPs, law enforcement officials, and a party in a lawsuit.

Employers

Employers are concerned about:

- The possibility of employees leaking sensitive information, either trade secrets or client information, via e-mail

- Compliance with personal, financial, and health care privacy regulations regarding customer information

- Prevention of sexual harassment lawsuits

These concerns have led many companies to implement an (often unstated) policy of monitoring employee e-mail. Thirty percent of all companies and 43% of firms with more than 20,000 employees hire staff to monitor and read outbound e-mail, according to one study.[6] Another study revealed that 25% of employers have fired employees for misusing office e-mail.[7]

While employers may feel justified in monitoring e-mail and Internet use to avoid or curtail potential liability from discrimination or harassment lawsuits or disclosure of proprietary or confidential information, restrictions on personal e-mail and awareness that their every move is watched may result in resentment and low employee morale. Nonetheless, more than three-quarters of employers electronically monitor their employees.[8] Such monitoring includes e-mail, Internet use, videotaped camera surveillance and recording, and logging phone calls. Half of all companies store and review employees' computer files.[9] The test for whether such monitoring is legal or an impermissible invasion of privacy hinges on whether there is a *"reasonable expectation of privacy."* The trend has been for courts to find that there is no reasonable expectation of privacy for e-mail in the workplace.

In *Shoars v. Epson America*,[10] Alana Shoars was in charge of the e-mail system at the Epson plant in Torrance, California. After assuring Epson employees that their e-mail was private, Shoars discovered that her boss was reading all employee e-mail. When

Shoars refused to go along with the monitoring, she was fired. She sued for wrongful termination, based on a California law that prohibited electronic surveillance, but the court held that the statute's protections applied only to telephone communications and did not extend to e-mail. The court found that the Epson employees did not have a reasonable expectation of privacy in their business e-mail used primarily for Epson business purposes.

In _Smyth v. Pillsbury Company_,[11] despite the fact that Pillsbury had assured its employees that their e-mails would be treated as confidential and not intercepted and used as grounds for termination, Michael Smyth was fired for "unprofessional use" of Pillsbury's e-mail system. Smyth used his home computer to exchange e-mails with his supervisor, referring to his sales managers as "backstabbing bastards." He was fired after his employer found a printout of the e-mail and then read all of his other e-mails. Smyth sued for wrongful discharge. The court found that Pillsbury's interest in preventing inappropriate and unprofessional comments on its network precluded any reasonable expectation of privacy.

And in _Bourke v. Nissan Motors Corp._,[12] plaintiffs Bonita Bourke and Rhonda Hall were customer service representatives for a car dealership. During a demonstration of the company's e-mail system, a randomly selected e-mail from Bourke turned out to be of a sexual nature. This prompted a management review by Nissan, which revealed more sexual e-mails from both Bourke and Hall. Bourke resigned and Hall was fired. Both sued for wrongful termination, claiming invasion of privacy, but the court ruled that they had no reasonable expectation of privacy in their e-mail because they had signed an agreement with their employer that restricted use of the e-mail system to company business and because they knew that their employer sometimes monitored e-mail.

Employer monitoring of e-mail is just part of the employee monitoring process. More than $140 million of employee surveillance software is sold annually,[13] and the extent and degree of such monitoring is mind-boggling. Monitoring software can include periodic "screen shots" of employee's computers and keystroke software programs can recreate what an employee typed.[14] A software program called "Pornsweeper" even scans e-mail attachments for images that resemble human flesh.[15] Orchestria makes software that notices when certain are typed in documents or web forms and warns users that they are violating company policy or blocks the action.[16] Proofpoint software, employed by hospitals, routes outgoing e-mail through a special box, then scans it for confidential patient data (_e.g._, patient names, prescription histories, and Social Security numbers) and if it finds any, automatically encrypts the message.[17] Monitoring may also tip off an employer as to which employees are sending e-mail with "résumé attached" in the subject line. There are even "Smart" ID cards that track an employee's location as he walks through the workplace.[18] As monitoring software proliferates, the question *Qui custodiet ipsos custodes?* ('Who watches the watchmen?') arises. One prescient article suggests the ultimate creation of a new corporate position, that of the information compliance officer, to oversee "who in an organization can send what kind of data where." [19.]

Monitoring has some risks associated with it, such as the *risk of false inferences* derived from the monitored data. For example, an employee might accidentally visit www. whitehouse.com, a pornographic website, while attempting to access www.whitehouse. gov, the White House's website. While employee monitoring software can detect access to an inappropriate website, it cannot determine the employee's intent in accessing the website. Then there is the risk of running afoul of labor laws. Restricting employee communications may violate fair labor laws if such restrictions interfere with union activities.

Government employees may also be subject to monitoring. In some situations, the public can obtain access to government employee e-mails under state "public record" laws or the federal Freedom of Information Act. In one case, where a C.I.A. employee used a government computer to download pornography, the F.B.I. impounded and searched the employee's computer and e-mails. [20] The court ruled that because the government had a long-standing policy allowing audits of computer hard drives the employee had no expectation of privacy.

Ironically, even the U.S. Judiciary is not immune from monitoring. In 2001, some U.S. federal court judges discovered that court administrators were monitoring their Internet communications. The 9th Circuit Court of Appeal judges were concerned about privacy and confidentiality issues raised by the monitoring (at least as it applied to them) and disabled the monitoring systems. The court administrators who maintained the judicial computers sought to reinstate the monitoring and adopt a policy of no expectation of privacy in the workplace for federal judges and their staffs. The judges, meanwhile, argued that monitoring would threaten judicial independence. Finally, the Judicial Conference, the policy-making body of the federal judiciary, settled the dispute. It rejected the court administrators' policy that would have eliminated all expectation of privacy "at any time" while online at work and voted to end e-mail monitoring, but did approve limited monitoring of Internet use and prohibited the use of certain file-sharing programs. [21]

As you can see from the examples above, most claims against employer monitoring fall under Invasion of Privacy, and most cases have allowed employers to monitor e-mail and Internet use, finding no reasonable expectation of privacy for e-mail in the workplace. Often the key factor is whether employees were *informed in advance* that e-mail and Internet use were subject to monitoring.

As for the issue of sexual harassment, while many workplaces in the past merely displayed the once ubiquitous nude calendar, the Internet has increased the opportunity for pornography to enter the business place. Courts have held that exposure to pornography in the workplace can create a "hostile work environment" that can be a form of sexual harassment. Sexually explicit e-mail attachments, screen saver or wallpaper displays, or files stored on a company computer may all be factors deemed to create a hostile work environment. Unlimited office access to the Internet invariably leads to inappropriate use, including employees visiting pornographic websites. While a single offensive e-mail to a co-worker may not be enough to establish a hostile work environment, it may establish a pattern, which can then be used as the basis for a sexual harassment claim.

Hackers

Hackers using "sniffer" programs that look for key words in e-mails can intercept e-mail transmissions and then read your e-mail.

Mistaken Recipients

A simple typographical error in the address line of your e-mail can easily result in a confidential e-mail being sent to an unintended recipient. When the University of Kansas e-mailed 119 students who had failed their classes to inform them that they were at risk of losing their financial aid,[22] the e-mail address list included the names of all 119 students, so everyone on the list could see each other's names.[23]

Likewise, clicking the "Reply All" button instead of the "Reply" button on your e-mail program will forward your reply not just to the named recipient but to everyone he had carbon copied (cc:) in the original e-mail.

Internet Service Providers (ISPs)

The Electronic Communications Privacy Act (ECPA) permits an ISP to look through all stored messages, including e-mail awaiting you in your mailbox or recently sent and received mail.[24] Most ISPs temporarily store all messages that pass through their system. The Act does not directly refer to the Internet, but instead governs "wire, oral, or electronic communications."[25] It contains a "Service Provider Exemption," which is what allows ISPs access to *stored communication messages*. Some courts have used this exemption to permit a company providing hardware and software to access employees' e-mail.

The federal *Wiretap Act* governs unauthorized interception of communications.[26] The Wiretap Act, written before the Internet became a ubiquitous part of daily life, may not be adequate to address modern communications. As the *Councilman* case, discussed below, makes clear that the law has failed to adapt to the realities of Internet communications and must be updated to protect online privacy.[27]

The concept of e-mail privacy was set back in *Councilman*, when a federal appellate three-judge panel ruled 2–1 that an *e-mail provider did not break the law by reading its customers' communications without their consent.*[28] An online bookseller offered e-mail accounts through its website to its book-dealer customers, but secretly installed programming code to intercept and copy e-mails that its competitor Amazon.com sent to them. The bookseller read thousands of copied messages to learn which books its customers were seeking and gain a commercial advantage over its competitor. The court held that it did not violate the Wiretap Act because the e-mails were already in the RAM of the defendant's computer when they were copied and therefore the bookseller did not intercept them while they were in transit over wires, even though it copied the messages before the intended recipients read them. The court ruled that the messages were in *storage* rather than transit, and thus fell under the service provider exemption of the ECPA.

The dissent in *Councilman*, which contained a fascinating, detailed description of how e-mail works, argued that Congress never intended for e-mail temporarily stored in the transmission process to have less privacy than messages in transit. Whether the Act applies turns on the issue of *whether e-mail is "in transit" or "in storage."* In the view of this book's author, if an e-mail has not reached its final destination, *i.e.*, the addressed recipient, then even if in temporary storage, it should still be deemed in transit and the Act should apply.

As a result of the Councilman case, the *E-Mail Privacy Act* was introduced in Congress in 2004.[29] This proposed law would alter current laws to prohibit the form of e-mail eavesdropping that took place in *Councilman*. The bill provided that ISPs may intercept e-mail only "to the extent access is a necessary incident to rendition of service, protection of rights or property of the service provider or to honor a government request," and give e-mail intercepted in real-time transmission privacy protection under the Wiretap Act. A similar bill was introduced in the Senate in April 2005, but neither bill was enacted.

In October 2004, in response to a request from the U.S. Justice Department, the First Circuit Court of Appeals announced that it would rehear the *Councilman* case *en banc*. Appellate courts sometimes grant a rehearing of a case by all the judges of a court to reconsider the decision of a panel of the court, where the case concerns a matter of exceptional public importance or conflicts with an earlier decision. In August 2005, the full appellate court, in a 5–2 decision, reversed the lower court's decision, holding that interception of an e-mail communication in "transient" electronic storage violates the Wiretap Act, and it remanded the case.[30]

The issue of ISP monitoring of e-mail was raised again when Google launched "Gmail," a free e-mail service with one gigabyte of free storage capacity — more than 100 times that offered by its rivals Yahoo! Mail and Microsoft's MSN Hotmail. However, Google's computers would scan the e-mails (*i.e.*, sniffing) for keywords to use in sending targeted advertisements to Gmail users. Google would also keep copies of the e-mails *even after customers had deleted them.* Google's Gmail raised privacy concerns around the world, due to both the retention of e-mails and the sniffing for keywords. Gmail may violate Europe's privacy laws because it stores messages where users cannot permanently delete them. And even if the Gmail account holder is aware of and consents to the sniffing, consent can only be given by the Gmail account holder; those who send e-mail to a Gmail customer have no opportunity to consent to having their e-mail read for keywords.

Law Enforcement Officials

When armed with proper warrants or administrative subpoenas, law enforcement agents can gain access to your e-mail. See the discussion in Chapter Eight about the F.B.I.'s Carnivore software, and the USA PATRIOT Act, which allows the government to issue NSLs to ISPs to view all the e-mail subject headers in the target's e-mail account.[31] Also, while ISPs usually delete log files that are no longer needed for business purposes, such as network monitoring, fraud prevention, or billing disputes, the Electronic Communication Transactional Records Act of 1996 requires ISPs to retain any "record" in their possession for 90 days "upon the request of a governmental entity."[32] (See the discussion on data retention in Chapter 10).

A Party in a Lawsuit

A party in a lawsuit may gain access to your e-mails through the legal process known as "discovery." If your company is sued, all e-mails sent or received and now archived on its computers may be subpoenaed for review. The rationale is that e-mails and instant messages, unlike formal written letters, are composed "off-the-cuff" and in the heat of the moment people tend to be more blunt and therefore more honest in what they write (as in the Merrill Lynch e-mails discussed above).

"In almost every workplace lawsuit being filed today, e-mail is being subpoenaed as evidence," according to Nancy Flynn, executive director of the ePolicy Institute.[33] This might lead you to believe the safest course would be routinely to delete your e-mails or to delete e-mails and instant message archives if a lawsuit is anticipated. However, in at least one Florida case that approach proved very costly to the defendant.[34] When billionaire investor Ron Pearlman sued Investment firm Morgan Stanley for fraud, Pearlman made repeated requests for Morgan Stanley's internal e-mails, but the investment banker failed to preserve the e-mails. At the plaintiff's request, the court then agreed to instruct the jury that, since the defendant failed to preserve the e-mails, the e-mails unveiled a scheme to defraud him. The jury returned verdict of $604.3 million in actual damages and $850 million in punitive damages — with interest and attorney fees the verdict topped $1.58 billion! (The verdict was subsequently reversed, although Perelman has said he will appeal).[35]

The issue of whether the duty to preserve electronic evidence (*e.g.*, e-mails and instant messages) arises when a potential lawsuit is reasonably foreseeable or upon the actual filing of such a suit remains unclear at both the federal and state levels. Some federal courts have held that the duty arises as soon as the company has a reasonable belief that it may be subject to pending litigation.[36] While the 4th Circuit has found that the duty arises "when a party should reasonably know that the evidence may be relevant to an anticipated litigation,"[37] the 1st Circuit has found that the duty arises after persistent attempts to obtain the electronic evidence prior to filing the lawsuit.[38] And in some states, such as Florida, site of the Morgan Stanley case, the duty does not arise until the actual filing of the lawsuit.

And of course, deliberately deleting electronic data after receipt of a subpoena would be the crime of destruction of evidence. The only way to ensure a high degree of privacy for your e-mail messages is to encrypt them. The current encryption standard for e-mail is a software program called Pretty Good Privacy ("PGP"). PGP is based on "RSA encryption," which uses a "public key/private key" system. The sender encrypts his e-mail with his private key (known only to him) and delivers it to the recipient, who can decrypt the message using the sender's public key (which is available to everyone).

As discussed at the beginning of this chapter, the 2006 amendments to the FRCP have changed the nature of e-discovery. The FRCP are important because they affect anyone — individuals, businesses, and organizations — who becomes a party in a federal court lawsuit. (State courts have their own rules of civil procedure). Companies should institute litigation hold procedures to provides notice to all the relevant people within the firm as to *what* data must be kept and for *how long* it should be retained. As soon as a lawsuit is anticipated, a company must use its "litigation hold" procedures and not wait to be subpoenaed.[39]

A party must now identify the existence of electronic data that it has not searched for or produced because of the costs and burdens of accessing the data (*e.g.*, deleted files, backup tapes, data stored on systems no longer in use). If the other party insists on seeing this data, the party holding the data has the burden of proving to the court that he information is not reasonably accessible.[40]

The amended FRCP do have an exception for data that is privileged or subject to protection as trial preparation material.[41] The electronic data must be provided in a form in which it is ordinarily maintained or is readily usable; however, the requesting party may specify the form of production of the electronic data.[42] This is important because it may include electronic data in its original format (*e.g.*, the actual spreadsheet file and not a PDF reproduction) with its metadata (*e.g.*, file creator and creation date, and document changes; and in e-mails, routing details such as the sender, receivers, and subject line) intact.

PRIVACY AND WORK

So far in this chapter, we have focused on privacy at the workplace. Most people have a private life outside of work. Usually they have an expectation that their private life outside of work is separate from their work life and should not affect it. There are, of course, obvious situations when an extrinsic circumstance in one's private life may adversely affect one's career. For example, if a priest is caught soliciting sex from young boys; if a Disney starlet unintentionally circulates nude photos of herself on the Internet; if a Miss Teen USA's racy photos appear on the Internet — in all of these instances, the individual has engaged in behavior that reflects poorly on the organization that employed them. The employee knew when he or she was hired that the organization (*i.e.*, the Catholic church, Disney, and the Miss Teen USA Pageant) were built around reputations of high morality and wholesomeness and that as high profile employees, they would be seen as representatives of those organizations even in their private lives. A truck driver may spend the evening drinking with his friends at a strip club and not expect to have to defend his actions the next day at work; a congressman might have to spend the next morning holding press conferences in an attempt to keep his job.

Foolish employee behavior after hours was once merely the subject of next day banter around the office water cooler, but today, with the advent of digital technology (cell phone cameras and high resolution pocket cameras) and the Internet, poor judgment can be immortalized in living color on every work station by the next morning.

One question that must first be asked is, With the advent of digital technology and the Internet, do we have any privacy left? Closed circuit cameras film us as we walk down streets and enter businesses, Google Earth posts photographs of our homes and even our cars online, and people all around us routinely carry cell phone cameras and pocket digital cameras. Is any expectation of privacy even reasonable?

The next question to ask is, Have we waived our right of privacy? As we will discuss in a later chapter, the generation that has come of age with the Internet has also developed a lessened expectation of privacy. Thanks to the Internet (*e.g.*, website, social networks, and YouTube) Andy Warhol's guarantee of 15 minutes of fame for everyone has become a reality. Anyone can post a homemade video on YouTube and be viewed by thousands of people. The Internet Generation thinks nothing of posting the most intimate details of their lives in blogs or on sites like MySpace or LiveJournal, or vlogging about their lives, loves, and even the job or boss they hate. Many individuals have been fired for comments they posted in their blogs after work (see Chapter 13). Could it really have surprised reporter Rachel Mosteller to have been fired after blogging publicly about how much she hated her job?[43] Can a job applicant really be shocked to learn he has been "Googled" by his prospective employer and his Facebook page and LiveJournal posts have been taken into equal consideration along with his application and résumé?

Let us set out some fundamental propositions:

- Employees are entitled to a reasonable expectation of privacy in their off work hours

- Employees who have high profile public personas should have a diminished expectation of privacy

- Employees who work for organizations that promote certain codes of behavior should not engage in behavior antithetical to those codes even outside of work

How would these propositions be applied to real life situations? For example, if John Smith, the public spokesman appearing in advertisements for the anti-lung cancer organization GASP (Group Against Smoke Pollution), is filmed smoking in public at various night clubs, while he may be entitled to a reasonable expectation of privacy outside of work, that expectation must be tempered by his job-related high profile persona. More importantly, by publicly smoking while serving as the spokesman for an anti-smoking organization, he has triggered our third proposition. His behavior might have been less egregious had both the second and third propositions been met, *e.g.*, if he had been a secretary and not a high profile spokesman.

Stacy Snyder was a Pennsylvania college senior enrolled at Millersville University, where she was working as a teaching assistant at a local high school to fulfill her requirements towards earning her teaching degree. Like many college students, the 25-year-old had a MySpace page. Snyder posted a photo of herself at a Halloween costume party (presumably after work and not on the high school campus) on her MySpace page. The photograph, a head shot of Snyder in a pirate hat drinking from a yellow plastic cup bearing the words "Mr. Goodbar chocolate," did not show the cup's contents. The photo was captioned "Drunken Pirate."[44]

The MySpace photo came to the attention of university officials in May, immediately prior to Snyder's graduation. After being summoned to meet with university officials, Snyder was told that the photo was "unprofessional" and that had any of the high school students gained access to the page, they might have found it offensive (it is not known whether Snyder's MySpace page was "public" or accessible only by those designated by her).[45] She was also told that by posting the photo on her MySpace page she was "promoting underage drinking."[46] She was then told that she would not receive her B.S in Education degree but would instead receive a B.A. in English (her previous major).[47] The university's refusal to confirm that Snyder completed her student teaching requirements satisfactorily kept her from obtaining state teaching certification; as a result, she sought employment as a nanny.[48] Snyder sued the university for $75,000 in damages and injunctive relief requiring the university to grant her an Education degree.[49]

As there is yet no body of established case law in this area, perhaps courts might consider taking judicial notice of our three propositions and apply them to the facts of each individual case in their analysis.

Turning to the example above, most college students have MySpace or Facebook pages, most of which contain photographs (which range from innocent to raunchy). For better or worse, college life has become synonymous with fraternities, sororities, partying, drinking, and football games, in addition to education and these activities will no doubt be reflected in the content one finds on such student websites. While the photo was captioned "Drunken Pirate," there was no indication that Snyder was drunk, nor that there was alcohol in the cup. Such captions are often tongue-in-cheek, and this could have been a play on the "Yo-ho-ho and a bottle of rum" drunken pirate stereotype. Even if she had been drinking or inebriated, under our first proposition, employees are entitled to a reasonable expectation of privacy in their off work hours. Unless Snyder brought the photo or her MySpace page to the attention of her students, it would be unreasonable to think that she would not be allowed to act as any other college student.

Snyder did not have a high profile public persona. Her job as a student teacher did not make her famous, nor did it make her a role model, any more than posting the innocuous photo was "promoting underage drinking."

Did the organization (the university) promote certain codes of behavior? According to the pleadings filed in the case, the school did have a code of conduct but there was nothing cited in that code that prohibited Snyder from maintaining a MySpace page or posting photographs from a costume party.[50]

Obviously, any employment agreements or relevant labor laws would also be a factor in such a case-by-case analysis. The importance of the pre-existence of codes of conduct or behavior, stated employee rules, employment contractual terms, or existing labor laws is that they provide notice to the employee of what behavior outside of the office environment is considered acceptable or grounds for termination.

The technology of the Internet, through blogs, vlogs, and social networks, is eroding the barrier between our public and private lives. Both society and the law will have to recognize this overlap and craft rules that balance the reputational interests of employers with the reasonable expectations of privacy of employees.

Summary

Most business documents today are not printed but are stored on hard drives. E-mail can provide evidence for employees claiming discrimination, harassment, or retaliation, and for customers seeking to sue a firm. E-mails, and back-ups of e-mails, may exist on computer workstations, company servers, and ISP servers indefinitely. Employers, hackers, mistaken recipients, ISPs, law enforcement officials, and parties in lawsuits may all be able to read your e-mail.

Most employers monitor e-mail and Internet use to avoid or limit potential liability from discrimination or harassment claims or to prevent employees from disclosing proprietary or confidential information to others. The test for whether such monitoring is legal or an impermissible invasion of privacy hinges on whether there is a "reasonable expectation of privacy." The trend has been for courts to find that there is no reasonable expectation of privacy for e-mail in the workplace. The Electronic Communications Privacy Act does not refer to the Internet, but contains a "Service Provider Exemption," which allows ISPs to access stored communication messages. The federal Wiretap Act, written before the Internet became a ubiquitous part of daily life, may not be adequate to address modern communication modes.

Sexually explicit e-mail attachments, screen saver or wallpaper displays, or files stored on a company computer may all be factors deemed to create a hostile work environment. While a single offensive e-mail not be enough to establish a hostile work environment, it may establish a pattern, which can then be used as the basis for a sexual harassment claim.

The 2006 amendments to the FRCP have changed the nature of e-discovery. The FRCP are important because they affect anyone who becomes a party in a federal court lawsuit. (State courts have their own rules of civil procedure). The amended FRCP provide a safe harbor that protects companies from sanctions for deleting e-mail as part of "routine, good-faith operation." Deliberately deleting electronic data after receipt of a subpoena would be the crime of destruction of evidence. Companies should institute litigation hold procedures to provides notice to all the relevant people within the firm as to what data must be kept and for how long it should be retained. As soon as a lawsuit is anticipated, a company must use its "litigation hold" procedures and not wait to be subpoenaed.

Chapter Nine Notes

[1] Howard Mankoff, Electronic Discovery: The Final Frontier," *available at* www.marshalldennehey.com/CM/DefenseDigest/DefenseDigest294.asp (accessed September 25, 2007).

[2] NOW with Bill Moyers, May 31, 2002, *available at* www.pbs.org/now/politics/wallstreet.html (accessed September 25, 2007).

[3] During the discovery process, prior to the start of a civil trial, both the plaintiff and the defendant can use civil procedural tools such as interrogatories, depositions, requests for production, and subpoenas to compel the production of evidence, in preparation for the upcoming trial.

[4] Fed. R. Civ. P. 26(a)(1).

[5] Fed. R. Civ. P. 37(f). However, the Rules do not define "routine, good-faith operation."

[6] "Survey: 40% of Large Companies Read Employees' Outbound E-mail," Cincinnati Business Courier, July 12, 2004.

[7] Study by the American Management Association and the ePolicy Institute. *See* Ed Frauenheim, "Is Your Boss Monitoring Your E-mail?," CNET News.com, May 18, 2005.

[8] Ed Frauenheim, fn. 7, *supra*.

[9] *Ibid.*

[10] *Shoars v. Epson America*, Case No. B073243 (Cal. Ct. App. Apr. 14, 1994), *rev. denied*, Case No. S040065, 1994 Cal. LEXIS 3670 (June 29, 1994).

[11] *Smyth v. Pillsbury Co.*, 914 F. Supp. 97 (E.D. Pa. 1996).

[12] *Bourke v. Nissan Motors Corp.*, Case No. B068705 (Cal. Ct. App. July 26, 1993). This case is included in the Cases Section on the Issues in Internet Law website (www.IssuesinInternetLaw.com).

[13] Privacy Foundation Study, Linda Rosencrance, "Study: Monitoring of Employee E-mail Escalates," CNN.com, July 9, 2001, *available at* http://archives.cnn.com/2001/TECH/internet/07/09/employee.monitoring.idg/ (accessed September 25, 2007).

[14] Ed Frauenheim, fn. 7, *supra*.

[15] Manufactured by ZiBiz, Inc., *available at* www.zibiz.com/solutions/mime-sweep/ (accessed September 25, 2007).

[16] *Available at* www.orchestria.com/solutions.

[17] Brian Bergstein, "Software Makes Office Computer Monitoring More Sophisticated," Associated Press wire report, August 19, 2007.

[18] Phillip J. Trobaugh, Mansfield, Tanick & Cohen, P.A. website, "The Workplace Panopticon: Minnesota Privacy Law at Work," *available at* www.mansfieldtanick.com/CM/Articles/The-Workplace-Panopticon.asp (accessed September 25, 2007).

[19] Brian Bergstein, fn. 17, *supra*.

[20] *United States v. Simons*, 29 F. Supp. 2d 324 (E.D. Va 1998).

[21] Report of the Judicial Conference Committee on Automation and Technology (September 2001).

[22] "119 Students Who Failed Courses Get Group E-mail," Associated Press wire report, June 17, 2005.

[23] A commentator on the website TechDirt.com opined, presumably with tongue-in-cheek: "Even so, the mistake might not be all bad. After all, it was limited just to people who failed all their classes, so they simply discovered who their peers are. It's like social networking for failures. FlunkedIn, anyone?," (An allusion to the social network 'LinkedIn'), *available at* www.techdirt.com/articles/20050617/1340223_F.shtml (accessed September 25, 2007).

[24] Electronic Communications Privacy Act, 18 U.S.C. § 2510, *et seq.*

[25] *Ibid.*

[26] 18 U.S.C § 2511. Interception and Disclosure of Wire, Oral, or Electronic Communications Prohibited.

[27] *United States v. Councilman*, Case No. 03-1383 (1st Cir. June 29, 2004). Councilman, as vice-president of Interloc, the online bookseller specializing in rare books, managed Interloc's ISP activities. By providing its customers with e-mail addresses ending with "@interloc.com," Interloc was acting as an ISP.

[28] *Ibid.*

[29] E-mail Privacy Act of 2004 (HR 4956).

[30] *United States v. Councilman*, 418 F.3d 67, 79 (1st Cir. 2005).

[31] USA PATRIOT Act (Pub. L. No. 107-56).

[32] Electronic Communication Transactional Records Act, 18 U.S.C. § 2703 (f).

[33] Dawn Kawamoto, "Mind Those IMs — Your Cubicle's Walls Have Eyes," CNET News.com, October 25, 2004.

[34] *Coleman Holdings, Inc. v. Morgan Stanley & Co.*, 2005 WL 679071 (Fla 15th Cir. Ct. 2005).

[35] "Morgan Stanley-Perelman Judgment Flipped," Associated Press wire report, March 21, 2007.

[36] *Stevenson v. Union Pacific R.R. Co.*, 354 F.3d 739 (8th Cir. 2004).

[37] *Silvestri v. General Motors Corp.*, 271 F.3d 583, 591 (4th Cir. 2001).

[38] *Blinzler v. Marriott Int'l., Inc.*, 81 F.3d 1148, 1159 (1st Cir. 1996).

[39] Fed. R. Civ. P. 26(a)(1).

[40] Fed. R. Civ. P. 26(b)(2).

[41] Fed. R. Civ. P. 26(b)(5).

[42] Fed. R. Civ. P. 34(b).

[43] Evan Hansen, "Google Blogger: 'I Was Terminated,'" CNET News.com, February 11, 2005. *See also* the "Fired for Blogging" discussion in Chapter 13.

[44] "College Sued Over 'Drunken Pirate' Sanctions: Woman Claims Teaching Degree Denied Because of Single MySpace Photo," April 26, 2007; *see also* Anita Ramasastry, "Can Universities Take Adverse Actions Against Students Based on Their MySpace Profiles? It Depends in Part on Whether the University Followed its Own Code of Conduct," FindLaw.com, May 4, 2007.

[45] Complaint, *Snyder v. Millersville Univ.*, Case No. 2:2007cv01660 (E.D. Pa Apr. 25, 2007) *available at* http://casedocs.justia.com/pennsylvania/paedce/2:2007cv01660/228127/1/0.pdf (accessed September 25, 2007).

[46] *Ibid.*

[47] *Ibid.*

[48] *Ibid.*

[49] *Snyder v. Millersville Univ.*, Case No. 2:2007cv01660 (E.D. Pa Apr. 25, 2007).

[50] Complaint, *Snyder v. Millersville Univ.*, fn. 45, *supra.*

Chapter Nine Quiz

A group of librarians at the Florida Public Library file a sexual harassment charge with the Equal Employment Opportunity Commission (EEOC). The librarians claim that they are being forced to work in a hostile work environment, and are therefore effectively sexually harassed in violation of federal law, because of the unfiltered computers connected to the Internet where patrons can access pornography. Upon hearing this, Fetish Freddy, a student who frequently surfs the web in search of such websites, threatens to sue the library if filters are installed.

Meanwhile, Miss Grundy, a rather conservative old biddy, has filed a lawsuit against AOL, the ISP, for transmitting the pornographic images. Billy the Kid, a minor, while using the same library computer that Freddy had been using, stumbles across cached images of naked women and virtual child pornography accessed earlier by Freddy. Billy's mother is outraged and asks whom she can sue. Billy's father, Hoosier Daddy, visits the library to see the offending images for himself, and copies the JPGs of the naked women, which Freddy had downloaded from the Playboy website, and e-mails them to everyone in his office address book.

If you are using this book in a classroom, discuss the issues raised and the liability of all parties. Otherwise, try to list the issues involved and probable outcomes before turning to the answers in the Appendix.

[Answers in Appendix]

CHAPTER TEN

PRIVACY BASICS

> This chapter covers the Right of Privacy, the Right of Publicity, public records, voluntary disclosure of private information, data retention, and the expectation of privacy in chat, e-mail, and on the World Wide Web.

The Right to Privacy

THE RIGHT OF PRIVACY is not explicitly stated anywhere within the U.S. Constitution. In fact, in the earliest case to address the concept, the New York Supreme Court ruled that it did not exist.[1] In that case, a flour company used a picture of Abby Roberson on flyers it posted around town to advertise its product, without her consent. The young girl's family claimed that this caused her severe embarrassment and humiliation but in a 4-to-3 decision, the court ruled that she had no cause of action to sue. The public outcry was so fierce that the state legislature immediately enacted a statute making it a misdemeanor and a tort to use the name, portrait, or picture of any person for "advertising purposes or for the purposes of trade" without written consent. Three years later, the Georgia Supreme Court, in what would become the leading case on the issue,[2] resolved the same issue with the opposite result of the New York court, recognizing a distinct Right of Privacy, when an insurance company used a man's picture to sell insurance.

The Right of Privacy is what is known as a derived right, *i.e.*, a right logically drawn from those rights that are expressly enumerated, in this case inferred from the Fourth Amendment guarantees against unreasonable search and seizures. Privacy has been defined by the U.S. Supreme Court as the right of the individual to control the dissemination of information about oneself. The Right of Privacy stems from:

- A class of persons, *e.g.*, children or patients

- A specific type of information, *e.g.,* medical history or tax returns

- A set of circumstances, *e.g.*, intrusion into one's private affairs

There are four distinct categories of the tort of invasion of privacy, each based on different elements:[3]

- Appropriation of name or likeness

- Intrusion

- Public disclosure of private facts

- False light in the public eye

Appropriation

Appropriation involves the use of an individual's name, likeness, or identity for trade or advertising purposes without consent. It is the oldest of the forms of invasion of privacy. The right refers not merely to an individual's name but to one's identity.[4] The tort of appropriation is also inversely referred to as the "Right of Publicity," *i.e.*, a right to prevent the use of one's identifiable name or likeness by a third party for commercial purposes without consent. The commercial component implies an intrinsic value in the name or likeness, which usually means that the plaintiff will be a celebrity or public figure (although arguably a private individual could take the position that of course his name or likeness has an intrinsic value as well or else the defendant would not be using it for commercial gain). Defenses to a claim of appropriation are consent, newsworthiness (as in being used to advertise an upcoming publication or TV show), and failing to identify the individual.

State courts have applied different tests to determine if there has been appropriation. Some states, like Missouri, consider whether the use is predominantly commercial or expressive; whereas other states, like California, add an additional requirement to see if the defendant's use is transformative.

The California 2nd District Court of Appeal held that three video game companies could market a character based on a well-known former lead singer of a 1990s funk band.[5] However, the Missouri Supreme Court using the "commercial or expressive" test, found the creation of a comic book villain using the name and likeness of former St. Louis Blues hockey player Tony Twist in Todd McFarlane's *Spawn* comic book to be commercially exploitative, awarding Twist $5 million.[6]

Comic books fared better in California under the transformative test, when the California Supreme Court found DC Comics had substantially transformed two half-worm, half-human creatures with green tentacles sprouting from their chests (named the "Autumn brothers") from the likenesses of musicians Johnny and Edgar Winters (known as the "Winters brothers") in its *Jonah Hex: Riders of the Worm* comic book.[7] "Although the fictional characters * * * are less-than-subtle evocations of Johnny and Edgar Winter, the books do not depict plaintiffs literally. They are distorted for purposes of lampoon, parody, or caricature."[8]

Intrusion

Intrusion involves intruding on a person's solitude or seclusion, either physically (*i.e.*, by entering onto his property, *e.g.*, searching an employees locker or opening an employee's mail that is marked "personal" or "confidential,") or by electronic or mechanical means. The tort occurs at the stage of information gathering and does not require publication. The intrusion must be offensive and objectionable to a reasonable man. Therefore, it would not be intrusion merely to photograph a woman walking down a public street; however, photographing the same woman walking down a public street at the precise moment a gust of wind were to blow her dress up would be considered intrusion.[9] Defenses to a claim of intrusion are express or implied consent, and being on public property.

Google, in 2007, launched Street View, an application for its Google Maps, which provided panoramic camera views of city streets in selected cities (*i.e.*, Denver, Houston, Las Vegas, Los Angeles, Miami, New York, Orlando, San Diego, and San Francisco, at time of publication). Google claimed its cameras only filmed public property, comparing it to what people walking down a city street would see.[10.] Pedestrians were visibly identifiable and the detail was so fine that even license plates could be read. While most of the street scenes captured on Google Street Views tend to be innocuous, some of these recent examples do appear to intrude on one's solitude in public places:

- A man urinating on the side of a road

- A woman picking her nose

- A surfer changing into his swimsuit

- A man sitting inside his house in front of a window

- A man entering an adult bookstore

- A man entering a strip club

While the argument can be made (and has been by Google) that all of these activities occurred in public, instead of a handful of people viewing other pedestrians, millions of people can view individuals working outside, picking their noses or adjusting their clothes as they walk along the street, or sunbathing in bikinis on the lawn of Stanford University (the latter scene was so popular that it was posted to several blogs that solicit popular Google Street Views photos[11]). The ubiquitous nature of the closed circuit filming was best expressed by an ad in a San Francisco Nordstrom's department store window for fashion designer Kenneth Cole's clothing line — "You are on a video camera over 20 times a day. Are you dressed for it?"[12]

The issue of intrusion becomes of even greater concern when one considers the effect of inferences drawn from extrinsic facts when viewing the filmed subjects. For example, while filming someone walking down a public street might not in of itself be an intrusion into individual privacy, would that change if the individual were walking into:

- A rape counseling center?

- An Alcoholics Anonymous meeting ?

- A strip club?

- An adult bookstore?

- A Gay & Lesbian Community Center?

- A police station, as an informant?

Google announced that it would "try to not have identifiable faces and identifiable licence plate numbers in any Street View image in Canada" after the Canadian federal privacy commissioner voiced concerns over Street Views being imported to Canada.[13] Is Google's

Street Views an intrusion that would be offensive and objectionable to a reasonable man. Or is it merely the exercise of free speech to photograph public places and people in them, colliding with the privacy interests and expectations of individuals as they go about their daily routine?

Public Disclosure of Private Facts

Public disclosure of private facts involves the publication of private and embarrassing facts that are not related to matters of public concern (*i.e.*, non-newsworthy). It is premised on the notion that certain information about an individual is of such an intimate or offensive nature, and of so slight legitimate public interest and concern, that it can and should be completely removed from public discourse. The facts must be private (*e.g.*, medical conditions and treatment, sexual relations, personal letters, or income taxes) and there must be a reasonable expectation that they will remain private. Anything in the public record, regardless of how embarrassing or distasteful it may be, is not actionable. Also, the disclosure must be relatively widespread; while disclosure to a small group might not be actionable, this requirement will seldom if ever pose a problem on the World Wide Web). Defenses to a claim of public disclosure of private facts are that the facts are related to matters of public concern (*i.e.*, newsworthy), that the facts would not be offensive to a reasonable man, that the facts are a matter of public record, and consent. This tort is described in greater detail later in this chapter.

False Light

False light involves a statement that is false or misleading, and highly offensive (but not necessarily defamatory) and creates a false impression about the plaintiff in the public eye. While similar to the tort of defamation, the primary difference is that defamation must adversely harm one's reputation, whereas the false light tort requires that the representation to be "highly offensive to a reasonable person." For example, suppose a newspaper publishes an article on local police cracking down on prostitution, accompanied by a photograph of a man leaving a bordello. The obvious impression would be that the man was a customer; however, what if he had just delivered a pizza and was on his way out of the building to return to his car? The use of the photograph, especially in juxtaposition with and given the context of the article would have cast him in a false light in the public eye.

Unlike defamation actions, truth is not a defense in invasion of privacy actions. Defenses to invasion of privacy claims usually fall under consent, privilege (as in court records), information in the public record, matters of legitimate public concern, failed to prove one of the necessary elements of the tort, or in some cases expiration of the applicable statute of limitations.

Federal Laws Affecting Privacy

Although there are no *general* federal privacy laws, there are some federal laws protecting certain aspects of an individual's right to privacy.[14] The *Video Privacy Protection Act* of 1988 makes it illegal to disclose what videotapes an individual has rented.[15] Portions of the *Fair Credit Reporting Act* of 1970 govern creating, distributing, or using consumer reports on the Internet.[16] The *Electronic Communications Privacy Act* of 1986 (ECPA) does not refer to the Internet, but governs "wire, oral, or electronic communications."[17] The *Gramm-Leach-Bliley Act* of 1999 limits when financial institutions may disclose personal information; it also applies to companies, whether or not they are financial institutions, which receive such information.[18] And the *Health Insurance Portability and Accountability Act* of 1996 (HIPPA) limits what personal information may be disclosed by health, medical, and doctor's office websites.[19]

Absent specific federal privacy laws, the Federal Trade Commission (F.T.C.) has regulated collection and use of personal information over the Internet using its authority over "unfair" or "deceptive" commercial practices pursuant to § 5 of the F.T.C. Act. The F.T.C. defines "personal data" to include:

- First and last name

- Address

- E-mail address, instant messenger ID, or screen name that reveals e-mail address

- Phone number

- Social Security number

- Photograph with name

- A persistent identifier (*e.g.*, cookie retrieval)

Sometimes however, people may expressly or by implication waive a claim for appropriation, or even misuse, of their personally identifiable identification. *People often disclose much personal information on home pages*, including their home address, and photographs, names and details of themselves, their children, and even the family dog! Many intimate details of a person's life are often revealed in online diaries, or blogs. Some employers even search for and peruse the blogs of prospective employees before making a hiring decision. While people are free to disclose and share such information with the world, they must realize there is also a risk of the wrong people gaining unrestricted access to such personal information. Also, a *customer waiver in a click-wrap agreement* [20] may limit liability for misuse of personal information. Many firms are putting *waiver clauses* in their *click-wrap agreements* stating that the customer agrees not to sue the company in the event of a data breach if the company's database is hacked or stolen.

Public Records

Public records take many forms—birth, adoption, marriage and death certificates, recorded wills, deeds, census records, court documents, military records, motor vehicle records, licenses (*i.e.*, from pilot licenses to ham radio operator licenses), property tax records, criminal records, business filings, UCC filings, professional licenses, and campaign contributor lists—are just some of the types of records available to the public.

Until the advent of the Internet, much of an individual's sense of privacy came from realizing the lengths that anyone would have to go through to retrieve personal information from public records. The cumbersome and inefficient process of digging through public records was itself, in many cases, a barrier protecting individual privacy to a degree. When Arthur Dent, the protagonist in Douglas Adams' novel *"The Hitchhiker's Guide to the Galaxy,"* complains about the bulldozer poised to knock down his house to make way for a new by-way, he is informed that the plans for the roadway construction have been a matter of public record: [21]

"On display? I eventually had to go down to the cellar to find them."

"That's the display department."

* * * "It was on display in the bottom of a locked filing cabinet stuck in a disused lavatory with a sign on the door saying 'Beware of the Leopard.'"

Prior to the Internet, so-called "public" records were not much more accessible than the plans to the by-way going through Arthur Dent's house. Sure, the records were available to the public; but "availability" entailed traveling to the physical location of the records, during proscribed hours of operations, and following precise rules and regulations to obtain and view such materials. Thus, most "public" information was public only to the most intrepid, resourceful, and perseverant researcher. An occasional reporter might snoop amongst filed court records to ferret out gossipy tidbits relating to divorce records, arrests, medical histories, and other private matters of public record, but not until recently could one conjure the image of a neighbor seated at her computer in her nightgown scrolling through such files while sipping her morning coffee.

Public records thus present a challenge for those who favor open records and state "Sunshine Laws" and privacy advocates. If you can drive to the courthouse to view a public record, why not be able to view the same record online? On the other hand, does ease of availability increase the likelihood of identity theft?

Saying that public records should remain public—but not be made widely available—goes against the fundamental principle of open records laws. If "public means public" and all public records should be easily accessible, both in person and online, then perhaps the notion of what information should be classified as "public" in the first place needs to be re-examined.

One concern is that access to public records should not be limited to those who have the financial means to hire employees, law firms, or couriers to go to the courthouse to retrieve those records. Making public records available online ensures a level playing field so that anyone, from a poor individual to a wealthy corporation, can access the same information.[22]

Another concern centers around court records, where an individual may be accused (but not convicted, and even later vindicated) of a crime. The mere allegation could follow the individual forever, causing permanent long-term damage to his reputation. To avoid this, the federal courts and some states use a record-by-record decision-making process to shield certain records[23] from public view.[24] However, this process is only set in motion after an individual makes an official request to the judge. In some cases, this may be a time-consuming, expensive, or complex task.

In Florida, the state that pioneered the concept of "Sunshine Laws," all kinds of court documents were available online until February 2004, when Florida instituted a temporary ban on the release of all court documents on the Internet, partly in response to the clamor around Dale Earnhardt's autopsy photographs. (NASCAR driver Dale Earnhardt died in a race-car crash at the Daytona 500 in 2001, and under Florida law his autopsy records, including photographs, were public records.) Local newspapers sought copies of the photographs and amidst concerns that a Thai website would publish the photographs, Earnhardt's widow and fans lobbied the state legislature to prevent release of the photographs.

A lawsuit filed against the Florida Department of Law Enforcement (FDLE) in 2007 sought removal of a minor's name from the state's publicly accessible online database. The 13-year-old girl was arrested for allegedly stealing a can of soda.[25] Her attorneys claimed that online publication of her name and the details of the arrest violates Florida law mandating that minors' misdemeanor records be kept confidential.[26] The Florida database apparently also routinely listed a physical description of the arrested individual and his or her Social Security number.[27] The state website offered this information to anyone willing to pay the $23 per record charge, and the state has received $52.7 million from such fees for criminal histories.

The minor's argument was that once such information is exposed on the Internet, it is irretrievable and can permanently harm the child's future.[28] It was for that reason that, historically, juvenile court records were kept confidential to protect children, so as not to stigmatize them for the rest of their lives with a criminal record. However, as juvenile crime rates soared in the last quarter of the 20th century, more than 42 states made juvenile criminal records public to some extent; under Florida law, records of juveniles charged with felonies or three or more misdemeanors are public record.

Federal judges in South Florida and eastern Pennsylvania began removing plea and sentencing memos from online case files in 2007 after a website, WhosARat.com, was started with the purpose of exposing informants and undercover agents in criminal cases.[29] While removing the documents from their own websites, the judges still allowed them to be obtainable directly from the courthouse. Although it would seem that a motivated criminal would take the extra effort to go to the courthouse and retrieve a physical copy of the documents, these courts have effectively created two classes of "public" records based on accessibility — online records and in person records. This invites the question of whether effectively creating a new class of public record — one with more limited accessibility — is inherently unfair to those lacking the financial or physical (*i.e.*, those with physical disabilities that would preclude them from travelling to the courthouse) means to access the records.

Information Broker Liability

There have always been private investigators, using various resources to ferret out personal information about individuals. But now there are online *information brokers* who deal in supplying personal information about individuals to the general public. Most, but not all, of these data are from public records, which prior to the Internet were difficult to access but are now easily accessed, searched and collated. There are many legitimate uses for such information, such as tracking down an old school friend or a distant relative, or for genealogical purposes. But what liability does an information broker have if the information it supplies is used by a *stalker*?

In *Remsburg v. Docusearch*, online information broker Docusearch sold some information about Amy Lynn Boyer to a man named Liam Youens.[30] Youens had become obsessed with Boyer in school, stalked her for years, and chronicled his plans to murder her on his website. Although he already knew where she lived, Youens bought information, including her Social Security number and workplace address, from Docusearch.[31] He later drove to Boyer's workplace, fatally shot her, and then himself. Boyer's mother sued Docusearch.

The court held that the threats posed by *stalking* and *identity theft* meant that the *risk of criminal misconduct* was sufficiently *foreseeable* so that an investigator has a *duty to exercise reasonable care* in disclosing a third person's personal information to a client.

Chillingly, after ordering information on Boyer from Docusearch's website, Youens wrote in his online diary on his own website devoted to his planned murder of Boyer, "It's accually [sic] obsene [sic] what you can find out about a person on the internet [sic]."[32]

Insurer Liability

The Boyer case spawned a second lawsuit, this time raising the issue of insurer liability. Insurers insure against risks, but what liability do they have *for the risks posed by dissemination of information*? Boyer's mother had sued Docusearch, who in turn requested a defense and indemnity from its insurer, Preferred National Insurance. In *Preferred National Insurance Co. v. Docusearch, Inc.*, Preferred filed a declaratory judgment action seeking a determination that the insurance policy it had issued to Docusearch did not provide coverage for this situation.[33] Preferred argued that under the policy it had no obligation to defend the company or pay any claims resulting from assault and battery. The New Hampshire Supreme Court found for Preferred on the issue of coverage for assault and battery but the court remanded the case for consideration as to whether coverage applied to the invasion of privacy and state Consumer Protection Act claims, leaving open the issue of under what circumstances an insurer may be liable for an insured's dissemination of a third-party's personal information.[34]

Voluntary Disclosure

Sometimes the greatest threat to privacy may come from the individual himself. Many people maintain personal websites, where they list many details of their lives, including names of family members and pets (a security risk since people often use children's and pets' names as their passwords), pictures of their home and children, their address, and details about their lives. All of this could subject them to identity thieves, stalkers, or sexual predators. Children often maintain their own websites, giving out their names, ages, addresses, interests, and schools attended, as well as publishing their photographs and even their student photo-ID cards. The rise of social networking websites aimed at students, such as Facebook and MySpace, are filled with minors routinely posting their cell phone numbers, school names, and other personal information, as well as sexually provocative pictures of themselves on these websites. (This issue is discussed further in Chapter 12). [35] Blogs are an especially delicate area, as bloggers often treat their blogs as personal online diaries, forgetting that they are potentially viewable by millions of people. Bloggers often write about the most intimate details of their lives, which may include details about friends and family members who do not know that their private lives are being exposed on the web. In deciding what to share with the world, one must balance the desire to share with the associated risks.

The Internet is forever; everything ever posted is cached on some hard drive somewhere. Deleting a website may not make a difference. The Internet Archive, also known as "The Wayback Machine," archives cached copies of 85 billion web pages dating back to 1996. [36] The frivolous night of drunken revelry with friends may years later be summoned like a ghost from the digital graveyard, becoming an embarrassment during a job interview or political campaign. It may not even take years, as conservative candidate Alan Keyes found out when after making anti-gay remarks during his U.S. Senate race, his daughter's blog about being a lesbian made headlines. [37]

Job Search Websites

The Internet has opened up many opportunities for job seekers by allowing them to post their résumés online for prospective employers to peruse. However, many do not realize that their online résumé containing their name, address, phone number, educational background, employment history, and other personal information could be floating in cyberspace for years to come, possibly attracting the attention of an identity thief. Using an online résumé, an identity thief can slip into the victim's skin as if he were slipping into a warm coat.

There are some steps a job seeker can take to avoid becoming a victim. Using initials in place of names, a post office box instead of a home address, and a temporary e-mail address in online résumés can limit a job seeker's exposure to identity theft. Also, birth dates should be left off online résumés, as they are essential personal information for identity thieves.

Conversely, the Internet *is* one's online résumé; employers are just as likely to "Google" an applicant's name and read his blogs and social network pages as intently if not more so than they read his résumé. One commentator has labelled such employer actions as "the institutionalized abuse of social network sites." [38]

Virtual Tour Websites

Many real estate websites have begun offering "virtual tours," which let prospective home buyers virtually "walk through" a home, using 360-degree panoramic imagery software. However, as with personal websites and online résumés, there is a risk in disclosing one's personal information online. Concerns have arisen that burglars may be using virtual tours to case homes, seeking out valuables and unsecured entry points. [39]

Social Networking Websites

Social networking websites (see Chapter 17) might best be described as the "Me Generation" meets the Internet. Each network consists of members with "profile pages," *i.e.*, a web page where the member can tell the whole world about "me." Indeed, the largest social network is aptly named "MySpace." But often members do not stop to consider that not only their friends, but the entire online world may be perusing the personal information they have placed on their profile pages.

Some of the personal information typically posted on profile pages include: first name, last name, city and state, home and/or cell phone numbers, e-mail address, IM user name, birth dates, age, gender, sexual orientation, name of school or employer, student class schedules, and names of friends, family, and pets. Then there are also photographs and often intimate and highly personal blogs and/or vlogs, as well as a list of network interest groups the individual has joined. One social network called Twitter is set up so users can constantly update their friends with a blurb on what they are doing at that instant (*e.g.*, "Jane is doing homework" or "Jack is taking a shower.")

The voluntary disclosure of such personal information creates a very public forum for everyday interactions, as well as very intense online ties because of the quick disclosure levels involved. That is, in effect, the essence of social networking: the unabashed disclosure of both personal data and intimate blog revelations enables complete strangers sharing the network to feel that they know each other. Many social network members have virtual "friends" whose lives they know all about and who know all the intimate details of their lives, but whom they have never met in person. Such friends are but "a mouse click away" — a distance measured in both time (the time it takes to click a mouse) and space (from around the corner to around the world).

Social networks then inherently engender a willingness to disclose personal information to complete strangers. One IT security firm study found that 41 percent of Facebook users eagerly disclosed personal identification to a bogus member "Freddi Staur" (an anagram for "ID fraudster") made up by the firm. The personal information they disclosed was sufficient to target spear-phishing e-mails, guess their passwords, pretend to be them, or even stalk them. [40]

Social networks can be a gold mine of personal data for stalkers, private investigators, or even defense attorneys. In a Connecticut case, a recent high school graduate sued a school superintendent for failing to protect her from the sexual advances of a volunteer basketball coach. The student filed an anonymous "Jane Doe" complaint, however the superintendent's attorney uncovered her identity by searching for the profiles of the high school's class of 2005 on MySpace, which is widely used by high school and college students. He found two profiles for her that included her true first and last names, seven photos of her, and an autobiographical reflection on her life. Armed with this information, the attorney filed a motion to reconsider her anonymous status, arguing that she had waived anonymity by voluntarily publicizing her name, image and the "circumstances of her case on an Internet website." Her attorney responded with motions for contempt and sanctions on the grounds that his motion had violated the standing "Jane Doe" order. The judge agreed and fined the superintendent's attorney $1,000 and ordered the motions that revealed the student's identity to be sealed and later replaced with redacted copies. The student's MySpace profiles were removed from the website.[41]

The rise of the Internet Generation has spawned a privacy generation gap. Members of the Internet Generation beginning college in 2007 were born in 1989. They grew up in, and cannot imagine a world without:

- Desktop computers

- Laptop computers

- 3-dimensional video games

- The World Wide Web

- E-mail

- Cell phones

- CDs and DVDs

- Portable media players

- PDAs

- Digital cameras

- Cable television

All of these recent technological innovations are prosaic to them, whereas older generations marvel at phones without cords, cameras without film, and television with more than three channels. Children of that generation went to the movies; kids in today's Internet Generation make their own movies and upload them for other kids to watch and critique. The older generation has a greater expectation of privacy and is surprised to discover the degree to which personal information is available online. The Internet Generation having grown up in an environment of friends armed with cell phone cameras and surrounded by closed circuit television cameras in stores and on streets, has developed a diminished expectation of privacy.

Members of the Internet Generation photograph each other at parties and then post the pictures on their websites (or social networks); members of the older generation might look askance at being photographed at a party and would probably feel their privacy had been violated upon finding the photo posted on a website (in fact, most probably would not even have a MySpace or Facebook page). Internet Generation members not only have a diminished expectation of privacy; they are self-proclaimed "attention whores" posting intimate photos, online diaries, and even attempts at poetry, having concluded that privacy in the modern world was already an illusion. Their generational icon is Paris Hilton, "blurring as she does the distinction between exposing oneself and being exposed. We live in a time in which humiliation and fame are not such easily distinguished quantities." [42]

By the time they reach college, today's grade schoolers will have become inured to an ever-diminishing expectation of privacy as they "graduate" from one social network to the next. The pre-teen set can network at *Club Penguin*; migrate to *Xanga* during junior high; switch to *MySpace* in high school; join the college crowd at *Facebook*; and after graduation, network with their peers at *LinkedIn*.

A parent on a social networking site should exercise caution in posting revealing information about children, such as names, photos of the children, and names of the school they attend. Social networking sites offer many benefits, but members must carefully consider the consequences of what they post, as often the greatest threat to privacy may come from the individual himself.

Non-U.S. Privacy Laws

Each state may have its own privacy laws. Also, the laws of foreign countries may apply in certain circumstances. Two major areas of foreign privacy laws are the Canadian Privacy Laws and the European Union Privacy Directive.

Canadian Privacy Laws

Canada has two federal privacy laws: the Privacy Act, and the Personal Information Protection and Electronic Documents Act (PIPEDA).

The *Canadian Privacy Act of 1983* protects personal information collected by the Canadian government.[43] It allows Canadians to access information collected about them and provides the means to challenge the accuracy of such information. The Privacy Commissioner of Canada, who has the authority to investigate complaints, oversees the Privacy Act.

PIPEDA applies to the collection, storage, and use of personal information by non-governmental organizations.[44] The Act requires businesses to inform consumers who is collecting the information, why the information is being collected, and the purposes for which it will be used. The Privacy Commissioner of Canada also oversees this Act. All organizations in Canada are required to designate an individual to handle privacy matters and complaints. The Act also applies to information collected, used, or disclosed by federally regulated agencies, such as telecommunications companies, ISPs, broadcasters, airlines, banks, and to provincially-regulated private-sector organizations, such as insurance companies and retail stores, unless the province has passed "substantially similar" legislation.[45] PIPEDA requires *consent* when collecting, using, or disclosing an individual's personal information. The business or website requesting the information must provide the *right to access* the personal information and challenge its accuracy. The use of the collected information is *limited* to the stated purpose for which it was collected and the scope of the consent that was given. If the business or website wishes to use the information collected for another purpose, PIPEDA requires that *additional consent* must be obtained. PIPEDA applies retroactively to information collected prior to the Act's passage.

The European Union Privacy Directive

The *European Union Directive on Data Protection* requires European Union member nations to implement national legislation to protect the privacy of individuals.[46] The European Union, as of January 2007, consisted of: Austria, Belgium, Bulgaria, Cyprus, the Czech Republic, Denmark, Estonia, Finland, France, Germany, Greece, Hungary, Ireland, Italy, Latvia, Lithuania, Luxembourg, Malta, the Netherlands, Poland, Portugal, Romania, Slovakia, Slovenia, Spain, Sweden, and the United Kingdom.

The Directive broadly defines personal data as any information relating to an individual. European law allows personal information to flow outside Europe only if there is an adequate level of protection in the receiving country. It prohibits the transfer of personal data to non-European Union countries that do not meet its "adequacy" standard for privacy protection. However, with regard to the United States, the European Commission has approved a "safe harbor" arrangement whereby companies and organizations in the United States can commit themselves to comply with a set of data protection principles and thus be deemed to meet the adequacy standard.

The differences between the European Union and the United States in their approaches to privacy stem from a fundamental difference in their conception of the role of government in society. In the European Union, privacy is a Fundamental Right *requiring* the government to pass comprehensive legislation to protect personal information; in the United States, the First Amendment *restricts* the government's ability to control the free flow of information (including personal information).

Anonymity on the Web and the Expectation of Privacy

Most web surfers sitting behind their computers view their monitors as a one-way screen. But can the websites they visit "see" them? Are they leaving behind clues to their own identities and could those clues be used at a later date to identify the web surfer? In many cases, the answer is yes. Many websites record the IP address of each visitor (an IP address is a unique number assigned to every end-user's computer to identify a user's geographic location). Some websites will acknowledge this in their website privacy policies (see Chapter 11) but others may not. Furthermore, the user's ISP routinely logs certain user activity. Most ISPs delete these logs after a few days, however there is a movement among lawmakers to require ISPs to retain such logs for years or even permanently. Does a subscriber have a reasonable expectation of privacy for his subscriber information held by his ISP? Does someone using a screen name in a chat room have a reasonable expectation of privacy?

ISP Subscriber Information

An ISP may be asked to reveal a subscriber's identity for several reasons, including to determine if the subscriber was accessing illegal websites (*i.e.*, obscene websites such as those displaying child pornography), stalking or harassing someone, or engaging in criminal or terrorist activities. An ISP may also be asked to reveal a subscriber's identity by the plaintiff in a civil suit, such as in a defamation action.

In a 2003 case, an anonymous harassing e-mail sent to a political campaign was turned over to the police, who filled out a search warrant (but did not get a judge to sign it) and presented the unsigned warrant to the ISP, demanding the sender's identity. The ISP (AOL) faxed the police the subscriber's name, address, phone numbers, account status, membership information, software information, billing and account information, and his other AOL screen names. A Connecticut federal court subsequently held[47] that AOL had violated the ECPA by releasing customer information that did not fall within the exceptions listed in the Act.[48] The case has been appealed to the 2nd Circuit Court of Appeals.[49]

Nonetheless, a New Haven, Connecticut superior court, in a motion to suppress evidence in 2006, ruled that by voluntarily giving subscriber information to the ISP, the subscriber had assumed the risk of the information being turned over to a third-party.[50] (Although it could be argued that by issuing each subscriber a screen name to mask his identity, the ISP was in fact creating an expectation of privacy). This case is not unique; in most cases where the issue of an Internet user's expectation of privacy in his subscriber information has arisen, courts have held there is no Fourth Amendment protection. Here, a university traced the IP address of a harassing e-mail sent to a student from his ex-girlfriend.[51] Pursuant to a search warrant, the police seized three computers from the ex-girlfriend's house. The ex-girlfriend filed a motion to suppress the evidence and a request to return the computers, but the court denied both, stating that "it is clear that the (plaintiffs) ceded any expectation of privacy in their underlying subscriber information, such as their residential address and other information, when they voluntarily entered into an agreement for (the ISP) to provide them with an Internet account servicing their home."[52]

Search Queries

Search engines *record and retain* every query in their logs. Not only do they retain the typed phrase, but also the date and time of the search and the IP address from which it was entered. They also store a cookie containing a unique identifier on the searcher's computer that can be used to identify subsequent searches by the user. (Even if the searcher logs on later with a different IP Address, the search engine will still be able to recognize the cookie identifier; to avoid this, the searcher must either delete the cookie or use another terminal). Depending on the firm, some companies' search engine will record other information, such as the type of browser; the native language; whether the search was for text, image, or video; and what links are clicked on the search results page.[53]

Armed with this data, a search firm could tell what phrases were searched from a specific IP address, or which IP addresses looked up certain phrases.

Imagine the U.S. government in the 1950s being able to print out a list of everyone who had expressed interest in the phrase "Communist Party."

Search phrases one enters into a search engine may reveal personal information about the individual, such as that he has a specific medical condition, is shopping for a divorce lawyer, is looking for a gay bar, or has kinky interests. Most people believe that what they type into a search engine cannot be connected to them personally; however, such data is logged by the search engine, even though search engine firms have neither the time, manpower, or inclination to spy on their users. The search firms usually strip out search terms that could be useful to their advertisers and subsequently delete old logs. But they do have the data and they know the IP address, which can be traced (by reverse DNS lookup) to the ISP who issued it to the user. Whether by subpoena or voluntarily, the ISP could reveal who, according to its logs, accessed the search engine at a specific time.

Likewise, if one is logged into an MSN or Yahoo! account and conducts a search in that firm's search engine, it might be possible for the firm to correlate its search log data with account registration form data previously entered by members.[54] Google offers its account holders a "web history" feature that allows members to "view and search across the full text of the pages you've visited, including Google searches, web pages, images, videos and news stories," which means users' web visits (not just searches) are being recorded and retained.[55] And the potential for correlating data will become enormous if and when Google's planned acquisition of DoubleClick goes through, as Google would be able to track its users Internet searches *and* their website visits!

Bush administration federal prosecutors in 2006 attempted to force major search engine firms to surrender logs that would reveal information about their customers' online Internet searches.[56] Google, Microsoft, Yahoo!, and America Online were subpoenaed and all but Google complied. The Bush administration then turned to a California federal court to force Google to comply with the subpoena. Google's log files record search terms used, websites visited, and the IP address and browser type of the computer for each search done through its website. While the information subpoenaed alone probably could not be used to identify a particular individual, the Bush administration claimed it needed the data about search patterns to bolster its case against anti-pornography filters. (The administration had been defending the constitutionally-challenged Child Online Protection Act [COPA, discussed further in Chapter 14] by arguing that criminal prohibitions are more effective than technological filtering methods and presumably wanted to use this data to support its claim.) Ultimately the federal court granted part of the administration's request for access to part of Google's index of websites but denied access to users' search queries.[57] The court stated its concerns about the "perception by the public that this is subject to government scrutiny" when people type search terms into Google.com but added that the government had demonstrated a "substantial need" for Google's random sampling data, although nonetheless admitting the government had been vague about its purposes for studying the URL sampling.[58]

Data Retention

As server space is limited, ISPs routinely delete log files they no longer need for business purposes (*e.g.*, network monitoring, fraud prevention, or billing disputes).[59] However, should a request be presented to an ISP from a law enforcement agency, the Electronic Communication Transactional Records Act of 1996 (ECTRA) requires ISPs to retain any "record" in their possession for 90 days "upon the request of a governmental entity."[60] Wanting to go further, in 2006 the Bush administration sought to require ISPs to record and save logs of their customers' online activities.[61] The proffered rationale for such a broad and invasive request stemmed from claims by law enforcement agencies that by the time they contact the ISPs, the customers' records may have been routinely deleted. Although the rationale suggests that only a small fraction of the customer records would belong to individuals under investigation by law enforcement, all of the ISPs' customer records would have to be retained, including the majority of "innocent" customers. The administration has also expressed interest in legislation that would require search engines to preserve logs.

A bill[62] proposed in 2007 would require ISPs to track customers' online activities (*e.g.*, Web browsing, instant message exchanges, and e-mail) to assist police investigations, with penalties of fines and imprisonment for noncompliance.[63] The Internet Stopping Adults Facilitating the Exploitation of Today's Youth Act of 2007 (SAFETY Act) would allow the U.S. Justice Department to order the companies to store those records forever.[64] It would also require, under threat of imprisonment, owners of sexually explicit websites to post warning labels. The irony of the proposed law (besides the fact that it bears the same name as a 2006 bill[65] sponsored by Rep. Mark Foley, who resigned from Congress that year after it was revealed he had sent sexually explicit instant messages to teenaged boys) is that by mandating indefinite storage of customer data, it would subject even more private individuals' data to potential breaches by hackers.

Data retention has been a topic of recent concern in Europe as well. The *European Union Data Retention Requirement*, scheduled to become effective in 2008, calls for communications providers in its member countries to retain subscriber data for at least six months and for no longer than two years. It applies to the identity of the individual contacted by the subscriber; the date, time, and length of phone calls and Internet logins; and e-mails (but content is not supposed to be retained).[66]

While most U.S. companies disclose their online data collection and retention practices in their website privacy policies (see Chapter 11), such privacy policies tend to be about notice, not control, as consumers rarely have a choice, other than to leave the website.[67] One concern, as pointed out above, is that the longer data is retained, the greater the risk of it being stolen or misused. As of 2007, Google (except for its Web History feature and any backup data) and Microsoft followed policies of removing identifying information from search logs after 18 months, while Yahoo! and AOL retained user data for 13 months.[68] Ask.com, the first search engine to address the issue of choice rather than control, stated it planned to offer users the option to block its search engine from recording search terms and IP addresses (although Ask's advertising partner Google would get and could keep the data).[69]

Whether voluntarily or by legislative decree, data retention means that companies will be storing large amounts of personal information about consumers. For example, the U.S. Treasury Department has proposed requiring Internet businesses to collect personal information about their customers and report it to the Internal Revenue Service (I.R.S.).[70] An entire underground economy has sprung up on the Internet as ever-increasing numbers of people make their primary or secondary income from selling items on auction websites like eBay and Amazon.com. The U.S. Treasury Department would like to get a bite of this unreported small business income, but to do so would require a list of all of the sellers and their Social Security numbers. The initial proposal would only affect sellers who make more than 100 separate transactions of $5,000 or more; however from an administrative standpoint, most websites would simply collect the personal data from all customers up-front. A Canadian court has already ruled that eBay Canada must turn over contact information and gross sales data for high-volume sellers based in Canada to the Canada Revenue Agency, even though the customer data is stored servers in San Jose, Calfornia and owned by the parent company eBay. However, the court noted: "The information can be summoned up in Canada and for the usual business purposes of eBay Canada. The situation may be different if the information never had been used in Canada."[71] Imagine a database with the names, addresses, and Social Security numbers of every eBay seller — a hacker or phisher's dream!

The flip side of data retention is the risk of data breaches by hackers. From our previous discussions of identity theft and phishing, you realize that such a database, holding as it does the keys to one's identity, is a virtual treasure trove for identity thieves. But rather than being housed in Fort Knox, the data is often kept in the equivalent of a cardboard shoebox on a shelf. Identity thieves function technologically at state-of-the-art level, while most businesses are ill-equipped to provide adequate security for such data (witness the large number of data breeches in major corporations frequently reported in the news). Small businesses are even less equipped to protect such data adequately. Perhaps the government should mandate set periods for data destruction instead of data retention if it is truly interested in protecting its citizens. [72]

Expectation of Privacy in Chat

An Internet "*chat room*," is a web page which, using chat software, can display typed messages in *real time*. This differs from a *message board* or *forum* where messages are posted on a page and maintained in static form for an indefinite period, often even permanently archived and searchable. In chat, messages scroll down the page and eventually disappear from view. When several people are logged on to the same chat page, each person can type brief messages, often with standardized abbreviations or emoticons (*e.g.*, smiley faces), onto the page. Each message, as well as replies from others in the chat room, are immediately visible to all the participants as sequential lines beginning with the identification of the author, usually a nickname or "screen name" created especially for the chat session.

Obviously, since everyone logged onto the page can view the "conversation," there is *no expectation of privacy in a public chat room*. Additionally, anyone can print out a transcript of the chat or save it to a file. The chat room conversation may also be logged and archived by the chat website, or any participant.

Another feature of chat is the private message (PM) or instant message (IM), which allows private messages to be exchanged between two parties. The parties may carry on a private side text conversation between themselves while still in the main chat room, but they do not necessarily need to be in a chat room to use the IM function. Each party knows that only the other party can see what he types in the IM. Does this fact create an expectation of privacy for IMs? What if one party copies the IM conversation and pastes it into the main chat room? Or what if one party saves the IM conversation to a file and later e-mails it to a third-party? Or what if law enforcement authorities use special electronic eavesdropping software to read an IM sent from one person to another?

One attorney argued that a chat room transcript should not be admitted into evidence because it was an *illegal eavesdropping* by police. The particular state (Illinois) law defined eavesdropping as "using any device capable of retaining or transcribing conversations or electronic communications without the consent of all parties involved in the communication." The attorney argued that the police computer was a device capable of retaining or transcribing electronic communication. The case involved 43-year-old lawyer who had arranged through chat conversations to meet a 14-year-old girl for sex. [73] However, the 14-year-old girl was, in reality, an undercover police officer. Police had created the imaginary girl's Internet profile using a picture of a real 14-year-old girl who had participated in the police department's Explorers youth program and had agreed to have her picture used. As the defendant ultimately ended up pleading no contest to the charges in a plea arrangement to avoid serving prison time, the issue of illegal eavesdropping was never ruled on by a court; however, it remains a viable legal argument.

In fact, in 2004, a New Hampshire judge threw out chat log evidence against an accused pedophile.[74] In a fact pattern similar to the Illinois case above, a police officer logged onto a chat room disguised as a 14-year-old girl. A man in the chat room then solicited the "girl" for sex. A police detective used screen capture software to create a record of the chat session. The defense filed a motion to suppress the results of the recorded conversation as a violation of the New Hampshire wiretap statute.[75] New Hampshire law requires that all parties to a conversation *consent* before the conversation can be intercepted or recorded. The court held that the chat log was an unlawful wiretap and could not be admitted into evidence. Note that it was perfectly legal for the detective to pose as a 14-year-old girl and chat with the suspect; U.S. law allows law enforcement agents to deceive, defraud, and lie in criminal investigations.[76] Where the detective ran afoul of the law was in recording the chat without the consent of the other party (the suspect). The decision, the first of its kind to apply that standard to online chats, struck down a technique routinely used by law enforcement, employers, and ISPs. Like New Hampshire, the states of California, Connecticut, Delaware, Florida, Illinois, Maryland, Massachusetts, Michigan, Montana, New Hampshire Pennsylvania, and Washington, require *all* parties to the communication to consent to a recording before it is legal.

However, in Washington, a court allowed a chat transcript to be admitted as evidence in a case where a man solicited a "girl" who was in reality an undercover detective.[77] The detective created the identity of "Amber," a 13-year-old girl with a Hotmail e-mail account and a chat room screen name "ambergirl87." A 26-year-old man was approached by the detective in a chat room and, after a series of e-mails and chat conversations, agreed to meet "Amber" at a local hotel, whereupon he was charged with attempted rape of a minor and other crimes. The difference here was that the chat software used, a program called ICQ, had a *default setting* to make a permanent record of the conversation. The appellate court noted that ICQ expressly advised users that: "Some versions of the software allow any party to an ICQ session to record the content of the session (messages, chat, URL, chat request, and other events). The ICQ program default in some versions is set to record message and other event dialog and traffic."[78] Using a combination of *imputed knowledge* and *implied consent*, the court reasoned that the defendant should have known about the default setting, and thus effectively consented to the making of the recording under Washington's "both party" consent statute. "By using the ICQ client–to–client communications, Mr. Townsend impliedly consented to recording of the communications by the intended recipient."[79] The appellate court ruled that the e-mail and ICQ messages were private communications protected by the Washington Privacy Act but that "because Mr. Townsend impliedly consented to the recording of the messages, there was no violation. The trial court correctly concluded the messages were admissible." [80]

Imputing knowledge of all of the features of a software program may be a large leap for a court to make. In this case, the default setting was to archive all conversations. What if the chat software has archiving capability but the default is set to not archive? Does the mere presence of archiving capability within the software eliminate any reasonable expectation of privacy and imply consent to recording of the conversation? If so, how is that different from knowledge of the existence of external tools, like screen capture software, which can be used to record IM conversations?

One common feature in the three cases above was that all of the defendants were charged with using Internet chat to solicit sex from minors who were in reality not minors but actually police officers. This raises the interesting issue of whether one can be charged with a crime against a minor when there is no minor involved. While some might consider such a scenario to be a form of entrapment, some courts have focused on the *mens rea* or "state of mind" of the defendant. Those courts look at whether the defendant had a guilty mind and took steps toward bringing the criminal act about, such as showing up at an agreed upon location to meet the "minor." For example, in 2006 the Connecticut Supreme Court upheld a man's attempted sexual assault conviction after a detective posed as a 13-year-old girl on the Internet in a police sting operation. He had arranged a meeting with what he believed was a 13-year-old girl in a chat room but "Danuta333" was really a police officer who arrested him when he showed up to meet the non-existent girl at a local shopping mall. [81]

Even the use of a commercial spyware program may be deemed to be an illegal "wiretap." [82] A woman was convicted of violating Florida's wiretapping statute after she installed a spyware program on her husband's computer to catch him chatting with his lover. [83] The court found that she had "intercepted the electronic communication contemporaneously with transmission" in contravention of the state's wiretap act when she obtained the online chat records of a Yahoo! Dominoes chat game between her husband and his lover. Further adding to the wife's troubles, the court also ruled that she could not reveal or use the illegally obtained conversations in the couple's pending divorce case.

Expectation of Privacy in E-Mail: Love Me Do

Does volunteering your personal information in a private context waive your privacy rights? This was the issue raised when a man posted a raunchy sex classified ad on Craigslist. com, an Internet-based classifieds page. Pretending to be a submissive 27-year-old woman seeking a dominant man to humiliate and abuse her, the poster — a 30-year-old male graphic designer from Seattle, Washington — collected the replies and posted them on Encyclopedia Dramatica, a website devoted to parodies and satires online.[84] The result: 178 responses with 145 photos of men, including nude photographs of the respondents and their genitalia, their names, e-mail addresses, phone numbers, IM accounts, and other contact information.[85] He also collected voice message and posted them as well. Most of the responses contained detailed descriptions of deviant sex acts. At least one respondent wrote "I'm married and looking to fill the needs not being done at home," followed by his name, cell phone number, e-mail, and four photographs.[86] How long before someone recognized him and tipped off his wife is open to speculation, but the potential harm the respondents could suffer from public exposure of what they believed to be private communications is evident.

The only redeeming feature of this otherwise grotesque prank is that rather than targeting love-sick singles seeking romance online, the perpetrator went bottom-fishing on the Internet, trawling for the type of losers who would respond to an ad that said, in part: "i am looking 4 a white or Latin only, str8 brutal dom muscular male 30-35 yo who is arrogant, self-centered, nasty, egotistic, sadistic who likes 2 give intense pain and discipline … it drives me krazy 2 get … , cuffed, … spanked with welts and bruises … i have a leg spreader, crop, cane and metal cuffs. spit on me, verbally abuse…" (the rest of the ad was too explicit to quote here) accompanied by a photograph of a woman bent over, her jeans pulled down, spreading her bare posterior.[87]

Craigslist said the perpetrator's actions violated the its Terms of Use policies.[88] Craigslist itself is protected under the CDA § 230, which protects service providers from liability for postings by their users. The perpetrator, who having already achieved his desired 15 minutes of fame need not be further identified here, might possibly be subject to civil liability for *invasion of privacy*. As discussed at the start of this chapter, one form of invasion of privacy is the tort known as *public disclosure of private facts*. The elements of this tort are: (1) the disclosure must be public, (2) the facts must be private, (3) the plaintiff must be identified, (4) the publication must be "highly offensive," and (5) there must be an "absence of legitimate concern to the public" with respect to the publication.[89] This is an example of a situation where all of the elements for this particular invasion of privacy tort appear to have been met.

Expectation of Privacy in E-Mail: 'Til Death Do Us Part

Most ISPs, absent a court order, will vigorously protect their subscribers' privacy. This, of course, makes sense. The subscriber is the ISP's customer and it is bad business to divulge a customer's private matters to third parties. Few customers would remain with an ISP that routinely disclosed customer e-mails and files to anyone who asked. Therefore there is an expectation of privacy and non-disclosure, either implied or often expressed in the service contracts with ISPs.

But what if the customer dies? What happens to the customer data (*e.g.*, e-mail or files) residing on the ISP's server? Can or should the ISP delete the data to protect the deceased customer's privacy? Or can or should the ISP turn over the data to an estate administrator or spouse or other family member? And if so, what constitutes a family member for this purpose (*e.g.*, a child, a parent, a cousin, an unmarried common-law spouse, or a homosexual partner)? Who decides where the line is drawn? Do the digital data become part of the deceased's estate, giving his heirs a property right in the data? Or are the data subject to the terms of the contract the decedent entered into with the ISP?

In November 2004, 20-year-old Marine Lance Cpl. Justin Ellsworth was killed by a roadside bomb in Falluja, Iraq. Adhering to the Marines' system of returning personal items to families and next-of-kin, the Ellsworth family would receive Justin's possessions at the time of his death, including any personal possessions he had left behind at Camp Pendleton, California before shipping out to Iraq. All letters destined for mail are sent to their recipients and received mail, including opened letters, are sent to the families. Since the government does not provide e-mail accounts to soldiers on the front line many, like Justin, use commercial ISPs like AOL, MSN, or Yahoo! for their e-mail. [90] Justin had a Yahoo! e-mail account. Justin's father sought access to his late son's e-mail account but did not know Justin's password. Yahoo! refused to reveal Justin's password to his father, citing its privacy policy in its "Terms of Use" agreement with Justin. [91] Yahoo! also has a policy of deleting e-mail accounts after 90 days of inactivity. This created a public relations nightmare for Yahoo!, which was in the position of publicly announcing its intention to delete the last words of a dying son without allowing a mourning father to read them first. Yahoo! justified its position by saying that it was protecting the privacy rights of the deceased and those with whom he corresponded. Yahoo!'s position is understandable. The senders of e-mail in Justin's account believed their mail would only be read by Justin; should not their privacy interests be protected? Conversely, Justin wrote e-mails to the intended recipients of those e-mails residing in his account with the expectation that his words were meant to be read only by those intended recipients. Suppose there was something within those e-mails that he did not want anyone else, even his family, to see? Should not his privacy interests be respected and protected? Indeed, Yahoo! might well respond that if Justin had wanted his father to read his mail then he would have previously forwarded it to him. On the other hand, soldiers killed in action might have important information in their e-mail accounts that could assist their families in resolving personal matters.

Thus the issue becomes one of balancing the privacy interests of the decedent and his correspondents with the presumed property interest of the decedent's family or heirs. On an episode of the TV series "*Married With Children*," Peggy Bundy asked her husband Al "What are you thinking?" to which he replied "If I wanted you to know what I was thinking, I'd be talking." Or to paraphrase, if I wanted you to read my e-mail/files, etc., I would have sent them to you (or provided you with the password or other access). Would the average person want his parents to read his e-mail correspondence or diary? Perhaps a decedent would want his or her gay lover to have access to the account; on the other hand, the same decedent might not want a parent or child to see messages relating to his or her heretofore unrevealed lifestyle. Also at risk would be the privacy of third parties discussed in the e-mails. The easiest solution would be for subscribers to share their passwords with those individuals they wish to have access (perhaps leave the password in a safe deposit box with a will and other testamentary papers) and for ISPs to have clear, stated policies on the matter. AOL, for example, permits next-of-kin to access e-mail accounts upon submitting documents proving the relationship and faxing a copy of the death certificate.[92] ISPs could ask subscribers to designate an "account beneficiary" to be allowed access to the account in the event of the subscriber's death, similar to naming a beneficiary on an insurance policy.

In the Ellsworth case, Yahoo!'s "Terms of Use" agreement contained a clause that read: "You agree that your Yahoo! account is non-transferable and any rights to your … contents … terminate upon your death." Setting aside the emotional impact of the situation, from a legal standpoint this would appear to support Yahoo!'s refusal to release the contents of the account.[93] However, in April 2005, an Oakland County, California probate judge ordered Yahoo! to turn over the contents of the e-mail account to Ellsworth's parents.[94] Yahoo! gave the family a CD with more than 10,000 pages of material (presumably a large amount of undeleted spam the account had received) and a hard copy printout. Yahoo! chose not to appeal the ruling, presumably grateful for the opportunity to end the negative publicity while remaining true to its policy to protect user privacy (unless compelled by court order), leaving the legal status of the issue unsettled.

Spyware

Although detailed at greater length in Chapter Eight in the discussion of cyber crimes, spyware deserves mention here as well, as it is an obvious invasion of privacy. Online advertisers in concert with certain file-sharing networks have placed programs on users' computers to monitor their activity or to use their computers' processors for other purposes. Many users are frequently *unaware* that they are being monitored for commercial purposes. Though some spyware may violate communications and computer trespass laws, many programs are *protected by agreements* buried in long, detailed disclosures that users click on when they download other programs. Besides being intrusive and an invasion of privacy, spyware can crash computers or slow down their performance and is often difficult to find and remove.

Terrorism Information Awareness Project

In 2003, to the relief of privacy advocates, the U.S. House of Representatives eliminated funding for the Terrorism Information Awareness Project, effectively ending the controversial Pentagon anti-terrorism plan. The project sought to compile computerized dossiers on American citizens. If fully implemented, the Terrorism Information Awareness Project would have linked databases from *credit card companies, medical insurers, and motor vehicle departments* for law enforcement purposes to track terrorists, making it perhaps the greatest governmental invasion of privacy to date.

Summary

The Right of Privacy is not explicitly stated anywhere within the U.S. Constitution. It is a derived right inferred from the Fourth Amendment guarantees against unreasonable search and seizures. The four distinct categories of the tort of invasion of privacy, each based on different elements, are: appropriation of name or likeness, intrusion, public disclosure of private facts, and false light in the public eye. Appropriation involves the use of an individual's name, likeness, or identity for trade or advertising purposes without consent. It is also inversely referred to as the "Right of Publicity," a right to prevent the use of one's identifiable name or likeness by a third party for commercial purposes without consent. Intrusion involves intruding on one's solitude or seclusion, either physically or by electronic means. Public disclosure of private facts involves the publication of private and embarrassing facts that are not related to matters of public concern. False light involves a statement that is false or misleading, and highly offensive (but not necessarily defamatory) and creates a false impression about the plaintiff in the public eye. Unlike defamation actions, truth is not a defense in invasion of privacy actions.

Although there are no general federal privacy laws, some federal laws protect certain aspects of an individual's right to privacy, including the Video Privacy Protection Act of 1988, the Fair Credit Reporting Act of 1970, the Electronic Communications Privacy Act of 1986, the Gramm-Leach-Bliley Act of 1999, and the Health Insurance Portability and Accountability Act of 1996. The Federal Trade Commission polices collection and use of personal information over the Internet through its authority over "unfair" or "deceptive" commercial practices pursuant to § 5 of the F.T.C. Act.

People often voluntarily disclose much personal information on home pages, blogs, résumés posted on job search websites, through virtual tours of their homes, and on social network profile pages. Bloggers often write about the most intimate details of their lives, which may include details about friends and family members who do not know that their private lives are being exposed on the web.

Online information brokers deal in supplying personal information about individuals to the general public. One court held that the threats posed by stalking and identity theft make the risk of criminal misconduct sufficiently foreseeable to impose on information brokers a duty of reasonable care in disclosing a third person's personal information to a client.

ISP routinely logs certain user activity. Most ISPs delete these logs after a few days, However, should a request be presented to an ISP from a law enforcement agency, the Electronic Communication Transactional Records Act of 1996 requires ISPs to retain any "record" in their possession for 90 days "upon the request of a governmental entity." There is a movement among lawmakers to require ISPs to retain such logs for years. Search engines record and retain every query in their logs. Armed with this data, a search firm could tell what phrases were searched from a specific IP address, or which IP addresses looked up certain phrases. Search phrases entered into a search engine may reveal personal information about the individual.

Data retention policies tend to be about notice, not control. The longer data is retained, the greater the risk of it being stolen or misused.

In most cases where the issue of an Internet user's expectation of privacy in his subscriber information has arisen, courts have held there is no Fourth Amendment protection. In cases where defendants were charged with using Internet chat to solicit sex from minors who were in reality police officers, courts have focused on the *mens rea* or "state of mind" of the defendant — whether the defendant had a guilty mind and took steps toward bringing the criminal act about, such as showing up at an agreed upon location to meet the "minor."

Canada has two federal privacy laws: the Privacy Act and the Personal Information Protection and Electronic Documents Act. The European Union Directive on Data Protection requires European Union member nations to implement national legislation to protect the privacy of individuals. The differences between the European Union and the United States in their approaches to privacy stem from a fundamental difference in their conception of the role of government in society. In the European Union, privacy is a Fundamental Right requiring the government to pass comprehensive legislation to protect personal information; in the United States, the First Amendment limits the government's ability to regulate the flow of information (including personal data).

Chapter Ten Notes

[1] *Roberson v. Rochester Folding-Box Co.*, 171 N.Y. 538, 64 N.E. 442 (1902).

[2] *Pavesich v. New England Life Ins. Co.*, 122 Ga. 190, 50 S.E. 68 (1905).

[3] Prosser, Restatement (Second) of Torts, §§ 652A-652I.

[4] Many people may share the same name, but identity is unique. A VCR manufacturer ran a TV ad showing a blonde robot flipping over cards on a game show; Vanna White, the blonde star of the game show "*Wheel of Fortune*," claimed it was her likeness and won her appropriation suit, as flipping over cards on a game show *was* her identity! *White v. Samsung Elecs. of America, Inc.*, (9th Cir. 1992).

[5] *Kirby v. Sega of America*, Case No. B183820 (Cal. 2nd Ct. App. Sept. 25, 2006)(Unpublished).

[6] *Doe a/k/a Tony Twist, v. TCI Cablevision*, 110 S.W.3d 363 (Mo. 2003); verdict *aff'd on appeal*, *John Doe a/k/a Tony Twist v. McFarlane*, Case No. ED 85283 (E.D. Mo. App. 2006).

[7] *Winter v. DC Comics*, 30 Cal. 4th 881 (2003).

[8] *Ibid.*

[9] *Daily Times Democrat v. Graham*, 276 Ala. 380 (1964).

[10] Miguel Helft, "Google Zooms In Too Close for Some," New York Times, June 1, 2007.

[11] LaudonTech's Google Street View Sightings Website, *available at* http://streetviewgallery.corank.com (accessed September 25, 2007).

[12] "Eye Spy," The Chandler Times, Phoenix, AZ, 2007. Ironically, the ad was visible on Google Street Views.

[13] Carly Weeks, "Street View Blurred by Canadian Privacy Concerns," CanWest News Service, September 24, 2007.

[14] Other than the Federal Privacy Act, 5 U.S.C. § 552a, which protects individuals by regulating when and how local, state, and federal governments and their agencies can request that individuals disclose their Social Security numbers.

[15] Video Privacy Protection Act, 18 U.S.C. § 2710 *et seq.*, *see* Electronic Privacy Information Center, *available at* www.epic.org/privacy/vppa/ (accessed September 25, 2007) for general overview of the Act and Cornell University Law School, *available at* http://www4.law.cornell.edu/uscode/html/uscode18/usc_sec_18_00002710----000-.html (accessed September 25, 2007) for text of the Act.

[16] Fair Credit Reporting Act, 15 U.S.C. § 1681 *et seq.*, *available at* www.epic.org/privacy/fcra/ (accessed September 25, 2007) for general overview of the Act and F.T.C. website, *available at* www.ftc.gov/os/statutes/fcra.htm (accessed September 25, 20076) for text of the Act.

[17] Electronic Communications Privacy Act, 18 U.S.C. § 2510, *et seq.*

[18] Gramm-Leach-Bliley Act, 15 U.S.C., Subchapter I, § 6801-6809.

[19] Health Insurance Portability and Accountability Act, 42 U.S.C. § 300gg and 29 U.S.C. § 1181 *et seq.*

[20] Click-wrap agreements are discussed further in Chapter 15.

[21] Douglas Adams, "*The Hitchhiker's Guide to the Galaxy.*"

[22] This is particularly important in a lawsuit where an individual may be suing a corporation with vast financial resources.

[23] Such as adoption records or other records concerning children, probate estate inventories, or records with personal financial data or Social Security numbers, for example.

[24] "Public Debates Online Access," Florida Bar News, December 15, 2004.

[25] Forrest Norman, "Florida Dept. of Law Enforcement Sued over Online Access to Juvenile Arrest Data," Daily Business Review, January 10, 2007.

[26] Florida Statutes § 985.04(2) makes juvenile criminal records confidential unless the minor is arrested on a felony or has three or more misdemeanors.

[27] Cathy Corry, "We've Been Duped! — Juvenile Arrest Records Not Confidential…," Justice4Kids.org, April 29, 2005, available at http://www.justice4kids.org/duped.htm (accessed September 25, 2007).

[28] Forrest Norman, fn. 25, supra.

[29] "Courts Keeping Records off Web to Shield Informants," Associated Press wire report, July 25, 2007.

[30] Remsburg v. Docusearch, Inc., 816 A.2d 1001 (N.H. Feb. 18, 2003). This case is included in the Cases Section on the Issues in Internet Law website (www.IssuesinInternetLaw.com).

[31] Since Youens knew where Boyer lived and had been stalking her for years, it is questionable how much of a factor the release of information by Docusearch was in her murder, since Youens could easily have followed her to or from work.

[32] www.amyboyer.org/mind.htm; this was a replica of Youens' website, displayed by Boyer's family to raise awareness of the circumstances surrounding their daughter's murder. As of September 21, 2005, the website was no longer accessible.

[33] Preferred Nat'l. Ins. Co. v. Docusearch, Inc., Case No. 2002-729 (N.H. Aug. 19, 2003). This case is included in the Cases Section on the Issues in Internet Law website (www.IssuesinInternetLaw.com).

[34] After the court dismissed the claim for damages based on assault and battery, Boyer's family and Docusearch settled their lawsuit for $85,000 in March 2004.

[35] Janet Kornblum, "Social Websites Scrutinized," USA Today, February 12, 2006.

[36] Available at www.archive.org/web/web.php. The "Wayback Machine" is a reference to the time machine used by cartoon characters Sherman and Mr. Peabody (the talking dog) in the classic TV cartoon "The Rocky and Bullwinkle Show."

[37] "Blog It Now, Regret It Later? Public Entries Intended for Friends Could Have Repercussions Later," Associated Press wire report, July 10, 2005.

[38] Helen A.S. Popkin, "Friends Don't Let Friends Join MySpace: Posting on Networking Sites is Like a Tattoo — Only Worse," MSNBC, May 16, 2007.

[39] David Lazarus, "Web Tours A Boon for Burglars," San Francisco Chronicle, June 3, 2005.

[40] Nicholas Carlson, "Report: Facebook Users Loose with the Info," Internet.com, August 14, 2007.

[41] Thomas B. Scheffey, "'Jane Doe' Status is Not Compromised by MySpace Postings," Connecticut Law Tribune, October 18, 2006.

[42] Emily Nussbaum, "Kids, the Internet, and the End of Privacy: The Greatest Generation Gap Since Rock and Roll," New York Magazine, February 12, 2007.

[43] Privacy Act (R.S. 1985, c. P-21) available at http://laws.justice.gc.ca/en/P-21/index.html (accessed September 25, 2007).

[44] Personal Information Protection and Electronic Documents Act (2000, c. 5) available at http://laws.justice.gc.ca/en/P-8.6/index.html (accessed September 25, 2007).

[45] As of this book's publication, Quebec is the only province that has been deemed to have met this standard.

[46] Directive 95/46/EC of the European Parliament and of the Council of 24 October 1995 on the protection

of individuals with regard to the processing of personal data and on the free movement of such data, Center for Democracy and Technology, *available at* http://eur-lex.europa.eu/smartapi/cgi/sga_doc?smartapi!celexapi!prod!C ELEXnumdoc&lg=EN&numdoc=31995L0046&model=guichett (accessed September 25, 2007).

[47] *Freedman v. AOL, Inc.*, 303 F. Supp. 2d 745 (D. Conn. 2004).

[48] Electronic Communications Privacy Act, fn. 17, *supra*. Exceptions to the Act are listed in §§ 2702-2703.

[49] Lisa Siegel, "Online Service Provider Rats Out User," The Connecticut Law Tribune, January 25, 2006.

[50] *Ibid.*

[51] *Ibid.*

[52] *Ibid.*

[53] "Mary Brandel, "What Search Engines Store About You," Computerworld, July 10, 2007.

[54] *Ibid.*

[55] Google Web History page, *available at* https://www.google.com/accounts/ServiceLogin?hl=en&continue=htt p://www.google.com/history%3Fhl%3Den&nui=1&service=hist (accessed September 25, 2007).

[56] Declan McCullagh and Elinor Mills, "Feds Take Porn Fight to Google," CNET News.com, January 19, 2006.

[57] Anne Broache, "Judge: Google Must Give Feds Limited Access to Records," CNET News.com, March 17, 2006.

[58] *Ibid.*

[59] Google retains search data for a certain period to assist in improving services and fighting computer attacks and fraud, however the search engine has refused to disclose the length of time that it typically retains such data. *See* Anick Jesdanun, "Control Over Online Data Rests with Companies — Consumers' Only Option for Privacy is Often Logging Off," Associated Press wire report, October 16, 2006.

[60] Electronic Communication Transactional Records Act, 18 U.S.C. § 2703 (f).

[61] Anick Jesdanun, fn. 59, *supra*.

[62] A bill must be passed by both the House and Senate and then be signed by the president before it becomes law. At the end of each session, any bills not passed into law are cleared from the books.

[63] Declan McCullagh, "GOP Revives ISP-tracking Legislation," CNET News.com, February 6, 2007, and Beth Pariseau, "ISPs Fear SAFETY Act Retention Requirements," SearchStorage.com, March 2007.

[64] H.R. 837 [110th Congress]: Internet Stopping Adults Facilitating the Exploitation of Today's Youth Act (SAFETY) of 2007, introduced on February 6, 2007 by Rep. Lamar Smith [R-TX].

[65] H.R. 5749 [109th Congress]: Internet Stopping Adults Facilitating the Exploitation of Today's Youth Act (SAFETY) of 2006, introduced on July 10, 2006 by Rep. Mark Foley [R-FL].

[66] Directive on Mandatory Retention of Communications Traffic Data: Directive 2006/24/EC of the European Parliament and of the Council of 15 March 2006 on the retention of data generated or processed in connection with the provision of publicly available electronic communications services or of public communications networks and amending Directive 2002/58/EC, *available at* http://eur-lex.europa.eu/ LexUriServ/LexUriServ.do?uri=CELEX:32006L0024:EN:NOT (accessed September 25, 2007).

[67] Anick Jesdanun, fn. 59, *supra*.

[68] Catherine Rampell, "Google Calls for International Standards on Internet Privacy," Washington Post, September 15, 2007, p. D01.

[69] "Search Engine Ask to Stop Keeping Search Data Upon Request," Associated Press wire report, July 20, 2007.

[70] Jaikumar Vijayan, "IRS Wants Data on Users from Internet Firms," Computerworld, May 08, 2007.

[71] Ian Austen, "Canadian Court Opens Up eBay Data to Tax Agency," New York Times, October 1, 2007.

[72] In 2006, Rep. Edward Markey [D-MA] sponsored a bill, H.R. 4731 [109th Congress]: Eliminate Warehousing of Consumer Internet Data Act of 2006, that proposed mandating that website owners destroy obsolete personally identifiable data such as credit card numbers, bank numbers, and date of birth, home address, and Social Security numbers. The bill did not become a law.

[73] "Legality of Internet-Based Arrest Draws Challenge," Belleville News Democrat, March 10, 2004.

[74] Mark Rasch, "Chat, Copy, Paste, Prison," Security Focus, April 12, 2004, *available at* www.securityfocus.com/columnists/233 (accessed September 25, 2007).

[75] New Hampshire Revised Statutes Chap. 570-A: Wiretapping and Eavesdropping.

[76] Law enforcement officers routinely pose as minors in chat rooms to arrest potential sex offenders, however Maryland's supreme court (known as the Maryland Court of Appeals) has unanimously held that an individual could not be found guilty of committing a crime with a non-existent victim (*i.e.*, a "minor" who in reality is a legal adult). *See* Fredrick Kunkle, "Court Overturns Child Porn Conviction — MD Ruling Squelches Tactic Used to Find Potential Molesters," Washington Post," September 8, 2005, p. B02.

[77] *State v. Townsend*, Case No. 19304-7-III, (Slip Op., Apr. 5, 2001), Keene, New Hampshire city website, *available at* www.ci.keene.nh.us/police/Townsend.html (accessed September 25, 2007).

[78] *Ibid.*

[79] *Ibid.*

[80] *Ibid.*

[81] Belinda Yu, "Connecticut Rules Against Internet Sex Predator," Reuters wire report, February 2, 2006.

[82] However, at least one federal court in California has held that keystroke logging devices do not violate the federal Wiretap Act, since there is not necessarily any "transmission in interstate commerce" when keystrokes are logged. *United States v. Ropp*, Cr. 04-3000-GAF (C.D. Cal. Oct. 8, 2004). In that case, allegedly attempting to collect evidence of his employer's wrong-doing, a disgruntled employee installed a keystroke logging device on a cable connecting his employer's computer to the keyboard. Prosecutors had argued that the Wiretap Act was applicable since outgoing e-mails were also logged by the device.

[83] Lester Haines, "Cheated Wife on Spyware Wiretap Rap," The Register, February 16, 2005.

[84] *Available at* www.encyclopediadramatica.com (accessed September 25, 2007).

[85] Anick Jesdanun, "Legal Concerns Raised Over Exposing Replies to Online Sex Ad," Associated Press wire report, September 12, 2006.

[86] *Available at* www.encyclopediadramatica.com/index.php/RFJason_CL_Experiment#From_small_prank_to_huge_debate (accessed September 25, 2007).

[87] *Ibid.*

[88] Craigslist's Terms of Use policies include the following provisions:

You agree not to post, email, or otherwise make available Content:

a) that is unlawful, harmful, threatening, abusive, harassing, defamatory, libelous, invasive of another's privacy, or is harmful to minors in any way;

b) that is pornographic or depicts a human being engaged in actual sexual conduct including but not limited to (i) sexual intercourse, including genital-genital, oral-genital, anal-genital, or oral-anal, whether between persons of the same or opposite sex, or (ii) bestiality, or (iii) masturbation, or (iv) sadistic or masochistic abuse, or (v) lascivious exhibition of the genitals or pubic area of any person;

***

h) that includes personal or identifying information about another person without that person's explicit consent;

i) that is false, deceptive, misleading, deceitful, misinformative, or constitutes "bait and switch";

***

t) collect personal data about other users for commercial or unlawful purposes;

see www.craigslist.org/about/terms.of.use.html (accessed September 25, 2007).

[89] Restatement (Second) of Torts § 625e (1977).

[90] Only officers outside the front lines are issued official Marine e-mail accounts. If the officer is killed, the Marines delete the accounts after retrieving military-related messages. *See* Jim Hu, "Yahoo! Denies Family Access to Dead Marine's E-mail," CNET News.com, December 21, 2004.

[91] Yahoo!'s policy is to turn over the account to family members only after they go through the courts to verify their identity and relationship with the deceased. *Ibid.* However, Yahoo!'s policy of deleting inactive accounts after 90 days might result in the account and all the e-mails being deleted before the matter could reach a judge.

[92] Earthlink and Microsoft's MSN Hotmail have similar policies.

[93] The Ellsworth case is not unique. Parents of the late Marine Corps reservist Karl Linn complained that ISP Mailbank.com, Inc. would not release their son's digital data after his death. Mailbank, like Yahoo!, cited the privacy interests of its clients as the reason for its refusal. The family of Army Spec. Michael J. Smith met with the same resistance when trying to obtain private portions of their late son's online journal on LiveJournal.com. Ariana Eunjung Cha, "After Death, A Struggle For Their Digital Memories," Washington Post, February 3, 2005.

[94] "Yahoo! Provides Family with E-mail Account of Marine Killed in Iraq," Associated Press wire report, April 21, 2005.

Chapter Ten Quiz

ClassmateFinders.com is a website where people set up accounts entering their name, address, age, e-mail address, schools attended, occupation, employer, and other personal information about themselves, their lives and their families, hoping to reconnect with former classmates and friends. The website charges a $25 fee to open an account and while it has a form requesting certain information it also contains blank spaces for the individual to enter any additional information he chooses to add. Any member can read any other member's account profile. Hannah Hottie listed her name, address, employer, and a history of her life since graduating from school. Oliver Obsessione had a huge crush on Hannah in high school but lost track of her after graduation. Now, many years later, he joined ClassmateFinders.com and received access to her profile with her contact information. He began by sending Hannah erotic anonymous e-mails and then progressed to phoning her at home and at work. Later, he would leave disturbing notes on her doorstep describing the clothes she had worn and the places she had visited that day. Realizing that Oliver was a cyberstalker, Hannah sought a restraining order against him and filed a civil lawsuit against ClassmateFinders.com, the source of the information he had used to stalk her. What will be her arguments for finding ClassmateFinders.com liable and is she likely to prevail?

Meanwhile, Hannah's 14-year-old daughter Holly Hottie was in a chat room when she was approached by Pete-the-Perv, a 38-year-old haberdasher. Holly reported Pete to the ISP who in turn reported Pete to the police. Detective Dick Tracy took over Holly's account and, pretending to be the 14-year-old girl, engaged in two dozen instant messages (IMs) with Pete, who made sexual advances toward "her," culminating in an arranged meeting at a local hotel for sex. Pete was arrested and transcripts of the chat room IMs were the main evidence against Pete. What are the legal arguments for and against admitting the chat room transcripts into evidence?

[Answers in Appendix]

CHAPTER ELEVEN

WEBSITE PRIVACY POLICIES

> This chapter discusses website privacy policies, focusing on the elements of a good privacy policy. It also examines the California Online Privacy Protection Act, and the practice of behavioral marketing.

Define "Never"

A "HOMESTEADER" WAS A 19TH Century man who, for a nominal fee, acquired and settled on U.S. public land. Nearly two centuries later, GeoCities revived the "homesteading" concept, revamped for the Internet, by allowing customers to build their own free web pages on its servers. GeoCities did not charge for the pages, but it made money by placing banner ads on its customers' web pages. But GeoCities had other ideas on how to profit from its customers. GeoCities homesteaders were required to fill out an application, which required the customer's first and last name, e-mail address, zip code, gender, date of birth, and member name. Additionally it asked for, but did not require, education level, marital status, occupation, and interests. Having millions of customers provide this type of information is highly lucrative and desirable to marketers. GeoCities also asked if they wanted to receive "special offers" from advertisers; presumably, if they said "no," GeoCities would not share their personal information with advertisers. To encourage people to complete the form, GeoCities included a privacy statement, which read in part, "... *we will **never** give your information to anyone without your permission.*" However, GeoCities "sold, rented, marketed, disclosed" the information, including information from children, to marketers, according to an F.T.C. complaint.[1] The F.T.C. charged GeoCities with misrepresenting why it collected personal information from adults and children. Ultimately, GeoCities agreed to a settlement with the F.T.C.

Toysmart, an online toy retailer, explained that when it stated in its website privacy policy that it would never disclose customer data, it meant 'unless someone wants to buy it.' *"What part of 'never' don't you understand?"* was the question raised in the F.T.C.'s lawsuit against the toy retailer.[2] Although <u>Toysmart.com</u> had promised its customers that it would never sell the personal information it solicited from them, after Toysmart filed for bankruptcy protection, the customer information became an asset of the bankruptcy estate, and a potentially valuable asset at that. Indeed, the bankruptcy estate had a duty to liquidate the firm's assets to pay off its creditors. This created an interesting conflict between the firm's obligation to adhere to its promise not to sell its database of personal information and the bankruptcy trustee's obligation to liquidate the firm's assets for the benefit of its creditors. The company tried to sell its customer records to the highest bidder, despite the promise in its privacy policy that it would never do so. Toysmart advertised the sale of its customer list and database in Wall Street Journal. The F.T.C. charged that the attempted sale violated § 5 of the F.T.C. Act,[3] which prohibits unfair or deceptive acts, and that it also violated the Children's Online Privacy Protection Act of 1998 (COPPA) by collecting personal information from children without their parents' consent.[4] The database was ultimately destroyed with the approval of the Bankruptcy Court.[5]

Geocities *chose* to ignore its stated privacy policy; Toysmart had *no choice*: its database was a company asset, and in bankruptcy all assets had to be sold to pay off the creditors. Toysmart was placed in a "no-win" situation by virtue of its circumstances. One proposed solution might have been for the buyer to take over the database subject to the terms of the original debtor's privacy policy. Alternatively, the Bankruptcy Court could have declared that the database was not an asset and order it destroyed (however, a customer list is a very valuable asset). Ideally, Congress should amend the Bankruptcy Act to deal with this conflict.

If a website privacy policy states that the website will never give out information to third-parties but later modifies its online policy, does the change apply retroactively to previously collected information? Gateway Learning Corp., makers of the "Hooked on Phonics" products, subsequently modified its privacy policy to permit it to share information with third-parties.[6] The F.T.C. considered that a deceptive and unfair practice in violation of § 5 of the F.T.C. Act. Under the consent agreement, Gateway was prohibited from sharing any of its previously collected customer information without first obtaining express "opt-in" consent from customers and in the future Gateway could not retroactively apply material changes to its privacy policy without first obtaining customer consent.

Website Privacy Policies

Many e-commerce websites, often out of necessity, collect personal information from their customers. Personal identifiable information, such as name, address, date of birth, occupation, income, age, gender, and hobbies, is highly valued by marketers to reach *targeted* audiences. The problem is that a website could obtain personal information, promise to use that information only for stated purposes, but then later market the information to other companies. To address this problem, many e-commerce websites have posted privacy policies explaining how they collect personal information and what they do with it. But as we have seen in the GeoCities and Toysmart cases, once a firm has a stated privacy policy, it must abide by it. For that reason, a website's stated privacy policy is the greatest restriction on website's ability to collect and use customer information. With certain exceptions, discussed below, a website is not required to have a privacy policy. In fact, some lawyers advise their website clients *not* to have a privacy policy, on the theory that one can not violate what one does not have. So why have one? Most e-commerce websites chose to have privacy policies because they make websites appear *trustworthy*.

Some websites are required by law to have posted privacy policies, such as websites collecting information from California residents, children under 13, or European customers.

California requires that any commercial website or online service operator that collects personally identifiable information about consumers residing in California provide individuals with notice of its privacy policies. The *California Online Privacy Protection Act*[6] requires websites to: (1) identify the categories of personally identifiable information collected and categories of third-parties with whom it may share it; (2) describe how to review and changes one's personally identifiable information, if the website allows review and changes; (3) describe how to learn of changes in the privacy policy; and (4) state the effective date of the privacy policy. It defines "personally identifiable information" as: first and last name, home or other physical address, e-mail address, phone number, social security number, and "any other identifier that permits the physical or online contacting of a specific individual," as well as any other information that the website collects from the user. The Act also requires a hyperlink from the main page to the privacy policy page.

Websites that collect personal information from children or are aimed at children are subject to the Children's Online Privacy Protection Act of 1998 (COPPA). This topic is discussed at length in the next chapter, Chapter 12.

Websites with customers or business operations in the European Union (EU) are subject to the European Union's Data Protection Directive, which requires them to inform users that their data may be collected and used for direct marketing, and to give them the right to object (*i.e.*, an "opt-out" provision). The Directive prohibits the transfer of personal data to non-European Union nations that do not meet its "adequacy standard" for privacy protection spelled out within the Directive. The U.S. Commerce Department and the European Commission have devised a "safe harbor" framework of data protection principles to enable American businesses to satisfy the EU's requirement of adequate data protection for personally identifiable information transferred from the EU to the United States. (The European Union's Data Protection Directive is also discussed in Chapter 10).

Ingredients for a Good Privacy Policy

If you are a webmaster, you either need or choose to have a privacy policy you should make it simple and straight-forward. A good privacy policy should be easily understandable by visitors to your website, not filled with indecipherable legalese. Your privacy policy should be reviewed periodically and updated as necessary. Your employees should be familiar with your privacy policy, both so they can respond to questions about it and so that they do not violate it.

If you are a website visitor, you need to understand the privacy policy of the website you are visiting. Websites collect two kinds of data: personally identifiable information and aggregate information. *Personally identifiable information* is identifiable to a specific individual, *e.g.*, your name, e-mail address, phone number, home or other address, name of school attended or business employed at, Social Security number, credit card number, bank account number, or any other information that tells someone who you are. *Aggregate information* is general demographic information that does not identify any individual.

General Elements

The necessary elements of a privacy policy should include:

- *What* personally identifiable information is collected

- *Who* collects the information

- *How* information is used

- *With whom* information may be shared

- What *choices* visitors have about collection, use, and distribution of information

- What *security procedures* are used to protect against loss, misuse, or alteration of information (*i.e.*, data breaches, hacking, employee data theft)

- How visitors can *correct inaccuracies* or update information

Specific Elements

• Company contact information: The name of the company, address of main office (possibly branches as well), phone numbers, e-mail address, and the effective date of the privacy policy

• What information (*e.g.*, IP addresses, browser type, ISP, referring/exit pages, operating system, date/time stamp, and clickstream data) the server automatically collects for its log files

• If the webmaster collects any of the following (and if collected, is it retained, and if so, for how long?):

◊ e-mail address of visitors to the web page

◊ e-mail address of visitors referred to the web page by previous visitors

◊ the referring URL of visitors to the web page

◊ e-mail address of people who send or receive e-mail through the website

◊ e-mail addresses of visitors who post messages to the message board

◊ e-mail addresses of visitors who post in the chat room

◊ logs of chat room conversations

◊ information on which pages visitors access (and if such information is general or user-specific)

◊ information voluntarily submitted by visitors

◊ payment information (*e.g.*, name, billing address, shipping address, phone number, e-mail address, bank account number, credit card number and expiration date)

◊ transaction information (*e.g.*, dates on which customers made purchases, dollar amounts, quantity, and item description of purchases)

- The disposition of information collected

    ◊ used to improve the content of the web page

    ◊ used to analyze trends, administer the website, track users' movements around the website, and to gather demographic data

    ◊ used to notify visitors about website updates

    ◊ used to contact visitors for marketing purposes (*i.e.*, targeted marketing)

    ◊ shared with third-parties for marketing purposes (*i.e.*, targeted marketing)

    ◊ shared in the aggregate (non-user specific) with third-parties for marketing purposes (*i.e.*, demographics, aggregate reports and market research)

    ◊ not shared with anyone for any purpose

    ◊ disclosed when legally *required* to do so by law enforcement or government agencies (*i.e.*, when subpoenaed)

    ◊ disclosed when *requested* to do so by law enforcement or government agencies (*i.e.*, without presentation of subpoena)

    ◊ to protect against misuse or unauthorized use of the website, or violation of the Terms of Use

    ◊ to a successor entity in the event of sale of the business, merger, bankruptcy, or other ownership change

    ◊ used to create a "profile" of the user based on information collected through cookies, log files, and web beacons, that is then tied to user personally identifiable information and purchasing history

- The length of time information is retained, if at all

- Whether the website sets cookies on the visitor's computer and if so, for what purposes

  ◊ A cookie is a small text file stored on a user's computer to allow the website to authenticate the user's identity, speed up transactions, monitor user behavior, and personalize the presentation

  ◊ Whether the website links the information it stores in cookies to personally identifiable information submitted by the user to the website

  ◊ Whether the website uses both session ID cookies (that expire when the browser is closed) and persistent cookies (that remain on the user's hard drive for an extended period)

  ◊ Whether the session ID cookies and persistent cookies are encrypted

  ◊ Whether any cookies are set by third-party content or service providers

- Whether the website uses web beacons or "clear GIFs" (*i.e.*, small one pixel GIF files embedded in a web page that either transmit information back to a home server or place a cookie on the visitor's computer)

  ◊ These are used to track the online movements of users

  ◊ Web beacons, or clear GIFs, are embedded invisibly on web pages and are about the size of a period

  ◊ Whether the data collected by the web beacons is tied to personally identifiable data

  ◊ Whether web beacons are used in HTML-based e-mails sent to users

- If web visitors must register as members (*i.e.*, create a user name and password) what information must they provide during the registration process?

  ◊ How long will it be retained?

  ◊ Will it be shared with third-party advertisers?

- If web visitors must register to participate in a survey or contest, what information must they provide during the registration process?

  ◊ How long will it be retained?

  ◊ Will it be shared with third-party advertisers?

- Instructions on how to opt-out of having personally identifiable information used to deliver marketing offers through e-mail. (For webmasters, it is better to offer an opt-in option than to automatically send e-mail to the addresses collected as that might be considered sending unsolicited bulk e-mailings, *i.e.*, spamming.)

- Whether affiliated ad servers, if any, may collect information such as the visitor's domain type, IP address, and clickstream information (*i.e.*, a record of all pages on the website visited, number of times an ad is viewed)

- What methods, if any, are available for the visitor to correct errors in previously collected information or update or delete that information

- If and under what circumstances visitors are redirected to a secure server to transfer sensitive information, using secure socket layer technology (SSL) to encrypt the information

- How is the user notified of changes to the privacy policy?

- Are there links to third-party websites that do not subscribe to this privacy policy?

If No One Heard the Tree Fall, Did It Make A Noise?

Are the terms of a privacy policy are enforceable if the aggrieved party never read the terms? In *In re Northwest Airlines Privacy Litigation*, the plaintiffs charged that the airline had violated laws and its own privacy policy by giving passenger name records, flight numbers, credit card information, hotel and car rental reservations, and names of travel companions to NASA for research on improving airline security following the September 11th terrorist attacks.[8] The court ruled that the lawsuits against Northwest had no merit, in part because the privacy policy posted on airline's website was unenforceable *unless plaintiffs claimed to have read it*. Since the plaintiffs did not actually read the privacy policy prior to providing Northwest with personal information, their "expectation of privacy was low," the court reasoned. Privacy advocates argue that *rather than focus on what the plaintiffs actually read, the focus should be on what Northwest said it would do.*

In a similar case, JetBlue Airways was sued by customers after it disclosed passenger name records to the U.S. Defense Department, which turned over the records to a data mining company it had hired to analyze the personal characteristics of individuals who sought access to military installations and predict which ones posed a security risk to those installations.[9] One of the claims in the lawsuit was breach of contract. Unlike <u>Northwest Airlines</u>, this court found that JetBlue's website privacy policy formed a valid contract between JetBlue and its website visitors. The court made no distinction between those who had read the policy and those who had not. However, the court nonetheless dismissed the contract claims because the plaintiffs were unable to show any economic damages; only damages for loss of privacy, which are not recoverable for breach of contract under New York law.

Behavioral Marketing

A website privacy policy should disclose whether the website uses behavioral marketing. Recall our discussion of keyword advertising in Chapter Five. When a user types a keyword into a search engine, in addition to his search results targeted ads related to the keyword appear on the page. Delivering relevant ads based on content is an example of *contextual marketing*.

Now imagine that you are surfing the web shopping for a new car. After looking at several automobile manufacturers' websites, you decide to check the sports page of your local newspaper's website where, as soon as the page loads an ad for a new Toyota Prius pops up. Coincidence? Serendipity? No, you've just experienced (or been victimized by) "behavioral marketing."

Behavioral marketing differs from contextual marketing in that it targets consumers based on their behavior on websites, instead of by the content of pages they visit. The basis of behavioral marketing is to track the websites the consumer visits, creating a profile of what products interest the consumer, and then deliver related targeted advertising to the consumer. By using clickstream data and IP information, advertisers can follow an individual's online activities, such as the websites visited or the keywords entered into search engines, and then deliver the targeted ads based on that information. Marketing companies are able to track this information through the use of *third-party cookies*, which are set by a website other than the one the individual is currently visiting. (Regular cookies are set by a website at the time an individual is visiting). Newer browsers have privacy settings that allow users to accept regular cookies but automatically decline third-party cookies.

It is estimated that U.S. firms, which spent $575 million on behavioral marketing in 2007, will nearly double their spending to $1 billion in 2008, and account for $3.8 billion of online ads by 2011.[10]

Although an advertising industry group issued guidelines to bar collection of personally identifiable data about Internet users and restrict web marketers from merging online data with personally identifiable data from offline databases, there is no assurance that marketers will adhere to these guidelines.

Some websites are now offering visitors the choice of receiving either the same ads as everyone else or a selection believed to be more relevant to their interests, based on its behavioral marketing results. A website's behavioral marketing practices may or may not be revealed in its privacy policy, although an advertising industry trade association, the Network Advertising Initiative, published a set of "NAI Principles" that would require disclosure of behavioral marketing practices in a posted privacy policy, along with "a clear and conspicuous link to opt out of the use of their information."[11]

Failure to disclose in its privacy policy the use of web beacons and clear GIFs by a third-party contractor cost Toys R Us $900,000 and its contractor almost half that amount. Toys R Us hired Coremetrics, who used cookies, web beacons, and clear GIFs on the Toys R Us website and linked the information obtained to personally identifiable visitor information. However, Toys R Us stated in its privacy policy that it did not share "any" personally identifying data with "anyone outside of Toysrus.com, its parents, affiliates, subsidiaries, operating companies and other related entities."[12] Privacy policies must clearly explain the website's use of cookies, clear GIFs, or other features that might result in linking browsing information with personally identifiable information.

Summary

Many e-commerce websites collect personal information from their customers. Personal information—such as name, address, date of birth, occupation, income, age, gender, and hobbies—is highly valued by marketers to reach targeted audiences. Many e-commerce websites have posted privacy policies explaining how they collect personal information and what they do with it.

Once a firm has a stated privacy policy, it must abide by it. For that reason, a website's stated privacy policy is the greatest restriction on its ability to collect and use customer information. A company cannot retroactively apply material changes to its website privacy policy without first obtaining customer consent.

Most e-commerce websites chose to have privacy policies because they make websites appear trustworthy. California requires that any commercial website or online service operator that collects personally identifiable information about consumers residing in California provide individuals with notice of its privacy policies. Websites with customers or business operations in the European Union are subject to the European Union's Data Protection Directive, which requires them to inform users that their data may be collected and used for direct marketing, and to give them the right to opt-out. Websites that collect personal information from children are subject to the Children's Online Privacy Protection Act of 1998. Both require the posting of privacy policies.

A good privacy policy should be easily understandable, not filled with legalese, and should be reviewed periodically and updated as necessary.

Behavioral marketing is the practice of tracking an individual's online activities, such as which websites he visits or which keywords he enters into search engines, and then delivering targeted ads based on that information. Behavioral marketing differs from contextual marketing in that it targets consumers based on their behavior on websites instead of by the content of pages they visit. A website's behavioral marketing practices may or may not be revealed in its privacy policy. However, Privacy policies must clearly explain the website's use of cookies, clear GIFs, or other features that might result in linking browsing information with personally identifiable information.

Chapter Eleven Notes

[1] Complaint *In re GeoCities* (1998), F.T.C. website, *available at* www.ftc.gov/os/1998/08/geo-cmpl.htm (accessed September 25, 2007). The complaint filed by the F.T.C. in this case is included in the Cases Section on the Issues in Internet Law website (www.IssuesinInternetLaw.com), Geocities, F.T.C. Docket No. C-3849 (Feb. 12, 1999).

[2] *F.T.C. v. Toysmart.com, LLC, and Toysmart.com, Inc.*, Civil Action No. 00-11341-RGS (D.C. Mass. filed July 10, 2000, amended July 21, 2000).

[3] Federal Trade Commission Act (1914), 15 U.S.C. §§ 41-51.

[4] Children's Online Privacy Protection Act (COPPA), 15 U.S.C. § 6501 *et seq.*

[5] Greg Sandoval, "Judge OKs Destruction of Toysmart List," CNET News.com, January 31, 2001.

[6] *In re Matter of Gateway Learning Corp.*, F.T.C. Docket No. C-4120 (2004).

[7] California Business and Professions Code § 22575-22579.

[8] *In re Northwest Airlines Privacy Litigation*, Civil File No. 04-216, 2004 US Dist. Lexis 10580 (D.C. Minn. June 6, 2004).

[9] *In re JetBlue Airways Corp. Privacy Litigation*, 379 F.Supp.2d 299 (E.D.N.Y. 2005).

[10] Michele Gershberg , "Where Were You Online? Advertisers Know," Reuters wire report, June 20, 2007.

[11] D. Reed Freeman, Jr., "Privacy and the Future of Behavioral Marketing," December 15, 2004, *available at* www.imediaconnection.com/content/4791.asp (accessed September 25, 2007).

[12] *In re Toys R Us, Inc., Privacy Litigation*, MDL No. M-00-1381-MMC (N.D. Cal. 2001).

Chapter Eleven Quiz

Lovebirds.com is an online dating website. Its posted privacy policy states that Lovebirds.com respects the privacy of its members and will never rent or sell any information supplied by members. A year later, Lovebirds.com is sold to a rival dating website, MeetYourMatch.com, which sells copies of its membership list, which includes the Lovebirds.com members, to various marketers interested in reaching the singles market. MeetYourMatch.com in its privacy policy reserves the right to rent or sell member information.

If you are using this book in a classroom, discuss the issues raised and the liability of all parties. Otherwise, try to list the issues involved and probable outcomes before turning to the answers in the Appendix.

[Answers in Appendix]

CHAPTER TWELVE

PRIVACY AND CHILDREN

This chapter explores privacy on the Internet as it relates to children and their social interaction in the cyber environment, with particular attention to F.T.C. regulation and the Children's Online Privacy Protection Act.

Soupy Sales ... and the Naiveté of Kids

IN 1965, SOUPY SALES, so the story goes, was somewhat perturbed at having to work on New Year's Day. With a few minutes to kill at the end of the live broadcast of his children's TV show, Soupy Sales looked into the camera and ad-libbed, "Hey kids, last night was New Year's Eve, and your mom and dad were out having a great time. They are probably still sleeping and what I want you to do is tiptoe into their bedroom and go in your mom's purse and your dad's pants and take out some of those funny green pieces of paper with all those nice pictures of George Washington, Abraham Lincoln, and Alexander Hamilton, and send them to your old pal, Soupy, care of WNEW, New York." Shortly thereafter, cash-filled envelopes trickled into the studio, as did complaints from outraged parents. Sales was suspended for a week for his prank, but it serves as a classic example of the ease with which the naiveté of children can be exploited by the power of a mass medium like television or the Internet.

Protecting Children from Marketers and Other Predators

Just imagine what Soupy Sales could have done on the Internet! Studies have shown that *children are less able to appreciate the ramifications of disclosing personal information on the Internet.* One psychiatrist even told a Federal Trade Commission (F.T.C.) workshop on privacy that young children do not understand what personal information is, and they look up to fictional characters and tend to do what they ask of them.[1] Some countries and provinces, recognizing the seriousness of the threat to children, have restricted marketing targeted at children. Sweden has banned advertising targeted at children under 12 and Quebec prohibits print and broadcast advertising targeting children under 13.[2] However, the United States *has never had a law that prevented marketing to children*; to the contrary, marketers have historically specifically targeted children. Examples of marketing targeted at children include cereal and toy commercials, magazine subscriptions in children's names, sponsored radio and TV show (*e.g.*, Superman hawking Cheerios in commercials on the Adventures of Superman radio and television shows), and the classic Johnson and Smith comic book novelty ads (*e.g.*, x-ray glasses and sea monkeys).[3] A walk down the cereal aisle of any supermarket reveals how products are heavily marketed to children. Movies now have "tie-in" products aimed at children; see the Spider-Man movie, then buy Spider-Man ravioli and a Spider-Man toothbrush before getting into your Spider-Man pajamas and crawling under the Spider-Man sheets (and remember to turn on the Spider-Man nightlight!). The marketers' goal is to get kids to nag their parents until they give in and buy the products. Mom may not have intended to buy ravioli tonight, but ultimately she will succumb to her kids' nagging prompted by the picture of Spider-Man on the can.

American children spend more time watching television than in the classroom.[4] The average American child sees 40,000 television commercials a year.[5] In fact, many school districts broadcast the commercial-laden Channel One's news broadcasts to a captive audience of students.[6] How pervasive is advertising? American adults and children are exposed to countless ads all day long on television, radio, billboards, bus benches, store floors, gas pumps and in magazines, newspapers, and movie theaters — both before the feature film begins and during movies through product placement in films. One enterprising marketer has proposed placing ads on egg shells![7]

The United States has 4.5 percent of the world's population, but buys 45 percent of the global toy production.[8] In 2004, U.S. children spent $35 billion of their own "pocket money," but they influenced $670 billion worth of parental purchases.[9] Advertisers spend $15 billion annually marketing to children.[10] Advertisers realize that children comprise three distinct market segments: (1) their own disposable income (*e.g.*, allowances, after-school jobs), (2) influencing their parents' income (*i.e.*, the "nag" factor), and (3) their future spending as they mature into adulthood (*i.e.*, creating brand loyalty today yields loyal customers tomorrow). Toyota, in 2006, paid for product placement of its Scion automobile in an online interactive community website aimed at 8–to–15-year-olds.[11] While obviously not planning to buy a Scion with their paper route earnings, these children could influence their parents' decisions when it came time to buy the new family car and they might well become predisposed to Toyota's brand by the time they start driving.

Kids want to be seen as "cool." Since "coolness" is usually defined by peer pressure, advertisers use "buzz marketing" to get the coolest kids in a community (be it at school or online) to use or wear their product, thus creating a buzz about their product among the target adolescent market. On the Internet, this can take the form of postings in newsgroups, chat rooms, and blogs.[12] Children and young adults of the Internet Generation, most of whom grew up playing interactive video games, are especially drawn to the Internet not only because of its graphics, but because of the interactivity it provides, as contrasted with the unilateral experience of passively viewing television. Savvy marketers create websites with interactive features, such as polls and flash-based games to attract children while at the same time marketing to them. Many of the games are actually advertisements for products that reinforce logos and characters associated with the manufacturer's products and the polls are often used to elicit personal information from children for marketing purposes.[13] Some games even tie purchases of the product into the game, *e.g.*, where a cereal company places coupons with codes inside specially marked packages — the codes can then be used in the online games to provide a shield or weapon to a character during a game.[14]

All of this shows that children are a major market for advertisers, especially for the Internet Generation, for whom screen time has replaced playtime. Advertisers crave data to target the children's market, and the naiveté of children combined with the power of a mass medium like the Internet poses the prospect of abusive collection and use of private information from children.

Children's Online Privacy Protection Act (COPPA)

To address this issue, Congress passed the Children's Online Privacy Protection Act (COPPA).[15] COPPA controls how websites can collect and/or maintain personal information about children. It is the only Internet-specific U.S. federal privacy law. The Act defines a "child" as under age 13. COPPA applies to "websites directed at children" or where the "site knows it is collecting information from children." COPPA applies only to commercial websites and not to non-profit websites.

COPPA requires that the website:

• Provide parents with notice of the website's information practices. This means *what* information is collected, *how* it is used, and *to whom* it may be disclosed

• Obtain prior verifiable parental consent to collect, use or disclose personal information *before* collecting such information from a child

- Provide the parent, upon request, with the right to *view* information submitted by the child

- Provide the parent with the opportunity to *refuse to permit the further use*, maintenance, or future collection of the child's personal information

- Limit collection of personal information required to participate in games or prize offers

- Provide reasonable procedures to protect the confidentiality, security, and integrity of personal information it receives

Under COPPA, the website must provide notice about its information collection practices. The notice must be posted from a link *on the home page and on each page where information is collected from children*. The website must obtain verifiable parental consent before collecting, using, or disclosing any information from a child. In addition to collecting information from online forms, under COPPA "collection" also encompasses permitting children to post messages in a chat room or on a message board, and providing them with e-mail accounts or instant messaging.

In 2003, the F.T.C. fined Mrs. Fields Cookies $100,000 for violating COPPA by knowingly collecting personal information from children under 13 from more than 84,000 children, without first obtaining parental consent. [16] The company set up a website aimed at children by promoting birthday clubs and explicitly stated that "only children twelve years old or younger may participate." [17] Upon joining, children were mailed a birthday greeting and a coupon for a free pretzel or cookie.

Some websites have given up collecting information collection from children, citing the process of compliance with COPPA as too burdensome. However, the website does not need verifiable parental consent if it is responding directly on *one-time basis* to a child and the information is *not retained*, or if it is reasonably necessary to protect *safety of child* or to protect the *security and integrity of the website*.

COPPA and COPA

Do not confuse COPPA with COPA. COPPA is the *Children's Online Privacy Protection Act*. COPPA is valid and enforced by the F.T.C., as you may recall from the Toysmart case in the previous chapter, where the F.T.C. charged Toysmart with, among other charges, violating COPPA by collecting personal information from children without their parents' consent. COPA is the *Child Online Protection Act*, which makes it a federal crime to use the World Wide Web to communicate for *"commercial purposes"* material *"harmful to minors."* [18] The 3rd Circuit ruled that COPA violated the First Amendment, however the U.S. Supreme Court did not go that far but it has blocked COPA from being applied. [19] COPA is discussed in greater detail in Chapter 14.

Social Interaction in the Cyber Environment

The World Wide Web was created as a cyber environment for the exchange of ideas, communication, and eventually entertainment and commerce. But with the rise of topic-specific forums and later social networks, complete strangers connected with one another, forming "cyber friendships," often with deep emotional bonds. These friendships were formed within the framework of a cyber community, either though a forum where members shared a common interest (*e.g.*, pet lovers, support group) or a social network of similar persons (*e.g.*, high school students, college students). One survey even found that more than 40% of respondents believed their cyber friends were equally as important as their real world friends. [20] This makes sense when one pictures the cyber friend as a real person sitting in front of his or her computer somewhere far away. However, a more cynical observer would argue that a cyber friend is actually a cipher; without having personally met the cyber friend, everything one knows about the friend could be false, since the only source of information about the cyber friend comes from the cyber friend himself.

With the advent of Internet three-dimensional gaming, (*e.g.*, games like "Second Life") a whole new level has been added to the cyber environment. Players choose avatars to represent themselves in interactive pseudo-lifelike games in vivid fantasy worlds where they (through their avatar) often engage in violent or socially objectionable behavior. Psychologists disagree on whether this encourages similar behavior in the real world; some argue it has no effect and some even contend it may serve as a positive way to let off steam and aggressive feelings. [21]

It is against this backdrop that children's social interactions on the World Wide Web must be viewed. Often they view their audience not as complete strangers they have never met, but as intimate friends, even a part of their own support network. And after all, you can tell your friends everything, right?

"Show And Tell" on the Internet

COPPA applies to commercial websites directed at children under age 13; however, it does not apply to children in their teen years, 13-to-17. That is why social networking websites aimed at teenagers and young adults, like MySpace, prohibit members under age 13. But that may put teenagers at even greater risk than younger children because neither the collection of personal information nor its disclosure is regulated or protected. These teenagers' privacy rests solely on the privacy policy of the particular website and on their own judgment in what they publicly disclose online.

In grade school, "Show and Tell" was a daily ritual where students would share intimate details of their personal or home lives with their classmates, often accompanied by the occasional prop (*e.g.*, a stuffed animal, a favorite toy, or a science project gone awry). Today, "Show and Tell" has moved from the classroom to the Internet and the audience has become practically anyone in the world who wishes to tune in. Andy Warhol's promise of "15 minutes of fame" now seems quaint in this world of web pages, uploadable photos, webcams, blogs, vlogs, MySpace, Facebook, and YouTube.

Children are voluntarily posting a wide array of personal information online for everyone to see. Often they do not stop to think that others besides their intended friends will be able to view this information; other times they do not care who may view it. On the following pages we will review what they are posting, where they are posting it, and whether this is a good or bad thing.

What Kids are Posting

Children, as any parent will attest, have a weird view of privacy. They will pen their most intimate thoughts in a poem and then bring that poem to school to read before their classmates but should their mother stumble across it while cleaning their bedroom, teenaged cries of "how dare you invade my privacy" will reverberate throughout the neighborhood. The same teens who hide their diaries under the mattress lest their darkest secrets and teen angst be revealed to the eyes of prying parents routinely publish the same words on their blogs (online diaries) on the Internet for the whole world, both friends and strangers, to read. For example:[22]

["I'm 14 and I'm gay. I'm out to everyone, except my parents."] ... ["Looking for 420-friendly[23] friends"] ... ["That was close! His mom almost walked in while I was giving him a blow job!"] ... ["I tried to kill myself last night. Guess I didn't take enough pills because I'm still here, lol."] ... ["Well, this is the first time I have admitted in public that I am bi. I wonder if my parents will find out and if they will be upset. I guess I don't care — I am who I am."] ... ["I had a fucking horrible day today. I was asked to leave (name deleted) Christian Academy. You know why, because I am a faggot. Yeah isn't that the sickest thing you have ever heard. You know what the most fucked up part about it is? They found out from my Myspace Profile."]

Teens are active bloggers and heavy users of social networks, often posting their names, addresses, phone numbers, school names, and even their school schedules. Personally identifiable information is not all they reveal; they also post photographs of themselves — girls wearing thongs and bikinis in provocative poses and shirtless boys in boxers or bikini briefs, with sexually-charged captions. Some profiles have more cleavage and crotches than a Victoria's Secret catalog. Many parents do not even know that their children belong to social network websites. An MSNBC reporter interviewed one parent who, after discovering her daughter's MySpace profile, said, "I sat my daughter down and said, 'Do you realize how inappropriate and how dangerous this is? Here's your face. Here's the town you come from. Do you realize how many sick people are out there?'"[24]

The law can only be expected to do so much. Parents have to take a proactive role by examining their children's online profiles to see if they are too detailed or if the photographs are provocative. Rather than over regulating the Internet with potentially unconstitutional laws aimed at protecting children, parents should discover who their children's cyber friends are. Who are they talking to and what are they disclosing? And just as parents lock their house to keep strangers out, they should tell their children to "lock" their profiles to keep strangers out; most social networks allow users to "privatize" their profiles so that they can control who gets access to view the full profile.

Where Kids are Posting

While some kids set up their own web pages, either through their own URLs or through a free web page service like Yahoo!, most use blogs or social networking websites. Some of the more popular blog websites include LiveJournal.com, Blogspot.com, and Blogger.com. These are basically online diaries with a worldwide audience, although some blogs have a feature to limit readers to pre-selected "friends." One study[25] showed that 51.5% of all blogs were written by teenagers (ages 13 – 19) and the same research company describes the typical blog as written by a teenage girl "twice a month to update her friends and classmates on happenings in her life."[26]

Social networking websites popular with teenagers include MySpace, Xanga, and Bolt. Whereas a blog is merely an online diary, a social network offers the user a personalized web page with a user profile that may contain not only a blog but personal information (*e.g.*, name, nicknames, screen names, age, date of birth, birthplace, current city and state, schools attended, hobbies and interests, brief biographies, instant messaging contact information, and e-mail addresses), uploaded photographs, links to friends' profiles, and comments left by friends. A popular student may have links to her entire class on her profile. Even if a teenager is careful not to include personally identifiable information on his profile, his friends may inadvertently reveal such information in the comments they post to his page. For example, "Happy Birthday today, David, how does it feel to be 15? I hear you're going to celebrate at Fisherman's Wharf tonight!" We now know that the student is a 15-year-old boy named David, whose birth date was 15 years ago to the day, and he lives in San Francisco, California. A click on the poster's name opens his profile, revealing him to be a student and classmate of "David's" at Pope Pius IX High School. So we can now extrapolate the neighborhood David lives in, the school he attends, and his religion. A few more comments like this and think what a stranger can learn.

Is it a Good or Bad Thing?

While some studies contend that teenagers reveal too much personal information in their blogs and social networking websites, fears of an army of child predators ensconced on websites like <u>MySpace.com</u> may be more media-fueled mass hysteria than truth.[27] Even the MSNBC report referred to above admits the "article could not cite a single case of a child predator hunting for and finding a child through a blog."[28] Not to say that at some point, somewhere, there will not be such a situation, it is equally likely that a determined predator would find such information in a school newspaper, yearbook, or other such non-Internet source.

There are many positive aspects to teenage social networking. Shy children often develop new friends far more easily online than in the offline world. Often the socially outcast teens, considered nerds or geeks at their schools form meaningful friendships online with others like themselves. A gay teen in a small rural conservative town may find solace and support from a sympathetic gay teen from a liberal city across the country. Students at all-girls and all-boys schools can create a virtual coed environment and develop friends of the opposite gender that would not be possible in their school social settings. Blogs and social networks can play an important role by connecting teens and helping them learn to express themselves. Teens will often engage in lively debates about current events, on topics as diverse as religion, homosexuality, war, and politics. By conversing with their peers from all walks of life and from literally the four corners of the globe, teenagers are exposed to differing views and perspectives and challenged to think and re-evaluate their own views and perspectives.

Perhaps most surprisingly, social networking websites can serve as an outlet for collective group grief. More than ever, teenagers are encountering loss of a peer, whether through suicide, drunk driving, school shootings, gang violence, AIDS, drug overdose, or accidents. When a teenage skateboarder was hit and killed by a driver "driving under the influence," his classmates created a photo montage of the deceased student set to music in a Flash movie, uploaded it to YouTube,[29] then linked to it so that the video memorial could play from each of their MySpace profiles; then they posted "farewell" comments onto the deceased student's own MySpace profile,[30] turning his MySpace page into a highly emotional shrine dedicated to the memory of their deceased friend — and serving as a mass cathartic outlet for teens sharing, and trying to come to grips with, a common grief.

Summary

Children are less able to appreciate the ramifications of disclosing personal information on the Internet. The United States has never had a law that prevented marketing to children; to the contrary, marketers have historically specifically targeted children. Advertisers crave data to target the children's market, and the naiveté of children combined with the power of a mass medium like the Internet poses the prospect of abusive collection and use of private information from children. Tools used by advertisers aimed at children include product placement, buzz marketing, and interactive online features such as games and polls.

To protect children, Congress enacted the Children's Online Privacy Protection Act, (COPPA), which controls how websites can collect and/or maintain personal information about children. It is the only Internet-specific U.S. federal privacy law. The Act defines a "child" as under age 13. COPPA applies to commercial "websites directed at children" or where the "site knows it is collecting information from children."

Teenagers, while still children, are not protected by COPPA. Teens are voluntarily posting a wide array of personal information online for everyone to see, mostly through blogs or social networking websites including MySpace, Xanga, and Bolt. There are many positive aspects to teenage social networking, especially for shy or socially outcast teens. Blogs and social networks help teens learn to express themselves and expose them to differing views, challenging them to think and re-evaluate their own perspectives. Social networking websites can serve as a cathartic outlet for collective group grief among teenagers experiencing their first encounters with death and loss.

Chapter Twelve Notes ▰▰▰▰▰▰▰▰▰▰▰▰▰

[1] Michael Brody, spokesperson for the American Academy of Child and Adolescent Psychiatry, *see* Susan Gregory Thomas, "Pushing Products To Young Consumers," U.S. News & World Report, June 23, 1997).

[2] "Special Issues for Young Children," *available at* www.media-awareness.ca/english/parents/marketing/marketers_target_kids.cfm (accessed September 25, 2007).

[3] The "sea monkeys" were actually brine shrimp.

[4] American Academy of Pediatrics and surveys by the non-profit Kaiser Family Foundation.

[5] Richard Zoglin, "Is TV Ruining Our Children?," Time, October 15, 1990.

[6] Donnell Alexander and Aliza Dichter, "Ads And Kids: How Young Is Too Young?," *available at* www.mediachannel.org/atissue/consumingkids/index.shtml (accessed September 25, 2007).

[7] Renuka Rayasam, "They'll Pay to Have Ads Put on Shells? Egg-cellent!," U.S. News & World Report, November 5, 2006.

[8] Juliet B. Schor, "Born to Buy: The Commercialized Child and the New Consumer Culture," (Scribner 2004).

[9] *Ibid.*

[10] *Ibid.*

[11] Julie Bosman, "Hey, Kid, You Want to Buy a Toyota Scion?," New York Times, June 14, 2006.

[12] "How Marketers Target Kids," Media Awareness Network, *available at* www.media-awareness.ca/english/parents/marketing/marketers_target_kids.cfm (accessed September 25, 2007).

[13] Adrian Humphreys, "Internet Marketing Targets Children," Edmonton Journal, July 3, 1997.

[14] Marni Goldberg, "Is It A Game Or An Advertisement?," Chicago Tribune, July 20, 2006. *See also* Janet Raloff, "How Advertising Is Becoming Child's Play," Science News Online, July 29, 2006, *available at* www.commercialexploitation.org/news/advertisingischildsplay.htm (accessed September 25, 2007).

[15] Children's Online Privacy Protection Act (COPPA), 15 U.S.C. § 6501 *et seq.*

[16] F.T.C. press release, February 27, 2003, *available at* www.ftc.gov/opa/2003/02/hersheyfield.htm (accessed September 25, 2007).

[17] *United States v. Mrs. Fields Famous Brands, Inc.*, complaint, Civil Action No. 2:03 CV205 JTG, *available at* www.ftc.gov/os/2003/02/mrsfieldscmp.htm (accessed September 25, 2007).

[18] Child Online Protection Act (COPA), 47 U.S.C. § 223, *et seq.*

[19] *ACLU v. Reno*, 31 F.Supp.2d 473 (E.D. Pa 1999), *aff'd* 217 F.3d 162 (3rd Cir. 2000).

[20] Annenberg School Center for the Digital Future at the University of Southern California survey, Bernadine Healy, "Alone in a Parallel Life," U.S. News & World Report, May 21, 2007, p. 66.

[21] *Ibid.*

[22] These quotes from teenage blogs, unlike all of the other quotes throughout this book, are deliberately not attributed to protect the identity of the minors who wrote them.

[23] Slang for pot-smoking.

[24] Bob Sullivan, "Kids, Blogs and Too Much Information: Children Reveal More Online Than Parents Know," MSNBC, April 29, 2005, *available at* http://msnbc.msn.com/id/7668788 (accessed September 25, 2007).

[25] According to a 2003 study by Perseus Development Corp., "The Blogging Iceberg," Perseus Development

Corp., *available at* http://perseus.com/survey/resources/perseus_blogging_iceberg.pdf (accessed September 25, 2007).

[26] *Ibid.*

[27] The MSNBC report cited a study by the Children's Digital Media Center at Georgetown University; *see* Bob Sullivan, fn. 24, *supra.*

[28] *Ibid.*

[29] *Available at* http://youtube.com/watch?v=wls5zwHbl-s (accessed September 25, 2007).

[30] *Was available at* www.myspace.com_tylerlitton01.htm (last accessed November 5, 2006; **as of September 25, 2007 the site was no longer accessible**).

Chapter Twelve Quiz

Krusty the Clown has a website where children enter various contests by submitting their names, ages, addresses, and other personal information online. Krusty wants to make sure that his website does not violate COPPA. What does Krusty need to do to be in full compliance with COPPA?

If you are using this book in a classroom, discuss the issues raised and the liability of all parties. Otherwise, try to list the issues involved and probable outcomes before turning to the answers in the Appendix.

[Answers in Appendix]

PART FIVE

1st AMENDMENT FREE SPEECH / FREE PRESS

CHAPTER THIRTEEN

FREE SPEECH

> This chapter examines free speech under the First Amendment; student speech, anonymous speech, Strategic Lawsuits Against Public Participation (SLAPPs), and gripe websites; the Communications Decency Act; defamation, personal attack websites, vlogging, and blogging (by employees, soldiers, and journalists); breach of contract, tortious interference with business, and securities fraud; and the "Marketplace of Ideas."

THE FIRST AMENDMENT TO the U.S. Constitution guarantees the right of freedom of speech. But *freedom of speech* is not absolute and sometimes speech can provoke a lawsuit. To bring a lawsuit, the suing party needs a valid legal cause of action, *i.e.*, the legal "grounds" for the lawsuit. Four primary causes of action against speech on the Internet are: *defamation, breach of contract, tortious interference with business,* and *securities fraud.*

Once it has been established that a cause of action exists, the next question is "Who is liable?" The author who wrote the words? The website owner or webmaster on whose website the words appeared? The Online Service Provider (OSP) who provides interactive content (*e.g.*, Amazon.com reviews, eBay feedback, YouTube videos)? The hosting company on whose server the website is hosted? Or the ISP who distributed the content?

The courts have applied the publisher-distributor analogy from the print medium to the Internet. A *publisher* is a provider of *content*, either its own or someone else's; *e.g.*, eBay.com and CNN.com. A *distributor* is a provider of a *pipeline* for the flow of services, *e.g.*, Bellsouth and Earthlink. A *hybrid* provides both content and the pipeline, *e.g.*, AOL and Prodigy. Under this analogy in the print medium, a publisher is liable for defamation, but a distributor is not. The concept is that one sues the newspaper, not the newsboy.

When an ISP exercises editorial control over the content of messages posted on an Internet message board, it is acting more like a newspaper publisher than a distributor. Since *only publishers, not distributors, can be liable for defamation,* the New York Supreme

Court ruled in _Straton Oakmont and Porush v. Prodigy_ that the ISP was liable based on the publisher analogy when the ISP screened and edited messages posted on its bulletin boards. [1]

After this decision, OSPs would be left with two choices: either do not remove offensive material posted by others, lest the OSP then be deemed a publisher and subject to liability; or simply do not allow any third-party postings. This decision was seen to have the potential to stifle the budding growth of the Internet and Congress realized that what worked for the traditional media might not be appropriate for the Internet. With that in mind, Congress enacted § 230 of the Communications Decency Act (CDA), [2] as a response to _Stratton_. It provided that "No provider or user of an interactive computer service shall be treated as publisher or speaker of any information provided by another information content provider." Section 230 establishes the _most important legal protection for ISPs and others who publish content on the Internet_ by overriding the traditional treatment of publishers, distributors, and speakers under statutory and common law. As a matter of public policy, Congress decided not to treat providers of interactive computer services like other information providers, such as newspapers, magazines, TV, and radio stations, all of which may be held liable for publishing or distributing obscene or defamatory material written or prepared by others. Thus, the _CDA immunizes ISPs from liability for defamatory or obscene material posted by someone else._

The rationale for immunizing ISPs is that ISPs are merely conduits (_i.e._, distributors of content) that provide a connection to the Internet. Some ISPs also act as hosting companies, storing website content on their servers. ISPs may have tens or hundreds of thousands, or even millions of customers; it is not practical to assume that they could constantly monitor all of the web content posted by their customers.

Courts have extended this broad immunity to other OSPs, including hybrids (_i.e._, provide both content and the pipeline) and Web 2.0 interactive content providers (_e.g._, <u>Amazon. com</u> reviews, eBay feedback, YouTube videos, and social networks like MySpace) based on the same rationale. Once again, this makes sense when one considers the sheer volume of products on Amazon and eBay and videos on YouTube; self-policing to screen out defamatory or obscene material is simply too manpower intensive to be a practical solution.

But there are three corollaries to these propositions that have been overlooked by most courts:

1. Rather than a grant of absolute immunity, OSPs could be given conditional immunity, _i.e._, immunity from liability conditioned on their removal of the defamatory or obscene material upon notification (similar to the "notice and takedown provision" of the DMCA).

2. Self-policing, while not a complete solution, could work hand-in-hand with a notice and takedown provision scheme.

3. Smaller interactive content providers, *e.g.*, a message board with 200 posts, are not so unwieldy that they cannot be adequately self-policed, especially in conjunction with a notice and takedown provision.

As we shall see in the _Barrett v. Clark_ case later in this chapter, a broad grant of immunity to every website with third-party comments (especially where such comments are often posted anonymously) can become a license to libel. Indeed, some websites, hiding behind the skirts of the CDA, actively solicit potentially defamatory comments (*see* the discussion of DontDateHim.com and AutoAdmit.com later in this chapter). Courts, such as the 9th Circuit, have stepped further into the breach. In _Perfect 10, Inc. v. CCBill_, the 9th Circuit held that § 230 can provide immunity from liability for ISPs where their users have violated state laws, such as Right of Publicity and trademark statutes.[3] The 9th Circuit would still not immunize ISPs in cases of federal copyright and criminal laws.

As discussed in Chapter Eight, at least one court has begun to step back from an absolute grant of immunity for OSPs, holding that OSPs are only immune from lawsuits for information they transmitted but did not create.[4] The question of what constitutes "creation" is subjective however. At some point, courts may determine that editing of content is equivalent to control over that content, making the OSP a content producer rather than merely a conduit. However, in _Ramey v. Darkside_, where a nude dancer sued a website publisher after one of its advertisers used a photograph of her on the website without her permission,[5] the court held that *online publishers are not responsible for the content of ads created by others.* The court ruled that Darkside *did not lose its CDA § 230 immunity by making "minor alterations"* to the advertisement, such as putting its own web address and a watermark on images. (Note that the dancer might have a claim against the advertiser directly for appropriation [*i.e.*, the Right of Publicity, discussed at further length in Chapter 10],[6] and depending on where it obtained the photograph, possibly copyright infringement.)

Defamation

Defamation is a "_published_ _intentional_ _false_ _communication_ that _injures_ a person or company's _reputation_." Each one of these elements must be present for the tort of defamation to exist.

For example, suppose that Bill posts this statement in a chat room: *"Lacy is a cheap whore!"* Is this defamatory? Yes? What if Lacy has 26 prostitution arrests — this month alone? Truth is a defense to defamation. What if Lacy's prostitution business increased 25% after the posting? In that case, there would be no injury to her reputation, since it had increased her business. But what if Lacy is a high-priced madam? In that case, being called a *cheap whore* might adversely affect her business and result in monetary injury to her reputation.

Defenses to Defamation

There are several defenses to a defamation action:

- Truth — is an absolute defense to a defamation action

- Privilege — is a legal concept protecting statements made in court by witnesses, attorneys, or judges; or on the floor of a legislative body

- Fair Comment — A statement of *opinion*, as opposed to fact, is not actionable as defamation. Likewise, *parody* is usually not actionable since defamation requires a "statement of fact" and most parody, because of its fictional nature, would fall under "Fair Comment"[7]

Forums for Potential Defamation

There are several possible forums for defamation on the Internet. Real time forums include *chat rooms* and *instant messages.* These postings disappear shortly after being made, but they can be preserved by archiving or screenshot programs. Static forums include websites, blogs, e-mail, message boards or forums, ListServs (e-mailed compilations of newsgroup or forum postings), Usenet newsgroups, and archived newsgroups (*e.g.,* Google Groups). Keep in mind, any of these can be archived and/or printed out.

Participants in message boards and chat rooms, in addition to posting defamatory statements, might also post *confidential, false, or misleading information* about *businesses* and *financial securities.* These types of postings might include disclosure of business or trade secrets or falsehoods designed to affect the stock price of a publicly-traded company. While chat room posts disappear shortly after posting, message boards often stay archived indefinitely and search engines can add *permanence* to such statements. The fact that most forums, message boards, and chat room posters use screen names or aliases makes *identification* of the individual who posted the comment difficult.

The Classmates.com Case

Classmates.com is a commercial website where individuals can track down and reunite with former classmates. In 2001, Oregon district attorney candidate Jim Carpenter, created a Classmates.com account using the name of a former high school acquaintance.[8] The acquaintance, now a high school teacher, had been rumored to have had an extramarital affair with a student. Carpenter, impersonating the teacher on the Classmates.com website, "confessed" to having sex with female students. He later claimed it was a practical joke. The Oregon Supreme Court, however, found that his "joke" raised questions about his "trustworthiness and integrity" to practice law as a member of the state bar.[9]

After Carpenter posted the message on Classmates.com, someone sent a printed copy of it along with an angry letter to the high school's principal, the school superintendent, and members of the school board. The principal started a formal investigation into the teacher's conduct. The teacher denied both having posted the message and having sexual relationships with students. The principal then told teacher to discover who had posted message. Classmates.com refused to disclose the identity of the person who had created account. The teacher turned to the police, who subpoenaed Classmates.com's records and discovered that Carpenter had created the account. Carpenter apologized and dropped out of the district attorney's race after a local newspaper learned about the incident. The Oregon Bar Association, the state's professional regulatory body for attorneys, filed a formal complaint against him. And the Oregon Supreme Court reprimanded him:[10]

> He had heard that the teacher had engaged in an extramarital affair with a (student) ... He knew the teacher, whose reputation was in question in at least some parts of the community, was uniquely vulnerable to the content of the message, because it pretended to be an admission by the teacher that the community rumors about inappropriate conduct were true.

The Classmates.com case raises several issues. *Should Classmates.com be entitled to rely on the publisher defense since it refused to disclose the author of the comments?* There is an inherent Catch-22 here.[11] The plaintiff sues the website, which shields itself under § 230 of the CDA by saying, "we're just the publisher, not the author of the defamation," but then refuses to reveal the author, leaving the plaintiff with no identifiable defendant to sue. In the opinion of this author, where the publisher refuses to disclose the identity of the author, there should be a *rebuttable presumption* that the publisher is the author, which would effectively force the publisher to identify the author. *Does the teacher have a valid defamation action? Or is truth a defense?* Here we must recall the elements of a defamation claim: "*Published* (yes) *intentional* (yes) *false* (unknown) *communication* (yes) that *injures* a person or company's *reputation*" (yes). Here all of the elements of defamation are met, with the possible exception of falsity, since we do not know if the statement that the teacher had affairs with students was true. Carpenter said he based this statement on rumors. Stating as true something that is based on mere rumor would indicate a reckless disregard of the truth. In <u>New York Times v. Sullivan</u>, the U.S. Supreme Court held that in order for a *public figure* to prevail in a defamation claim, he must meet a *higher* standard than a non-public figure, by showing that the defendant had "knowledge of falsity *or reckless disregard of truth*" when making the comment. [12] Here, the teacher (unlike Carpenter) was not a public figure and, while not required to, would nonetheless have met that higher bar in this case.

Barrett v. Clark [13]

Dr. Stephen Barrett, a retired psychiatrist and a medical journalist, ran a website called <u>Quackwatch.com</u>, a guide to health fraud and quackery. Barrett testified that he had written 48 books, 10 chapters in various textbooks, and "hundreds of articles" in lay and scientific publications. The defendants were "alternative medicine" advocates — Hulda Clark, an unlicensed naturopath operating clinics in California and Mexico who claimed that "all cancers are caused by parasites, toxins, and pollutants" and that "cancer can be cured within a few days by herbs and administration of low-voltage electric current" from a battery-operated "zapper" she marketed, and Ilena Rosenthal, who moderated an Internet newsgroup. Clark hired Tim Bolen to handle her public relations. Bolen wrote a letter that accused Dr. Terry Polevoy (one of the plaintiffs) of stalking a woman.

The interesting aspect of the case is that Rosenthal republished Bolen's letter in her newsgroup. Barrett and Polevoy sued Clark and Rosenthal for libel. Rosenthal argued that she should not be held liable for libelous comments that she had not written but had merely reposted.

The trial court held that a *newsgroup user* who posts an allegedly libelous message written by someone else was immune from liability because she was not the "publisher," only the poster. The court wrote: "As a user of an interactive computer service, that is, a newsgroup, Rosenthal is not the publisher or speaker of Bolen's piece. Thus, she cannot be civilly liable for posting it on the Internet. She is immune." Recall that publisher is also immune, under § 230 of the CDA. The result is a *free pass to libel*. While CDA § 230 states that ISPs cannot be held liable for third-party postings, the trial court's decision would have extended § 230 to apply to individuals as well as ISPs. This was bad case law and fortunately the California 1st District Court of Appeal overturned the decision. [14] However, the case, now retitled <u>Barrett v. Rosenthal</u>, was appealed to the California Supreme Court, which reversed the appellate decision. [15] In effect, the California court's decision allows individuals to republish defamatory content online even if they were notified that it was defamatory. Even the court was not totally at ease with it's decision, stating: [16]

> We acknowledge that recognizing broad immunity for defamatory republications on the Internet has some troubling consequences. Until Congress chooses to revise the settled law in this area, however, plaintiffs who contend they were defamed in an Internet posting may only seek recovery from the original source of the statement.

Should Congress follow the court's suggestion and amend the statute, it might draft a safe harbor provision similar to that of the DMCA which requires removal of the offending content upon notice to the ISP. While it is reasonable to provide protection for third-parties who republish content, upon notification that such content is defamatory it does not make sense to allow the third-party to continue to distribute what it knows to be defamatory content.

Defamation in a Blog

Blogs, short for "web logs," are basically *online diaries or commentaries* by everyday people. When you type words into your blog, it may feel as though you are writing in your diary, but in reality, your words potentially will be seen by millions of readers. Many diary-type blogs are rife with defamatory comments that the writer might not otherwise have published in a more traditional, less instantaneous medium. Other blogs purport to be news or social commentaries. However, unlike professional journalists, who are trained to avoid libel lawsuits by labeling opinions as such and substantiating and verifying facts before presenting a comment as true, bloggers "shoot from the hip," often without regard to the consequences of their actions.

Three months short of the November 2004 election, a Republican congressman dropped his re-election bid after a blogger accused him of having solicited homosexual sex. The blogger posted an audio file on his blog purporting to be the voice of the Virginia congressman requesting homosexual encounters. [17] The blogger offered no proof to back up his claims or that the voice in the audio file was really that of the congressman, although there had been rumors for several years that the congressman was gay. Nor did anyone else substantiate the claim and the congressman did not comment on it. However, in just 11 days, its posting on the Internet was enough to lead to the congressman's withdrawal from the race. While no defamation lawsuit was filed in this case, it illustrates the ease with which an unsubstantiated rumor can be disseminated to large numbers of people very quickly via the Internet and the potential damage to reputations and careers that can result.

Defamation can be written (*libel*) or spoken (*slander*). Truth is a defense to a charge of libel or slander. Libel can occur on a website as well as in a blog or on a message board. When a professor posted a student essay on the school's website, both Oakland University and Professor Donald Mayer were sued for libel.[18] In the allegedly libelous essay about business ethics, the student recounted how he had been urged by his employer to steal software and documentation from his previous employer for the benefit of his then-current employer. The current employer then insisted that the school remove the paper from its website and publish a retraction; the university did the former but refused the latter. The current employer then filed its libel lawsuit, and although a lower court granted summary judgment to the defendants,[19] the Michigan Appeals Court reversed that decision, allowing the case to proceed.[20] The appellate court based its reversal on the fact that Mayer was negligent in not having read the paper closely before posting it "given Mayer's education as a lawyer, his position as a professor of business law and that he teaches defamation in the course at issue."[21]

Judging from a survey of recent articles on the subject, there seems to be a great deal of confusion amongst commentators (and therefore presumably amongst bloggers themselves) about the applicability of libel laws to bloggers. One article describes "a mind-set that has long surrounded blogging: that most bloggers essentially are 'judgment-proof' because they — unlike traditional media such as newspapers, magazines, and television outlets — often are ordinary citizens who don't have a lot of money."[22] Any blogger who believes this absurdity is in for a rude awakening. Being poor does not grant one a license to libel. In fact, as we will see from some of the cases discussed below, anyone from students[23] to homeless hurricane victims[24] can be sued for defamation. While most bloggers "shoot from the hip," unlike a speaker who, too late, wishes he could stuff the spoken words back into his mouth, the blogger still has time to reread and edit comments before posting them. This is the point at which the blogger must shift his brain out of neutral and ask himself "Did I just type something that might cause me to be sued?"

Money is not always the primary motivator of a defamation suit. The plaintiff may feel a need for vindication and sue even if there is no hope of economic recovery. Case in point: in September 2006, a Florida jury awarded against an impoverished defendant what may be the largest judgment over postings on a blog or Internet message board.[25] Louisiana resident Carey Bock sought Florida resident Sue Scheff's aid in withdrawing Bock's sons from a Costa Rican boarding school After her children had been withdrawn, Bock had a dispute with Scheff and posted critical messages about her on <u>Fornits.com</u>, a website for parents with troubled children in boarding schools. Scheff responded with a defamation lawsuit. Bock retained an attorney but when she could no longer could afford his fees she was left unrepresented by legal counsel. Then Hurricane Katrina devastated Louisiana in August 2005 — Bock's house was flooded and she was forced to relocate temporarily to Texas, eventually returning to Louisiana in June 2006. It appears that during that time, according to court records, copies of pleadings (and presumably subsequent notice of trial) mailed to Bock's destroyed home in the disaster area were returned by the Post Office. Bock's Mandeville, Louisiana home was less than 35 miles north of the flooded-ravaged New Orleans, separated only by Lake Pontchatrain. Upon returning to her home, Bock has stated that she knew the trial was pending but did not know the date and in any event could not afford an attorney. When she did not show up for the trial, the judge entered a default judgment for the plaintiff. The issue of damages was left to a jury, which returned a judgment of $11.3 million ($6.3 million in compensatory and $5 million in punitive damages)![26]

Bock had posted messages calling Scheff a "crook," a "con artist" and a "fraud." She probably did not receive proper notice. She could not afford legal counsel and was not represented at, nor did she attend, the trial. As a result she had an $11.3 million judgment entered against her. Bock has stated that she does not have the financial means to appeal, so the judgment will stand. If nothing else, this case should put to rest the mindset that bloggers who are judgment-proof cannot be sued.[27]

Another misconception is that since false posts on the Internet can be edited and replaced instantly, the damage to one's reputation (and thus recoverable money damages) are minimal.[28] There are three major flaws in this theory. First, a visitor may read the original post but may never return to read the correction, thereby continuing to believe the damaging libel. Second, other blogs may repost the original post but fail to post the subsequent correction, leaving all of their readers believing the damaging libel. And third, websites — like The Wayback Machine[29] and Google — cache and archive web pages so someone could easily come across the original post on a cached page without ever seeing the correction.

Yet another misconception is that "a blogger is [not] entitled to the same sort of free speech protection others are."[30] Bloggers are entitled to free speech; however they are not entitled to the abuse of free speech, or to libel others in a capricious or malicious manner. When David Milum fired the lawyer representing him in a drunk driving case after a dispute, he requested return of his $3,000 retainer. The lawyer refused and Milum responded by accusing him in his blog of bribing judges on behalf of drug dealers. The attorney sued and since Milum could not produce any evidence to prove the truth of the libelous statement, he earned the dubious distinction of becoming the first known blogger to lose a libel suit in a jury trial;[31] the Georgia Court of Appeals subsequently upheld the $50,000 jury verdict.[32]

Remember, a statement is not libelous because it says something bad about a person; it is libelous because it says something that is untrue and negatively affects his reputation. Some defamation suits may be filed merely to silence critics, such as in the case of SLAPP actions or gripe sites (both discussed at length below). In these cases, courts must factor in the motivation for bringing the suit, and the public interest served by preserving a forum for consumers to vent, along with the truthfulness of the statement and the degree of damage to reputation, if any.

At least one federal court has held that bloggers are "publishers" and thus protected by § 230 of the CDA from liability for comments posted by third-parties on their blogs. [33] The court ruled that even if the blogger exercised some editorial control over the anonymous postings he is still protected. However, this does not mean that the blogger is not responsible for his own comments; nor does the CDA relieve third-parties of responsibility for the comments that they post.

Then there are the blogs and message boards that almost seem to be inviting libel from their posters. Disgruntled waitresses can now complain about bad tippers by name at bitterwaitress.com. A cursory review of the website reveals that "cheapskate" is one of the nicer epithets a tightwad tipper may expect to see next to his name. But that pales by comparison to the comments found on DontDateHimGirl.com, where women post bad date reviews that identify their dates by name and label them as rapists, pedophiles, or carriers of sexually-transmitted diseases, with no concern for the truthfulness of their statements.

As commentator Kim Ficera succinctly summed up in her own blog: [34]

> Scorned women no longer need to waste time and energy boiling pet rabbits; they can now simply log in to DontDateHimGirl.com, post their exes' pictures and names, and begin destroying the reputations of the men who've done them wrong, all in the name of revenge and in the comfort of anonymity.

And therein lies the problem: with the assurance of anonymity, posters fear no consequences from the comments they post. Truth becomes the first casualty in the lack of accountability. A criminal defense lawyer sued the website for libel, after several posts allegedly from women he dated, appeared on the website along with his photograph. One post claimed that he had herpes, another alleged that he had infected a woman he once dated with a sexually transmitted disease, while a third said that he was gay. [35] The plaintiff argued that the website operator was liable because the site solicited negative comments but did not screen them for truthfulness.

DontDateHimGirl.com sought to fall under the safe harbor provisions of the CDA but the lawsuit attempted to distinguish a website from an OSP (such as AOL or Yahoo!). More important is the distinction between third-party posts to generic blogs and message boards and those blogs and message boards that literally invite and solicit potentially libelous comments. It is one thing to propose that the CDA provide the operator of a website, message board, or blog with a safe harbor for comments made in the heat of debate on topics of public interest. However, where the sole purpose of the forum is to solicit posters to "talk trash" about specific individuals without regard to the truth or falsity of their comments, it would be both inequitable and legally reckless to allow such forums to find shelter under the safe harbor umbrella.

The Allegheny County (PA) Common Pleas court did not address that issue, stating that it lacked jurisdiction to hear the case (see Chapter One), even though the plaintiff was a Pennsylvania resident and Pennsylvanians posted messages on the Florida website.[36]

Separate from the defamation issue is a privacy issue. Assuming for the moment that the allegations made on DontDateHimGirl.com were true — that the man had herpes and was gay — would not posting such personal details on the Internet for the whole world to see be an invasion of privacy? What about a post revealing that a man was HIV positive, or that he had served time in prison? Or that he had been sexually abused as a child? The technology of the Internet, through instant access to a worldwide audience, enables a single individual to destroy the reputation of another, either through false statements or revelation of private matters. As a society, we must ensure that our laws protect against both threats while not chilling legitimate free speech.

This type of website can be defined as a *Personal Attack Website, i.e.*, websites that solicit online postings containing personal attacks and offensive content that can be archived indefinitely and easily accessed through a search engine query. Usually, these sites take the form of message boards or forums where users can start a thread and post comments to it. The websites are archived by search engines so names posted on the message boards will show up in search query results. As we discussed in a previous chapter, an increasing number of employers are conducting Google searches on job applicants. Suppose such a search by an employer turned up negative or potentially defamatory comments on a personal attack website?

That's exactly what one woman believes happened to her. A Yale law student interviewing with 16 firms for a summer job, the woman did not receive a single offer, which she attributes to postings about her on a law school-related message board. The Phi Beta Kappa student had been the topic of derogatory chat on AutoAdmit.com, a message board for law school students run by Anthony Ciolli, a third-year law student at the University of Pennsylvania (the site is not operated with school resources) and Jarret Cohen, a 23-year-old insurance agent.[37] Users post anonymously with no accountability for their comments, which often include general ad hominem attacks on racial and religious minorities as well as targeted attacks on specific individuals. Sometimes the personal attacks are accompanied by photographs of the victim, lifted from Facebook or other social network websites, and increasing the sense of personal violation on the part of the victim. It was reported that one user threatened "to sexually violate" the Yale student while another user posed as her on the board to make it look as though she were participating in the chat.[38]

Another Yale law student, whose picture and breasts were the topic of explicit discussion on the message board, said she was afraid to venture out after posters encouraged her classmates to shoot and post photos of her with their cell phones. The message board operators were quoted as saying that the women invite attention by posting their photographs on social networking sites; a comment that is wrong on so many levels that it bears repeating if only to offer a glimpse into the mindset of those who would run personal attack boards.[39] (It should also be noted that copying someone's photographs from their social networking site and republishing them without permission on a message board is copyright infringement).

Ironically, the message board operators were quoted as saying that their users posted anonymously because they did not want to "worry about employers pulling up information on them," showing that they and their users were (hypocritically) aware of the negative consequences of Google searches by prospective employers on the victims.[40]

While the CDA may or may not protect personal attack websites, there is nothing in the Act to prevent such sites from removing offensive content once notified of its existence. However, from anecdotal experience, most, if not all such websites do not remove the material. While theoretically the poster can be sued for defamation, it is not always easy to uncover the poster's identity. Also, the damage has been done by the initial posting, by its continued presence on the site, and by the fact that the defamatory comments will be searchable forever through archived caches.

Some misguided free speech advocates contend that the solution is to counter the defamatory speech with more speech, *i.e.* a rebuttal. (The "Marketplace of Ideas" is discussed at the end of this chapter). The problem with this approach is that in defamation cases, it merely reinforces the defamation by repeating it and adding another layer to the cached and searchable content. Suppose for example, that an anonymous poster writes that John Smith is a child molester, and John Smith writes back "I am not a child molester." Five years later, after a job interview, a prospective employer conducts a Google search on John Smith's name and finds his statement "I am not a child molester." The employer may think "Why would someone write that?," draw his own inferences, and not bother to search any further.

Defamation versus Anonymous Free Speech

The U.S. Supreme Court has held that the First Amendment protects the right to anonymous speech.[41] Anonymity, the court reasoned, helps speech stay free. However, a conflict arises when an anonymous Internet poster makes a defamatory comment on a blog or website. The right to free speech does not include a right to defame, but how does one sue a faceless entity?

A New Jersey Superior Court fashioned a three-prong test for a defamation plaintiff seeking to discover the identities of anonymous Internet posters. In that case, a corporation sued multiple "John Doe" defendants for allegedly defamatory messages posted on a bulletin board and sought discovery of their identities.[42] In denying discovery, the court announced the *Dendrite* test: the plaintiff must (1) show it has attempted to notify the anonymous posters that they are the subject of an application for an order of disclosure; (2) identify to the court statements made by the posters; and (3) establish a prima facie cause of action for defamation against the posters. Only after the three prongs of this test have been met can the trial court then "balance the defendant's First Amendment right of anonymous free speech against the strength of the prima facie case presented and the necessity for the disclosure of the anonymous defendant's identity to allow the plaintiff to proceed."[43]

A subsequent lawsuit, filed in 2007 by a plaintiff upset that a website revealed his identity in response to a subpoena, may lead the court to extend or curtail the *Dendrite* Test.[44] The plaintiff had posted anonymous comments on a message board, calling his target a "litigation terrorist," a "pathetic psychopath" and a "paranoid-delusional, over-paid-under-worked sicko." The plaintiff claimed that he was not notified of the subpoena and only learned his identity had been disclosed when the target of the attack outed him on the bulletin board. The case may clarify what means of attempted notification are satisfactory under *Dendrite*.

A Delaware court took a different approach toward protecting anonymous speech.[45] An elected official filed a "John Doe" suit to reveal the identity of an anonymous critic in a blog. The poster had referred to the politician's "character flaws," "mental deterioration," and "failed leadership."[46] The ISP notified "Doe" about the request to disclose his identity, leading "Doe" to seek an emergency protective order to prevent the ISP from releasing his identity.[47] The trial court denied the order, and "Doe" appealed directly to the Delaware Supreme Court, which reversed the trial court. The state supreme court acknowledged the importance of the right to speak anonymously, particularly on political issues, while at the same time noting that the First Amendment does not convey a right to defame others. It recognized the need to balance these competing interests but thought the *Dendrite* test went too far:[48]

> [T]he *Dendrite* standard goes further than is necessary to protect the anonymous speaker and, by doing so, unfairly limits access to the civil justice system as a means to redress the harm to reputation caused by defamatory speech. Specifically, under *Dendrite*, the plaintiff is put to the nearly impossible task of demonstrating as a matter of law that a publication is defamatory before he serves his complaint or even knows the identity of the defendant(s). Indeed, under *Dendrite*, the plaintiff is not even able to place the alleged defamation in context by describing the

relationship between the plaintiff and the speaker because the speaker's identity is protected until the prima facie case against him has been established.

Frankly, the court's rationale makes little sense, as it implies that one must know the context in order to determine if a statement is defamatory. While context is necessary to show *libel per quod*, it is not necessary in cases of *libel per se*. If someone writes that you are "a deadbeat, a thief, and a drunken wife-beater" that is libel per se (absent a showing of truth, which is an affirmative defense) and far from "an impossible task" to demonstrate the defamatory nature of the comments (at least in terms of surviving a motion for summary judgment). In *libel per quod*, the statement may be harmless by itself but becomes defamatory when placed in the context of other facts. Most defamation lawsuits are *per se* and public figures have a higher standard to prove defamation.[49] Nonetheless, the court reached the correct decision, realizing that "there is reason to believe that many defamation plaintiffs bring suit merely to unmask the identities of anonymous critics" holding that the plaintiff must present evidence creating a genuine issue of material fact for each element of the defamation claim before a Delaware court orders an anonymous speaker's identity to be disclosed.[50] Applying that standard, the court had no difficulty finding that the phrases "character flaws," "mental deterioration," and "failed leadership," were merely opinion and not defamatory.

The right of anonymous free speech is immensely important to a free society, especially in the political arena. However, it is not absolute and must be balanced with the interests of individuals to protect themselves from defamatory comments posted anonymously. A Pennsylvania trial court, choosing not to follow either the New Jersey or Delaware rationale discussed above, found in favor of the plaintiff compelling the operator of two websites to reveal the identities of anonymous posters of comments about a Philadelphia law firm.[51] The posters referred to the lawyers as "thieves," who committed "fraud" and had "lied to a judge."[52] The court ruled that the statements on the websites were "*defamation per se*" because they amount to accusations of criminal conduct.[53] The court went on to state that it chose not to fashion a balancing test as the New Jersey and Delaware courts had done because it believed the state's existing civil procedure rules that prohibit discovery sought "in bad faith" or that would "cause unreasonable annoyance, embarrassment, oppression, burden or expense to the deponent or any person or party" would afford sufficient protection to both interests.[54] Under that standard, the court concluded that the statements were defamation per se, and as such not entitled to First Amendment protection.

SLAPPs

A Strategic Lawsuit Against Public Participation (SLAPP) is a civil lawsuit without substantial merit brought by private interests to stop citizens from exercising their political rights or to punish them for having done so. The plaintiffs bringing the SLAPP lawsuits usually do not prevail on the merits, since the merits are often specious. The charges are often flimsy and the damage claims ridiculously large. Most of these lawsuits wind up being dismissed and of those that do make it to trial the defendants win more often than not. However, the goal of companies and organizations filing SLAPPs is not to win monetary judgments but to harass, intimidate, and distract their opponents. A lawsuit can last an average of two–to–three years and even if the defendant wins, the costs and legal fees can total tens of thousands of dollars, not to mention the toll of emotional stress, loss of time, and expenditure of effort on the defendant, his family, and supporters.

Many companies are now suing anonymous messages board posters. Of course, not all such lawsuits are SLAPPs; some may indeed have merit. But many are merely attempts to silence anonymous corporate critics and intimidate others. This "chilling effect" of a SLAPP lawsuit often silences others on the message board, which is the actual goal of the SLAPP, *i.e.*, to halt public discussion of an issue that the plaintiff prefers remain undiscussed.

The elements of a SLAPP are:

- The *defendants' speech* forms the basis of the lawsuit

- There is *no true legal merit* to the lawsuit (although the lawsuit may claim defamation, breach of contract, and/or trade secret violations)

- The lawsuit is usually filed as a *"John Doe" lawsuit*, where the pseudonym "John Doe" is used to represent the name of the unknown defendant, since most message posters use screen names in lieu of their real names

- The plaintiff *attempts to discover the poster's identity* from his ISP

- There is a resulting *chilling effect* on the speech of others

California is at the forefront in addressing SLAPPs. In California, once an anti-SLAPP motion (the "special motion to strike") is filed, all discovery is stayed (*i.e.*, frozen). Thus, the plaintiff's attempts to discover information about the poster's identity must wait until after the court determines whether or not the company's lawsuit has a "probability of success." If an anti-SLAPP motion to strike is *granted*, then the lawsuit is dismissed and the prevailing defendant is entitled to recover attorney's fees and costs. If the motion is *denied*, then the anti-SLAPP statute does not apply and the litigation (and discovery) proceeds.[55]

Blog Wars

There was a time, in pre-Internet days, when one wrote down one's inner-most thoughts and feelings in a diary, a small book with a lock, which usually lay hidden under lock and key in a desk drawer. Today, many people bare their souls in online diaries, called web logs, or "blogs" for short. Unlike the locked diaries, blogs are accessible by the entire world, yet often their authors, known as "bloggers," forget that their words may be read by anyone and everyone and that their words carry consequences. A remark that lies unread in a locked diary is harmless but an offensive remark broadcast to the world–at–large may be actionable as defamation, breach of contract, or grounds for dismissal from employment.

Breach of Contract

If an employee posts *information* (*e.g.*, regarding products, sales, management, employees, or rumors) *about his employer in a public forum*, and he had previously signed a *confidentiality agreement*, then the employee may have breached his fiduciary duty to the company and be in breach of contract.

Sometimes an employee (*i.e.*, a "whistle-blower") will post anonymously on an Internet message board to disclose corporate wrongdoing within the company that employs him, or perhaps merely criticize his employer. Absent a confidentiality agreement, if the anonymous poster is later revealed as employee, can the company fire him? Or does the employee have a First Amendment free speech right to criticize his employer?

Fired For Blogging

In 2004, Friendster, a social networking website, fired one of its employees for comments she made in her personal blog on her own website.[56] Joyce Park, a web developer, made three posts about Friendster in her blog. The posts related to the new programming she had developed for the Friendster website that made the website run much faster. The information in her blog was all publicly available information. Friendster did not have a stated policy about web comments and did not give Parks any warning or ask her to remove her comments before firing her. Park had written:[57]

> As most of you probably know, I've spent the last six months working at Friendster.
> I have not managed to release any code in that entire time. Finally on Friday we
> launched a platform rearchitecture based on loose-coupling, web standards, and a

move from JSP (via Tomcat) to PHP. The website doesn't look much different, but hopefully we can now stop being a byword for unacceptably poky site performance. I also want to call out our first new user-facing feature in a long time, Friends in Common (upper left corner of your friends' profiles). Try it out and let me know what you think.

Presumably, someone in Friendster's management did not like the reference to "being a byword for unacceptably poky site performance." Imagine how management must have felt upon reading the 4,630 comments (culled from a Google search in September 2004) resulting from the negative backlash to Park's firing. Many outraged commentators and fellow bloggers urged readers to cancel their Friendster memberships in protest, proving once again that companies need to realize that the Internet is not a vacuum and must beware the backlash to their actions.

Park was not the first employee to lose her job for comments made in a blog. Microsoft fired contractor Michael Hanscom in 2003 after he took pictures of Apple G5 computers being unloaded onto the software company's campus and posted them to his blog under the title, "Even Microsoft wants G5s."[58] (Despite the implication in the blogger's caption, Microsoft had good reason to order Apple computers, as it is a major producer of software for Apple).

Then there was the case of Ellen Simonetti, a Delta Airlines flight attendant fired after posting suggestive pin-up photos of herself in her Delta uniform on her blog.[59] Simonetti shot back by re-titling her blog "Diary of a Fired Flight Attendant." And Mark Jen was working for Google for only 11 days when he was fired for comments he made in his blog. Jen diaried his impressions and criticisms of his new employer, which set management at Google agoggle.[60] Reporter Rachel Mosteller blogged about how much she hated her job: "I really hate my place of employment. Seriously."[61] While not naming her place of employment — the Durham (N.C.) Herald-Sun — her employer sought to relieve her obvious suffering by giving her a pink slip the next day.[62] There have been so many "fired for blogging" cases that there is now a name for it — getting "dooced." The phrase was coined by web designer Heather B. Armstrong in 2002 after she was fired for comments about her co-workers in her blog on her website, Dooce.com.[63]

Beyond the private sector, government employees and contractors risk dismissal for blogging too. A CIA contractor was fired after she posted her opinion that American interrogation methods violated the Geneva Conventions in her blog.[64]

The National Labor Relations Act might protect employees from being fired for their blog comments related to union organizing activity, although there has been no case law on this scenario yet.[65] However, it would not shield against firing for defamatory comments or disclosure of trade secrets in a blog. Union contracts (as well as some non-union employment contracts) that require "just cause" for firing may afford the blogger some protection. The blogger would still be subject to termination for "just cause" if the blog violated the employer's work rules. Non-union workers are at greater risk of losing their jobs over blogging; they could risk firing if they criticize the company or disclose confidential information. An "at will" employee is one who works for a private employer and has no union contract, and can be fired for any reason not specifically prohibited by law. Employers in "at–will" states can fire employees even if they wrote the blog on their own time on their own computer outside of the office.

Employee blogs raise the issue of balancing freedom of speech with an employer's right to protect the company's public image. Some bloggers have begun adding disclaimers stating that they do not represent the company for whom they work. Ideally, companies should establish written policies about blogging. But often, it is a matter of common sense. As one blog reader put it, "Make your boss look bad, find another job. It's a no–brainer."

Student Blogs

Can a school punish or expel a student based on the content of his blog? Later in this book we discuss the limits of student free speech, which often turn on whether the school is a private school or a public school (public schools administered by state governments are constrained by the First Amendment in limiting student speech) and on whether the student used the school's computers, website, or web hosting.

The U.S. Supreme Court has ruled that students have free speech rights under the First Amendment and that any regulation of such speech by public school administrators must be to prevent "substantial disruption" in the classroom.[66] However, those speech rights have been curtailed by subsequent decisions: schools may prohibit "indecent speech" (e.g., a high school student's sexual innuendo laced speech during a student assembly),[67] or speech at school events (even off school property) promoting illegal drug use.[68] One highly controversial decision held that schools can regulate, for legitimate educational reasons, the content of non-forum, school-sponsored newspapers (a forum being where school officials have "by policy or practice" opened a publication for unrestricted use by students).[69] The case is controversial because it concluded that a student newspaper did not constitute a forum for student expression. The court appears to distinguish between a student publication produced as part of a journalism class project (non-forum) and one produced extracurricularly, open to participation by all students (forum). As the court has held that non-forums are entitled to a lesser degree of First Amendment protection, it remains to be seen if the court will consider the Internet to be a public forum.

When a middle school principal found a MySpace page purported labelled as his own profile, he found that a student, identified as "A.B.,"[70] had commented:[71]

> Hey you piece of greencastle shit.
>
> What the fuck do you think of me [now] that you can['t] control me? Huh? Ha ha ha guess what I'll wear my fucking piercings all day long and to school and you can['t] do shit about it! Ha ha fucking ha! Stupid bastard!
>
> Oh and kudos to whomever made this ([I'm] pretty sure I know who).

The comment referred to her displeasure over the school's policy on body piercings. A.B. did not create the fake page; she merely posted a comment on it. Nonetheless, the state "filed a delinquency petition alleging A.B. committed acts that, if committed by an adult, would have constituted identity deception,"[72] and one count of identity theft, although it is not clear where there was any identity deception or identity theft committed by A.B. since she did not create the fake profile. The state must have also realized this, as it dismissed the identity theft charge but A.B. was still adjudicated by the juvenile court to be a "delinquent child" and placed on nine months probation.

The Juvenile Court opinion stated:[73]

> [A.B.'s comment] is obscene. As the well known U.S. Supreme Court decision "One knows Pornography when one sees it," this [c]ourt finds that such language is obscene in the context used by [A.B.]. [A.B.] was not exercising her constituted rights of free speech in such a tirade — but to use the most vulgar language she could. Moreover she was not expressing her opinion in her writing.

We will discuss obscenity in the next chapter, which leads off with the famous quote by Justice Potter Stewart that he could not define obscenity but he knew it when he saw it. However, it should be noted that the humorous offhand comment was a quote within the Justice's opinion, and not a holding or decision; any judge who cannot tell the difference between a quote within an opinion and an actual Supreme Court decision has no business sitting on the bench of any court.

The Indiana Court of Appeals agreed with the appellant's argument:[74]

> A.B. asserts that her message, made in a public forum and criticizing Gobert, a state actor, in implementing a school policy proscribing decorative piercings is a legitimate communication envisioned within the bounds of protected political speech.

A.B. openly criticizes Gobert's imposed school policy on decorative body piercings and forcefully indicates her displeasure with it. While we have little regard for A.B.'s use of vulgar epithets, we conclude that her overall message constitutes political speech.

Students do have a right of free speech under the First Amendment.[75] They may not be as articulate as one might wish, falling back on "vulgar language" to express themselves, but it is expression, which is protected when it concerns policies implemented by state school officials. Compare this case with the Anna Draker case in Chapter 16 where students created a fake profile of an educator and that allegedly defamed her, with no apparent political message.

In another case, a University of Miami student posted a raunchy rap song recorded two years earlier by members of the school's football team, describing their sexual exploits with coeds in their dorm room. After attracting 64,000 visitors and the attention of ESPN to his usually inconspicuous blog, the student was summoned to the dean's office and advised to withdraw from the school.[76] Word of the misogynist rap song had spread to local and national media, and the football team — the school's cash cow — was looking more like a filthy pig. Five days later, after school officials discovered what the student called a satirical suicide note on his blog, the school ordered the student to undergo a "comprehensive battery of tests from a licensed psychologist"[77] and to move out of the university residence hall and into a motel because the university "has an obligation to ensure the health and well-being of its students."[78] According to news reports,[79] the student typed his blog on his own laptop and appeared to use a URL not connected to the university, although the school, in a letter to the local newspaper, contended that the student had used the university's "computer network" and "computer systems" — presumably this meant that the student connected his laptop to the Internet via the school's ISP.[80] The school's contention that removing the student from the structured supervised environment of a residence hall to a dingy motel room was for the student's own welfare and not punitive appears questionable. The university's letter also contended that the student's removal was unrelated to the posting of the rap song on his blog. The school's athletic director later apologized for the "demeaning tape" however there is no record of any of the football team members who actually made the tape having been expelled from the school.[81]

Lawyer Blogs

Many lawyers have begun using blogs, either as marketing tools or simply to discuss a wide range of legal topics with their clients on a regular basis. This raises the issue of whether lawyer blogs fall under advertising (which is regulated by state bar associations) or political free speech. State bar associations are revising their attorney advertising and ethics rules to address the issue of whether lawyer blogs should be regulated as advertising.

Most state bars regulate all advertising by their attorneys, but the scope of what is considered "advertising" can encompass business cards, letterheads, print ads, radio and television commercials, direct mail, and the Internet. The first question is when does an attorney blog cross over from free speech to regulated advertising. Lawyers may blog about current court decisions, political events, or subjects within their practice (*e.g.*, criminal law, bankruptcy, personal injury, litigation, etc.) or their blogs may be more personal in nature, such as discussing their last family vacation. As with most blogs, readers may be permitted to make their own third-party posts to the blog. But even these seemingly innocuous topics may be viewed by state bars as marketing-focused with the purpose of attracting or retaining clients. In an attempt to fend off criticism from state bars, some attorneys have taken to attaching a disclaimer identifying the blog's purpose, *e.g.*, that it is not intended as advertising and does not represent the views of the firm. However, it is more likely that content rather than disclaimers will sway the bar associations in their determinations. The second question is whether requiring attorneys to submit their blogs for review by a state bar committee would stifle blog discussions. Indeed, there is an inherent contradiction between the spontaneity and immediacy of blogging and the red tape of review committees.

Another issue raised by lawyer blogs is whether comments could run afoul of lawyers' professional liability insurance company guidelines for coverage. One of the largest legal professional liability carriers, Chubb Group of Insurance Companies, stated its policy would be to insure blogging by attorneys so long as the blog fell within certain parameters.[82] The insurer differentiated "informational blogs" that merely inform about the law and pose minimal risk from "advisory blogs" that might be construed as offering legal advice. The idea that a Q and A format blog would be equivalent to offering legal advice, or actually establish an attorney-client relationship (and hence potential malpractice liability) is subject to debate. Most attorneys would argue that to have an attorney client relationship, the attorney must first actually meet his client.

Military Blogs

What if your employer is the government, or specifically, the U.S. military? The Iraq War has put a new spin on blogging. Many soldiers are eschewing old-fashioned letters to the home-front in favor of online military blogs. These *milbloggers* (*i.e.*, military bloggers) offer details of the war that do not make it into most hometown newspapers. Raw war reporting with varied themes, including photographs snapped by the soldiers themselves and online diary entries, fill the milblogs. Some milblogs are political; some question the war while others enthusiastically embrace it. Many milblogs accounts are filled with examples of military absurdity, the 21st century "e-version" of Joseph Heller's "*Catch-22*" novel of the same theme.[83]

Milbloggers must be careful not to reveal any information, such as names and locations, that might be useful to enemies. Sometimes what may seem harmless, such as soldiers posting photographs of the scene of an enemy attack in their blogs might unwittingly provide the enemy with valuable damage assessment data. Such revelations could not only be harmful to troops but also subject the milbloggers to punishment under Article 15 of the Uniform Code of Military Justice (UCMJ). During the Iraq war, a 40-year-old Arizona National Guardsman on active duty in Baghdad was demoted from specialist to private first class and fined $820 per month for two months after a military tribunal concluded that he had revealed classified information in his milblogs.[84]

The UCMJ prohibits soldiers from disclosing or "encouraging widespread publication" of classified or specific information about troop movement and location, military strategy and tactics, and soldiers who have been wounded or killed.[85] The latter restriction, which also includes photographs of casualties, is to prevent families from learning of a loved one's injury or death before official notification by the military. Additionally, milbloggers are forbidden from disclosing planned raids, itineraries of senior leaders, photographs of new technology, or details that could compromise their location.[86]

While most milbloggers are cautious not to reveal any information, some still have been shut down by commanding officers. Cheryl Irwin, a Defense Department spokesperson told the Associated Press in 2004:[87]

> [The Pentagon has] no specific guidelines on blogging per se…Generally, they can do it if they are writing their blogs not on government time and not on a government computer. They have every right under the First Amendment to say any darn thing they want to say unless they reveal classified information, and then it becomes an issue as a security violation.

Despite that assurance, servicemen have reported instances of being ordered to shut down their milblogs for reasons other than security violations. Beginning in April 2005, all military personnel in Iraq were required to register their blogs and the content is subject to quarterly monitoring by their commanding officers to ensure they are not violating operational security and privacy restrictions.[88] Unit commanders are authorized to establish more restrictive requirements if they feel it is necessary, such as reviewing individual blog postings.

Both the U.S. Army and the Defense Department have programs set up to monitor blogs and websites. The Army Web Risk Assessment Cell, based in Virginia, monitors official and unofficial blogs and other websites for threats to security, such as official documents, personal contact information, and photographs of weapons or camp entrances.[89] The Defense Department's Joint Web Risk Assessment Cell program only monitors official military sites. Procedurally, the Web Risk Assessment Cell will first contact the soldier to have him remove any objectionable content; if he does not do so, then they contact his commanding officer. According to an Army investigative report, official Army websites violated operational security more than milbloggers.[90] Army Web Risk Assessment Cell audits revealed at least 1,813 violations of operational security on 878 official military websites as opposed to 28 on 594 milblogs (from January 2006 to January 2007).[91]

While it is likely that the military will eventually promulgate guidelines on milblogging, the boundaries between the military employer's need to control speech for security purposes and the servicemen's First Amendment right to free speech through milblogging have not yet been defined by the courts.[92]

News Blogs

Some blogs present themselves as offering news and commentary on social issues or industry-related topics. The question then arises, is a "news blogger" a journalist?[93] If so, is the news blogger entitled to the same statutory protections under state shield laws as professional journalists? (Although most states have shield laws, which protect journalists from being compelled to reveal sources, there is no federal shield law). Can a news blogger claim First Amendment protection?

The issue arose when Apple Computer sued a news blogger[94] and two other websites[95] to force them to reveal the identity of the Apple employee who had leaked advance product information to them. Apple claimed that revelations about unreleased products were trade secret violations.[96] A San Jose, California (Santa Clara) County Superior Court ruled[97] that the state "shield law"[98] did not apply to news bloggers or the other two information technology news websites and that they could be subpoenaed to reveal their sources. The decision was reversed on appeal and Apple declined to appeal the reversal.[99] Apple had contended in its complaint that the First Amendment and the California "shield law" only applied to "legitimate members of the press."

But what is a "legitimate member of the press?" Unlike many countries, such as Italy, where one must first pass an examination and be licensed by the government to become a professional journalist, in the United States there is no litmus test to determine who is a journalist. The high school newspaper reporter may be covering a news story for his readership just as the Washington Post reporter does for his constituency. A journalist may write on behalf of readers of a trade publication, a special interest magazine, or even a small town newspaper with only a few hundred readers. Why then, would a writer for an online publication with hundreds of thousands of readers not be considered equally "legitimate?"

The First Amendment to the U.S. Constitution states: [100]

> Congress shall make no law respecting an establishment of religion, or prohibiting
> the free exercise thereof; or abridging the freedom of speech, or of the press; or
> the right of the people peaceably to assemble, and to petition the government for
> a redress of grievances.

Nowhere within the First Amendment does it state that freedom of the press applies only to organizations or "legitimate members of the press." Indeed, no doubt the inspiration for "freedom of the press" came from Thomas Paine who in 1776 used a printing press to print pamphlets like "Common Sense" that led to the American Revolution. The First Amendment was drafted, not to protect an organized body called "the press," but to preserve the right of any individual to express and publish his views freely, as Paine did. The Internet allows every individual to have his own version of an electronic printing press that can reach practically anyone in the world who wishes to read it. In this context, Apple's comments about the First Amendment appear uninformed, disingenuous, and even ludicrous.

Since state "shield laws" are drafted by each state's legislature, their applicability in this type of situation would hinge on how each statute defined "journalist." For example, would the author of a controversial or exposé book be considered a "journalist" under the "shield law?"

Ironically, in the Apple case, the judge's comments were more ludicrous than Apple's. Santa Clara County Court Judge James Kleinberg stated: [101]

> Unlike the whistleblower who discloses a health, safety or welfare hazard affecting
> all, or the government employee who reveals mismanagement or worse by our
> public officials, [the sites] are doing nothing more than feeding the public's
> insatiable desire for information.

Is not "feeding the public's insatiable desire for information" the very job definition of what journalists and newspapers are supposed to do and have been doing for centuries?

A bill called the Free Flow of Information Act introduced in 2007 would create a federal shield law and define a journalist as one who derives "financial gain or livelihood" from the practice of journalism, which it defines as "gathering, preparing, collecting, photographing, recording, writing, editing, reporting or publishing of news or information that concerns local, national or international events or other matters of public interest for dissemination to the public."[102] Theoretically, ad-supported bloggers would qualify under the bill. Despite the "financial gain or livelihood" requirement, the bill is an improvement over previous attempts that based the definition of a journalist on ties to an established media entity rather than on one's function.

Even professional journalists have encountered problems as bloggers. A Louisville (KY) Courier-Journal reporter had his media credentials revoked and was evicted from a NCAA college baseball playoff game for violating NCAA rules against blogging from the event.[103] In mid-game, the reporter-blogger was told by college athletic staff that if the school did not revoke his credential it would jeopardize its chances of hosting another NCAA baseball game. The newspaper admitted that the college had sent an NCAA memo prior to the game stating that no blogging was allowed during the game because blogs were considered a "live representation of the game," however it contended the blog was merely reporting facts, not broadcasting a recreation of the game. Live blogging has become common at many sporting events as the technology of Wi-Fi is enables reporters to get Internet connectivity in the field. A decade earlier, when pagers and not Wi-Fi were state-of-the-art, a similar case arose. The National Basketball Association (NBA) challenged a text-message service developed by Motorola, that was designed to give subscribers updates of basketball scores. The 2nd Circuit held that the NBA did not have a valid copyright claim over the factual, statistical information about the game and that Motorola's Sports Trax product was not a substitute for the product offered by the NBA (*i.e.*, the ability to be physically present at the game or watch it on TV).[104] Following that logic, the blogger might also prevail in court.

Vlogs

The newest form of blog is the vlog, short for video log. With the easy availability of webcams and the rising popularity of "post your own video" websites like YouTube and Google Video, many bloggers have become vloggers. Vlogs can range from one sitting in front of a webcam discussing whatever is on her mind that day to attempts at very stylish productions. Viewers can then leave text comments below the video.

Many vloggers produce regular shows and develop a following of viewers. Some vloggers have tens of thousands of subscribers to their videos, turning bedroom broadcasters in to Internet celebrities. A few vloggers have gone beyond vlogging to sign recording contracts or TV deals. This presents an interesting issue: would a celebrity vlogger be considered a "public figure" in a defamation suit?

To prove defamation, one must show a published intentional false communication that injures one's reputation. However, the statement must also have been made with "actual malice," which means knowledge of falsity or reckless disregard of the truth, if the defamed individual is a public figure. This standard, first enunciated by the U.S. Supreme Court in _New York Times v. Sullivan_ [105] to apply to _public officials_, has been extended to _public figures._

> 'Public figures' are those persons who, though not public officials, are 'involved in issues in which the public has a justified and important interest.' Such figures are, of course, numerous and include artists, athletes, business people, dilettantes, anyone who is famous or infamous because of who he is or what he has done. [106]

The U.S. Supreme Court, in _Gertz v. Robert Welch, Inc.,_ has also defined public figures as those who have "thrust themselves to the forefront of particular public controversies in order to influence the resolution of the issues involved." [107] One can also become a "limited public figure" by engaging in actions that generate publicity within a narrow area of interest. In _Gertz_, the court noted that public figures "invite attention and comment" and "usually enjoy significantly greater access to the channels of effective communication and hence have a more realistic opportunity to counteract false statements than private individuals normally enjoy." [108] That would seem to describe a YouTube "celebrity" who posts videos to invite attention and comment (YouTube allows both text comments to be posted below the video and "response videos" by others) and has access to channels of effective communication by posting his or her own response video or text comments.

Tortious Interference

To file a cause of action for tortious interference, the plaintiff must show all of the following:

1. The existence of a _contract or business relationship_
2. Intentional _interference_
3. _Causation_
4. _Damage_

In one case, the defendant, an Internet activist, upon receiving spam, complained to the spammer's ISP, who promptly disconnected the spammer.[109] The spammer then sued the Internet activist for tortious interference with his business contract with his ISP.

In another case, the defendant used frames to put content from the Washington Post website within its own framed website, allowing users to bypass the Washington Post's website which included paid ads.[110] The Washington Post sued for tortious interference with its business relationship with its advertisers, claiming that the framing made performance of its advertising contracts more burdensome.

In yet another case, the defendant, a disgruntled former Intel employee, sent e-mails criticizing Intel to thousands of its employees at their workplace e-mail addresses.[111] Although recipients could opt-out from future mailings and the defendant apparently honored all opt-out request, Intel claimed that the content of the e-mails disrupted its workplace and was tortious interference.

These three examples of tortious interference claims are presented here to familiarize you with the concept and breadth of the tortious interference cause of action, not necessarily to illustrate successful claims. In fact, Intel lost its claim, as the court found that the defendant had a First Amendment right to send e-mail (*i.e.*, Intel had only objected to *content* of the e-mails, not that it was an e-mail attack against its servers).

Securities Fraud

Securities fraud can serve as another cause of action against certain speech on the Internet. Both criminal and civil lawsuits can result in response to *wrongful posts in online forums attempting to manipulate securities prices* (*e.g.*, rumors) or attempts to manipulate stock prices by e-mailing fake press releases or information, or creating phony websites. In a *"Pump and Dump"* scheme, an individual may enter a message board or chat room and talk up stocks she already owns and then surreptitiously sell them into the artificial demand she has created. The S.E.C. has estimated that 100 million stock spam e-mails are sent each week, causing sharp spikes in share prices and trading volume that the spammers then sell into.[112] E-mailed stock spam is more efficient boiler rooms and cold calls, as one study showed the spam can boost a stock price by six percent.[113]

In addition to civil lawsuits, criminal enforcement actions can arise from violation of the laws governing securities fraud. These laws include state securities laws and common law fraud statutes, and federal statutes such as the Securities Act of 1933[114] and the Securities and Exchange Act of 1934.[115] The laws are enforced, respectively, by state securities administrators and divisions, and the United States Securities and Exchange Commission (S.E.C.). Stockbrokers are also regulated by the National Association of Securities Dealers (N.A.S.D.), a self-regulating organization that does not make or enforce laws.

Marketplace of Ideas

Supreme Court Justice Oliver Wendell Holmes first enunciated the "marketplace of ideas" metaphor in his dissent in _Abrams v. United States_ in 1919.[116] The idea behind his metaphor is that ideas compete for acceptance against each other — with the underlying faith that the truth will prevail in such an open encounter. Applying this concept to the Internet, the injured party can counter the damaging effects of Internet postings by _rebutting_ them in same forum. However, there is the _time factor_ until a rebuttal can be made to be considered. An individual may not learn of a defamatory posting until long after many people have seen it. And while a rebuttal can be made almost instantaneously on the Internet, so too can a defamatory comment be seen or reposted instantaneously. The rebuttal must also avoid defamatory comments itself. One problem with this approach is that, in defamation cases, it merely reinforces the defamation by repeating it and adding another layer to the cached and searchable content. And in some cases, where a public company seeks to rebut a defamatory statement, there may be _securities laws restrictions_ on what public statements a company can make and when it can make them.

Cyber Gripers

The Internet has evened the playing field by allowing aggrieved consumers to criticize companies that they feel have cheated them. Indeed, the Internet is the world's largest soapbox, a cyberspace version of Hyde Park. A housewife or Joe Sixpack suddenly has the power to tell millions of people about the bad experience he or she had with a company's product or services.

However, the _cyber griper, must avoid violating defamation, trademark, or copyright laws_ while airing her gripe, lest she open herself up to a retaliatory lawsuit from the company. Many firms seeking to silence their critics and stem negative publicity counter with a lawsuit for defamation, trademark infringement, or even tortious interference with business. Although courts tend to side with the cyber gripers upholding their free speech rights, the expense of defending such lawsuits often has the same chilling effect as a SLAPP lawsuit. (One might argue they are identical to SLAPP lawsuits as there is a public interest component in the cyber gripers speech).

And _companies must weigh the public relations repercussions_ of attempts to quash cyber gripers; unwanted negative publicity from a lawsuit may exceed the reach of the cyber griper's small website, blog, or message board posting. Consider the case of Toys"R"Us, who took umbrage at a website titled "Roadkill"R"Us," a humor website listing prices paid for various roadkill (*e.g.,* "field mouse 10¢, armadillo $1.25, lawyer TOP $$$ — CALL!!!").[117] A cease and desist letter from Toys"R"Us claiming trademark infringement resulted in the creation of a second website[118] devoted to detailing the ongoing legal battle and the addition of giraffes[119] at $88.25/linear neck inch on the Roadkill website.

There is even a website, WebGripeSites.com, which lists cyber gripe websites, such as: BMWlemon.com, FordReallySucks.com, MySuzukiLemon.com, FordLemon.com, BoycottDelta.org, AmexSux.com, PayPalSucks.com, EarthlinkSucks.net, VerizonEatsPoop.com, AllstateInsuranceSucks.com, and even GWBush.com (a parody website "which reportedly prompted the Bush campaign to buy preemptively a number of domain names such as BushSucks.net and BushSucks.org").[120]

One website listed is CrownPontiacNissan.com, a gripe website about an automobile dealer, Crown Pontiac Nissan. Where the entire name of the website URL is identical to the entire name of the business, it would appear at first glance that it might violate the business' trademark rights. However, the trend in the same circumstances has been for courts to favor the cyber griper over the trademark holder, absent a showing of a pecuniary motive. One federal court denied a plaintiff's application for injunctive relief under the Anti-cybersquatting Consumer Protection Act (ACPA), stating that consumers were not likely to be confused as to the source of the gripe website or believe that it was created by or affiliated with the plaintiff, even though it bore the plaintiff's name.[121] The injunction was also denied under the Lanham Act (see Chapter Four), which requires a showing that the defendant used the plaintiff's trademark in commerce, as the court determined the gripe website to be a non-commercial use. And in *Lucas Nursery and Landscaping Inc. v. Grosse*, the 6th Circuit held that, absent a bad faith intent to profit from the use of another's trademark in a domain name, a use solely to criticize the trademark owner cannot be enjoined under the ACPA.[122] More recently, a disgruntled customer of Seattle-based Bosley Medical Institute launched bosleymedical.com to hair, er, air his gripes about the hair restoration company.[123] Bosley sued, claiming that his use of the company's name in the domain name amounted to trademark infringement. The 9th Circuit Court of Appeals disagreed on the grounds that the website was not created to confuse current or potential customers nor was it motivated by a profit motive. The ruling further solidified the notion that consumers can use a trade name as the domain name for a company that they wish to criticize.[124]

Many of the "sucks sites" cases — where the griper simply adds the suffix "sucks.com" to the trademarked brand name — have been decided on whether the web surfer would realize that "sucks" is a pejorative term and would not confuse it with the company's website (confusion on the part of the consumer being the test for a finding of trademark infringement, as discussed in Chapter Four). Most American cases have held that consumers usually do not confuse "suck sites" with official trademarked websites. However, in non-American jurisdictions where the slang meaning of the term "sucks" may not be familiar to the general public, trademark infringement claims have been upheld. The World Intellectual Property Organization (WIPO) sided with Air France in its arbitration claim for cybersquatting against a Florida corporation that had registered the domain name AirFranceSucks.com, citing possible confusion of international customers.[125]

Typically in a retaliatory lawsuit, the company will charge trademark infringement and the defendant will raise First Amendment free speech rights as a defense. A Georgia couple faced a retaliatory lawsuit[126] from a siding company after creating a cyber gripe website.[127] Unhappy with the sprayed-on siding applied to their house, Alan and Linda Townsend launched a website to complain and provide a forum for other dissatisfied customers. Visitor postings to the website's message board said the product, "Spray on Siding," cracked, bubbled, and buckled. The product's manufacturer, North Carolina-based Alvis Coatings Inc., sued the Townsends, claiming their website infringed on the company's trademarks, intentionally misled and confused consumers, and defamed its product. Alvis claimed that the name of the Townsends' website, spraysiding.com, "is confusingly similar" to Alvis' website, sprayonsiding.com, as well as its trademark "Spray on Siding." Alvis also charged tortious interference with business relationships, but the complaint did not list any specific relationship or how a specific relationship was interfered with; it merely implied that publication of negative comments would deter potential customers from doing business with them.[128] (Tortious interference requires the presence of an existing contractual relationship, not a potential relationship with unknown parties). The Townsends rejected settlement offers that would have barred them from talking about the product and required them to sell their website's domain name to the company, choosing to fight, they said, so other potential customers could be better informed about the product. The lawsuit sought $75,000 in actual damages plus punitive damages and attorney fees, leading the couple to remark that they could lose their home.[129] As the Internet is a worldwide medium and the cost of a website is negligible, the Townsends' website may be their only viable means of communicating with other dissatisfied Alvis customers.

In a similar case, a New Jersey builder sued both gripe site RipOffReport.com and Google over an anonymous post that characterized his home construction as a "shoddy nightmare" and claimed he had "ripped off" her and "99 percent of the people" in her development. The builder claimed that he was rejected by three banks after they found the posts on a Google search.[130] RipOffReport.com refused to remove the comments but said it provided an opportunity for rebuttals to be posted on its site. The builder countered that the poster was subsequently "satisfied by a payment of a claim" and the gripe site should therefore remove the post, but the website refused, stating its policy was to keep all complaints on the website to maintain a "working history on the company or individual in question." [131]

In a case like this, the website would probably be protected by the CDA, and while the poster's opinions would be protected, she would have to substantiate any factual claims that would otherwise be defamatory.

Courts will usually side with the cyber griper over the trademark owner in these types of cases. It is difficult for companies to overcome the First Amendment argument and the resulting publicity of a lawsuit could backfire, bringing the company unwanted negative publicity and a potential public relations nightmare.

Social Boundaries of Free Speech

The First Amendment prevents the government from interfering with free speech. The U.S. Supreme Court has held that that protection is not absolute; there are certain categories of speech that have lesser protection or no protection, and some circumstances that affect how speech is protected. Commercial speech has a lesser degree of protection than political speech. Obscenity is not protected by the First Amendment (although non-obscene pornography is protected, but child pornography is not). One cannot yell "Fire" in a crowded theater (unless there is actually a fire) but can yell "Fire" on a target range.

Criminal conduct is not protected by the free speech guarantees of the First Amendment. In a recent case where a website sold material to teach people how to avoid paying taxes (allegedly) legally, a federal court held that the First Amendment did not protect the two organizations that operate the website, or their founder, because the website incited criminal conduct by "instructing others how to engage in illegal activity and [supplying] the means to do so." [132] (Ironically, the organizations had solicited donations that it claimed were tax deductible). [133]

But what about speech that society may find offensive and that may be illegal in some but not all jurisdictions? Since the Internet extends across all jurisdictions, how should such cases be handled?

In 2007, cockfighting was illegal in every U.S. state except Louisiana. At that time, Amazon. com offered subscriptions on its website to two cockfighting magazines, *The Feathered Warrior* and *The Gamecock*. The Humane Society sued Amazon.com, claiming that it was violating animal cruelty laws by selling magazines promoting illegal behavior, and that the magazines were effectively catalogs for illegal goods since they carried ads for blades that attach to birds' legs.[134] There is no doubt that cockfighting is a form of animal cruelty and a reprehensible "sport." But Amazon contended that since the magazines themselves were legal to sell that it should not be cast in the role of a censor simply because some individuals object to the content.

YouTube, which is owned by Google, reportedly hosted video clips of a 1940 anti-Semitic propaganda film and music videos of a banned far-right German rock band that contain scenes of World War II Nazi military operations.[135] Such material would be illegal under German laws that prohibit the expression of pro-Nazi sentiments and the production of pro-Nazi materials; in the United States there are no corresponding laws.

In both of these instances, the speech and the underlying activities (illegal in some jurisdictions) are abhorrent, yet under U.S. laws would be considered protected speech.

Prisoners and Free Speech

State and federal inmates do not have direct access to computers and are not allowed to access the Internet directly. The rationales for this policy include: prisoners might download instructions on making weapons, like pipe bombs; prisoners might harass their victims or victims' families online; and prisoners forfeit their rights when convicted.

The free speech issues involving inmates are: Should inmates have direct access to computers or the Internet? Should inmates be allowed to receive correspondence or material from the Internet indirectly? Family, friends, and prisoner advocacy groups often attempt to mail inmates material they have downloaded online, arguing that the First Amendment protects the right of inmates to receive such downloaded material. A solid argument can be made that inmates should be allowed to avail themselves of the Internet to communicate with the outside world or to do legal research; many inmates file their own appeals *pro se* from their prison cells. Some inmates — through family and friends — have created websites and opened e-mail accounts to voice grievances, seek legal aid, and express political views.[136]

Georgia prison guards confiscated a package containing legal research that had been downloaded by a prisoner's girlfriend, following the Georgia Department of Corrections policy prohibiting inmates from receiving printed material downloaded from the Internet. In 2007, the inmate sued in federal court to challenge the policy.[137]

The trend has been running in favor of prisoners. A California federal appeals court ruled against a state policy that prevented inmates from receiving mail with Internet-generated information.[138] In Colorado, a district court ruled against a similar prison policy.[139] And in Arizona, a court declared state law prohibiting inmates from exchanging written mail with ISPs or creating profiles on websites via outside contacts unconstitutional.[140]

Many inmates already have websites, created indirectly by family or friends. At least 30 death row inmates in Texas have MySpace pages.[141] While MySpace does not want to become known as the cyber haunt where kids meet killers, the company has stated that it will only remove prisoner profiles that violate its terms of service.[142]

Summary

The U.S. Supreme Court has held that First Amendment free speech protection is not absolute; there are certain categories of speech that have lesser protection or no protection, and some circumstances that affect how speech is protected. Commercial speech has a lesser degree of protection than political speech. Obscenity and child pornography are not protected, although non-obscene pornography is protected. Criminal conduct is not protected. Students have a right of free speech to protect expression when it concerns policies implemented by state school officials. The First Amendment protects the right to anonymous speech; however, a conflict arises when an anonymous Internet poster makes a defamatory comment on a blog or website.

Four primary causes of action against speech on the Internet are defamation, breach of contract, tortious interference with business, and securities fraud. The CDA § 230 immunizes ISPs from liability for defamatory or obscene material posted by someone else. The rationale is that ISPs are merely conduits (distributors of content) that provide a connection to the Internet and it is not practical to assume they could constantly monitor all of the web content posted by their customers. Courts have extended this broad immunity to other OSPs, including hybrids (that provide both content and the pipeline) and Web 2.0 interactive content providers based on the same rationale.

Defamation is a "published intentional false communication that injures a person or company's reputation." Defamation can be written (libel) or spoken (slander). If the defamed individual is a public figure, he must show the statement was made with "actual malice" (knowledge of falsity or reckless disregard of the truth) to prevail. Defenses to a defamation action are truth, privilege, and fair comment (a statement of opinion, as opposed to fact).

Blogs (short for "web logs") are online diaries or journals. Many are rife with defamatory comments that the writer might not otherwise have published in a more traditional, less instantaneous medium. The ease with which an unsubstantiated rumor can be disseminated to large numbers of people very quickly via the Internet underscores the potential damage to reputations and careers that can result.

Some blogs present news and commentary on social issues or industry-related topics. The question then arises, is a "news blogger" a journalist? If so, is the news blogger entitled to the same statutory protections under state shield laws as professional journalists? What is a "legitimate member of the press?"

Employee blogs raise the issue of balancing freedom of speech with an employer's right to protect the company's public image. Non-union workers are at greater risk of being fired if they criticize the company or disclose confidential information in their blogs. Employers in "at–will" states can fire employees even if they wrote the blog on their own time on their own computer outside of the office. Ideally, companies should establish written blogging policies. State bar associations are revising their attorney advertising and ethics rules to address the issue of whether lawyer blogs should be regulated as advertising.

Beyond the private sector, government employees and contractors risk dismissal for blogging too. The boundaries between the military employer's need to control speech for security purposes and servicemen's First Amendment right to free speech through milblogging have not yet been defined by the courts. Milbloggers must be careful not to reveal any information that might be useful to enemies or they risk punishment under Article 15 of the Uniform Code of Military Justice. Military personnel must now register their blogs and the content is subject to quarterly monitoring by their commanding officers to ensure they are not violating operational security and privacy restrictions.

The newest form of blog is the vlog, short for video log. Many vloggers produce regular shows and develop tens of thousands of subscribers, turning bedroom broadcasters in to Internet celebrities. This presents an interesting issue: Would a celebrity vlogger be considered a "public figure" in a defamation suit?

A Strategic Lawsuit Against Public Participation (SLAPP) is a civil lawsuit without substantial merit brought by private interests to stop citizens from exercising their political rights or to punish them for having done so. SLAPPs also have a "chilling effect," silencing other critics on message boards.

A cause of action for tortious interference requires a showing of a contract or business relationship, intentional interference, causation, and damage. Both criminal and civil lawsuits can result in response to attempts to manipulate stock prices through making wrongful posts in online forums, e-mailing fake press releases or information, or creating phony websites.

The "Marketplace of Ideas" metaphor is that ideas compete for acceptance against each other, with the underlying faith that the truth will prevail in such an open encounter. One problem with this approach is that, in defamation cases, it merely reinforces the defamation by repeating it and adding another layer to the cached and searchable content.

Personal attack websites — sites that solicit online postings containing personal attacks and offensive content that can be archived indefinitely and easily accessed through a search engine query — may or may not be protected by the CDA. There is nothing in the Act to prevent such websites from removing offensive content once notified of its existence, but most, if not all such websites do not remove the material. While theoretically the poster can be sued for defamation, it is not always easy to uncover the poster's identity. Also, the damage has been done by the initial posting, by its continued presence on the site, and by the fact that the defamatory comments will be searchable forever through archived caches.

The Internet has created an unprecedented way for dissatisfied consumers to criticize companies that they feel have wronged them. The cyber griper, however, must be careful to avoid violating defamation, trademark, or copyright laws while airing his gripe, lest he open himself up to a retaliatory lawsuit from the company. And companies must consider the public relations ramifications of attempts to silence cyber gripers.

Chapter Thirteen Notes

[1] _Stratton Oakmont, Inc. v. Prodigy Servs., Co._, 1995 WL 323710 (N.Y. Sup. Ct. 1995). This case is included in the Cases Section on the Issues in Internet Law website (www.IssuesinInternetLaw.com).

[2] Communications Decency Act (CDA), 47 U.S.C. § 230.

[3] _Perfect 10, Inc. v. CCBill, LLC_, Case No. 04-57143, 04-57207 (9th Cir. Mar. 29, 2007). _See also_ Anne Broache, "Adult Site's Legal Battle Could Aid Web Hosting Services," CNET News.com, March 30, 2007 _available at_ http://news.com.com/2100-1030_3-6172184.html (accessed September 25, 2007). The same article appears verbatim as Samuel Fineman, "Communications Decency Act Protection Extended to State Law: 9th Circuit Weighs in on Hotly Anticipated Perfect 10 Decision," Law.com, May 7, 2007, _available at_ www.law.com/jsp/article.jsp?id=1178269481477 (accessed September 25, 2007).

[4] John Borland, "Suit Against Craigslist Claims Discriminatory Ads," CNET News.com, February 8, 2006.

[5] _Ramey v. Darkside_, Case No. 00-1415, (D.C.D.C. May 2004).

[6] The Right of Publicity prevents unauthorized commercial use of someone's identity, including name, image, or likeness.

[7] _Hustler Magazine, Inc. v. Falwell_, 485 U.S. 46 (1988).

[8] "Lawyer's Joke Earns Reprimand From Court," The Oregonian, August 03, 2004.

[9] Jim Carpenter Public Reprimand OSB #00436, Oregon State Bar Bulletin, October 2004, _available at_ www.osbar.org/publications/bulletin/04oct/discipline.html (accessed September 25, 2007).

[10] Oregon State Bar complaint against Jim Carpenter, November 7, 2003, (OSB 02-32; SC S50321), _available at_ www.publications.ojd.state.or.us/S50321.htm (accessed September 25, 2007).

[11] The phrase "Catch-22," derived from the 1961 novel of the same name by Joseph Heller about the madness of war, has evolved into common use to mean a cyclical conundrum.

[12] _New York Times v. Sullivan_, 376 U.S. 254 (1964). This case is included in the Cases Section on the Issues in Internet Law website (www.IssuesinInternetLaw.com).

[13] _Barrett v. Clark_, 2001 WL 881259, 2001 Extra LEXIS 46 (CA Super. Ct. 1996). This case is included in the Cases Section on the Issues in Internet Law website (www.IssuesinInternetLaw.com).

[14] _Barrett v. Rosenthal_, 114 Cal.App.4th 1379, 9 Cal.Rptr.3d 142 (2003).

[15] _Barrett v. Rosenthal_, 06 C.D.O.S. 10651 (Cal. Sup.Ct. 2006).

[16] _Ibid._

[17] _Available at_ www.blogACTIVE.com (accessed September 25, 2007).

[18] Declan McCullagh, "Professor's Web Posting at Center of Libel Suit," CNET News.com, January 25, 2005.

[19] A summary judgment is a ruling by the court that there is no material issue of fact to be tried, and therefore the cause of action should be dismissed.

[20] _Ben-Tech Industrial Automation v. Donald Mayer and Eric Kaczor_, Case No. 02-040847-CZ, (Oakland Circuit Ct. Jan. 11, 2005).

[21] Declan McCullagh, fn. 18, _supra_.

[22] Laura Parker, "Courts Are Asked to Crack Down on Bloggers, Websites," USA Today, October 2, 2006.

[23] In _Wagner v. Miskin_, 660 N.W.2d 593, 2003 ND 69 (N.D. Sup. Ct. May 6, 2003), _cert. denied_, 540 U.S. 1154 (2004), a University of North Dakota student's website alleged that a professor had harassed her with sexually

provocative phone calls; the professor sued and won $2 million for libel, $500,000 for slander, and $500,000 for interference with his business relationships. *See also* the Anna Draker case discussed *infra* in Chapter 17.

[24] Laura Parker, "Jury Awards $11.3M over Defamatory Internet Posts," USA Today, October 11, 2006.

[25] _Scheff v. Bock_, Case No. CACE03022837 (Fla. Cir. Ct. default verdict Sept. 19, 2006).

[26] Laura Parker, fn. 24, *supra.*

[27] This case is disturbing in several respects. First, there is the issue of whether there was proper notice of trial. Normally notice sent by U.S. Mail is sufficient for proper service; however in a situation where court papers sent to a federally-declared disaster area where entire homes (and presumably mailboxes) are several feet under water are returned as undeliverable by the Post Office, and the defendant admits she was not aware of the trial date, one might question the sufficiency of the notice. Second, while default judgments are a common occurrence, it nonetheless seems to fly in the face of notions of due process and equity to proceed with a trial against a defendant who is precluded from personally attending the trial due to lack of proper notice and precluded from being represented by counsel due to lack of funds. Third, while the phrases "crook," "con artist," and "fraud" are undeniably perjorative and damaging to one's reputation, $11.3 million seems rather excessive, unless the plaintiff had an extremely lucrative business and these three words were proven to cost her that amount (or at least the $6.3 million in compensatory damages) from her bottom line.

[28] Laura Parker, fn. 22, *supra.*

[29] *Available at* www.archive.org/index.php.

[30] Laura Parker, fn. 22, *supra.*

[31] _Banks v. Milum_, Case No.A06A2394 (Ga. Super. Ct., Jan. 27, 2006).

[32] Greg Land, "Ga. Appeals Court Upholds Libel Verdict Against Blogger," Fulton County Daily Report, March 9, 2007.

[33] _DiMeo v. Max_, Case No. 06-1544 (E.D. Pa. May 26, 2006), *aff'd. on appeal*, _DiMeo v. Max_, 2007 WL 2717865 (3rd Cir. Sept. 19, 2007).

[34] Kim Ficera, "Don't Quote Me: Online Anonymity Fosters Prejudice," AfterEllen.com, October 5, 2006, *available at* www.afterellen.com/column/2006/10/quote-online2.html (accessed September 25, 2007).

[35] _Hollis v. Joseph_, Case No. GD 06-12677 (Allegheny County, PA 2007).

[36] Joe Mandak, "Judge Tosses Date-Dissing Website Suit," Associated Press wire report, April 11, 2007.

[37] Ellen Nakashima, "Harsh Words Die Hard on the Web: Law Students Feel Lasting Effects of Anonymous Attacks," Washington Post, March 7, 2007; p. A01.

[38] *Ibid.*

[39] *Ibid.*

[40] *Ibid.*

[41] _MacIntyre v. Ohio Elections Comm'n._, 514 US 334 (1995).

[42] _Dendrite Int'l. v. Doe_, 342 N.J. Super. 134 (July 11, 2001).

[43] *Ibid.*

[44] _Gallucci v. New Jersey On-Line, LLC_, docket number unavailable, (N.J. Super. Ct., Bergen County Feb. 5, 2007).

[45] _Doe v. Cahill_, 884 A.2d 451 (Del. Oct. 6, 2005).

[46] "Delaware Supreme Court Protects Anonymous Blogger," Electronic Frontier Foundation website, *available*

at www.eff.org/news/archives/2005_10.php (accessed September 25, 2007).

[47] As required by the federal Cable Communications Policy Act of 1984, 47 U.S.C. § 551(c)(2).

[48] *Doe v. Cahill*, fn. 45, *supra*.

[49] *Gertz v. Robert Welch, Inc.*, 418 US 323 (1974).

[50] *Doe v. Cahill,* fn. 45, *supra*.

[51] *Klehr Harrison Harvey Branzburg & Ellers v. JPA Dev. Inc.*, 2006 WL. 37020 (Pa. Com. Pl. Jan. 4, 2006).

[52] Shannon P. Duffy, "Law Firm's Defamation Claim Found to Trump Critics' Internet Anonymity," The Legal Intelligencer, January 23, 2006.

[53] *Ibid.*

[54] Pa. R. Evid. 4011.

[55] *Batzel v. Smith*, 333 F.3d 1018, (9th Circuit, 2003), included in the Cases Section on the Issues in Internet Law website (www.IssuesinInternetLaw.com), is an interesting case that discusses many of these topics — publisher analogy, *Straton Oakmont v. Prodigy*, CDA § 230, forums for potential defamation and SLAPPs — in great detail.

[56] Stefanie Olsen, "Friendster Fires Developer for Blog," CNET News.com, August 31, 2004.

[57] Joyce Park's Blog entry, *available at* http://troutgirl.com/blog/index.php?/archives/22_Friendster_goes_PHP. html (last accessed November 5, 2006; entry was **unavailable as of September 25, 2007**).

[58] David Becker, "Microsoft Photo Prompts Blogger's Regret," CNET News.com, November 3, 2003. Hanscom's version of the incident is recorded on his blog *available at* www.michaelhanscom.com/eclecticism/2003/10/of_ blogging_and.html (accessed September 25, 2007).

[59] Time Magazine, December 19, 2004.

[60] Evan Hansen, "Google Blogger: 'I Was Terminated,'" CNET News.com, February 11, 2005.

[61] Amy Joyce, "Free Expression Can Be Costly When Bloggers Bad-Mouth Jobs," Washington Post, p. A01, February 11, 2005.

[62] *Ibid.*

[63] *Ibid.*

[64] David E. Kaplan, "Hey, Let's Play Ball," U.S. News and World Report, October 29, 2006.

[65] National Labor Relations Act, 29 U.S.C. § 157.

[66] *Tinker v. Des Moines Indep. Cmty. Sch. Dist.*, 393 U.S. 503 (1969).

[67] *Bethel Sch. Dist. v. Fraser*, 478 U.S. 675 (1986).

[68] *Morse v. Frederick*, 551 U.S. __ (2007) where a student was suspended after displaying a banner reading "Bong Hits 4 Jesus" at a school-sanctioned and school-supervised event.

[69] *Hazelwood Sch. Dist. v. Kuhlmeier*, 484 U.S. 260 (1988).

[70] As a minor, initials were substituted for the girl's name in court documents.

[71] *A.B. v. Indiana*, Case No. 67A01-0609-JV-372 (Ind. Ct. App. Apr. 9, 2007).

[72] *Ibid.*

[73] *Ibid*, quoting the Juvenile Court opinion.

[74] *Ibid.*

[75] The Indiana Court of Appeals decided *A.B. v. Indiana*, fn. 71 *supra*, on the free speech clause in the state constitution, Art. 1, § 9, of the Indiana Constitution, and having determined that the appellant's free speech rights had been violated, did not proceed further to analyze it under the free speech clause of the U.S. Constitution.

[76] Nicholas Spangler, "UM Student Thrown for Loss After Blog Shames Canes," Miami Herald, November 24, 2005.

[77] Ibid.

[78] Ibid.

[79] Ibid.

[80] Jerry Lewis, "UM Student's Removal Not Related to Rap Song," Miami Herald, November 28, 2005.

[81] Jorge Milian, "UM Athletic Director Apologizes for 'Demeaning' Tape," Palm Beach Post, November 15, 2005.

[82] Lisa Brennan, "'Dear Abby' Law Firm Blogs a No-No, Insurance Carrier Says," New Jersey Law Journal, April 17, 2007.

[83] The phrase "Catch-22," derived from the 1961 novel of the same name by Joseph Heller about the madness of war, has evolved into common use to mean a cyclical conundrum.

[84] "Private First Class Leonard Clark Press Release," CENTCOM press release, July 2005. Leonard Clark was charged with violating UCMJ "Article 92 (Failure to obey order), 11 specifications; by releasing classified information regarding unit soldiers and convoys being attacked or hit by an improvised explosive devices on various dates, discussing troop movements on various dates, releasing Tactics, Techniques, and Procedures and Rules of Engagement used by the unit on various dates, in violation of a lawful general order prohibiting the release of such information and Article 134 (Reckless endangerment), 2 specifications, by releasing specific information, on various dates regarding Tactics, Techniques, and Procedures and Rules of Engagement used by his unit and encouraging its widespread publication, such that the enemy forces could foreseeably access the information, such that with that information it was likely that the enemy forces could cause death or serious bodily harm to U.S. forces engaged in the same or similar mission."

[85] Ibid.

[86] "Soldier Bloggers Told to Guard Information," Associated Press wire report, May 2, 2007.

[87] Associated Press wire story, September 27, 2004.

[88] Martha Brant, "Soldiers: War on 'Milblogs,'" Newsweek, August 8, 2005.

[89] Michael Felberbaum, "Army Monitors Soldiers' Blogs, Websites," Associated Press wire report, October 30, 2006.

[90] Robert Weller, "Report: Official Sites, Not Bloggers, Breaching Army Security," Associated Press wire report, August 22, 2007.

[91] Ibid.

[92] In May 2007, the Pentagon banned service members from using the military's computer system to access certain websites that allow uploading of videos. The ban encompasses video-sharing sites YouTube, Metacafe, IFilm, FileCabi, and StupidVideos; social networking websites MySpace, BlackPlanet, and Hi5; music sites Pandora, MTV, 1.fm, and live365; and the photo-sharing site Photobucket. The ban does not apply to private Iraqi Internet cafés. Ironically, the defense department uploads videos of soldiers in Iraq to some of the banned websites as a recruitment tool. See "Military Puts MySpace, Other Sites Off Limits," Associated Press wire report, May 14, 2007 and Sam Diaz, "Military Says Bandwidth Alone Forced Web Site Blocking," Washington Post, May 18, 2007, p. D01.

[93] Random House Unabridged Dictionary defines a "journalist" as "a person who keeps a journal, diary, or other record of daily events," which would seem to qualify all bloggers as journalists.

[94] Nicholas M. Ciarelli's blog, available at www.thinksecret.com (accessed September 25, 2007). The 19-year-old student's blog is listed in Google as "Think Secret is the source for Apple Macintosh inside information and industry news scoops."

[95] PowerPage, *available at* www.powerpage.org (accessed September 25, 2007), and Apple Insider, *available at* www.appleinsider.com, (accessed September 25, 2007).

[96] The facts of the case are discussed in the Trade Secrets section of Chapter Six.

[97] "Judge Says Websites Can Be Forced to Reveal Sources," Mercury News, March 04, 2005.

[98] Many states have "shield laws," which protect journalists from being compelled to reveal their sources.

[99] *Apple Computer, Inc. v. Doe*, Case No. 1-04-CV-032178 (Cal. Super. Ct. Mar. 11, 2005), appeal pending *sub. nom.* *O'Grady v. Superior Ct. of Santa Clara County*, Case No. H028579 (Cal. App. 6th Dist. May 26, 2006).

[100] U.S. Supreme Court decisions have held that the 14th Amendment extended the prohibition against government abridgement of free speech or press to state governments as well as the federal government.

[101] Andrew Orlowski, "Bloggers Must Reveal Sources — Judge," The Register, March 12, 2005.

[102] H.R. 2102: Free Flow of Information Act of 2007.

[103] Rick Bozich, "Courier-Journal Reporter Ejected from U of L Game," Louisville Courier-Journal, June 11, 2007.

[104] *Nat'l Basketball Ass'n. v. Motorola, Inc.*, 105 F.3d 841 (2nd Cir. 1997).

[105] *New York Times v. Sullivan*, fn. 12, *supra*.

[106] *Cepeda v. Cowles Magazines and Broad., Inc.*, 392 F.2d 417, 419 (9th Cir. 1968). *cert. den'd* 393 U.S. 840 (1968).

[107] *Gertz v. Robert Welch, Inc.*, fn. 50, *supra*.

[108] *Ibid.*

[109] Bruce W. McCullough, "Internet Jurisdiction," Findlaw.com, *available at* http://library.lp.findlaw.com/articles/file/00563/002296/title/Subject/topic/Civil%20Procedure_Personal%20Jurisdiction/filename/civilprocedure_2_887 (accessed September 25, 2007).

[110] *Washington Post v. TotalNews*, Case No. 97 Civ. 1190 (PKL) (S.D.N.Y. 1997). This case is included in the Cases Section on the Issues in Internet Law website (www.IssuesinInternetLaw.com).

[111] *Intel Corp. v. Hamidi*, 71 P.3d 296 (Cal. Supreme Ct. June 30, 2003). This case is included in the Cases Section on the Issues in Internet Law website (www.IssuesinInternetLaw.com).

[112] Karey Wutkowski, "SEC Cracks Down on Spam-driven Stocks," Reuters wire report, March 8, 2007.

[113] Kit R. Roane, "Taking Penny Stocks Out of the Boiler Room," U.S. News & World Report, June 4, 2007, pp. 55-56.

[114] Securities Act of 1933, text available at U.S. Securities and Exchange Commission website, *available at* www.sec.gov/divisions/corpfin/33act/index1933.shtml (accessed September 25, 2007).

[115] Securities and Exchange Act of 1934, text available at U.S. Securities and Exchange Commission website, *available at* www.sec.gov/divisions/corpfin/34act/index1934.shtml (accessed September 25, 2007).

[116] *Abrams v. United States*, 250 U.S. 616 (1919).

[117] "Roadkill"R"Us" website, *available at* www.rru.com (accessed September 25, 2007).

[118] "Roadkill"R"Us" gripe website, *available at* www.rru.com/tru (accessed September 25, 2007).

[119] Geoffrey the Giraffe is the Toys"R"Us mascot.

[120] *Available at* www.webgripesites.com/gripesites.shtml (accessed September 25, 2007).

[121] *Northland Ins. Cos. v. Blaylock*, 115 F. Supp.2d 1108, Civ. No. 00-308 DSD/JMM (D. Minn. Sept. 25, 2000).

[122] *Lucas Nursery & Landscaping Inc. v. Grosse*, 359 F.3d 806 (6th Cir. Mar. 2004).

[123] "Court Rules Man Can Disparage Company on Web," Associated Press wire report, April 5, 2005.

[124] However, the appellate court did reinstate a portion of the lawsuit in which Bosley alleged that Kremer

violated the Anti-cybersquatting Consumer Protection Act by allegedly offering to sell the website to Bosley. *Ibid.*

[125] *Societé Air France v. Virtual Dates, Inc.*, Case No. D2005-0168 (May 24, 2005), WIPO Arbitration and Mediation Center, *available at* http://arbiter.wipo.int/domains/decisions/html/2005/d2005-0168.html (accessed September 25, 2007).

[126] *Alvis Coatings, Inc. and Alvis, Inc. v. Townsend*, Civil Action No. 3:04-CV-482-K (D.C.NC 2004).

[127] Associated Press wire service report, November 6, 2004.

[128] *Alvis Coatings,* fn. 126, *supra.*

[129] *Ibid.*

[130] *RSA Enters. v. Rip-Off Report.com*, Case No. 2:2007cv01882, (D.N.J. Apr. 23, 2007), *dismissed by stipulation,* Aug. 7, 2007.

[131] Jim Lockwood, "Builder Sues Web Site and Google Over Posting," (New Jersey) Star-Ledger, April 27, 2007.

[132] *United States v. Schulz*, Case No. 1:07-cv-0352, (N.D.N.Y. Aug. 9, 2007). Of course the free speech issue could have been avoided had the website been shut down under anti-fraud laws.

[133] David Cay Johnston, "Judge Orders a Website Selling Tax-Evasion Advice to Close," New York Times, August 30, 2007. The Times article reported that the judge also ordered that the names, addresses, telephone numbers, e-mail addresses, and Social Security numbers of every person who merely received materials from the website be turned over to the government so the Internal Revenue Service could identify them and the Justice Department could prosecute them for tax crimes. One wonders if persons ordering material marketed as "How to LEGALLY Avoid Paying Taxes" would have the demonstrated requisite criminal intent to be prosecuted if they honestly believed they were receiving information on some sort of legal tax shelter.

[134] Andrew Adam Newman, "Humane Society Has Its Sights on Amazon.com," New York Times, August 27, 2007.

[135] Nicola Leske, "YouTube Criticized Over Neo-Nazi Clips," Reuters wire report, August 27, 2007.

[136] Kevin Johnson, "Inmates Go to Court to Seek Right to Use the Internet," USA Today, November 23, 2006 and Vesna Jaksic, "Prisoners' Right to Internet Materials Contested," National Law Journal, December 26, 2006.

[137] *Williams v. Donald*, Case No. 5:01-CV-292-2 (M.D. Ga.).

[138] *Clement v. California Dept. of Corrections*, 364 F.3d 1148 (9th Cir. 2004).

[139] *Jordan v. Hood*, Case No. 03-cv-02320 (D. Colo. 2004).

[140] *Canadian Coal. Against the Death Penalty v. Ryan*, Case No. CV02-1344 PHX EHC (D.C.Ariz. May 2003).

[141] Andy Cerota, "Dozens of Condemned Killers Have MySpace.com Accounts," ABC13.com, November 11, 2006.

[142] Kevin Johnson, fn. 136, *supra.*

Chapter Thirteen Quiz

Beetle Bailey is an employee of Food Services Corp., an independent contractor for the U.S. military. Bailey travels to foreign U.S. military bases to survey the quality of the food supplied to U.S. troops by Food Services Corp. On one such trip, Bailey noticed that many of the soldiers were keeping milblogs on the Internet so Bailey decided to start his own blog. Bailey read an entry in Private Blabbit's blog stating that the base cook, a local restaurateur who had a contract to prepare meals for the base using the food supplied by Food Services Corp., was actually selling the food shipped by Food Services Corp. on the black market and substituting cheaper, poor quality foodstuffs.

Bailey reprinted Blabbit's entire blog entry in his own blog, "Food for Thought." The base cook sued Bailey for defamation and tortious interference with his business. Food Services Corp. fired Bailey for having added in his blog, "If the base chef has been substituting foodstuffs then he must be a superb chef because his meals taste better than the usual Food Services Corp. fare I've tasted in other units." Bailey countered by suing Food Services Corp. for wrongful termination. Upset over the controversy, the base commander ordered all milblogs shut down.

If you are using this book in a classroom, discuss the issues raised and the liability of all parties. Otherwise, try to list the issues involved and probable outcomes before turning to the answers in the Appendix.

[Answers in Appendix]

CHAPTER FOURTEEN

FREE SPEECH: THE DARK SIDE OF THE WEB

This chapter examines restraints on free speech: pornography, obscenity, child pornography, hate speech, online harassment, prior restraint, and totalitarian restraints. The Children's Internet Protection Act of 2000 and the Child Protection and Obscenity Enforcement Act of 1988 are also discussed.

PORNOGRAPHY, HATE SPEECH, AND REPRESSION

"But I know it when I see it" — Justice Potter Stewart [1]

Pornography and Obscenity

IN 1957, IN <u>Roth v. United States</u>, the Supreme Court ruled that prosecution for possession or distribution of obscene material is lawful and that the *Constitution does not protect obscene speech.* [2] Pornography is entitled to First Amendment protection *unless it is obscene* [3] *or child pornography.* [4] Thus the question becomes, what is the definition of obscenity? This is a question that the courts have been unable to answer satisfactorily, although many attempts have been made. Supreme Court Justice Potter Stewart even admitted that he could not define obscenity, adding "but I know it when I see it." [5]

The current test for determining obscenity is the <u>Miller</u> test, first enunciated in 1973 in <u>Miller v. California</u>: "Whether to the *average person*, applying *contemporary community standards*, the *dominant theme* of the material *taken as a whole* appeals to *prurient interest*." [6] Although still nebulous to apply, prior to the advent of the Internet, defendants could limit liability by avoiding geographic areas with restrictive standards. However, the borderless nature of the Internet makes applying community standards impossible. Since the Internet reaches every community, only the lowest common denominator (*i.e.*, most restrictive) community standards would apply. However, the Supreme Court has more recently said that "community standards" need not be defined by a precise geographic area.

The Communications Decency Act (CDA) § 223

Earlier in this book, we discussed § 230 of the Communications Decency Act (CDA). Another section of the same act, § 223, made it illegal to transmit indecent material or display *patently offensive* material on the Internet.[7] In 1997, in *Reno v. ACLU*, the Supreme Court in a 9–0 decision ruled that the *CDA restrictions violated the First Amendment* because the terms "indecent" and "patently offensive" were too broad.[8]

The Supreme Court turned down the chance to set online obscenity standards in 2006 when it rejected an appeal from a photographer who claimed that the CDA violated her free-speech rights to post pictures of sadomasochistic sexual behavior online.[9] A three-judge federal panel had held that the photographer — by not providing hard data on how many websites might have their free speech at risk from inconsistent applications of the *Miller* test by local juries — failed to meet the evidentiary burden of proving the statute unconstitutional.[10] Barbara Nitke — whose website featured her bondage and sadomasochistic (often homoerotic) photographs — and the National Coalition for Sexual Freedom argued that the fear of prosecution created a "chilling effect" on artists who might otherwise post such materials online, even if it would be legally protected speech in their own communities. In Nitke's case, what might not be considered "obscene" by the community standards of her native New York City might well be deemed "obscene" by a more conservative community (*e.g.*, the Bible Belt or Salt Lake City). Nitke argued that this chilling effect demonstrated that the CDA was overbroad. (The overbreadth standard holds that if a statute designed to prevent illegal speech instead has the effect of inhibiting protected speech, then that statute would be deemed overbroad and thus unconstitutional.)[11] However, by declining to hear the appeal, the Supreme Court let stand the earlier three-judge panel decision, with the result that since the CDA is a federal law, federal prosecutors retain the option of selecting where to file obscenity charges. Obviously, under the *Miller* test, their venue of choice would be the most conservative community. The problem, of course, is that the Internet, unlike other methods of communication, is not targeted to a discrete audience but is available worldwide without any geographic boundaries. Hence the borderless nature of the Internet effectively renders the *Miller* test obsolete, a reality that the Supreme Court has yet again declined to address.

The Child Online Protection Act of 1998 (COPA)

After the Supreme Court struck down § 223 of the CDA, Congress made yet another attempt to restrict Internet pornography. Hoping to resolve the First Amendment issues that had plagued the CDA, Congress enacted the Child Online Protection Act (COPA). [12] COPA criminalized publication of "any communication for *commercial* purposes that includes sexual material that is *harmful to minors, without restricting access* to such material by minors." "Harmful to minors" was defined in the Act as lacking "scientific, literary, artistic, or political value" and offensive to local "community standards." The maximum penalty for violations was a $50,000 fine, six months in prison, and additional civil fees. The "restricting access" requirement of the Act required adults to use access codes or credit cards for age verification to view objectionable material.

However, *COPA never took effect*. The 3rd Circuit [13] upheld a lower court's injunction of COPA as *unconstitutional*. [14] The Supreme Court let the injunction stand, although it cast doubt on the appellate court's reasoning in dicta. [15] But in May 2002, after rejecting the lower court's ruling that the use of "community standards" to define what is harmful to children was unconstitutional, the Supreme Court pointed out other constitutional problems that the lower court failed to address. [16] The lower court in turn looked at law again and promptly said, for the second time, that it violated the First Amendment. [17] Then, in 2004, in <u>Ashcroft v. ACLU</u>, the Supreme Court sent the issue back to lower court for a new trial, citing rapid changes in technology that would make filtering software a more effective tool to block access than the more restrictive means proffered in COPA, such as age verification and use of a credit card. [18] (Indeed, how does one *really* verify online an individual's age or that the individual is the true owner of the credit card used online?) In March 2007, a federal district court again ruled the law unconstitutional, noting that the government's "own study shows that all but the worst performing filters are far more effective than COPA would be at protecting children from sexually explicit material on the Web." [19]

Several factors led to COPA being held unconstitutional. First, there was the obvious *constitutional issue*: the case pitted the First Amendment *free speech* rights of adults against the power of Congress to control *interstate commerce*, derived from Article I, § 8 of the U.S. Constitution. *Vagueness* and *overbreadth* are two characteristics that violate the First Amendment. Here the statute was overbroad because adults would be denied access to "material harmful to children" (itself a vague phrase). Secondly, children could still access harmful material on foreign and non-commercial websites (since COPA only applied to commercial, U.S. websites) and via Internet protocols other than the World Wide Web, such as chat, message boards, instant messaging, and Usenet.

Child Pornography

In 1982, in <u>New York v. Ferber</u>, the Supreme Court ruled that *child pornography was not entitled to First Amendment protection.*[20] Prior to this decision, child pornography had been treated as any other pornography, *i.e.,* requiring a showing of obscenity to be deemed unprotected speech. The rationale for declaring child pornography de facto obscenity was *to protect children from physical abuse.*

Congress, in 1996, enacted the *Child Pornography Prevention Act* (CPPA).[21] The stated goal of this Act was *to protect children* from sexual exploitation. However, the Act went further, by prohibiting *"virtual child pornography,"* *i.e.,* images that were completely computer-generated or morphed and images of young-looking adult actors used to create the appearance of minors engaging in sexually explicit conduct. Thus the Act would impose criminal penalties of up to 15 years imprisonment *even where there was no real child involved.* Banning virtual child pornography ran counter to the rationale of protecting children, since no actual child is physically abused. In 2002, the Supreme Court, in <u>Ashcroft v. Free Speech Coalition</u>, ruled that the *CPPA violated the First Amendment.*[22] In fact, the Supreme Court in <u>Ashcroft</u> referred to previous decisions suggesting that where it was necessary for literary or artistic value to denote what would otherwise be child pornography, "a person over the statutory age who perhaps looked younger could be utilized," adding that "simulation outside of the prohibition of the statute could provide another alternative."[23] Thus the CPPA had outlawed the very safe harbor advocated by the court as a constitutional alternative.

Undeterred, Congress the following year enacted the *PROTECT Act* of 2003, also known as the *Amber Alert Bill.*[24] The Act established a national AMBER Alert Program to locate missing children and primarily authorized wiretaps for crimes using the Internet to lure children for sexual abuse and sex trafficking. Few congressmen would dare to vote against a bill to "protect children" (the PROTECT Act passed 98–0 in the Senate and 400–25 in the House), but *tacked on to the bill were two items with significant First Amendment implications.*

In response to <u>Ashcroft</u>, the 2002 Supreme Court decision that struck down key portions of the CPPA, the PROTECT Act amended child pornography laws to make *virtual child pornography illegal.* The Act banned "a computer image, computer-generated image, or digital image that is of, or is virtually indistinguishable from that of, an actual minor," thus criminalizing images that were merely indistinguishable, even if computer-generated or using youthful-looking adult models.

It would appear that Congress had enacted a near identical version of the CPPA, itself already declared unconstitutional only a year earlier. And it did it by slipping it into a bill designed to locate and protect missing children, which no one was likely to vote against.

The first edition of this book stated "Nevertheless, it stands to reason that this portion of the Act will most likely be held *unconstitutional* for the same reasons, if challenged."[25] Sure enough, an 11th U.S. Circuit Court of Appeals panel unanimously struck down[26] that portion[27] of the PROTECT Act as too broad and vague in April 2006. The ruling affects only the jurisdiction of the 11th Circuit — Florida, Georgia, and Alabama; however, the case was appealed to the U.S. Supreme Court, with oral argument slated for October 30, 2007.[28]

As discussed in Chapter Five, the PROTECT Act also makes it illegal to use misleading domain names with the intent to deceive a *person into viewing obscenity* on the Internet (with penalty of a fine or up to two years imprisonment or both) or a *minor into viewing material that is harmful to minors* on the Internet (with penalty of a fine or up to four years imprisonment or both). The terms *"misleading," "obscenity,"* and *"harmful to minors"* are inherently vague, and therefore subject to a First Amendment challenge.

The absurdity of the recent drive on the part of some conservative senators to outlaw virtual child pornography is reminiscent of an incident where a store owner faced child pornography charges for selling a comic book. The comic book featured illustrations (no photographs) of elves — short, ancient magical creatures with pointy ears and child-like appearance. Despite the fact that no children (or even real people) appeared in the comic book, it was cited as child pornography by local authorities. This is a far cry from the stated purpose of the child pornography laws, *i.e.*, protecting children from being sexually exploited in photographs and movies.

In 2004, a federal court held unconstitutional a Pennsylvania statute designed to prevent viewing websites containing child pornography. The statute tried to place the burden of enforcement on the ISPs, rather than on the violators posting the content, who are frequently hard to locate or located overseas. The court found that the 2002 law violated First Amendment free speech rights because it caused more than a million legitimate websites to be shut down while blocking only about 400 violators. The statute let prosecutors demand ISPs block access to offending websites or face potential criminal penalties. However, blocking entire IP addresses also shut down many websites with sub-addresses that contained legitimate content. This was because websites hosting companies, which are assigned blocks of addresses, often assign sub-addresses to individual websites since IP addresses are scarce. These sub-addresses were difficult if not impossible for the ISPs to block individually, so shutting down the IP address resulted in shutting down the sub addresses as well.

The Children's Internet Protection Act of 2000 (CIPA)

The Children's Internet Protection Act of 2000 (CIPA) denies federal funds (*i.e.*, e-rate funds that provide technology discounts to public libraries and schools, and Library Services and

Technology Act funds) linked to Internet access to public libraries and schools that refuse to put filter software on their Internet-accessible computers. [29] It requires blocking of visual depictions of obscenity, child pornography, or "material harmful to minors" (minors are defined as under age 17 in the Act). It does not apply to text. The Act provides that libraries disable the filters on request of adult patrons. The law initially was not widely enforced, as its constitutionality was questioned (because of its limits on access to free speech), but the Supreme Court upheld the law in June 2003, [30] and now libraries across the country must rethink their Internet safety policies. Some libraries have even refused federal funds to be able to continue offering unfiltered Internet access.

CIPA does not force public libraries and schools to use filtering software; it only threatens loss of federal funds if they do not comply. By 2007, 21 states had Internet filtering laws applicable to public libraries and schools. Most merely required public libraries and school boards to adopt policies to keep minors from accessing sexually explicit, obscene or "material harmful to minors," but some states additionally required filtering software. In California, an appellate court ruled that CDA § 230 protected a public library from attempts to use state law causes of action to force it to use filtering software. [31] In Phoenix, Arizona, the city council, in 2004, ended unrestricted Internet access for adults on public library computers, [32] attributing the policy change to a recent arrest of a child molester who admitted downloading child pornography at the Phoenix Public Library. The prior policy required that filters remain on at all times in the libraries' children's areas and for patrons under age 17, but allowed adults the option of disabling the filters. The filters block obscene images and web pages by targeting key words, phrases, or graphical images. Free speech advocates argue that when libraries do not allow adults to turn off the filters, the adult patrons are denied access to websites that deal with non-pornography issues such as breast cancer, AIDS research, or sexual education, which might be mistakenly filtered.

The Child Protection and Obscenity Enforcement Act

The Child Protection and Obscenity Enforcement Act of 1988 requires that certain adult media, *e.g.*, magazines and videos, maintain onsite records to verify that all models or actors are of legal age. [33] The purpose of the Act is to ensure that minors are not engaged in the production of pornography. In 2005, the Act was extended to encompass websites. Webmasters who run adult-oriented websites are required to keep and provide extensive documentation about their performers, including legal name, date of birth, and copies of documents with a photographic ID. However, the expanded rules do not extend to ISPs. The age regulations were inspired by congressional outrage at a hardcore video performance by then 15-year-old porn star Traci Lords.

What Is "Possession?"

At the beginning of this chapter, we stated that the Supreme Court has ruled that prosecution for possession or distribution of obscene material is lawful. But what constitutes "possession" in cyberspace? A Georgia man was sentenced to 20 years in prison for possession of child pornography.[34] The images were found on his computer in his Internet browser's cache. The cache temporarily stores files automatically downloaded from visited websites. Suppose the man had arrived at the website unintentionally, or with no idea of its content and left immediately; the images would still reside in his computer's cache. The user has no control over the images being downloaded to the computer cache; should he be subject to criminal penalties of up to 20 years imprisonment? Does the existence of the images in his cache amount to possession?

Online Harassment

Online harassment occurs when the harasser uses the Internet to cause *substantial emotional distress* to the victim. It can be through e-mail, chat, instant messages, newsgroup or message board posts, or even words or images posted on websites or social networks. Harassment is distinct from, but may be in conjunction with, cyberstalking or hate groups. Rude people, unpopular ideas, spam, or simple disagreements — annoying as they may be — do not rise to the level of harassment.

In one form of harassment, *e-mail spoofing*, a fake e-mail is sent using real addresses. The fake e-mail is usually highly inflammatory, resulting in hundreds or thousands of angry recipients responding to the legitimate address on the e-mail. The only problem is the recipient of this unleashed anger never actually sent the original e-mail. Spoofing can waste the victim's time receiving and/or responding to thousands of e-mails, damage the victim's reputation and even cause the victim's e-mail account to be suspended. And finding the perpetrator is difficult since he is using someone else's identity. One spoofer was particularly vindictive, using his victim's legitimate e-mail address requesting return receipts for each message; when the victim returned from a three-week vacation, he was greeted by 55,000 messages in his e-mail inbox.[35]

Perhaps the greatest degree of online harassment occurs among teenagers. Adults are often so concerned with protecting children from adult "online predators" that they forget that sometimes children need to be protected from other kids. Teens are often impulsive and lack empathy for their peers, leading them to bring adolescent bullying from the schoolyard into cyberspace.[36] Female teen bullies, who naturally prefer emotional over physical harassment and like to avoid direct confrontation, gravitate to online bullying. Teenage boys tend to make significantly more sexually explicit remarks online than they do in person.[37] In short, the new technologies associated with the Internet have intensified normal adolescent cruelty, creating an uber-bully — the "cyber bully." By enabling kids to harass their peers from a distance, without having to view the results of their actions, the Internet has inflicted a deeper level of cruelty.

Cyber bullies use websites, chat rooms, message boards, social networks, e-mail, instant messaging, and text messages via cell phone calls to make their anonymous threats and harass their victims. (Instant messaging is the lifeline to the Internet Generation's teenager, just as the telephone was to the previous generation's teens.)[38] Teachers cite students in class upset over incidents from the previous night, where they may have been harassed online by, or in front of, their peers.[39] Such online harassment usually goes on unseen by adults and is often publicly humiliating, as e-mail and blogs allow gossip, put-downs, and embarrassing photographs to be distributed amongst their peers.

"Private" videos and photographs often wind up forwarded by the recipient to friends, who also pass them around like satellites orbiting in cyberspace. One boy made a video of himself singing a song for a girl he liked; the object of his affection posted it on the Internet, much to his chagrin. A Quebec teen, Ghyslain Raza, found that a video he made of himself practicing his *Star Wars* light saber moves and left on a shelf in the school TV studio had been discovered by other classmates and digitally tweaked and circulated to millions via the Internet, where he quickly gained notoriety as "the Star Wars Kid."[40] He later sued his classmates for $351,000 in damages for subjecting him to global ridicule by uploading the digitalized versions of "May the Farce Be with You." The case was settled out of court three years later. A girl made a "dirty dancing" video that she ended with the words "If you show this to anyone else..." followed by a hand motion slicing across her neck; undeterred, the boy to whom she sent it apparently decided to share it with a few million of his closest friends on the Internet. Another high school girl e-mailed a nude photograph of herself from her cell phone to her boyfriend, who promptly e-mailed it to all of his friends, who then circulated it online. Perhaps the most infamous incident was the eighth-grader at Horace Mann School in the Bronx, New York, who in an attempt to win over a classmate e-mailed her crush a video of her masturbating while declaring her love for him. The video soon made its way onto a popular file-sharing network and there were reports that her classmates would even go online at school and view the video.

Students often have their own web pages and blogs, where they post insulting or derogatory comments about classmates. Some student blogs include online lists ranking their male classmates as "stud or dud" and their female classmates as girls as "hottest" and "ugliest." Other student blogs discuss rumored sexual promiscuity of particular girls at the school, listing their names and cell phone numbers. Online harassment among teenagers can even extend to using another teen's screen name to send inflammatory or embarrassing messages to the victim's friends or crushes.

Unlike typical adolescent bullying, cyber bullying does not necessarily occur during school hours or on school property.[41] Running home and locking the door does not provide relief from cyber bullying, as it can continue 24 hours a day, invading the victim's home, computer, and cell phone.[42] Unlike schoolyard bullies, the cyber bully has an infinite audience, a degree of protection through anonymity, and the ease of striking repeatedly through only a mouse click.[43]

A Vermont eighth-grader found herself the subject of a website created by two classmates entitled called "Kill Kylie Incorporated" that was "devoted to show people how gay Kylie [last name omitted] is," and concluded with, "Kylie must die."[44] Then another classmate posing as Kylie, sent instant messages to her female field hockey teammates asking them out on dates and attempting to portray her as a lesbian.[45] The girl had to receive professional help and change schools twice, even being home-schooled for a semester.[46]

Another Vermont teen, a 13-year-old boy who was cyber bullied for two years, committed suicide. His classmates had spread rumors online that he was gay and a girl from school befriended him online, merely to lead him on so she could get him to reveal embarrassing personal details that she would then forward to her friends.[47]

Sometimes online harassment may even be unintentional. A college student snapped some pictures at a San Diego hardcore rock concert and posted them on his online photo gallery.[48] One photo of an unknown girl awkwardly "moshing" in mid-step motivated gallery visitors to contribute retouched photographs of the mosher, now dubbed "Moshzilla," morphed into various poses and scenarios (such as where she confronts Godzilla in hand-to-hand combat across the Tokyo skyline). The photographs were then reposted to multiple message boards and seen by millions of people. While the original poster of the initial photograph stated he had no malicious intent when posting it, the teenage girl dubbed "Moshzilla" said, "Some of the pictures that were Photoshopped were amazing, some were pretty malicious and cruel. So even though some of those pictures I laughed at hysterically with my boyfriend, you can't help but realize that you are being humiliated across the country. In a nutshell, I feel shitty."[49]

Online harassment is a crime in certain states. For example, in New York, online harassment carries a penalty of up to one-year imprisonment, and/or a $1,000 fine. Anyone harassed online should archive or log the conversations and report them to the ISP and local law enforcement.

An outgrowth of online harassment is the new trend of "*happy slapping*," where the perpetrators record physical assaults on cell phones that can record video and distribute the recorded videos to other phones and websites through video messaging, e-mail, or Bluetooth wireless connection. The happy slapping craze began in London, England but has begun to spread thanks to the Internet.[50] The craze has been linked to the popularity among teens of TV shows like MTV's "*Jackass*," where people are filmed doing dangerous or outrageous stunts. With a cell phone camera and an Internet connection, anyone can become a mini-movie producer with worldwide distribution. Many of the videos show up on message boards or P2P networks. Of course, if the perpetrators are caught, the photographs or video can often become the best evidence against them.

Nonetheless, this has not deterred the happy slappers. Instances of happy slapping can range from walking up to a classmate and slapping his or her face unexpectedly to violent assault. Three 14-year-old boys raped an 11-year-old girl and filmed the attack, then within minutes sent the video to hundreds of the girl's classmates at her school.[51] Two other happy slapping teens shot a 17-year-old girl in the leg with a pellet gun to create their video.[52] A 16-year-old girl was brutally punched and knocked unconscious by teen happy slappers and shortly thereafter a fellow student showed the video to the girl's 13-year-old brother.[53] And two teens were arrested after a happy slapping incident where they set fire to a man sleeping in a bus station.[54]

A 2007 French law to prevent happy slapping makes it illegal for anyone except professional journalists to film and broadcast violent events in France. French happy slapping incidents include a student using his cell phone camera to film a classmate attacking a Porcheville high school teacher, and photos of a young girl gang-raped in Nice being e-mailed around her school.[55]

Hate Speech On the Internet

Hate speech is speech that denigrates or attempts to inflame public opinion against certain groups of people. *Hate speech is protected in the United States* by the First Amendment guarantee of freedom of speech. Hate groups usually attack their targets on the basis of skin color, race, religion, ethnic origin, age, gender, or sexual orientation. They often circulate elaborate conspiracy theories to blame the targeted groups for a wide array of social, economic, or political ills. Frequently, hate groups will use the Bible to justify their positions, as in the case of Rev. Fred Phelps of the Westboro Baptist Church of Topeka, Kansas, who created his website godhatesfags.com.

Hate groups have found a home on the Internet where hundreds of them maintain a web presence. From 2000 to 2007, the number of hate websites increased from about 2,700 to 7,000 websites.[56] Activities of hate groups were once limited by geographical boundaries; now the Internet allows even the smallest fringe group to spread hate and freely recruit members online. This is because the Internet is an *inexpensive* and *effective* means for hate groups to communicate their message. The Internet is also a powerful *recruitment tool* for hate groups. Hate groups depend on recruitment for survival and their primary target is often impressionable teenagers. Many hate websites are specifically designed to attract and indoctrinate children using racist and anti-Semitic music and games. One of the most popular forms of racist music is "white power" rock 'n' roll, a mix of loud and violent music with hostile lyrics calling for the murder of blacks or a racial holy war. More than 50,000 white power rock 'n' roll CDs are sold annually. [57] One hate website sells a computer game called "Ethnic Cleansing" where players dress as Klansmen or skinheads in their quest to kill "subhumans" (*i.e.*, blacks and Latinos) and their "evil masters," the Jews. [58] The game's website promotes it as: [59]

> … the most politically incorrect video game ever made. Run through the ghetto blasting away various blacks and spics in an attempt to gain entrance to the subway system, where the Jews have hidden to avoid the carnage. Then, if YOU'RE lucky… you can blow away Jews as they scream 'Oy Vey!' on your way to their command center.

The fact that the game's website admits that the game has many programming bugs that the creator does not know how to fix may be indicative that many (but not all) hate websites are small (even one-man) operations set up by individuals long on hate but short on the intellect one would expect from their talk of being a "superior race." Hate groups find the Internet to be a fertile hunting ground for disaffected youths, who spend an enormous amount of each day in the "virtual world."

Some hate websites disguise themselves as legitimate sources of information but really contain racist propaganda or "revisionist history." Other hate websites bring in revenue that helps fund hate groups through merchandise sales and donations.

Most ISPs regulate but do not ban hate speech. Yahoo! has stated that "hate clubs" violate its "Terms of Service" agreement. Private businesses like Yahoo! are allowed to limit speech through "Terms of Service" agreements because the First Amendment only applies to the government. AOL has clear guidelines regulating what is and is not acceptable behavior on its servers, whereas Earthlink states that it "supports the free flow of information and ideas over the Internet" and does not actively monitor the content of websites it hosts.

Online hate speech remains protected in the United States under the First Amendment in most cases. The *exception* is when hate speech crosses into *threats and intimidation*. Threats involving *racial epithets* or motivated by *racial animus* are *not* protected under the First Amendment if they are directed at *specific individuals*; however, *blanket statements* of hatred toward an ethnic, racial, or religious *group* are protected.

Speech inciting *imminent violence* is also not protected.[60] In 1999, a coalition of anti-abortion groups was fined more than $100 million for providing information for a website called the "Nuremberg Files" that threatened the lives of doctors and clinic workers performing abortions. The website posted photographs of abortion providers, their home addresses, license plate numbers, and the names of their spouses and children. On three occasions following the murder of a doctor listed on the website, a line was drawn through the name of each murdered doctor. Although the website did not directly call for attacks on the physicians, the jury found that the information provided by the website amounted to a real threat of bodily harm.

Student Hate Websites

High schools and colleges routinely provide students with access to computers networked into the schools' server, as well as with e-mail accounts and web page hosting on their servers. Suppose a student wishes to set up a hate website on the school server. Can the school prevent students from using its computers, servers, and network for the promotion of hate views? *Private* schools are not agents of government and therefore can prohibit students from publishing offensive speech using university equipment or services. However, *public* schools, as agents of the government, must follow the First Amendment's prohibition against speech restrictions based on content or view. But, public schools may choose to restrict student use of their server and computers to academic activities only; this would likely prevent a student from creating a hate website or sending hate e-mail from his student e-mail account.

Remedies to Hate Speech

The anonymity of the Internet makes it difficult to track down and prosecute individuals and hate groups who use the Internet threaten their intended victims. But there are some remedies to hate speech online. As seen in the Nuremberg Files case, civil lawsuits with huge fines are a powerful remedy that can financially cripple an organized hate group. Then there is the *"Marketplace of Ideas"* view that the best antidote to hate speech is more speech, *i.e.*, rebuttal.

Hate filters are often proposed as another remedy to online hate speech. Filters are software that can be installed along with a web browser to block access to certain websites that contain inappropriate or offensive material. The Anti-Defamation League created "HateFilter," which blocks access to websites that advocate hatred, bigotry, or violence towards Jews or other groups on the basis of their religion, race, ethnicity, sexual orientation, or other immutable characteristics.

Hate Speech in Foreign Jurisdictions

The United States and the rest of the world are diametrically opposed on the issue of hate speech on the Internet. While hate speech is *constitutionally protected* in the United States, in most other countries legislation prohibits and, in some cases, even criminalizes hate speech. In the United States, the First Amendment protects hate speech and U.S. law prohibits interfering with the *content* of electronic communications. Europe, in contrast, is moving toward establishing international standards to define and regulate hate speech. But the United States has repeatedly stated its constitutional objection to any international legal means to outlaw hate speech and has indicated that it will not join Europe in such a venture.

Publishing material likely to incite racial hatred is illegal in the United Kingdom under the Public Order Act of 1986, but there is nothing that can be done under U.K. law if the offending company's servers are located in another country, such as the United States. In Germany, promoting Nazi ideology is illegal, while in many European countries it is illegal to deny the reality of the Holocaust. Britain, Canada, Denmark, France, and Germany have all charged people for crimes involving hate speech on the Internet.

Under American law, the United States will not extradite a person for engaging in a constitutionally protected activity even if that activity violates a criminal law elsewhere. Since hate speech is protected in the United States, it has become a safe harbor for hate group websites seeking to escape Europe's strict hate speech laws. By hosting their hate websites from a U.S.–based server, European hate groups can avail themselves of the United State's broader protections, while their websites still remain accessible anywhere in the world, even in countries where the subject matter may be prohibited by law.

Once again, we see the problem of enforcing conflicting laws on a medium that transcends geographical boundaries. In 2001, there were reports that Germany was contemplating initiating denial of service attacks against U.S. servers hosting neo-Nazi websites. While that would, of course, prevent German citizens from viewing the objectionable material, it would also prevent anyone, anywhere from viewing it, including U.S. citizens who have a constitutional right to view it. It would also effectively shut down all of the other, non-neoNazi hate websites also hosted on the server. And, had such a plan been implemented, it would not only mean that a foreign government had launched an attack against physical assets (the servers) in the United States, but also that a foreign government would have been able to shut down U.S. websites based solely on their content. The German proposal, to date, has not been implemented.

A French court, in 2000, held that Yahoo! violated French anti-hate laws when it allowed online auction listings of about a thousand Nazi-related items.[61] While Yahoo! removed the Nazi paraphernalia from its French subsidiary yahoo.fr, it did not remove them from its parent website yahoo.com, which is also accessible within France. Yahoo.com is accessible worldwide, even though it is hosted in California. The lawsuit was brought by two anti-hate groups in Paris.[62] Yahoo! faced a daily $13,000 fine unless it blocked access within France to all Nazi objects listed on Yahoo.com (by 2006, the fine had reached $15 million). Rather than appeal the ruling in France, *Yahoo! filed a complaint in the U.S.* District Court for the Northern District of California, seeking a declaratory judgment that the *French court's orders were not enforceable under U.S. laws* and a ruling that the French judgment could not be collected in the United States. The district court ruled in 2001 that websites operated by Yahoo! were not subject to French laws, as the French court order posed a direct threat to Yahoo!'s First Amendment rights.[63] The court stated: "what is at issue here is whether it is consistent with the Constitution and laws of the United States for another nation to regulate speech by a United States resident within the United States on the basis that such speech can be accessed by Internet users in that nation," and continued "although France has the sovereign right to regulate what speech is permissible in France, this court may not enforce a foreign order that violates the protections of the United States Constitution."[64] However, in August 2004, the 9th Circuit *reversed the decision*, ruling that *U.S. courts did not have blanket power to block foreign countries from enforcing their laws against U.S. websites* such as yahoo.com, adding that obeying other nations' laws is the price of doing international business.[65] The 9th Circuit found that U.S. courts do not have jurisdiction to override the orders of a foreign court without that foreign government first bringing the dispute into the U.S. legal system. But the court added that should the French government turn to the U.S. courts to enforce its order, then Yahoo! would be free to raise its First Amendment defense. The court wrote: "If Yahoo! violates the speech laws of another nation, it must wait for the foreign litigants to come to the United States to enforce the judgment before its First Amendment claim may be heard by a U.S. court."[66] Of course, a French judgment could still be enforced against whatever assets, if any, Yahoo! might have in France. This decision could *expose U.S.–based websites to the more restrictive speech laws of other nations.* In January 2006, a 6–5 majority of the 9th Circuit dismissed the case, leaving unresolved the primary issue of whether U.S.–based websites are liable for damages in foreign courts for displaying content that is unlawful overseas but protected in the United States.[67]

These cases illustrate the *fundamental conflict of values* between the United States, which views the alternative as ceding to foreign governments the authority to censor Internet speech contrary to the constitutional guarantees of free speech granted in the First Amendment to the U.S. Constitution, and the other nations of the world, which feel that the United States' position essentially forces American speech values on the rest of the world.

Repression of Online Speech

In the 16th Century, the English government controlled the printing presses through a system of patent grants, monopolies, and licensing. Licensing was a form of prior censorship or prior restraint. A *prior restraint* is a law that requires an individual to obtain permission from the government before speaking or conveying information. The practice of licensing continued into the American colonies but ended in the 1720s. Prior restraint by the government in the United States was ultimately prohibited by the First Amendment (adopted in 1791). Indeed, in *Near v. Minnesota*, the Supreme Court stated that "the chief purpose" of the First Amendment was to prevent prior restraints and that post-publication punishment was the preferred remedy for libel or defamation.[68] In that case, a state statute allowed suppression of a newspapers or periodicals as a public nuisance. However, the court did note some limitations to the doctrine against prior restraint:[69]

> [T]he protection even as to previous restraint is not absolutely unlimited. But the limitation has been recognized only in exceptional cases. 'When a nation is at war many things that might be said in time of peace are such a hindrance to its effort that their utterance will not be endured so long as men fight and that no Court could regard them as protected by any constitutional right.' ... No one would question but that a government might prevent actual obstruction to its recruiting service or the publication of the sailing dates of transports or the number and location of troops.

The concept of "permissible prior restraint in matters of national security," first hinted at in *Near v. Minnesota*, reared its head again 40 years later in what has become known as "The Pentagon Papers Case."[70] In that case, the Nixon White House turned to the Supreme Court to prevent the New York Times and the Washington Post from publishing a stolen, classified document entitled, "The History of U.S. Decision-Making on Viet Nam Policy" on grounds that publication would endanger "national security." While each Justice offered his own view on prior restraint, the court held that the government had failed to meet the "heavy burden" required to sustain a prior restraint.

Perhaps the most straight-forward case of prior restraint versus national security was *U.S. v. Progressive*, where the federal government filed suit to enjoin *The Progressive*, a left-wing magazine, from publishing its cover story entitled "The H-Bomb Secret: How We Got It and Why We're Telling It."[71] The government argued that a "how-to" manual for anyone wanting to build a hydrogen bomb was a "clear and present danger" and should be prevented from publication.[72] However, the issue was rendered moot when the article was published outside the United States.[73]

An early Internet case illustrates the difficulty of balancing the First Amendment protection from prior restraint against an individual's right to privacy (see Chapter 10).[74] William Sheehan sued several credit reporting agencies for violating the Fair Debt Collections Practices Act[75] and the Fair Credit Reporting Act[76] and also created a gripe site (see Chapter 13). Sheehan's gripe site contained disparaging comments about one of the credit agencies and contact information for its employees and attorneys. The contact information posted on the website included home addresses, street maps, home phone numbers, fax numbers, and Social Security numbers. Sheehan claimed that he obtained all of the contact information from public sources. The credit agency sought and received a temporary restraining order against Sheehan's website.

The agents and employees of the credit agency had legitimate concerns about the disclosure of their private information. As made clear by the Amy Boyer case (see Chapter 10), the threats of *cyberstalking* and *identity theft* posed by disclosure of such private information are sufficiently foreseeable.[77] But did they rise to the level of outweighing the constitutional protection against prior restraint? Whose right should prevail in such a conflict — Sheehan's right of free speech without prior restraint or the agency employees' right of privacy?

As you may recall from Chapter 10, one of the four invasion of privacy torts is *public disclosure of private facts.* The employees might well have a valid civil claim against Sheehan; however, a defense to that tort is that the facts are not "private" and Sheehan claimed he obtained the information from public sources. Should a jury determine that to be the case, then Sheehan would have an adequate defense to an invasion of privacy claim.

Courts will issue a prior restraint on speech if the speech contains incitement to imminent unlawful action.[78] In this case, the court initially denied the agency's motion to issue a temporary restraining order (TRO) against the allegedly defamatory speech but granted the TRO against the disclosure of the private information fearing that it could be an incitement to imminent unlawful action (*i.e.*, the foreseeability of cyberstalking).

After a TRO is granted, a hearing date is set for the court to decide whether to vacate (*i.e.*, eliminate) the TRO or to issue a preliminary injunction based on the TRO. Note however that until the hearing the TRO effectively was a prior restraint. Obtaining a preliminary injunction requires a showing of both a strong chance of success on the merits and the possibility of irreparable harm. Here the court concluded that since the information had been "available on plaintiff's website since early 1997, and there is no evidence that anyone has ever been harassed, approached, or contacted by a person who viewed the site" the posting could not be deemed an incitement to imminent unlawful action.[79] The court summed up the case:[80]

Restraining orders and injunctions 'are classic examples of prior restraints' and as such are presumed to be unconstitutional…The First Amendment does not tolerate even temporary suppression of speech that might ultimately be found to be protected…In the absence of incitement to imminent unlawful action, the motion for a preliminary injunction must be denied.

The First Amendment also protects commercial speech from government repression. A California law that prohibited a website from advertising homes for sale unless the website was first licensed by the state as a real estate broker was challenged on First Amendment grounds. The California law required Internet advertising companies to be licensed real estate brokers in order to list or advertise homes online. The law was written broadly to include anyone acting as an agent or advertising or listing homes for a fee, but it specifically exempted newspapers.[81] In *ForSaleByOwner.com v. Zinneman*, the federal district court ruled in favor of web publisher ForSaleByOwner.com, concluding that the statute, by requiring websites to obtain a license but specifically exempting newspapers that publish the same information, was "wholly arbitrary" and violated the First Amendment guarantees of free speech and freedom of the press.[82] The court stated "[T]here appears to be no justification whatsoever for any distinction between [either medium, *i.e.*, newspapers and websites]."

In Canada, courts are allowed to issue gag orders on the press attending public hearings.[83] The rationale for this ban on publication of details of the proceedings is to ensure a fair trial for the defendant, since, unlike the United States, Canada does not sequester its jurors. The gag order is meant to protect jurors from learning information that the court does not want them to see. However, this has led to the odd situation where a reporter covering the trial is prohibited from revealing information from a government proceeding that is open to the public. With the advent of blogs, Canadian judges are now contending with bloggers who gain access to public hearings and then publish the information online while their press counterparts must remain silent or face judicial sanctions. In a recent situation, a conservative American blogger from Minneapolis published in his blog[84] detailed reports of Canada's Adscam hearings, provided by a confidential source present at the hearings.[85] The blogger reported a tenfold increase in news-hungry Canadian visitors to his blog. Ironically, when interviewing the blogger, the Canadian press was barred from even publishing the blog's URL. The chilling effect on speech was evident by one Canadian blogger's stated fear of even linking to the U.S. blogger's website after Canadian government attorneys hinted that they might charge Canadian web publishers with contempt of court if they even link to the American blog.

In another case of a democratic government repressing speech, ironically South Korea tried to ban access to a North Korean university website.[86] South Korea feared that the Korean-language website (ournation-school.com) would spread Communist ideology amongst its Internet-using youth. One South Korean official was quoted as saying, "We need to block access to resources of one-sided information or knowledge which ordinary people can obtain easily," a comment one would more likely associate with a Communist regime like North Korea than with a democracy.[87] Certainly, it is hardly an acceptance of the "marketplace of ideas" theory! And in 2007, a new South Korean law required citizens to disclose their name and ID number before they opine online.[88]

Indeed, if the approach to Internet speech by democratic Western nations contrasts so sharply with that of the United States, how does the approach of totalitarian or communist governments compare?

Web Speech Under Communism

The borderless nature of the Internet makes it difficult for governments to control the flow of information. Communist China has been engaged in a constant struggle to gain and maintain control over its citizens' use of the Internet. The Chinese government has clamped down on Internet speech by blocking certain keyword searches and entire websites and forcing cyber cafés to keep records of users and the web pages they visit. China has even formed a special task force of undercover online "commentators" whose job is to defend government positions when they are criticized on online message boards, in an attempt to sway public opinion on controversial issues.[89] The Chinese government, which has 11 agencies overseeing Internet use, has installed video cameras and monitoring software in Shanghai's Internet cafés and bars to prevent customers from viewing "forbidden websites." If the software detects an Internet user viewing a banned website, it automatically sends a message to a "remote supervisory center." Banned websites are those deemed *pornographic,* or *"superstitious"* (such as those discussing the outlawed Falun Gong spiritual group), or websites that criticize the government or the Communist Party. Dozens of people have been imprisoned for posting or downloading such materials from banned websites. China has installed filters on public Internet terminals to prevent access to these websites. All computer users in Internet cafés or bars must enter their ID card numbers (or passport number for foreigners) to access the Internet.[90]

Bloggers have become a major concern to the Chinese government. Through an arm of its Ministry of Information Industry, known as the Internet Society of China, it proposed in late 2006 that bloggers be required to use their real names when they register blogs although they would still be allowed to write under a pseudonym.[91] The result, of course, would be that the bloggers would be anonymous to everyone except the government. The plan was subsequently abandoned as technologically impractical to administer, and instead the government promoted a voluntary registration system by having bloggers sign a "self-discipline pledge."[92] Second only to the United States in the number of Internet users, China has 137 million citizens online, of whom 30 million are registered bloggers, while 100 million are regular blog readers.[93]

The Chinese government also requires ISPs to police online content and weed out any criticism of the government. China recently called on ISPs to sign a "self-discipline pact" to stop the spread of "information that could harm national security." The pact describes the "basic principles of self-discipline for Internet" as "patriotism, observance of law, fairness, and trustworthiness." In accordance with the pact, ISPs must promise not to spread information "threatening national security, social stability, or containing superstitious or erotic content." ISPs must also make sure they do *not provide links to other websites with "inappropriate material."* The pact also requires Internet cafés to direct web users to "healthy online information," and urges respect for intellectual property rights.[94] All of these efforts are part of Communist China's struggle to gain and maintain control over Internet use by its online citizens.[95]

Even U.S. websites have felt the repressive grasp of Communist China. Google recently launched a search engine in China after agreeing to omit search results from government-banned websites. The results are omitted if the search requests are made through computers connecting to the Internet in China. The same search queries submitted through a U.S. connection would retrieve the blocked website links. Google voluntarily had agreed to exclude Chinese results from at least eight websites, including <u>voanews.com</u>, the Voice of America website.[96]

Like China, Vietnam sees the Internet as a potential threat to the government, recognizing the capability of the Internet as a powerful tool for recruitment and spreading dissent. Few Vietnamese can afford Internet connections, let alone their own computers, so Internet cafés have become a popular refuge for the country's online users, estimated at 20% of the nation's population of 83 million. Under Vietnamese law, Internet cafés are obligated to inform on their customers, and cafés that do not comply are closed down. This has created a climate of fear and has chilled free speech. The Vietnamese government claims that it filters the Internet to protect its citizens from socially objectionable topics like pornography, but according to a recent study only material related to politics, religion, and human rights was being filtered out.[97]

Web Speech in the Arab World

Arab nations have placed limits on web speech as well. Syria sentenced a man who downloaded material from a banned émigré website and e-mailed it to others to two-and-a-half years in prison for the crime of "publishing false news that saps the morale of the nation." Four other

Syrians faced similar charges. Amnesty International has called the verdict a "political decision that quells the right of expression in Syria," and urged Syria to release all five of the detained men.[98] Another Syrian man has been imprisoned since July 2003 after posting photographs of a Kurdish demonstration in Damascus on the Internet. Syrian state-run media is still closely controlled, and the government bans any websites deemed offensive or anti-Syrian.

In Bahrain, every website is required to register with the government, providing the names, addresses, and telephone numbers of website operators and then post a government-issued ID number on the website.[99] While not a prior restraint on what the webmasters may wish to publish, it does have a chilling effect on web speech by serving as a constant reminder that Big Brother is watching over their shoulder.

Summary

The Constitution does not protect obscene speech. Pornography is entitled to First Amendment protection unless it is obscene or child pornography. Thus the question becomes, what is the definition of obscenity? Despite many attempts, courts have been unable to answer that question satisfactorily. The current test for determining obscenity is the _Miller_ test, _i.e._, "Whether to the average person, applying contemporary community standards, the dominant theme of the material taken as a whole appeals to prurient interest." However, the borderless nature of the Internet makes applying community standards impossible.

The Children's Internet Protection Act of 2000 denies federal funds for Internet access to public libraries and schools that refuse to put filter software on their Internet computers. The Child Protection and Obscenity Enforcement Act of 1988 requires that certain adult media, _e.g._, magazines and videos, maintain onsite records to verify that all models or actors are of legal age.

The United States has laws against child pornography and obscenity but statutes must not be vague or overly broad or they will be held unconstitutional in violation of the First Amendment.

Online harassment occurs when one uses the Internet to cause substantial emotional distress to the victim. It can be through e-mail, chat, instant messages, newsgroups or message boards posts, or words or images posted on websites or on social networks. Online harassment is a crime in certain states.

Hate speech is speech that denigrates or attempts to inflame public opinion against certain groups of people. It is protected in the United States by the First Amendment. Threats involving racial epithets or motivated by racial animus are not protected if they are directed at specific individuals; however, blanket statements of hatred toward an ethnic, racial, or religious group are protected. The Internet is a cheap and effective means for hate groups to communicate their message. It is also a powerful recruitment tool for hate groups, which depend on recruitment for survival and target impressionable teenagers. Some hate websites disguise themselves as legitimate sources of information but really contain racist propaganda or "revisionist history." Most ISPs regulate but do not ban hate speech. Private schools are not agents of the government and therefore can prohibit students from publishing offensive speech using university equipment or services; but public schools, as agents of the government, must follow the First Amendment's prohibition against speech restrictions based on content or view. While hate speech is constitutionally protected in the United States, in most other countries legislation prohibits and, in some cases, even criminalizes hate speech.

A prior restraint is a law requiring an individual to obtain permission from the government before speaking or conveying information.

The borderless nature of the Internet makes it difficult for governments to control the flow of information. Communist nations are engaged in a constant struggle to gain and maintain control over their citizens' use of the Internet. The Internet is a potential threat to Communist governments because it is a powerful tool for recruitment and spreading dissent. Registration of web users creates a chilling effect on free speech.

Chapter Fourteen Notes

[1] *Jacobellis v. Ohio*, 378 U.S. 184 (1964).

[2] *Roth v. United States*, 354 U.S. 476 (1957). This case is included in the Cases Section on the Issues in Internet Law website (www.IssuesinInternetLaw.com).

[3] *Miller v. California*, 413 U.S. 15 (1973). This case is included in the Cases Section on the Issues in Internet Law website (www.IssuesinInternetLaw.com).

[4] *New York v. Ferber*, 458 U.S. 747 (1982).

[5] *Jacobellis v. Ohio*, fn. 1, *supra*.

[6] *Miller v. California*, fn. 3, *supra*.

[7] Communications Decency Act, 47 U.S.C. § 223 *et seq.*

[8] *Reno v. ACLU*, 521 U.S. 844 (1997).

[9] *Nitke v. Gonzales*, 2006 WL 684668 (Mar. 20, 2006), *aff'g Nitke v. Gonzalez*, 2005 WL 3747954 (S.D.N.Y., July 25, 2005).

[10] *Nitke v. Gonzalez*, 2005 WL 3747954 (S.D.N.Y., July 25, 2005).

[11] *Broadrick v. Oklahoma*, 413 U.S. 601 (1973).

[12] Child Online Protection Act (COPA), 47 U.S.C. § 231.

[13] *ACLU v. Reno*, 217 F.Supp. 3d 162 (2000).

[14] *ACLU v. Reno*, 31 F. Supp.2d 473 (E.D. Pa. 1999).

[15] "Dicta" is a portion of a judicial opinion that is merely a judge's editorializing and does not directly address the case at hand.

[16] *Ashcroft v. ACLU*, 535 U.S. 564 (2002), *vacating ACLU v. Reno*, 217 F.3d 162 (3d Cir. 2000).

[17] *ACLU v. Ashcroft*, 322 F.Supp. 3d 240(2003).

[18] *Ashcroft v. ACLU*, 542 U.S. 656 (2004), *aff'g ACLU v. Ashcroft*, 322 F.3d 240 (3d Cir. 2003).

[19] *ACLU v. Gonzales*, (Final Order, 98-5591, E.D.Pa Mar. 22, 2007) [originally *ACLU v. Reno*, then *ACLU v. Ashcroft*].

[20] *New York v. Ferber*, 458 U.S. 747 (1982).

[21] Child Pornography Prevention Act, 18 U.S.C. § 2252.

[22] *Ashcroft v. Free Speech Coalition*, 122 S.Ct. 1389 (2002). This case is included in the Cases Section on the Issues in Internet Law website (www.IssuesinInternetLaw.com).

[23] *Ibid.* The court wrote:

> The second flaw in the Government's position is that *Ferber* did not hold that child pornography is by definition without value. On the contrary, the Court recognized some works in this category might have significant value, see *id.*, at 761, but relied on virtual images — the very images prohibited by the CPPA — as an alternative and permissible means of expression: "[I]f it were necessary for literary or artistic value, a person over the statutory age who perhaps looked younger could be utilized. Simulation outside of the prohibition of the statute could provide another alternative." *Id.*, at 763. *Ferber*, then, not only referred to the distinction between actual and virtual child pornography, it relied on it as a reason supporting its holding. Ferber provides no support for a statute that eliminates the distinction and makes the alternative mode criminal as well.

[24] PROTECT Act of 2003 (Pub. L. No. 108-21, 117 Stat. 650).

[25] Keith B. Darrell, *Issues in Internet Law*, p. 163, Amber Book Company (1st edition, 2005).

[26] *United State v. Williams*, Case No. 04-15128, (11th Cir. Apr. 6, 2006).

[27] Section 2252A(a)(3)(B) of the PROTECT Act of 2003 (Pub. L. No. 108-21, 117 Stat. 650).

[28] *United State v. Williams*, Docket: 06-0694 (2007).

[29] Children's Internet Protection Act, 47 U.S.C. § 254(h) and (l), (Pub. L. No, 106-554).

[30] *United States v. American Library Ass'n.*, 539 U.S. 194 (2003). This case is included in the Cases Section on the Issues in Internet Law website (www.IssuesinInternetLaw.com).

[31] *Kathleen R. v. Livermore*, 104 Cal.Rptr.2d 772 (Cal. App. Dist. 1, 2001).

[32] Teri Metros, "Phoenix Public Library Filtering Policy Changed Due to City Council," Mountain Plains Library Association website, *available at* www.mpla.us/documents/reports/state/az/20041021.html (accessed September 25, 2007).

[33] Child Protection and Obscenity Enforcement Act, 18 U.S.C. § 2257.

[34] Nathan Frick, "Lawyers in Walker County Child Porn Case Hope to Redefine Law," Walker County Messenger, June 14, 2005.

[35] Noah Shachtman, "Return to Sender — 55,000 Times," Wired News, August 23, 2002, *available at* www.wired.com/news/culture/0,1284,54708,00.html (accessed September 25, 2007).

[36] Amy Harmon, "Internet Gives Teenage Bullies Weapons to Wound from Afar," New York Times, August 26, 2004.

[37] *Ibid.*

[38] Amanda Lenhart, Mary Madden, and Paul Hitlin, "Teens and Technology Youth are Leading the Transition to a Fully Wired and Mobile Nation," Pew Internet & American Life Project, July 27, 2005. Pew observed that "instant messaging has become the digital communication backbone of teens' daily lives," and that "roughly 32% of all teens — use IM every single day."

[39] *Ibid.*

[40] Tu Thanh Ha, "'Star Wars Kid' Cuts A Deal with His Tormentors," (Quebec) Globe and Mail, July 4, 2006.

[41] Andrew Childers, "Bullying Moves to the Internet," Hometownannapolis.com, September 5, 2006.

[42] "1 of 3 Teens are Victims of Cyber Bullying" Spero News, August 17, 2006.

[43] Anne Marie Chaker, "Schools Act to Short-Circuit Spread of 'Cyberbullying," Wall Street Journal, January 24, 2007, p. D1.

[44] Suzanne Struglinski, "Schoolyard Bullying Has Gone High-Tech," Deseret News (Salt Lake City, UT), August 21, 2006.

[45] Anne Broache, "Anticrime Group Calls for Laws to Curb 'Cyber Bullying,'" CNET News.com, August 21, 2006, and Nicholas Zifcak, "Bullying Rampant in Cyberspace," Epoch Times, August 21, 2006.

[46] Suzanne Struglinski, fn. 44, *supra.*

[47] John Flowers, "Cyber Bullying Hits Community, Addison County Independent, October 19, 2006.

[48] Leslie Katz, "When 'Digital Bullying' Goes Too Far," CNETnews.com, June 22, 2005.

[49] *Available at* www.moshzilla.com (accessed September 25, 2007).

[50] Leslie Katz, fn. 48, *supra.*

[51] Tosin Sulaiman, "Girl's Rape 'Filmed by Teenagers on Mobile,'" London Times, June 18, 2005.

[52] *Ibid.*

[53] *Ibid.*

[54] *Ibid.*

[55] "New French Law Aimed at `Happy Slapping,'" Associated Press wire report, March 07, 2007.

[56] "Hate Websites Continue to Flourish," The Register, May 10, 2004, and Andy Levy-Ajzenkopf, "Online Hate Sites Grow Again, Wiesenthal Report Says," JUF News, August 24, 2007.

[57] Ros Davidson, "Web of Hate," Salon, October 16, 1998.

[58] "Racist Groups Using Computer Gaming to Promote Violence Against Blacks, Latinos, and Jews," Anti-Defamation League, *available at* www.adl.org/videogames/default.asp (accessed September 25, 2007).

[59] *Available at* www.resistance.com/ethniccleansing/catalog.htm (accessed September 25, 2007).

[60] *Brandenburg v. Ohio*, 395 U.S. 444 (1969). This case is included in the Cases Section on the Issues in Internet Law website (www.IssuesinInternetLaw.com).

[61] *UEJF v. Yahoo! Inc.*, Case No. 00/05308, (Tribunal de Grande Instance de Paris Nov. 20, 2000).

[62] France's Union of Jewish Students and the International Anti-Racism and Anti-Semitism League.

[63] *Yahoo!, Inc v La Ligue Contre Le Racisme Et L'antisemitisme*, 169 F. Supp. 2d 1181 (N.D. Cal. 2001).

[64] *Ibid.*

[65] *Yahoo!, Inc. v. La Ligue Contre Le Racisme et L'Antisemitisme*, 04 C.D.O.S. 7742 (2004).

[66] *Ibid.*

[67] David Kravets, "Court Dismisses Yahoo Free Speech Suit," Associated Press wire service report, January 12, 2006.

[68] *Near v. Minnesota*, 283 U.S. 697 (1931). Overturning an injunction obtained by Minnesota state officials that prevented Jay Near from publishing a scandal sheet that routinely attacked state officials, under a state statute that provided that anyone who published "(a) an obscene, lewd and lascivious newspaper, magazine, or other periodical, or (b) a malicious, scandalous, and defamatory newspaper, magazine, or other periodical, is guilty of a nuisance, and all persons guilty of such nuisance may be enjoined."

[69] *Ibid.*

[70] *New York Times v. United States*, 403 U.S. 713 (1971).

[71] *United States v. Progressive, Inc.*, 467 F. Supp. 990 (W.D. Wis., Mar. 28, 1979).

[72] A hydrogen bomb, which is fusion-based, can be many hundreds of times more powerful than a fission-based atomic bomb.

[73] *The Progressive* then proceeded to publish the article.

[74] *Sheehan v. King County Experian*, Case No. C97-1360WD (W.D. Wash. order denying preliminary injunction, issued July 17, 1998).

[75] 15 U.S.C. § 1692 *et seq.*

[76] 15 U.S.C. § 1681 *et seq.*

[77] *Remsburg v. Docusearch, Inc.*, 816 A.2d 1001 (N.H. Feb. 18, 2003). This case is included in the Cases Section on the Issues in Internet Law website (www.IssuesinInternetLaw.com).

[78] *Brandenburg v. Ohio*, fn. 60, *supra.*

[79] *Sheehan v. King County Experian*, fn. 74, *supra.*

[80] *Ibid.*

[81] The California statute broadly defined "real estate broker" to include any person who, for a fee, "sells or offers

to sell, buys or offers to buy, solicits prospective sellers or purchasers of, solicits or obtains listings of, or negotiates the purchase, sale or exchange of real property."

[82] *ForSaleByOwner.com v. Zinneman*, Case No. CIV-5-03-1019 MCE (GGH), (E.D. Cal. Nov. 18, 2004). Paula Reddish Zinnemann was the Commissioner of the California Department of Real Estate.

[83] *Dagenais v. Canadian Broad. Corp.*, [1994] 3 S.C.R. 835, 1994 CanLII 39 (S.C.C.), *available at* www.canlii. org/ca/cas/scc/1994/1994scc102.html (accessed September 25, 2007), holding that publication bans did not violate Canada's charter of rights and freedom.

[84] Declan McCullagh, "U.S. Blogger Thwarts Canadian Gag Order," CNET News.com, April 5, 2005.

[85] The Adscam hearings concerned allegations of corruption and illegal campaign contributions in Canada's Liberal party.

[86] "Seoul May Ban North Korea College Website," Reuters wire report, November 12, 2004.

[87] *Ibid.*

[88] Dan Simmons, "Cyber Bullying Rises In S. Korea," BBC Click Online, November 3, 2006, *available at* http://news.bbc.co.uk/2/hi/programmes/click_online/6112754.stm (accessed September 25, 2007).

[89] "China Goes Undercover to Sway Opinion on Internet," Reuters wire report, May 19, 2005.

[90] Associated Press wire service report, April 22, 2004.

[91] "China Moves Toward 'Real Name System' for Blogs," Reuters wire report, October 23, 2006.

[92] Jason Leow, "Why China Relaxed Blogger Crackdown: Registration Plan was Dropped in Face of Tech-Industry Protests," Wall Street Journal, May 17, 2007.

[93] "Chinese Blog Providers 'Encouraged' to Register Users with their Real Names," Associated Press wire report, August 22, 2007.

[94] "China Encourages ISPs to Sign 'Self-Discipline Pact,'" Washington Post, June 21, 2004.

[95] "China Goes Undercover to Sway Opinion on Internet," Reuters wire report, May 19, 2005.

[96] Associated Press wire report, September 25, 2004.

[97] John Boudreau, "Vietnam Tightens Grip on Internet; Cafés Closed for Not Reporting Dissenters," (San Jose, CA) Mercury News, October 24, 2006.

[98] BBC News, June 21, 2004.

[99] "Bahrain Site Registration Sparks Protests," Associated Press wire report, April 28, 2005.

Chapter Fourteen Quiz

Charlie Brown is a black student at Ecumenical High School. Each student is given 14mb of space on the school's server to use for e-mail accounts and personal websites. Charlie has used his space to set up a website promoting his theory that blacks are a superior race and that Caucasians and Asians are inferior races. His website includes links to anti-Hispanic and anti-Semitic websites. He has an online game on his website called "Honk When You Kill a Honkey," where players earn points by killing white people. Charlie also has a "hit list" page on his website where he lists "Lucy, Linus, and Patty" as white classmates he would like to see dead. He has also posted a nude picture of his 15-year-old girlfriend "Snoopy" on his website. Last week, Charlie used his account to send hate e-mail to every student in the school.

If you are using this book in a classroom, discuss the issues raised and the liability of all parties. Otherwise, try to list the issues involved and probable outcomes before turning to the answers in the Appendix.

[Answers in Appendix]

PART SIX

WEB CONTRACTS

CHAPTER FIFTEEN

This chapter explores online contracts, legal capacity to contract, online signatures, sales contracts, website user agreements, and website development contracts.

CONTRACTS

IN THIS CHAPTER WE will discuss common contracts one might find on the web, who has or lacks the legal capacity to be bound by a contract, and what constitutes a "signature" online. Two common forms of contracts encountered online are *website user agreements* and *sales contracts to make an online purchase*, which often take the form of click-wrap or browse-wrap agreements.

Binding Contracts

Capacity to Contract

Minors (children under 18) and mentally disabled individuals lack the legal capacity to enter into contracts. A contract with a minor is unenforceable by the other party and *voidable at the minor's option*. As long as the minor does not cancel the contract, it is *binding on the other party*. Even though a minor may cancel a contract, a minor cannot be unjustly enriched by the ability to cancel a contract. Thus, if a minor makes a purchase and cancels the contract, the minor will have to *return anything received* under the contract.

Notification of Changes

Companies must notify customers of any changes they make to their contracts. Under contract law principles, a unilateral change to a contract is not binding; instead it results in the revised contract becoming an offer. The other party must then be notified so she can accept or reject this offer; upon assenting to the new terms, the contract will become a binding agreement.

A recent case illustrates the issue of 'What is proper notice?' Joe Douglas had contracted for phone service through a division of AOL that was subsequently acquired by Talk America, Inc. After the acquisition, Talk America made several important changes to the contract (a price increase, an arbitration clause, a class-action suit waiver, and choice-of-law provision pointing to New York law). It posted these changes on its website but did not send any notification directly to individual customers. After using the service for four years, Douglas became aware of the changes and sued Talk America. The trial court ruled that pursuant to the revised contract, the case had to go to arbitration. On appeal to the 9th Circuit Court of Appeals, the trial court decision was overturned. The appellate court held that companies cannot change their contracts without first notifying their customers and that posting revisions online was not sufficient notification.[1] The court stated: "Parties to a contract have no obligation to check the terms on a periodic basis to learn whether they have been changed by the other side."[2]

Electronic Signatures

Only real estate contracts and contracts that cannot be performed within one year are required by the *Statute of Frauds* to be in writing. However, although *oral* contracts are valid, it is difficult to prove their terms. Therefore, most people follow the old adage, "Get it in writing." The verbal agreement of the parties *is* the contract; the writing is merely the memorialization of that agreement. However, once committed to writing, the Parol Evidence Rule provides that a written agreement is the final expression of the agreement of the parties, not to be varied or contradicted by prior or contemporaneous oral or written negotiations.

For centuries, a contract signing involved two people passing a pen to sign their names on a sheet of paper. Advances in technology have eliminated the necessity of both pen and paper, but the law has been slow to catch up with technology. As late as 1996, a court refused to accept the validity of a faxed signature on a legal document. In *Georgia Dept. of Transportation v. Norris*, Norris sought to sue the state department of transportation, after his wife was killed in an accident on what he claimed was a poorly maintained highway intersection.[3] Before Norris could sue, he was required to file a notice of claim in writing to the department of transportation. He faxed the notice within the specified time and followed up with a mailed notice that arrived a day after the deadline. The Georgia court held that he did not satisfy the notice requirement because even though the faxed notice was received in time, "*the transmission of beeps and chirps along a telephone line is not a writing.*" The Georgia Supreme Court later reversed the decision on grounds unrelated to whether a fax is a writing. The case, which has become derisively known as the "beeps and chirps" case, highlights the difficulty courts have applying new technologies to traditional legal transactions.

The Uniform Electronic Transactions Act (UETA)

The Uniform Electronic Transactions Act (UETA) is a *model statute* for states to adopt. A state's "version" of the UETA may contain significant state-specific variations. To date, 46 states and the District of Columbia have adopted it. The Act states that "*a record or signature may not be denied legal effect or enforceability solely because it is in electronic form.*" The UETA does not apply to wills.

The E-SIGN Act

Congress enacted the *Electronic Signatures in Global and National Commerce Act (the E-SIGN Act)* in 2000.[4] The Act's purpose is *to provide legal validity to contracts entered into electronically.* The E-SIGN Act does not replace the UETA; in fact, the Act specifically states that in any state that has adopted the UETA, the E-SIGN Act is pre-empted. The E-SIGN Act applies to e-mails, PDF documents, and digital signatures with encryption, but does not apply to wills, family law (*e.g.*, adoption, divorce) documents, court documents, cancellation of utilities or health insurance, public recalls, or notices of default, repossession, foreclosure, or eviction. Under the Act's provisions, if another law requires *written* information to consumers, then they must *affirmatively consent* to receiving the electronic version. The E-SIGN Act does not apply to intra-state transactions that do not affect interstate or foreign commerce.

The actual electronic "signature" can be either a scanned version of the signer's signature, the signer's name typed into the signature space, the clicking of an "I Accept" button, or a signature sent through encryption.

Wrap It Up — License Agreements

Shrink-wrap, click-wrap, and browse-wrap agreements are contracts where the terms are essentially offered on a "take-it-or-leave-it" basis and assent is expressed by some action or inaction other than an actual signature.

Shrink-Wrap Agreements

Agreements printed on back of, or included inside, a commercial computer software box are called shrink-wrap agreements. By *breaking* the cellophane shrink-wrap on the package, the purchaser *agrees to be bound* by the terms of the agreement. Shrink-warp agreements are *controversial*, especially if the agreement is inside the box and *not visible* until after purchase has been made and the box is opened, because the purchaser is agreeing to terms he has not been able to read, and the only way he can read them is to break the seal and thus automatically consent to the terms. The 7th Circuit has held that a shrink-wrap agreement was valid where there was a *notice outside of the box with terms inside* **and** *the right to return the software if the terms are unacceptable to the purchaser.*[5]

Click-Wrap Agreements

More and more web users are encountering click-wrap agreements, where an agreement is displayed on the website to web user, who *must click a link or button indicating acceptance* of the terms in order to proceed further. *Most click-wrap agreements are legally binding,* even if the offeree did not read the terms, so long as terms were available to be read.

However, in <u>Scarcella v. America Online</u>, the New York City civil court invalidated a choice of forum clause in AOL's click-wrap agreement.[6] The plaintiff had argued that AOL's 91-page click-wrap agreement was deceptive because it featured two "O.K., I Agree" buttons midway through the document which, when clicked, allowed customers to "sign" the agreement before reaching its end. The court appeared to accept the plaintiff's argument, adding that AOL might even be seen as discouraging customers from reading the agreement by referring to it as "detailed" and "lengthy." But the court did not go so far as to rule it a "deceptive practice," instead basing its decision to invalidate the provision on public policy grounds. The court ruled that a "contractual choice of forum clause should be held unenforceable if enforcement would contravene a strong public policy of the forum in which suit is brought." The court added that there was a strong public policy interest in providing access to a low cost, informal, local small claims forum rather than forcing the plaintiff to bear the expense of traveling to AOL's choice of forum in Virginia to litigate the claim.

Browse-Wrap Agreements

Unlike a click-wrap agreement, a *browse-wrap agreement* is a contract that a user *may view online but need not do anything to indicate his acceptance.* Most website *"Terms and Conditions"* agreements would fall into this category.[7] Although it is hard to see how this would be considered a valid contract, since one party to be bound has not consented by any affirmative act, some courts, notably the 2nd Circuit, have upheld browse-wrap agreements as legally binding contracts.[8]

However, the logic of a browse-wrap agreement is similar to your neighbor saying, "If you walk past my house, you agree to pay me $200." If you then walk past his house, would he then be entitled to collect $200 from you? Does the act of walking past his house indicate an affirmative assent to a contract or the complete opposite, an act of defiance? A fundamental concept of contract law is that there must be a clear "meeting of the minds" between the parties. In *Ticketmaster Corp. v. Tickets.com, Inc.*, the California district court remarked that "It cannot be said that merely putting the terms and conditions [on the bottom of the web page] necessarily creates a contract with anyone using the website."[9]

Website Development Agreements

You or your company may decide to hire a web designer to create a website for yourself or your firm. Or you may be a web designer[10] about to accept a job from a potential client. In either case, both parties will need to agree on the terms and conditions pursuant to the job. This agreement, or contract, will take the form of a website development agreement.

Many companies do not realize that they do not own the intellectual property rights to the website created by the designer they have hired. As you may recall from Chapter Three, the *creator* of a copyrightable work is deemed by law to be the copyright holder, absent a "Work-Made-For-Hire" agreement or an assignment of rights. So by default, the web designer becomes the copyright owner unless the contract states otherwise. The contract may define "developer content" and "company content" and assign rights to each. The contract may grant the client a license to use a copyrighted work, while the actual copyright is still held by the designer. If the rights are not assigned to the company in the contract, the company may end up with a *limited license* to use the website, preventing it from making changes without the developer's permission.

No matter how detailed the contract, the project is likely to evolve in unforeseen ways. The website development agreement should be drafted in an attempt to cover foreseeable contingencies. Among the more important clauses to include in a website development contract are:

- *Warranties and Indemnification* — where the designer assures the client that the text and graphic elements used in constructing the website do not infringe on copyrights and the client warrants that he owns the rights to any materials provided to the designer for inclusion in the website

- *Payment* — a description of the initial deposit and a schedule for subsequent payments to be made at specified dates or "milestones." Note that some designers may charge an hourly rate because of the difficulty in determining in advance how long a specific project may take to complete. The contract may call for a combination of fixed fees and an hourly rate with a cap

- *Limitation of Liability* — limits the designer's liability to refunding client fees paid if the designer fails to perform as promised

Authorization & Definition Clauses

The website development agreement should begin with the client information. The *Authorized Contact clause* identifies the person with the decision-making authority. It should be clearly spelled out which person in the company has the authority to approve work and authorize changes. This prevents the situation where different members of the company or organization give the web designer conflicting instructions. The *Definitions clause* sets out the clear meaning and intent of the phrases used in the contract. This not only avoids confusion over what may, at first glance, appear to be clear, common terminology, but also enables the parties to refer to the stated definitions as a sort of shorthand throughout the document. The *Authorization clause* gives the designer permission to access the client's server to upload files and make changes to the website. The *Subcontractor clause* gives the designer permission to assign work on the project to subcontractors. The designer may need to bring in help to complete the project on time, or to assist in areas that require expertise outside of the designer's skill set. For example, a complicated website may require specialized programming that would necessitate the designer bringing in a software programmer; or the client may require specialized artwork to be created by a graphic designer.

Description of Services Clauses

The *Website Packages clauses* describe the various packages offered by the designer and allow the client to select the appropriate package desired. These clauses may be very detailed and spell out limitations and conditions. The *Maintenance and Hourly Rate clause* provides that additional work or maintenance of the website during the project phase will be billed at the stated hourly rate. This protects the designer from falling into the trap of setting a fixed price and then being inundated with changes and additional work from the client. Often a designer may set a flat minimum monthly maintenance fee for specified amount or number of additions, deletions, or other changes to the website, with the proviso that any work beyond the specified amount is billed at an additional hourly or piecemeal charge. The clause may also provide the option for the client to purchase a plan for website maintenance after the website construction has been completed and the contract has been fulfilled. Of course, the maintenance plan itself would require a separate contract. There may also be a provision to address a situation where the client brings in a third party to make changes to the website and the third party damages the website, requiring repair by the web designer. Such a provision might state that such repairs are not normal maintenance covered by the maintenance agreement but are additional hourly charges. Also there may be a hold harmless provision to protect the designer from liability for inadvertent harm caused by changes at the client's request (*e.g.*, making a typographical error in the price of an item or the date of an event listed on the website).

Performance Clauses

The *Conditional Upon Client Performance clause* makes the rates quoted conditional upon the client fully cooperating with, and not hindering, the designer. Obviously, if the client's actions, or inactions (*i.e.*, failing to provide necessary content in a timely fashion) prevent or delay or otherwise hinder the designer's efforts to complete the website within a certain time frame and for a certain price, then the designer reserves the right to adjust the quoted time frame or price accordingly. The *Changes in Project Scope clause* sets up a process where the client can request major changes (since the client's needs may change from the date of the contract signing) and the designer can evaluate the scope of the changes and advise the client if he is able to make the changes and what the additional cost will be. The client can then accept or reject the designer's proposal. The *Completion Date clause* establishes a completion date for the project, with allowances for delays and provisions for "rush" jobs.

Payment Clauses

The *Payment of Fees clause* describes the initial deposit and sets out a schedule for subsequent payments to be paid at predetermined intervals. These intervals may be specific dates or project milestones. The *Payment of Designer's Costs clause* allows for reimbursement to the designer for any out-of-pocket expenses incurred. These expenses may include travel, long-distance phone calls, postage or overnight shipping, courier services, and monies advanced by the designer to subcontractors. The *Timely Payment of Fees clause* establishes penalties for late payments. The *Web Hosting clauses* allow the designer to charge the client for temporary hosting on his server if the website must continue to be hosted there due to a delay of the completion date caused by the client. It may also provide that if the client wishes the designer to maintain the website after completion, the client must either allow the designer access to the web hosting service it selects, or chose to use the designer's hosting service. The *Initial Payment and Refund Policy clause* allows the client a predetermined number of days to cancel the contract, provided that the client pays for any work done prior to cancellation.

Representations & Warranties Clauses

The *Disclaimer of Warranties clauses* provide the designer does not warrant against error-free operation of the website or infringement on third-party copyrights and limits the designer's liability to the fees paid by the client. The *Copyright and Trademarks clause* states that the client represents that he owns the copyrights and trademarks to any material given to the designer for inclusion on the website. The *Client Representations and Warranties clause* assures the designer that the client has authority to enter into the contract on behalf of his company or organization, will obtain any necessary rights or licenses for content provided and will indemnify the designer for any claims arising from use of such content.

Penalty Clauses

The *Liquidated Damages clause* provides for compensation to the designer in the event the client breaches the contract. The *Termination of Agreement Other than by Performance clause* provides that if the contract is terminated prior to successful completion, the client will cease the use of and return any content provided by the designer and forfeit all rights and licenses under the contract. It also accelerates the balance payable, which becomes due immediately.

Litigation Clauses

The *Venue clause* establishes where disputes will be litigated or arbitrated. The *Sole Agreement clause* states that the entire agreement between the parties is embodied in this document and that there are no other written or oral agreements. The *Severability clause* provides that if any portion of the contract is deemed illegal or unenforceable, that portion will be stripped from the contract and the rest of the contract will be considered valid and enforceable.

Other Clauses

The *Laws Affecting Electronic Commerce clause* states that the client is solely responsible for complying with any new laws or taxes that may affect the website. The *Copyright to Web Pages clause* advises the client that the designer, by law, is the copyright holder of the website that he creates (as you may recall from Chapter Three) and provides for the assignment of various rights between the designer and the client. This clause may also spell out that a copyright notice on the website in the client's name applies only to the client content and not to the site design or designer content. The *Website Credits and Links clause* gives the client the opportunity to grant the designer permission to advertise the fact that he created the website

The *Acknowledgement Paragraph* at the conclusion of the terms should be printed in boldface type above the signature section. In plain English, it should spell out that the document the parties are about to sign is a legally-binding agreement, that the parties by signing are acknowledging their understanding of all of the terms and their agreement to those terms, and warn that if they do not understand or agree with the terms then they should not sign it. This is important because if the designer were to sue under the contract, and the client claimed that she did not fully understand the terms of the contract, the designer could point out to the judge where she signed immediately below the words **"DO NOT SIGN THIS AGREEMENT IF YOU DO NOT UNDERSTAND IT OR AGREE WITH IT, AS THIS IS A LEGALLY BINDING CONTRACT."**

Obviously all contract terms are subject to negotiation between the parties. This discussion has been presented merely to illustrate the issues that need to be addressed in a website development agreement. The specifics may vary from contract to contract. The reader is advised to obtain a contract drafted by a competent, licensed attorney in his jurisdiction to meet his specific needs.

Summary

Two common forms of contracts encountered online are website user agreements and sales contracts to make an online purchase, such as click-wrap or browse-wrap agreements. Minors (children under 18) and mentally disabled individuals lack the legal capacity to enter into contracts. A contract with a minor is unenforceable by the other party and voidable at the minor's option.

Companies must notify customers of any changes they make to their contracts; however, merely posting such changes on the company website is not sufficient notice. Under contract law principles, a unilateral change to a contract is not binding; instead it results in the revised contract becoming an offer. The other party must then be notified so she can accept or reject this offer; upon assenting to the new terms, the contract will become a binding agreement.

The Uniform Electronic Transactions Act states that "a record or signature may not be denied legal effect or enforceability solely because it is in electronic form." The E-SIGN Act provides legal validity to contracts entered into electronically.

Agreements printed on back of, or included inside, a commercial computer software box are called shrink-wrap agreements. Most click-wrap agreements are legally binding, even if the offeree did not read the terms, so long as terms were available to be read. Most website "Terms and Conditions" agreements are browse-wrap agreements.

A website development agreement is a contract between a website designer and his client. By default, the website designer becomes the copyright owner unless the contract states otherwise. If the rights are not assigned to the company in the contract, the company may end up with a limited license to use the website, preventing it from making changes without the designer's permission. The website development agreement should be drafted in an attempt to cover foreseeable contingencies. The contract should specify an authorized contact person and provide for changes in project scope. It should also allow the designer to assign work on the project to subcontractors to complete the project on time or to assist in areas that require expertise outside of the designer's skill set. A copyright notice on the website in the client's name applies only to the client content and not to the site design or designer content.

Chapter Fifteen Notes

[1] *Douglas v. Talk America, Inc.*, Case No. 06-75424 (9th Cir., July 17, 2007).

[2] *Ibid.*

[3] *Georgia Dept. of Transp. v. Norris*, 222 Ga.App. 361, 474 S.E.2d (1996).

[4] *Electronic Signatures In Global And National Commerce Act* ("E-SIGN Act") 15 U.S.C. § 7001-31 (2000).

[5] *ProCD, Inc. v. Zeidenberg*, 86 F.3D 1447 (7th Cir. 1996), *available at* www.law.emory.edu/7circuit/june96/96-1139.html (accessed September 25, 2007).

[6] *Scarcella v. America Online* (New York City Civ. Ct., Sept. 2004).

[7] In *Edwin Dyer v. Northwest Airlines Corp.*, 2004 U.S. Dist. Lexis 18010 (D. N.D. Sept. 8, 2004), the court held that a website privacy policy did not create a contract between the company and a website user.

[8] *Register.com, Inc. v. Verio, Inc.*, 126 F. Supp. 2d 238 (S.D.N.Y. Dec. 12, 2000) *aff'd* 356 F.3d 393 (2nd Cir. 2004).

[9] *Ticketmaster Corp. v. Tickets.com, Inc.*, 2000 U.S. Dist. LEXIS 4553 (C.D. Cal. Mar. 27, 2000).

[10] In this chapter, the terms "web designer" and "web developer" are used synonymously. In practice, a web developer specializes in applying programming-based applications (such as CGI, Perl, and database integration) to websites, whereas a web designer focuses on non-programming aspects (such as HTML and site design). Many web developers are also web designers, and many web design firms employ web developers, so the terms are used interchangeably throughout this chapter.

Chapter Fifteen Quiz One

Sixteen-year-old Joyce loves shopping online. She recently visited Sluts-r-Us.com to buy some accessories for her new fall outfits. Before entering the website, Joyce had to click "Yes" on a click-wrap agreement. The agreement was more than 100 pages long, so Joyce just scrolled down to the bottom and clicked yes without reading it. Joyce ordered and received a spiked collar but when it arrived she decided she did not like it and she mailed it back. Sluts-r-Us.com sent Joyce an e-mail stating that they had a "No Returns, No Refunds" policy, clearly stated on page 69 of their click-wrap agreement. Joyce then filed a lawsuit against Sluts-r-Us.com, who filed a motion to dismiss based on a clause in their online "Terms and Conditions Agreement" that conditioned use of their website on agreement that all disputes would be submitted to arbitration, not litigation.

If you are using this book in a classroom, discuss the issues raised and the liability of all parties. Otherwise, try to list the issues involved and probable outcomes before turning to the answers in the Appendix.

[Answers in Appendix]

Chapter Fifteen Quiz Two

The Skipper hired Gilligan to design a website for the island dwellers. Ginger ordered Gilligan to make the website as glamorous as possible. Mary Ann told Gilligan it had to be practical, not flashy. Mr. Howell insisted that Gilligan make the website a financial and business portal. The Professor instructed Gilligan to make the website an educational one. Whose instructions should Gilligan follow and what clause should Gilligan have included in his web development agreement to deal with this situation?

The Skipper gave Gilligan detailed coordinates to post on the website so that they could be rescued but Gilligan made a mistake and transposed the numbers. Due to Gilligan's negligent error, the castaways' rescue may be delayed indefinitely. The Skipper promised to sue Gilligan if they ever get off the island. What clause should Gilligan have included in his web development agreement to deal with this situation?

The Skipper, frustrated with Gilligan's mistakes, hired Mrs. Howell to type in the correct coordinates onto the website, but while Mrs. Howell correctly added the coordinates she inadvertently deleted several lines of HTML code and now the website will not load. The Skipper insists that Gilligan repair the website but Gilligan, referring to the website development agreement, demands to be paid on an hourly rate to do so. To which contract provision is Gilligan referring?

The Skipper refuses to pay Gilligan and instead asks the Professor to fix the website. The Professor not only fixes it but adds many of the features that he originally wanted included in the website. Gilligan then informs the Skipper that he plans to sue for copyright infringement. What is Gilligan talking about?

The Skipper tells Gilligan that he is crazy; the website clearly states "©2007 The Skipper" so Gilligan cannot sue for copyright infringement since the Skipper is clearly the copyright holder. Who is right, Gilligan or the Skipper?

The Skipper agrees to pay Gilligan to return the website to its original state. Gilligan says he will have to charge based on a "major structural change." The Skipper argues this is merely a "minor cosmetic change." What contract provision would address this issue?

After the website is completed, the Skipper wants to add a picture of his boat. Gilligan is not sure if the photograph supplied by the Skipper is copyrighted by the Skipper or the photographer. What contract provisions might be of some comfort to Gilligan?

If using this book in a classroom, discuss the issues raised and liability of all parties. Otherwise, try to list the issues involved and probable outcomes before turning to the answers in the Appendix.

[Answers in Appendix]

PART SEVEN

WEB 2.0 AND BEYOND

CHAPTER SIXTEEN

ISSUES ON THE HORIZON

> This chapter looks at the Internet and interstate commerce, website accessibility for the disabled, and Web 2.0 innovations — wikis, social networks, RSS, and podcasting.

L IKE A WHIRLING CYCLONE across the landscape of Internet law, the advent of technology, swift and often blinding in its onslaught, is a harbinger replete with portents of the shape of things to come in the Brave New World that lies ahead. As we contemplate new laws to address the issues raised by our present technology can we, any better than our forefathers, imagine the appearance of the technological landscape of the future, which those laws will have to address?

To some extent we can. As a boy, I fantasized about one day being able to capture the ephemeral television broadcasts of my favorite shows onto a permanent recording and ultimately having a library, not of traditional books, but of TV recordings. I also envisioned being able to catalog my growing comic book collection on a computer like the mammoth machines then in use by NASA. Of course, we already knew from Dick Tracy and Captain Kirk that we would one day have wireless communication, perhaps wristwatch radios or "*Star Trek*" 'communicators.' Now, of course, VCRs, videotapes, home computers, databases, and cell phones are prosaic items that today's generation seldom stops to realize did not exist a scant 30 years ago. Indeed, even these technological innovations are being supplanted by still newer advances, such as DVDs and PDAs. But even as imaginative a child such as I could not have envisioned an invention that would allow any individual in the world to communicate instantaneously with anyone else, friend or random stranger, in the world, or for that matter, simultaneously with the entire world at once.

The Internet is here to stay. Technology, like an evil djinn, once freed from the bottle cannot be recorked. Advances in the technology of the Internet will lead to new legal issues, some as yet unimaginable, but some equally foreseeable. The rest of this chapter will spotlight some of those areas.

Interstate Commerce and the Internet

Borders act as constraints. Just as the borders of this page constrain the words from running off the page, so too do geographic borders restrain interstate commerce. States determine their own laws regarding commerce, including what items may be shipped into or from the state and what taxes or tariffs may be applied to incoming goods.[1] States often maintain protectionist policies that aid local producers of goods while disadvantaging outside producers.

The borderless nature of the Internet will raise many questions about the constraints states will be able to place on commerce. Many states regulate or prohibit items that are not regulated or prohibited in other states. Drugs, cigarettes, alcohol, and lottery tickets are just some examples of this. The legal age may vary from state to state. A 14-year-old living in a state where gambling is legal for those over 14 may wish to purchase a lottery ticket online from a state where the legal age is 18. A New York woman may wish to order a bottle of wine online from a California winery, which may be prohibited by New York state law. A man in Illinois may view material on a Dutch server that would be considered obscene in America. Many states wish to collect sales tax on items sold to their citizens online by out-of-state sellers (the theory is that the state is losing the tax it would have received had the buyer made the purchase within the state).

As people experience the freedom of the Internet that comes from its borderless nature, states will have a hard time enforcing, let alone justifying, their constraints on interstate commerce. In May 2005, the U.S. Supreme Court overturned a 70-year-old ruling that had permitted states to prohibit out-of-state wineries from shipping wine to consumers within the state.[2] The court held that such protectionist laws, on the books in 23 states and that would bar online sales by out-of-state wineries to in-state residents, violated the Commerce Clause of the U.S. Constitution. As a result of this decision, states must now choose between allowing direct shipment to individual consumers residing within their territory by all wineries (within and without the state) or prohibiting direct shipment by local and out-of-state wineries. It remains to be seen what effect, if any, this holding will have on other Internet/interstate commerce conflicts.

Conversely, does Internet use automatically entail interstate commerce? When data travels across the Internet, is it travelling through interstate commerce? At first glance, one might say "Of course." However, one circuit court has said that the interstate nature of the Internet does not necessarily mean that connecting to the World Wide Web invariably equals data moving in interstate commerce.[3] The 10th Circuit Court of Appeals overturned a man's conviction for receipt and possession of images involving sexual exploitation of minors because the federal statute under which he was convicted required a showing that the images had traveled across state lines. The court reasoned that while most uses of the Internet involve movement of data between states, that cannot be assumed — it must be proved, at least in so far as to meet the statutory burden of proof. As the court stated:[4]

> Ultimately, the decision to uphold or overturn Mr. Schaefer's convictions turns on whether an Internet transmission, standing alone, satisfies the interstate commerce requirement of the statute. Mr. Schaefer asserts that [the statute]'s jurisdictional provisions requires movement across state lines, and it is not enough to assume that an Internet communication necessarily traveled across state lines in interstate commerce. We agree.

> [The statute] require[s] a movement between states. The government did not present evidence of such movement; instead, the government only showed that Mr. Schaefer used the Internet. We recognize in many, if not most, situations the use of the Internet will involve the movement of communications or materials between states. But this fact does not suspend the need for evidence of this interstate movement.

The First,[5] Third,[6] and Fifth[7] Circuits have taken a contrary position in similar cases, holding that connection to a website or server invariably involves data moving in interstate commerce.

Sales tax is another area where the Internet and interstate commerce are at odds. While states salivate at the prospect of taxing internet transactions, the U.S. Supreme Court has held that businesses can avoid paying sales tax to states where they have no physical presence.[8] In light of this ruling, most Internet business do not pay sales taxes in states other than where they are incorporated or have their principal place of business. However, the borderless nature of the Internet calls into question the concept of "physical presence." Ironically, a bookstore named "Borders" was found by California's 1st District Court of Appeal to owe that state sales tax on merchandise sold on its website.[9] Borders argued that it was not required to collect California sales taxes because its online division did not own or lease property in the state and all of its Internet orders were received and processed outside the state. Based in Ann Arbor, Michigan, Borders however also owned a 414,000 square-foot distribution center and 129 "Borders" and "Waldenbooks" stores in California. The court reasoned that the company's website (and therefore its online division) was too intertwined with its physical stores in the state, due to cross-promotion and the ability of customers to return merchandise purchased online to retail stores.

The Internet may not always remain a tax-free zone. Fifteen states are members of the Streamlined Sales Tax Agreement, a coalition to implement laws necessary to collect sales tax on Internet purchases, should Congress can enact a federal law authorizing states to do so. [10]

Internet Accessibility for the Disabled

The Workforce Investment Act of 1998 [11] includes the Rehabilitation Act Amendments of 1998 (RAA). [12] *Section 508* of the RAA requires that people with disabilities seeking information or services from a federal agency have access to and use of information and data comparable to that provided to non-disabled individuals. This means that *federal, state, and local government websites must be accessible to disabled individuals.*

But what about non-government websites? Under the Americans With Disabilities Act of 1990 (ADA), *places of public accommodation*, such as stores, restaurants, and hotels, must take reasonable steps to make themselves accessible to those with physical limitations. [13] Is the Internet a "place of public accommodation?" The law was written before the World Wide Web became a ubiquitous presence in society, and may or may not apply to online services and websites. The ADA does apply to common carriers like buses. Would it apply to cyber common carriers, *i.e.*, ISPs like AOL?

AOL was sued by the National Federation of the Blind alleging that AOL's Internet service was inaccessible to the blind in violation of the ADA. [14] The lawsuit was dropped after AOL agreed to make its software compatible with screen-access software for the blind. Screen-reading software reads content out loud (there are talking web browsers that read website text and alt tags that describe graphics) or translates it into Braille text. [15] Since the lawsuit was dropped, there is no court decision yet on this issue.

Extending the issue further, does the ADA apply to a *private business' website*? The first federal court to address that issue held that the ADA did not apply to private websites. In Access Now v. Southwest Airlines, the Florida district court ruled that the ADA applies only to physical spaces, such as restaurants and movie theaters, and not to the Internet. [16] The Act defines a "public accommodation" as a facility, operated by a private entity, whose operations affect commerce and fall within at least one of 12 specified categories, including hotels, restaurants, shopping centers, universities, and bowling alleys. The court reasoned that because Congress so meticulously specified what kinds of physical spaces are covered by the ADA that it clearly did not intend for it to apply to the Internet. The Sixth [17] and Ninth [18] Circuits have sided with the Florida district court, holding that a public place of accommodation must be a physical location. However, the First Circuit, while not specifically addressing the Internet, has said that the ADA is not limited to purely physical structures. [19]

However, in a bizarre move, New York Attorney General Elliott Spitzer, arguing that the ADA requires that *private* websites be accessible to blind and visually impaired Internet users, subsequently launched an "investigation" into the accessibility of two major travel services' websites. While New York has its own laws regarding disability access, it is unclear where the New York attorney general would draw the authority to attempt to enforce his own interpretation of a federal statute against two out-of-state corporations. Nonetheless, both Priceline.com and Ramada.com agreed to make changes to enable users with screen reader software and other disability aiding technology to navigate and listen to text throughout their websites. While the software and other devices, such as a vibrating mouse that lets the blind "feel" boxes and images on the computer screen, have existed for years, websites need special coding for the equipment to operate. Ramada and Priceline, which faced no charges and made no admissions of guilt, agreed to pay New York $40,000 and $37,500 respectively to cover the investigation's cost.

While the ADA applies to "places of *public* accommodation," unless Congress amends the ADA or conflicting federal court decisions arise, the ADA does not apply to private websites. To force the ADA onto private websites would have a devastating effect on millions of Internet websites, both commercial and non-commercial. [20] (This does not mean that websites cannot and should not try to follow web accessibility design standards). [21] Nonetheless, a recent case could have a profound impact on this issue. A class action lawsuit filed by the National Federation of the Blind (NFB) with a visually-impaired [22] college student as the lead plaintiff alleged that the Target department store chain's website was inaccessible to the blind because it did not use the ALT attribute in its HTML and parts of its shopping cart required the use of a mouse instead of a keyboard. [23] The lawsuit claimed that Target violated the ADA, the California Disabled Persons Act (a state law guaranteeing full and equal access for the disabled to all public places) and another state statute, the Unruh Civil Rights Act. Target moved to dismiss, arguing the state laws were inapplicable to websites as they are not "physical" places of public accommodation. In September 2006, the U.S. District Court for the Northern District of California rejected the motion and distinguished this case from *Access Now*: [24]

> In *Access Now*, the court held that plaintiff failed to state a claim under ADA because plaintiff alleged that the inaccessibility of southwest.com prevented access to Southwest's 'virtual' ticket counters. 'Virtual' ticket counters are not actual, physical places and therefore not places of public accommodation. Since there was no physical place of public accommodation alleged in *Access Now*,

the court did not reach the precise issue presently in dispute: whether there is a nexus between a challenged service and an actual, physical place of public accommodation.

The court appeared to require a nexus between the website and a physical "bricks 'n mortar" location. In other words, the ADA requires a physical place of public accommodation; a website by itself is not a physical place and therefore does not fall under the ADA; however, if the website is merely a tool of an existing physical place of public accommodation, i.e., it is using the Internet as a means to enhance services it offers at a physical location, then by extension it would then fall under the ADA. (In this case, Target customers could refill prescriptions and order photo prints for pick-up at a store via the website). The court reasoned that because the website served as a gateway to a place of public accommodation, and as blind individuals were unable to enjoy the services of the website, Target may have violated the ADA. This logic seems rather strained, as does the attempt to distinguish a "virtual ticket counter" from a virtual store checkout lane. The court parsed the language of the statute in a manner most likely not foreseen by its drafters, stating: [25]

> [The] statute applies to the services of a place *of* public accommodation, not services *in* a place of public accommodation. To limit the ADA to discrimination in the provision of services occurring on the premises of a public accommodation would contradict the plain language of the statute.

Rather than change its website to comply with California law, "Target could choose to make a [separate] California-specific website," the judge wrote, oblivious to the onerous burden of requiring a business to have multiple versions of the same website to comply with a multitude of often conflicting state requirements. [26] The judge added that "even if Target chooses to change its entire website in order to comply with California law, this does not mean that California is regulating out-of-state conduct," although arguably that is precisely the effect. Target, in this author's opinion, correctly argued that the Internet requires uniform, national regulations. While other jurisdictions may choose not to follow this court's path, and indeed, the court's interpretation of the reach of the statute may eventually be repudiated by the Supreme Court, at present the case is noteworthy because the court's order is believed to the first ruling that the ADA may apply to non-government websites on the Internet.

Internet accessibility for the disabled is a major issue on the horizon. While accessibility is required by law for government websites, the extent to which private websites may be required, if at all, to be accessible to the disabled is unclear. At least in the 9th Circuit it would appear that a physical business that has a tangential website may be subject to the ADA. However, even in the Ninth Circuit there is no indication that the ADA would apply to an online business with no physical retail environment, such as Amazon.com. [27]

Ambushed by Porn

Should an individual or institution be liable for downloading pornography if circumstances indicate they did not knowingly or intentionally do so?

A Norwich, CT substitute teacher, convicted of allowing her seventh grade students to view pornography on a classroom computer, was granted a new trial when the judge concluded that it was possible that spyware and adware programs might have been responsible for the pornographic pop-up ads viewed by students. The school computer did not have a firewall or anti-spyware software installed. The teacher had faced up to 40 years in prison after her conviction until a state crime lab released findings casting doubt on evidence presented at the trial by the state computer expert. [28]

A similar situation could be imagined in a public library (or cyber café), where the institution is charged with displaying pornographic images left on the computer from a patron's use. Should such institutions be liable for the use their patrons make of the technology they provide? Should they be required to apply filters to all of their computers? If so, would that violate the First Amendment free speech rights of the patrons?

A Georgia man was sentenced to 20 years in prison for possession of child pornography, after the images were found on his computer in his Internet browser's cache. The cache temporarily stores files that are automatically downloaded from visited websites. It is very possible for one to click a link in a pop-up ad, e-mail, or search engine result and wind up on an unknown web page. Suppose that the man had arrived at the website unintentionally, or with no idea of its content and left immediately; the images would still reside in his cache on his computer. The user has no control over the images being downloaded to the computer cache; should he be subject to criminal penalties of up to 20 years imprisonment? Does the existence of the images in his cache amount to possession? [29]

We have already discussed wardriving scenarios where an individual's Wi-Fi connection is hijacked, and the wardriver, piggy-backing on the individual's network, downloads child pornography. The downloads would be traced back to the innocent individual's network from his ISP's logs, not to the wardriver.

These are just four scenarios where innocent parties could find themselves liable for something they had little or no control over, and facing substantial penalties for acts of which they had no knowledge, nor intent to commit. Technology may be ahead of the law here, especially with the advent of Web 2.0 and user-generated content, such as blogs and other web pages that employ widgets that could contain malicious code to install spyware through a drive-by download. And while there are ways to guard against (although not entirely prevent) such ambushes by porn, not every computer user is sophisticated enough to install firewalls, anti-spyware software, filters, or to secure a Wi-Fi network.

"O' Brave New World That Has Such Things In It"

The rise of Web 2.0 has ushered in an era of web user-generated content and user interactivity. As a result, wikis, social networks, podcasts, and RSS are some of the areas where the newest issues in Internet law may arise.

A Wiki is Not Han Solo's Co-Pilot [30]

A *wiki* is server software that allows viewers to create and edit web page content using any web browser. Normally, a web page is written by its creator and read by the viewer. A wiki web page can be edited by anyone viewing the page. The changes made by the viewer are then visible to all subsequent viewers. For example, *Wikipedia* is an online encyclopedia where all the entries are constantly updated, added to, or modified by viewers who in fact become virtual contributors in what ultimately emerges as a community or consensus work. [31] The idea is that multiple individuals will be able to bring different aspects of knowledge to the project, resulting in a more complete and all-encompassing work — a collaborative aggregation of knowledge. The same people who sponsor the Wikipedia also sponsor the "Wiktionary" (a dictionary and thesaurus), "Wikiquote" (a collection of quotations), "Wikispecies" (a directory of species), "Wikinews" (a free content news source), and "Wikibooks" (free textbooks and manuals). Wikis are not limited to reference works; they can be tailored toward a focused audience or an affinity group, *e.g.*, a "*Star Wars*" wiki devoted to Wookies. The C.I.A. has its own wiki called Intellipedia. [32]

Usually there is no review before modifications are published on the web, so a major characteristic of wikis is the speed at which pages can be created or updated. This open philosophy of wikis could potentially be a drawback though, since libelous or defamatory comments, profanity, or hate speech could slip onto a page almost instantaneously. Another problem is the spread of "Wikispam," where spammers (or their robots) add hyperlinks to irrelevant websites in an effort to boost the search engine page rankings of the linked website. To deal with this eventuality, most wikis have a "revision history" feature that allows an editor to view and restore a previous version of the article. Wikis may also ban selected individuals from contributing by blocking their particular IP address. The wiki software also provides for setting the pages to a "read only" mode; however this obviously defeats the stated purpose of the wiki. Like any democracy, the greatest feature of a wiki, its openness, is also its greatest vulnerability. Another major characteristic of wikis is that each page contains a large number of hyperlinks. Pages often cite other related pages, including pages that have yet to be written.

A wiki is in some ways similar and yet in other ways completely different from a blog. Both offer ease of publication to anyone wishing to become a "web publisher." A blog may allow viewers to add replies to the blogger's comments, thus making the blog an interactive experience; however, the viewer cannot change the author's original text, which is not a limitation in a wiki.

Many of the issues that we discussed earlier in this book that relate to message boards and blogs, two areas where third-parties can add content to a website, may also become relevant to wikis as they develop. In 2007 there were several incidents reported of Wikipedia entries being changed to add defamatory content, to delete embarrassing facts, to "spruce up" one's own (or one's company's) entry or to add negative comments to a competitor's entry.[33]

During emergencies or natural disasters, wikis have proven to be important gathering sites not just for news reports but also to share resources, publish safety bulletins, locate missing person, post vital information, and even serve as a meeting place for virtual support groups. When Hurricane Katrina struck Mississippi and Louisiana in September 2005, "Katrina wikis" provided updates from residents on the scene and allowed people to post names of missing relatives or post their own names to show they had survived. One Katrina wiki even allowed users to post status notes (*e.g.*, "flooded," "destroyed," "still standing") on an aerial photo map of houses in the hurricane-stricken area.

Social Networks

In the mid-1990s, three college students devised a game they called "Six Degrees of Kevin Bacon," showing that every actor could be linked to actor Kevin Bacon within six steps.[34] The game was based on the John Guare play and movie adaptation "*Six Degrees of Separation*," which theorized that every individual is connected by six or fewer stages of circumstance or acquaintance. The notion that relationships between individuals can be mapped like an infinitely expansive geometric progression formed the basis for the establishment of social networking websites. If "A" has a circle of 10 friends or "contacts" (let us call them B_1 through B_{10}) as does each of the 10 "B"s (let us call them C_1 through C_{100}) then that means "A" now has 100 "friend of a friend" contacts. By trading on her own relationship with "B," "A" can gain instant credibility with 100 individuals who would otherwise be strangers. From a business perspective, this network creates instant entrée for "A" amongst any of the "C"s, as a close friend or business associate of one of their own close friends or business associates. One is more likely to do business with someone who knows or is referred by a mutual acquaintance than with a stranger. In a social environment, many individuals feel more at ease dating a "friend of a friend" than a complete stranger. Thus by listing only 10 contacts, "A"'s business or social network of three degrees contains 110 contacts (10 "B"s and 100 "C"s). Now if each "C" were to add 10 names (let us call them D_1 through D_{1000}) to the network, the size of the network would increase exponentially to 1,110 contacts (10 "B"s and 100 "C"s and 1,000 "D"s). Extending this concept to five degrees increases the contact list to 11,110 (10 "B"s, 100 "C"s, 1,000 "D"s, and 10,000 "E"s) and going to the full six degrees yields 111,110 contacts in A's social network (10 "B"s, 100 "C"s, 1,000 "D"s, 10,000 "E"s, and 100,000 "F"s). Of course, this is based on 10 names per person; a greater number would produce an even larger exponential result.

A number of companies realized the tremendous advantage to social networking and established websites such as <u>Friendster.com</u> and <u>LinkedIn.com</u> where individuals could start their own social networks by inviting contacts to register through the website. Then individuals related by varying degrees within the common network could see and contact each other, even though most were strangers to each other.

What possible liability might ensue, if any, from the creation of such social networks? In our litigious society, it is not hard to imagine a scenario where, regardless of the legal validity of such a lawsuit, a claim could arise where "B_{10}" through a social network meets and is date-raped by "E_{27}" or where "C_{78}" hires "F_{1212}" who ends up embezzling from "C_{78}." Or perhaps the website would also be named as a party in such a lawsuit. While the legal foundation for such liability would appear at first glance to be shaky (indeed, seismically so), it would not be the first time that a specious lawsuit made its way through the court system draining thousands of dollars from defendants forced to defend against such claims.

The most successful social networks have carved out a niche. The pre-teen set can play games at Club Penguin; migrate to Xanga during junior high; switch to MySpace in high school; join the college crowd at Facebook; and after graduation, network with their peers at LinkedIn. MySpace has the broadest appeal across all age ranges; in 2005 a quarter of its users were teenagers (12-17) but a year later that percentage had dropped by more than half while adult (35-54) membership had risen to comprise 40% of its membership.[35]

According to a 2006 survey of members of four social network sites (MySpace, Facebook, Xanga, and Friendster), the largest member age group was 35–54 years old, making up between 33.5%–to–40.6% of the sites' membership. The 12–17 age range accounted for 9.6% of the total Internet but a whopping 20.3% of Xanga membership. The 18–24 age range accounted for 11.3% of the total Internet but a staggering 34% of Facebook. The 24–34 age range accounted for 14.5% of the total Internet but a significant 28.2% of Friendster. The 35–54 age range accounted for 38.5% of Internet users and was evenly distributed across all of the sites. The over 55 age range accounted for 18% of Internet users but single digit membership in most of the studied social network sites.[36]

Contrary to popular opinion, social networks are not primarily the stomping grounds of kids. They are used to an even greater degree by adults, often as a business networking tool. However, some businesses complain about lost worker productivity due to employees spending too much time on their Facebook sites. An Australian study found that Facebook users potentially cost their employers up to $4 billion annually.[37]

But there are social networking sites specifically aimed at kids. Club Penguin, a 12 million member site targeting the 8–to–14 year old age range, blends interactive gaming with social networking. Children joining Club Penguin interact with other members using a customized penguin avatar. The site, launched in 2005, is very child safety-oriented, employing filtering software to prevent children from disclosing e-mail addresses and phone numbers, or using profanity. Members inhabit an arctic virtual world where they can play games, chat, or ski with other penguins in a "virtual sandbox." Penguins chat through word balloons above their heads, using either a list of pre-approved phrases or filtered chat software. They can ask another penguin "boy or girl?" and exchange virtual hearts or flowers in hope of attracting a little penguin boyfriend or girlfriend.[38]

Club Penguin members play arcade style games, where they can win "coins" to buy accessories (e.g., clothes, pets, or furniture) for their penguin or igloo (all penguins get a virtual igloo on their home page). As in real life, the more toys a penguin has, the more popular he becomes with other penguins. A penguin clothed in attire no longer available for purchase can expect to be flooded with "friend requests" and virtual "postcards." Club Penguin makes its money through subscriptions rather than advertising. Only subscribers can buy clothing or furniture; non-subscribers can only have blue or red penguins (out of 13 possible colors).[39]

Most other social networks targeting children follow an advertising-based business model. One competitor even allowed advertisers to do product placement in its virtual world, offering its members the chance to drive virtual Toyota Scions or append a mermaid tail to their avatar's body in advance of a "*Walt Disney's The Little Mermaid*" promotion (see Chapter 12).

Social networking websites are a global phenomenon not limited to the United States. CyWorld (short for Cyber World) is a South Korean social network that not only offers traditional features such as photo galleries, message boards, and friends lists but also provides each member with a virtual room inhabited by an avatar of the member's choice. To say that CyWorld has taken South Korea by storm would be an understatement — five million people (one-third of the nation's population) are members and among those in their late teens and early twenties that number rises to 90%.[40] CyWorld is expanding into the United States as well.[41] Mixi is the largest social networking website in Japan, with 4.8 million users as of July 2006.[42] Unlike MySpace, newcomer Mixi is an invitation-only service and does not allow members to edit their page layout.

Social networks can also provide a unique opportunity for criminals. In Brazil, drug dealers set up a "members-only" group on Google's "Orkut" social network and used the network to facilitate drug transactions, with group members buying and selling the drugs ecstasy and marijuana.[43] In Japan, a "crime mates" social network site matches up potential partners in crime. The website came to light after three men were arrested for allegedly meeting and conspiring online to kidnap and murder a woman. The woman was kidnapped on her way home from work one night, robbed of $600, beaten to death, and her body abandoned in a forest west of Tokyo, Japan. The alleged online conspirators reportedly never even told each other their names.[44]

Social networking can backfire on criminals too. A San Jose, California parole violator was captured by police after TV viewers recognized his photo from his MySpace page![45] And a young woman plotting the murder of her ex-boyfriend's new girlfriend turned to his MySpace page to get all the information she needed — including a photo of her intended victim — to recruit a hitman. (Recall the discussion in Chapter 10, about the dangers of voluntary disclosure of personal information on the Internet, and how a personal profile page on a social network can be a gold mine of information waiting to fall into the wrong hands.) Fortunately the "hitman" turned out to be an undercover cop.[46]

Perhaps one of the most interesting MySpace situations is one that is neither unique nor unexpected, given the social network's large base of students. Anyone can create a profile on MySpace and as a result there are a lot of fake profiles. As lampooned on the cover of this book, the anonymity of the Internet allows people to pretend to be anyone they want. This has allowed MySpace to become the technological equivalent of the schoolhouse bathroom stall: where students once scrawled derogatory comments about their peers or teachers on bathroom walls they can now create a profile for the target of their humiliation. Similarly to the Classmates.com case in Chapter 13, many students have created fake profiles purporting to be the pages of their fellow students, teachers, and principals.

In Pennsylvania, a school principal sued four former students claiming they falsely portrayed him as a pot smoking, beer guzzling, porno lover on a fake MySpace profiles.[47] As they find themselves similarly victimized, more school educators and administrators are filing such suits. In San Antonio, Texas, two boys reportedly decided to get back at their high school assistant principal who had repeatedly disciplined them by creating a profile for her on MySpace. The fake profile included her photograph, lewd comments, obscene pictures, and images of sexual devices, written as though the subject herself had posted the information. The profile also falsely identified her as a lesbian.[48] MySpace immediately removed the page after Anna Draker, the assistant principal, notified them that she had not posted the information. The school suspended the page's creator for three days and the District Attorney charged him with retaliation and identity theft, both third-degree felonies.[49] What makes this instance different from the multitude of "fake teacher" profiles — besides the criminal prosecution — is the fact that Draker filed a civil suit against the two students and their parents claiming defamation, libel, negligence, and negligent supervision.[50] The civil complaint raises a number of controversial issues:

- Do parents have a duty to supervise the activities of their children as they access the Internet?

- Can parents can incur liability merely by "furnish[ing] the instrumentality utilized by their children to create the MySpace web page, namely, their personal computer?"[51]

- Is it appropriate in this day and age for statements about someone's sexuality to be deemed libel per se as a matter of state law?

- Given the fact that most parents of high school students are struggling to meet the costs of impending college tuition, is filing a lawsuit seeking monetary damages from such parents — and thus possibly depriving the student from the means of attending college — a proper response by an educator to what is admittedly a mean-spirited and ill-advised juvenile prank?

There is no doubt that what these boys did was wrong and caused embarrassment and distress to Draker. But teachers have been the butt of students' malicious scribblings and pranks since the first little red schoolhouse was built. Children do not necessarily appreciate all of the consequences of their actions — they may view this as a harmless prank or satire, failing to grasp the deep emotional harm or long-term injury to reputation that their actions may cause. Do the potential consequences — a felony conviction and a civil judgment that could devastate a family or preclude a college education — fit the act? As a society, we must devise appropriate legal responses for abuse of new technology which, while serving as deterrents, are not Draconian.

A Draconian response is exactly what another student received from her MySpace posting. Julia Wilson, a 14-year-old high school student, found herself pulled out of her biology class by two Secret Service agents who then proceeded to interrogate her to the point of tears about her MySpace page. [52] The self-described "politically passionate" honor student apparently had posted a picture of President George W. Bush on her MySpace page with the words "Kill Bush" written across it. [53] While it is a violation of federal law to threaten to harm or kill a U.S. president, one would hope that the government could differentiate hyperbole or an inartful adolescent attempt at political expression from a legitimate threat to the chief executive. [54]

RSS

RSS (Really Simple Syndication) is a distribution system that lets publishers share web content, such as headlines and text, via XML feeds. The RSS feed (also known as a channel or stream) consists of a list of items, each containing a headline, description, and a link to a web page for the full version of the article. When a website has an RSS feed, it is said to be "syndicated." Many websites and blogs use RSS to display headlines from other websites, so as to provide additional content to their readers. RSS is highly targeted because it delivers headlines only to people who have signed up for them, similar to an opt-in mailing list. Readers use a feed reader or RSS news aggregator to subscribe to and read feeds. Some newer browsers include feed readers in their design. RSS data can also flow into other products and services, like PDAs, cell phones, e-mail ticklers, and voice updates. RSS can also be used to automate e-mail newsletters.

As with other aspects of publishing content online, concerns of defamation, profanity, obscenity, and copyright and trademark violation will have to be addressed in this new area. While the CDA will undoubtedly apply to RSS feeds, courts will have to determine if a webmaster (or blogger) providing an RSS feed is a publisher or a distributor; after all, syndication is a form of distribution.

Many websites publish RSS aggregated news headlines in a bid to lure more readers to their websites and thus provide more eyeballs for their advertisers. If a third-party creates an RSS news feed for the aggregated news headlines published on such a website, he would in effect be providing a means for the reader to access the information without viewing the ads. Recall the similar situation with framing and inline linking in Chapter Six, where the content appeared "filtered" on a third-party website without the ads. In this case, the headlines would be distributed via RSS feed, but none of the advertising would show up with the feed. On the other hand, while the selection and order of the headlines may be proprietary to the website publishing them, the actual content of those headlines, *i.e.*, the full articles, in most cases are not.

Podcasting — Invasion of the Byte-Snatchers

The concept of podcasting is similar to that of RSS feeds. The user subscribes to a collection of feeds and selects new content from the feeds, either individually or in the aggregate. The difference with podcasting is that instead of text feed, the feeds are audio (or video) files and instead of reading the feeds on a monitor, the user listens to them via portable mp3 players like the ubiquitous Apple iPod (hence the name "podcasting").

Websites like ipodder.org catalog pod feeds available for subscription. Subscribers automatically receive audio files downloaded to their computers, where they can play them at their convenience. Once downloaded, the podcast can be transferred to a portable mp3 player. Podcasts can consist of music, seminar lectures, or homemade talk shows. The growth of the popular new medium is spurred in part by the fact that most podcasts are distributed free and without commercials or advertisements (although that may change as the medium matures and podcasters need revenue to pay licensing fees or bandwidth expenses).

Unlike streaming (*i.e.*, continuous real-time) music offered by many Internet radio websites, podcasts are individual audio files meant to be downloaded and listened to at a later date. Anyone can be a podcaster and anyone can download a podcast. All it takes to become a podcaster is the right software, a computer, a microphone, a website, and sufficient bandwidth. Podcasts can be downloaded by any type of computer. If the Internet brought publishing to the masses, then podcasting promises to bring broadcasting to the masses. Even school children can now podcast and syndicate their own talk shows! The big media companies have also entered into podcasting; many large broadcasters, such as the BBC and NPR, are repackaging broadcasted segments into podcasts as marketing tools to promote their shows to a wider audience.

Since the content of the podcast rests solely with the podcaster it is important that the podcaster not include copyrighted material unless he has procured a license to do so. Apple announced plans for its new generation of iPods to have a podcast menu button to take users to its online iTunes Music Store, where they can subscribe to podcasts. [55] However, this raises the possibility of Apple offering a podcast containing infringing copyrighted material; unless Apple individually reviews every podcast, it cannot assure that a podcaster / wannabee DJ has not submitted a podcast with a copyrighted song. Another area of potential liability is podcasts whose content may be legal in one country but illegal in another; for example, a broadcast protected under the First Amendment in the United States might run afoul of British defamation laws.

Even radio stations need to pause before packaging broadcasted syndicated material into podcasts, as many syndication agreements give only broadcast rights while reserving all other rights. Of course, the radio station can also specify podcast rights in its syndication agreements or later acquire a license to podcast such material. As podcasts increase in popularity and downloads, the Recording Industry Association of America will probably seek to enforce copyright laws against infringers, as it has with mp3 downloads through P2P file-sharing networks. [56]

Unlike broadcasters, podcasters are not subject to regulation by the Federal Communications Commission (F.C.C.). That means both content and advertising are free from F.C.C. censorship. So not only is Howard Stern free to say whatever comes to mind on his podcast without fear of F.C.C. fines, but advertisers may also hawk products that the mainstream media might shy away from, as was the case with Durex, a condom manufacturer that became an early podcast advertiser. [57] Podcasts also allow advertisers to narrowcast to a discrete target audience; indeed, the allure of podcasting is that it provides an outlet for shows with formats so specialized that they could never appear on commercial radio.

For its consumers, the allure of podcasting can be summed up in four key points: access to highly specialized content, uncensored content, free distribution, and the option of time-shifting digital content. For the podcaster, like blogging, it is a low-cost version of "personal publishing." With podcasting, the consumer can choose exactly what he wants, free of F.C.C. regulations, and he can listen to it at his convenience.

Summary

The borderless nature of the Internet will raise many questions about the constraints states will be able to place on commerce. Many states regulate or prohibit items that are not regulated or prohibited in other states, such as drugs, cigarettes, alcohol, and lottery tickets. Most Internet business do not pay sales taxes in states other than where they are incorporated or have their principal place of business.

Section 508 of the Workforce Investment Act of 1998 mandates that federal, state, and local government websites must be accessible to disabled individuals. A federal court in Florida held that the ADA did not apply to private websites. Internet accessibility for the disabled is a major issue on the horizon. While accessibility is required by law for government websites, the extent to which private websites may be required, if at all, to be accessible to the disabled is unclear. At least in the 9th Circuit it would appear that a physical business that has a tangential website may be subject to the ADA. However, even in the Ninth Circuit there is no indication that the ADA would apply to an online business with no physical retail environment.

A wiki web page can be edited by anyone viewing the page. The idea of a wiki is that multiple individuals will be able to bring different aspects of knowledge, resulting in a more complete and all-encompassing work. During emergencies or natural disasters, wikis have proven to be important gathering sites not just for news reports but also to share resources, publish safety bulletins, locate missing person, post vital information, and even serve as a meeting place for virtual support groups. Like any democracy, the greatest feature of a wiki, its openness, is also its greatest vulnerability.

Social networks allow members to invite contacts to register through the website; then individuals related by varying degrees within the common network can see and contact each other, even though most were strangers to each other. The most successful social networks have carved out a niche. Contrary to popular opinion, social networks are not primarily for children; they are used to an even greater degree by adults, often as a business networking tool. However, some businesses complain about lost worker productivity due to employees spending too much time on such sites. A personal profile page on a social network can be a gold mine of information waiting to fall into the wrong hands. Social networking websites are a global phenomenon not limited to the United States.

RSS is a distribution system that lets publishers share web content, such as headlines and text, via XML feeds. The RSS feed (also known as a channel or stream) consists of a list of items, each containing a headline, description, and a link to a web page for the full version of the article. When a website has an RSS feed, it is said to be "syndicated." RSS is highly targeted because it delivers headlines only to people who have signed up for them.

The concept of podcasting is similar to that of RSS feeds. In podcasting, instead of text feed, the feeds are audio files and instead of reading the feeds on a monitor, the user listens to them via portable mp3 players. Podcasts can consist of music, seminar lectures, or homemade talk shows. Podcasting provides an outlet for shows with formats so specialized that they could never appear on commercial radio. For its consumers, the allure of podcasting can be summed up in four key points: access to highly specialized content, uncensored content, free distribution, and the option of time-shifting digital content. For the podcaster, like blogging, it is a low-cost version of "personal publishing."

Web 2.0 advances like wikis, social networks, RSS, and podcasts are at the forefront of Internet technologies where the newest issues in Internet law may arise. There will be innovations to follow them, of course. And with each wave of innovation, the courts and legislatures will be asked to tailor existing laws and legal concepts to deal with the issues raised by these technological advances. Most of the issues spawned by Internet technology will be resolved not by new laws created entirely out of whole cloth but by applying (and tweaking) existing laws and legal concepts in areas such as intellectual property (copyright, trademark, and patent law), criminal law (cyber crimes), privacy law, First Amendment law (free speech, free press, defamation, and obscenity), and contract law. The key will be to recognize the red flags on the information superhighway, the issues in Internet law.

Chapter Seventeen Notes

[1] "States" are referred to here both in the sense of nations as well as the individual states that comprise the United States of America, the difference being that international commerce is often subject to international treaties and agreements while interstate commerce within the United States is subject to federal regulation by the Commerce Clause of the U.S. Constitution.

[2] *Granholm v. Heald*, 03-1116; *Michigan Beer & Wine Wholesalers Ass'n. v. Heald*, 03-1120; and *Swedenburg v. Kelly*, 03-1274, (U.S. Sup. Ct., May 16, 2005).

[3] *United States v. Schaefer*, Case No 06-3080 (10th Cir. Sept. 5, 2007).

[4] *Ibid.*

[5] *United States v. Carroll*, 105 F.3d 740 (1st Cir., 1997), *cert. den'd*, 520 U.S. 1258 (1997).

[6] *United States v. MacEwan*, 445 F.3d 237 (3rd Cir., 2006), *cert. den'd*, 127 S. Ct. 208 (2006).

[7] *United States v. Runyan*, 290 F.3d 223 (5th Cir., 2002), *cert. den'd*, 537 U.S. 888 (2002).

[8] *Quill v. North Dakota*, 504 U.S. 298 (1992).

[9] "Appeals Court: Borders Must Pay Online Sales Tax," Associated Press wire report, June 14, 2005.

[10] "Arkansas Joins States to Push for Internet Tax," Associated Press wire report, July 30, 2007.

[11] Workforce Investment Act of 1998 (Pub. L. No. 105-220).

[12] Rehabilitation Act Amendments of 1993 (Pub. L. No. 103-73).

[13] Americans With Disabilities Act of 1990 (Pub. L. No. 101-336), 42 U.S.C. § 12101 *et seq.*

[14] Sheri Qualters, "Discrimination Case Opens Door to Internet ADA Claims," National Law Journal, September 28, 2006.

[15] *E.g.*, Simply Web 2000 talking browser, *available at* www.econointl.com/sw (accessed September 25, 2007).

[16] *Gumson v. Southwest Airlines* and *Access Now v. Southwest Airlines*, 227 F.Supp.2d 1312 (S.D. Fla. 2002) *appeal den'd*, 385 F.3d 1324, (11th Cir. Sept. 24, 2004).

[17] *Parker v. Metro. Life Ins. Co.*, 121 F.3d 1006 (6th Cir. 1997).

[18] *Weyer v. Twentieth Century Fox Film Corp.*, 198 F.3d 1104 (9th Cir. 2000).

[19] *Carparts v. Automotive Wholesaler's Ass'n.*, 37 F.3d 12, 22-23 (1st Cir. 1994).

[20] Statutes that prohibit private companies from discriminating against disabled individuals (and theoretically that prohibition would extend to their websites) tend to define discrimination as the act of treating disabled customers in a worse manner than non-disabled customers and do not require provision of special or better treatment. The notable exception is the Americans with Disabilities Act, which applies to issues of employment and accessibility to public accommodations, although even the ADA exempts smaller private companies from its provisions.

[21] The University of Wisconsin has an excellent resource page on web accessibility *available at* http://library. uwsp.edu/aschmetz/accessible/pub_resources.htm (accessed September 25, 2007).

[22] *National Fed'n. of the Blind v. Target Corp.*, __Supp.2d__, 2006 WL 2578282 (N.D. Cal. Sept. 6, 2006). The lead plaintiff, Bruce Sexton, is "legally blind" however "legal blindness does not necessarily mean total blindness; 90% of people who are legally blind have some remaining vision," *see* Bonnie Azab Powell, "Transfer Student Bruce Sexton Has Target-ed Independence for Blind People as a Major Goal," UC Berkeley News, March 20, 2006. Sexton's "vision is just enough to see general shapes and to distinguish between light and dark." *Ibid.*

[23] HTML or Hyper Text Markup Language, is the computer language web browsers use to format web pages. The ALT attribute allows text to be associated with a graphic on the pages so that when the page is loading or the graphics are turned off in the browser settings the images will be replaced with text describing the images. Such text can then be read out loud by a "talking" browser using screen-reading software.

[24] *National Fed'n. of the Blind v. Target Corp.*, fn. 22, *supra.*

[25] *Ibid.*

[26] "Target Lawsuit Tests Limits of U.S. Web Accessibility Law," OUT-LAW.com, September 12, 2006, *available at* www.out-law.com/page-7285 (accessed September 25, 2007).

[27] "Blind Web Users Fight, Sue for More Accessible Sites," Fox News.com, October 24, 2006.

[28] Stephanie Reitz, "Teacher Gets New Trial on Pop-up Porn," Associated Press wire report, June 7, 2007.

[29] Nathan Frick, "Lawyers in Walker County Child Porn Case Hope to Redefine Law," Walker County Messenger, June 14, 2005.

[30] Han Solo, a human pilot in George Lucas' film "*Star Wars*" was aided by his alien "Wookie" co-pilot Chewbacca.

[31] *Available at* http://en.wikipedia.org/wiki/Main_Page (accessed September 25, 2007). Wikipedia describes itself as "the free-content encyclopedia that anyone can edit." *Ibid.*

[32] Cass R. Sunstein, "A Brave New Wikiworld," Washington Post, February 24, 2007, p. A19.

[33] *Ibid.*

[34] Some credit the theory to Hungarian writer Frigyes Karinthy in his 1829 short story "*Chains.*"

[35] Source: comScore Media Metrix, October 2006, *available at* www.comscore.com/press/release.asp?press=1019 (accessed September 25, 2007).

[36] *Ibid.*

[37] "Facebook Surfers Cost their Bosses Billions," Reuters wire report, August 20, 2007.

[38] Elizabeth Weiss Green, "Clique on to Penguin: How A Virtual World is Changing Social Dynamics in Fifth-Grade Classrooms Across the Country," U.S. News & World Report, March 19, 2007, pp. 31-32.

[39] *Ibid.*

[40] "E-Society: My World Is Cyworld," Business Week, September 26, 2005.

[41] The U.S. version is *available at* http://us.cyworld.com (accessed September 25, 2007).

[42] Pete Cashmore, "Mixi, Japan's Biggest Social Network," July 8, 2006, *available at* http://mashable.com/2006/07/08/mixi-japans-biggest-social-network (accessed September 25, 2007).

[43] Gregg Keizer, "Brazilian Police Bust Dope Ring Built Around Google's Orkut," Informationweek.com, July 21, 2005, www.internetweek.com/software/166401648 (last accessed November 5, 2006; **as of September 25, 2007 the site was no longer accessible**).

[44] "Internet 'Crime Mates' Arrested After Japan Killing," Reuters wire report, August 27, 2007.

[45] Sandra Gonzales, "Profile on MySpace Proves to be S. J. Fugitive's Undoing," San Jose Mercury News, August 9, 2006.

[46] Tracey Christensen, "Police Foil MySpace Murder Plot," 11alive.com, October 10, 2006, www.11alive.com/news/usnews_article.aspx?storyid=85876 (last accessed November 5, 2006; **as of September 25, 2007 the site was no longer accessible**).

[47] Anne Broache, "Principal Sues Ex-students over MySpace Profiles," CNET News.com, April 9, 2007.

[48] "Assistant Principal Sues Students Over MySpace.com Page," Associated Press wire report, September 25, 2006. Interestingly, the complaint, fn. 50 *infra*, states that "statements regarding Ms. Draker's sexuality are considered libel per se under Texas law."

[49] Ken Rodriguez, "Lewd Web Posting About Principal Leads to Lawsuit, School Options," San Antonio Express-News, September 21, 2006; and Jenny LaCoste-Caputo, "Educator Sues Teens Over Page on MySpace," San Antonio Express-News, September 21, 2006.

[50] *Anna Draker v. Benjamin Schreiber, Lisa Schreiber, Ryan Todd, Lisa Todd, and Steve Todd*, Case No. 06-08-17998-CV (DC Medina County, Tex 2006), www.courthousenews.com/draker.pdf (last accessed November 5, 2006; **as of September 25, 2007 the site was no longer accessible**).

[51] *Ibid.*

[52] "It's Big Brother's Space, Too," Associated Press wire report, October 16, 2006.

[53] *Ibid.*

[54] 18 U.S.C. § 871(a), enacted in 1917 reads:

> Threats against President and successors to the Presidency:
>
> (a) Whoever knowingly and willfully deposits for conveyance in the mail or for a delivery from any post office or by any letter carrier any letter, paper, writing, print, missive, or document containing any threat to take the life of, to kidnap, or to inflict bodily harm upon the President of the United States, the President-elect, the Vice President or other officer next in the order of succession to the office of President of the United States, or the Vice President-elect, or knowingly and willfully otherwise makes any such threat against the President, President-elect, Vice President or other officer next in the order of succession to the office of President, or Vice President-elect, shall be fined under this title or imprisoned not more than five years, or both.

[55] Charles Arthur, "Apple Pushes Podcasts Through iTunes," The Register, June 28, 2005.

[56] In fact, ASCAP and BMI already offer a podcast license.

[57] "Durex Buys Condom Product Placements In Podcasts," AdAge.com, March 12, 2005.

APPENDIX

ANSWERS TO CHAPTER QUIZZES

The quizzes and their "answers" in this book are purely meant to be illustrative of emerging issues in Internet law. The answers are not definitive "right" answers; they merely serve as an analysis of the issues raised with speculation on how courts might rule, based on rationales of previous cases. They are presented to make the reader *think*; not to provide definitive answers to legal questions.

CHAPTER ONE

QUIZ ANSWERS

WHAT ARE THE CHALLENGES FOR LEGISLATORS POSED BY THE INTERNET?

Legislative bodies must struggle to understand the new medium and draft laws that will adequately address the issues surrounding it.

WHAT ARE THE CHALLENGES FOR COURTS POSED BY THE INTERNET?

The courts must interpret and apply existing laws and court decisions to issues of Internet law. Many of these laws, including, for example, the First Amendment to the U.S. Constitution drafted more than two centuries ago, were written by men who could not conceive of the new technologies to which their words would be applied today.

WHO CAN BENEFIT FROM STUDYING INTERNET LAW?

Anyone who comes in contact with the Internet can benefit from an understanding of the legal issues related to the Internet.

HOW MANY JURISDICTIONS ARE THERE IN THE UNITED STATES?

Fifty state jurisdictions and the federal government.

WHAT IS FEDERALISM?

A system of government where power is divided between a centralized government and a number of regional governments by a written constitution.

WHICH COURT HAS JURISDICTION TO HEAR APPEALS IN PATENT RIGHTS CASES?

The U.S. Court of Appeals for Federal Circuit.

HOW MANY FEDERAL CIRCUITS ARE THERE?

Thirteen — there are 11 federal circuits plus the District of Columbia and the Federal Circuit.

WHAT IS VENUE?

Venue is the proper location for trial of a lawsuit.

WHERE IS VENUE IN CRIMINAL CASES?

Venue in criminal cases is the judicial district or county where the crime was committed.

WHERE IS VENUE IN CIVIL CASES?

In civil cases, venue is usually the district or county where the defendant resides, where the contract was executed or is to be performed, or where the act occurred.

WHAT QUESTION DOES SUBJECT MATTER JURISDICTION ASK?

"Does the court have authority to hear the case?"

WHAT QUESTION DOES PERSONAL JURISDICTION ASK?

"Does the court have authority over the parties?"

HOW CAN A PERSON SUBMIT TO A COURT'S JURISDICTION ONLINE?

By consent through an online click-wrap agreement.

WHAT IS THE PUBLIC POLICY JUSTIFICATION FOR SMALL CLAIMS COURT?

The public policy interest of providing an inexpensive and informal venue for small claims.

WHAT IS AN ACTION IN REM?

An action in rem means that the plaintiff is proceeding against a "thing" as opposed to a "person."

WHAT ARE THE FOUR PARTS OF A COURT'S WRITTEN OPINION?

Facts, Issue, Holding, and Rationale.

WHAT IS THE PURPOSE OF STUDYING THE RATIONALES OF PREVIOUS DECISIONS?

To infer the direction a court might take on first addressing an issue or that an appellate court might take on resolving a split of opinion.

WHY DO COURTS ADHERE TO THE RULE OF PRECEDENCE?

Courts adhere to the rule of precedence because of the instability that would ensue from a constantly changing landscape of legal decisions continually being overruled.

CHAPTER TWO

QUIZ ANSWERS

Silly Sally has written an opera. It is automatically protected by common law copyright since original works are automatically protected once they are created and fixed in a tangible medium. She neglected to register her work with the copyright office but she is not required to, although it would be advisable to serve as public notice and a prerequisite for any infringement suit she might wish to file. However, Sally did not use a valid copyright notice when she placed "(c) 2008 Silly Sally" on the opera. She failed to use the © symbol and the word "copyright" or the abbreviation "Copr." Sally wrote the opera while she was working at Fred Flintstone's musical instrument repair shop. Fred claims he should be the copyright holder since it was a "Work-Made-For-Hire," but Sally's opera was not a "Work-Made-For-Hire" since it was not created within the scope of Sally's employment.

The ever-industrious Sally also invented a new type of guitar pick while working for Fred. Both agree that the guitar pick was developed within the scope of Sally's employment. Since this was within the scope of employment Sally's guitar pick was "Work-Made-For-Hire." However an invention cannot be copyrighted, although it can be patented. Absent a written agreement to the contrary Sally, as the employee, will own the patent rights.

Fred asked Betty Rubble to create a sales brochure for his business. Betty was not an employee of Fred's so she was an independent contractor. Betty started work right away after speaking with Fred and she was almost finished a week later when the contract Fred had mailed arrived on her doorstep. Fred wants to know if the brochure is "Work-Made-For-Hire." This depends on whether Fred and Betty are in a jurisdiction that follows the 2nd Circuit decision in _Playboy v. Dumas_ or the 7th Circuit decision in _Schiller & Schmidt, Inc. v. Nordisco Corp._ The 2nd Circuit held that the Copyright Act requires that the parties agree before the creation of the work that it will be a "Work-Made-For-Hire," but the actual writing memorializing the agreement does not need to be executed before the creation of the work, while the 7th Circuit requires a writing prior to the creation of the work. So the brochure would be "Work-Made-For-Hire" in the 2nd Circuit but not in the 7th Circuit.

Betty included in the brochure several photographs of the various types of musical instruments that "Flintstone's Fiddles" repairs. She used photographs from an educational book on musical instruments and believes this to be a "fair use." While educational uses may be a fair use, in this case Betty's use was for a commercial, not educational, use so it would not fall under the "fair use" defense.

Betty also added the copyright holder's information below each photograph, but that will not protect her from a copyright infringement lawsuit, although it may mitigate her damages. Betty also used a photograph of a Stradivarius violin that she found online for the cover of the brochure. Betty told Fred that since the photograph was on the Internet in public, it was O.K. to use it since it was obviously in the public domain. But just because something is on the Internet in public does not make it public domain. Unless the copyright has expired the photographs are not in the public domain and Sally and Fred have infringed on the copyright holder's rights.

CHAPTER THREE

QUIZ ANSWERS

Fred Flintstone hires web designer Barney Rubble to create a website for Flintstone's Fiddles Repair Shop. Barney asks Fred for a photograph of Fred to use on the website and Fred gives Barney a copy of a magazine that has a very flattering photograph of Fred accompanying an article on Flintstone's Fiddles. He tells Barney to use that photograph. If the magazine took the photograph of Fred then it is the copyright owner of the photograph and Fred cannot use it without permission. However, if the photograph belonged to Fred and he allowed the magazine to print it with the article, then Fred would be the copyright owner and the magazine merely had the right to use the photograph.

However, copying the text of the magazine article onto the website's "About Us" page, even if it is about Fred, would still be an infringement on the magazine's copyright.

Fred also gives Barney an old Flintstone's Fiddles brochure with a cover photograph of famous violinist Rock Granite. Fred assures Barney that the photograph was licensed and paid for to use in the brochure so they can use it on the website. However, while the photograph may have been licensed for that specific use, *i.e.*, the brochure, unless it was a broad license it may not extend to future uses or uses in another medium.

Barney has included a message board and guest book on the website. Fred is concerned because visitors have been posting product reviews from music magazines on the message board and Slate's Rock & Gravel Co. has been filling the guest book with spam. Fred is correct to worry about visitors posting material that is copyrighted on his message board, thereby infringing on the copyright holder's valid copyright. One solution would be to not allow third parties to post on the website. Another solution would be to make sure he has a moderator who is responsible for policing and cleaning up third-party postings on the message board. And instead of using a guest book that automatically posts user comments directly to the website, Fred could have the guest book form use a "Mailto: form" to send the comments directly to him to review before posting them, so that the spam would never appear on the website.

Barney has cleverly designed the website with frames so that on one page the eBay website auction listings for musical instruments appears framed within Fred's website. The problem with framing is that it could cause possible confusion about, or be used intentionally to misrepresent, an affiliation or endorsement by the framer of the framed website. The framed website loses control over the content surrounding it. The safest course would be for Fred to get express consent from the other website to frame its content.

On the home page Barney has used an inline link to cause a copyrighted photograph of Clay Limestone, a famous musician, to appear on the page. Barney assures Fred that there is no copyright concern here because the photograph is still hosted on the original server and has not been "copied" to Fred's server. While the legal status of inline linking has still not been completely resolved, even if not copied onto Fred's server, it is still "displayed" on Fred's website, and the right of display is an exclusive right of the copyright holder. The result is that the copyrighted work is effectively appearing as part of a web page belonging to someone other than the copyright holder. Inlining is more likely to violate copyright as it creates a potential for creating a derivative work and could cause confusion as to the association, if any, between the two websites. The safest course would be for Fred to get express consent from the copyright holder to use the photograph.

Meanwhile, Pebbles and Bamm-Bamm have been downloading music from Quartzaa, a decentralized P2P file-sharing network. The Bedrock United Record Producers are suing Mr. Quarry, owner of Quartzaa, as a contributory infringer. What defenses can he use? Quarry can start with the Betamax Test: Is the technology capable of commercially significant non-infringing uses? Next, to be a contributory infringer, one must (1) "know or have reason to know" of a direct infringement and (2) materially contribute to the infringing activity. Since Quartzaa is a decentralized file-sharing P2P service it could not actively facilitate and could not stop its users' infringing activity, and thus does not meet this test for contributory infringement. Most importantly, in _MGM v. Grokster_, the Supreme Court held that makers of decentralized P2P software are vicariously liable for their users' actions if they actively and knowingly induce or encourage the user's illegal use.[1] Mr. Quarry should point out that his marketing and promotion of Quartzaa never encouraged or induced users to use the service to infringe on copyrighted material.

BURP has subpoenaed Rocklink, the ISP, to discover the identity of the downloaders. What issues does this raise for both Rocklink and Pebbles and Bamm-Bamm? _RIAA v. Verizon_ held that the Recording Industry Association of America (RIAA) could not use the subpoena process under the DMCA to obtain the name of ISP customers suspected of file-sharing.[2] And a Pennsylvania U.S. District Court ruled that when ISPs are served with subpoenas demanding that they reveal the names of file-sharers, the ISPs must first provide a detailed notice to their customers advising them of their rights, so this decision would apply if Bedrock were within the jurisdiction of that court. However, if Bedrock were in Great Britain, ISPs there must reveal the names and addresses of Britons accused of file-sharing copyrighted songs when subpoenaed, the British High Court has ruled. If the subpoena is honored and the names released, upon being sued by BURP, Pebbles and Bamm-Bamm could fight back by filing a motion for summary judgment, arguing that it was a case of mistaken identity, based solely on their names, an IP address, and a list of songs flagged by file-sharing software.

Noticing Pebbles and Bamm-Bamm's growing interest in music, Fred has an epiphany and decides to expand his business to include music lessons to schoolchildren. So with the help of a good HTML book, a six-pack of Shale beer and a long weekend, Fred completely revamps the Flintstone's Fiddles website. A short time later, Barney files a copyright infringement lawsuit against Fred. Fred tells Barney that he cannot sue him for making modifications to his own website. Fred is wrong. As the creator of the website Barney is the copyright holder and modification of his work would be a derivative work, which is an exclusive right of the copyright holder. Fred would be infringing on one of Barney's exclusive rights.

Chapter Three Quiz Answer Notes

[1] *MGM v. Grokster*, 545 U.S. 913 (2005).
[2] *Recording Indus. Ass'n. of America, Inc. v. Verizon Internet Servs., Inc.*, 351 F.3d 1229 (D.C. Cir. 2003).

CHAPTER FOUR

QUIZ ANSWERS

Silly Sally has named her new guitar pick the "Noise Pick" and advertises it in a music industry magazine as the "Noise Pick®." However, Sally is not allowed to do this because the ® symbol can only be used for a trademark that has been registered with the U.S. Patent and Trademark Office. Since trademarks arise from use, Sally does have a common law trademark but it can only be demonstrated by use of the ™ symbol. Sally might still benefit from registering her trademark because registration would establish a public record of the trademark, allow for federal jurisdiction of any disputes arising from it and aid in preventing fake imports of the "Noise Pick."

Mr. Slate files an infringement and dilution lawsuit against Sally claiming her trademark is likely to cause confusion with his own trademark, the "Rockpick®," a large mechanical machine used to smash boulders. There is no dilution here because the "Rock Pick" is not a famous trademark like Coca-Cola or Pepsi. There is also no infringement, since both the names and the items they represent (a guitar pick and a boulder smashing machine) are sufficiently dissimilar to prevent any confusion between the two products in the minds of consumers.

Meanwhile, Dusty Grit has setup a website for his fictional product, a guitar pick that doubles as a nasal implement, which he calls the "Nose Pick™." The website goes into great detail describing the guitar pick that doubles as a nose pick. Sally, believing that the similarity will confuse her potential customers, files an infringement lawsuit against Dusty. Sally may have a good legal argument because the names and uses of the products are very similar and that similarity may create confusion between the two products in the minds of consumers. What defenses might Dusty raise? Dusty might claim that the website is merely a parody and thus protected under the free speech provisions of the First Amendment. However, the rationale of _PETA v. Doughney_[1] might not support this defense.

Dusty also has a message board on his website where visitors can "buy and sell picks of any kind." Some of the message board participants have been offering fake "Noise picks" on the message board. Sally could file suit against participants offering fake "Noise picks" as direct infringers and against Dusty as a contributory infringer since he "knowingly facilitated" and promoted the sale of the infringing products.

Chapter Four Quiz Answer Notes ▰▰▰▰▰▰▰▰▰▰▰▰

[1] _PETA, Inc. v. Doughney_, 113 F. Supp.2d 915 (E.D. Va 2000).

CHAPTER FIVE

QUIZ ANSWERS

Barney Rubble registers his domain name, Barney.com. Barney plans to post photographs of his little boy Bamm-Bamm lifting the family car and playing with his friend Pebbles. However, the creators of the children's icon "Barney the Brontosaurus," an anthropomorphic orange brontosaurus, have filed a trademark infringement lawsuit against Barney Rubble claiming that his Barney.com website is infringing on their registered "Barney" trademark. They point to the fact that Barney has placed the phrases "Barney" and "orange brontosaurus" in his website meta tags.

Under the Anti-cybersquatting Consumer Protection Act (ACPA) the plaintiff must show both that the domain name registrant had a "bad faith intent to profit from" a trademark and that the registrant registered, trafficked in, or used a domain name identically or confusingly similar to the trademark. Since there is no evidence of bad faith on Barney's part in registering Barney.com, the ACPA does not apply. Barney obviously has an interest in his own name and absent any reference to the trademarked item other than the common name "Barney" it would seem unlikely that the Barney creators would prevail in an infringement lawsuit. However, Barney did include the phrase "orange brontosaurus" in his meta tags, which seems an obvious reference to the trademarked item, "Barney the Orange Brontosaurus." If a website owner places someone else's trademark in his meta tags, has he committed trademark infringement? The answer depends on why he placed the trademarked terms in his meta tags. If his purpose was to divert traffic from the trademark owner's website to his own website, then he may have infringed on the owner's trademark rights. However, if he were merely using the trademarked terms to describe his content in a factual manner, it would be considered "fair use." Here it would appear that Barney was using the "Barney the Brontosaurus" trademark to drive traffic to his website. But it might appear different if Barney had used that phrase to describe the photograph on the website of Bamm-Bamm in an orange brontosaurus costume in his school play.

The creators of Barney the Brontosaurus have also filed suit against Sy B. Squatter, who has registered the domain names Barnie.com and BarnieTheBrontosaurus.com. When children mistakenly type in the misspelling of Barney's name at those websites they are taken to a pornographic website, MutantTeenageLesbianTurtles.com and every attempt to exit the website results in the appearance of a succession of pop-up ads for more sex websites.

Courts will find trademark infringement where the trademark owner's name has been intentionally misspelled in a bad faith attempt to divert visitors away from the targeted website to the violator's website. Mouse-trapping, where the visitor cannot leave a website without clicking on a succession of pop-up windows, is a common element in those cases. Sy B. Squatter is a cybersquatter, someone who deliberately and in bad faith registers domain names in violation of the rights of the trademark owners. He has violated the Truth in Domain Names Act, which makes it illegal to use a "misleading domain name" with the intent to deceive a person into viewing obscenity or to deceive a minor into viewing "material that is harmful to minors." He also violated the ACPA, having had a "bad faith intent to profit from" a trademark and having "registered, trafficked in, or used a domain name identically or confusingly similar to the trademark."

CHAPTER SIX

QUIZ ANSWERS

Wilma Flintstone is not your ordinary housewife. Wilma has invented a revolutionary new housecleaning apparatus, which she has named the "Wonder Broom." The Wonder Broom squirts a cleaning solution onto the floor that is specially formulated to lift up the dirt so that the broom can easily sweep it up. Wilma unveiled her invention two years ago in a two-page spread in *Good Housekeeping* magazine. Last week Wilma filed a patent application, however she did not reveal the formula for her special cleaning solution, either in the article or in her patent application, claiming it is a trade secret. Today she received an office action letter from the U.S. Patent & Trademark Office informing her that her patent application had been rejected. On what basis could the U.S.P.T.O. reject Wilma's application?

Unlike copyrights and trademarks, patents do not arise upon use; a patent application must be filed in a timely manner. Failure to file a timely patent application can result in effective donation of the patent rights to the public domain. The patent application must be filed within one year of description of the invention in a publication, or public use of the invention, or patenting of the invention by another, or offering to sell the invention. Here Wilma waited two years after publishing a description of the invention before filing an application. Another requirement to get a patent is that the inventor must make a full disclosure of the invention, *i.e.*, not hold back any secrets. In exchange for patent rights, the patent (*i.e.*, how the invention works) becomes public information. In this respect, patents are the opposite of trade secrets, another form of intellectual property. Here Wilma held back the details of the formula for her special cleaning solution.

CHAPTER SEVEN

QUIZ ANSWERS

Eddie Haskell has started a new online mail order business selling penis enlargers. Eddie invested $50 in harvesting software to "harvest" e-mail addresses from newsgroups and websites. He then sent a mass e-mailing to two million addresses advertising his "Eddie Haskell Penis Enlarger." He assured recipients of his e-mail that this was not "spam" because the message was in compliance with Bill S.1618 Title III, as the mailing contained the sender's valid e-mail address and a provision to opt out of future mailings.

However, Eddie is murking. A Murkogram is spam that includes a disclaimer stating that the message cannot be considered spam because it is in compliance with Bill S.1618 Title III, known as the Inbox Privacy Act. The bill he refers to was never enacted as a law. Eddie is also in violation of the CAN-SPAM Act by harvesting e-mail addresses and spamming them.

Wally Cleaver was one of the recipients of Eddie Haskell's e-mail and, angered at all the recent spam he had been receiving, Wally retaliated by sending a mail bomb to Eddie.

Wally has broken the law by sending a mail bomb, *i.e.*, a massive amount of e-mail sent to a specific person or computer network with the intention to disrupt service to all mail server customers.

Wally's younger brother Beaver also received Eddie's e-mail and had a marketing epiphany: he set up a website called "Beaver Sex Enhancement Products" where visitors could sign up for his weekly e-mail newsletter showcasing the latest sex toys.

Beaver, by allowing website visitors to opt-in to his mailing list, is engaging in permission-based e-mail marketing. Not all bulk e-mail is spam; only unsolicited bulk e-mail is considered to be spam.

CHAPTER EIGHT

QUIZ ANSWERS

Gilligan received an e-mail notifying him that his bank account would be closed in 24 hours unless he confirmed his account information by clicking on a link in the e-mail and entering his account information on the bank web page. He later discovered that his bank account had been emptied. E-mail spoofing is forgery of an e-mail header so that the message appears to have originated from someone or somewhere other than the true source. In this case, the criminal spoofed the e-mail to Gilligan so that it would appear to have come from Gilligan's bank. Often such spoofed e-mail claims to be from someone in a position of authority, asking for sensitive data, such as passwords, credit card numbers or other personal information — any of which can then be used for a variety of criminal purposes. E-mail spoofing is illegal under the CAN-SPAM Act. Phishing is an Internet scam in which unsuspecting users like Gilligan receive official-looking e-mails that attempt to trick them into disclosing online passwords, user names and personal information. The scam victims are usually persuaded to click on a link that takes them to a fake version of the real organization's website, such as Gilligan's bank. The fake page is set up to procure account numbers and passwords or other personal data from the visitor. The act of sending the visitor to the fake page is known as pagejacking.

Mary Ann visited a quilt-knitting website and now her computer is running very sluggishly. The Professor scanned her computer and discovered a spyware program on her hard drive was sending information from Mary Ann's computer to the quilt-knitting website. Mary Ann was probably a victim of a drive-by download, *i.e.*, a program that is automatically downloaded to a user's computer, often without the user's knowledge or consent. The drive-by download probably installed spyware on her computer. Spyware is any software that accesses and uses a user's Internet connection in the background without the user's knowledge or explicit permission. Spyware often includes programming code that tracks the user's personal information and forwards it to third parties, in this case to the quilting website, without the user's authorization or knowledge. Spyware can crash computers or slow performance, as in this case with Mary Ann, and is often difficult to find and remove. Spyware may violate communications and computer trespass laws.

The Professor drove around the island with his WIFI-enabled laptop until he found a wireless signal coming from Mr. Howell's hut. The Professor intercepted the signal and logged onto the Internet to download an X-rated movie Ginger had starred in. Wardriving is the practice of driving with a Wi-Fi enabled laptop mapping houses and businesses that have wireless access points. Piggy-backing is the use of a wireless Internet connection without permission. The theft of Internet access or bandwidth is the crime of telecommunications theft. The Professor is guilty of telecommunications theft for illegally piggy-backing on Mr. Howell's network without his consent. He may also have committed copyright infringement by downloading a copyrighted film.

The Professor, noting a sign reading "Free WiFi for All Patrons," stopped for lunch at Mrs. Howell's Cyber Café Hut. The Professor sends unsolicited e-mail containing a copyrighted photo of the S.S. Minnow to advertise his new business, "Ship Shape Computing." He launches a mail bomb at a rival's server on the mainland, uploads a Trojan horse to Mr. Howell's computer to seek out and relay Mr. Howell's stock tips and transactions to him, and then downloads some images from lolitas4u.ru, a Russian child porn website. Should Mrs. Howell face any liability for the Professor's actions?

While as yet there is no case law on point, an argument could be made that by providing the technology that enabled the Professor's actions, Mrs. Howell should be held contributorily liable. The Supreme Court has introduced the concept of contributory liability for one providing the enabling technology in copyright cases, and state dram shop acts impose a form of contributory liability for providing the means (alcohol) for the crime committed by a patron (drunk driving). Whether it would be practical to do so, or whether a greater societal interest is provided by allowing free and unfettered Internet access at public facilities and business is another matter.

Mr. Howell has been using a sock puppet in several investment chat rooms and on several message boards touting the stock of Howell Industries, revealing tantalizing insider information and watching the share price rise 500%, whereupon he quickly e-mailed his broker with instructions to sell all his shares in Howell Industries. A sock puppet is a false online identity to deceive others or promote a product or company. By making wrongful posts in an attempt to manipulate securities prices and stating false "facts," "rumors," and alleged "inside information," Mr. Howell has been engaging in a "Pump and Dump" scheme. Pumping up highly volatile share prices in small companies and then selling his own shares in those companies into the false demand that he has created is illegal and violates both state and federal securities laws. Mr. Howell has violated state securities laws, state common law fraud statutes, and the Securities Act of 1933.

Ginger, meanwhile, is frightened by the harassing e-mails that she has been receiving and the threatening messages she has been subjected to in the "Famous Actresses: Where Are They Now?" chat room. Cyberstalking is crime in which the attacker harasses the victim using electronic communication, such as e-mail, instant messaging, or messages posted to a website, chat room, or a discussion group. No federal law exists to protect victims so they must rely on state laws, which offer varying definitions, protections, and penalties.

She seeks out the Skipper, who is online with 17-year-old Gilligan gambling on the HighSeasHighStakes.com casino website. The U.S. government has made several unsuccessful attempts to ban online gambling, however most states prohibit or regulate most or all forms of gambling. The primary concern raised by online gambling is the increased accessibility to gambling for minors and pathological gamblers. Gilligan, being under the age of 18, is a minor. It is illegal in most jurisdictions for minors to gamble. The Skipper may be contributing to the delinquency of a minor. Since federal prosecutors contend that it is illegal for online gambling operators to solicit or accept bets from U.S. citizens, even if their operations are not in the U.S., the website that allowed Gilligan to gamble may be subject to prosecution under federal racketeering and mail fraud laws, the Wire Wager Act, and state laws. The website may have difficulty collecting Gilligan's money — the Unlawful Internet Gambling Enforcement Act makes it illegal for banks, credit card companies, and online payment systems to process payment to online gambling companies.

Gilligan finds a shipwrecked house boat in the lagoon and dutifully repairs it to seaworthiness. He then creates a website offering both day cruises and permanent housing on his house boat. Ginger complains that Mary Ann has posted a roommate notice on his website expressly stating that she does not want to room with lesbians. She enlists the aid of the Island Civil Liberties Union to file a lawsuit against Gilligan, claiming violation of the Fair Housing Act. Is she likely to prevail?

Mary Ann also sues Gilligan, claiming that Ginger's online roommate notice stating "women only" is in violation of the Fair Housing Act. Is she likely to prevail?

The first determination to be made is whether the FHA applies to temporary housing, such as a week-long cruise. What if, instead of a cruise, it was temporary housing in tent shelters set up for hurricane victims that could last for 12–to–24 months? Under the FHA, a "dwelling" is "any building, structure, or portion thereof which is occupied as, or designed or intended for occupancy as, a residence." However, under the "Mrs. Murphy exception," Gilligan would be exempted from the FHA if he rented four or fewer units and lived on the premises. (Mrs. Murphy being a fictional representation of a boarding house owner). The second determination to be made is whether the FHA applies to housing not on land. The Act itself does not address this issue and many people (e.g., cruise ship employees, fishermen, house boat owners) do actually reside "at sea." The FHA provides "for fair housing throughout the United States" and bodies of water, such as Gilligan's lagoon, are within the United States. Assuming, for the sake of argument, that the FHA was applicable to Gilligan's house boat, Ginger would still not prevail because sexual orientation is not a protected class under the FHA. However, Mary Ann might prevail because gender is a protected class under the FHA.

CHAPTER NINE

QUIZ ANSWERS

A group of librarians at the Florida Public Library file a sexual harassment charge with the Equal Employment Opportunity Commission (EEOC). The librarians claim that they are being forced to work in a hostile work environment, and are therefore effectively sexually harassed in violation of federal law, because of the unfiltered computers connected to the Internet where patrons can access pornography.

In an actual claim by librarians, the EEOC found in favor of the librarians' argument that unfiltered Internet connections created a hostile work environment exposing them to sexual harassment.[1]

Upon hearing this, Fetish Freddy, a student who frequently surfs the web in search of such websites, threatens to sue the library if filters are installed. Fetish Freddy raises the issue of his First Amendment right of free speech to have access to information (*i.e.,* the speech of others) in a public library.

Ironically, the public library is funded by the government and the Supreme Court has ruled that the federal government can deny funds for Internet access to public libraries and schools that refuse to put filter software on their Internet computers (*U.S. v. American Library Assn.,* discussed in Chapter 14).[2]

Miss Grundy, a rather conservative old biddy, has filed a lawsuit against AOL, the ISP, for transmitting the pornographic images. She will probably not prevail in her lawsuit, as the Communications Decency Act, discussed in Chapter 14, immunizes ISPs from liability for offensive material posted by someone else.

Billy the Kid, a minor, while using the same library computer that Freddy had been using, stumbles across cached images of naked women and virtual child pornography accessed earlier by Freddy. Billy's mother is outraged and asks whom she can sue. Billy's mother could sue the ISP, and would most likely lose, as would Miss Grundy. She might also sue the library, which would raise even more issues. Does the library have a responsibility to provide a separate filtered computer for minors? Is there a responsibility to supervise minors in a library, and if so, whose responsibility is it, the librarians or the parents?

Does the First Amendment protect "virtual" child pornography? Do state child pornography laws apply to "virtual" child pornography? While the PROTECT Act would appear to outlaw virtual child pornography, the Supreme Court decision in *Ashcroft v. Free Speech Coalition* makes the constitutionality of the PROTECT Act highly questionable.[3] (See the discussion in Chapter 14).

Billy's father, Hoosier Daddy, visits the library to see the offending images for himself, and copies the JPGs of the naked women, which Freddy had downloaded from the Playboy website, and e-mails them to everyone in his office address book. Did Hoosier Daddy violate Playboy's copyright by copying the downloaded images? Did he further infringe on Playboy's copyright by e-mailing them, *i.e.*, distributing them? Remember from Chapter Two that copying and distribution are exclusive rights of the copyright holder, so Hoosier Daddy has infringed on Playboy's copyright. By e-mailing the images to everyone in his office address book, can Hoosier Daddy be charged with sexual harassment? Or would this single incident not be enough to establish a hostile work environment?

Chapter Nine Quiz Answer Notes

[1] *Cynthia L. Smith v. Minneapolis Public Library*, Charge Number: 265A00651; FEPA Number: 0000 (May 23, 2001); *see also* EEOC Determination Re: Unrestricted Internet Access Policy of Minneapolis Public Library Creates Sexually Hostile Work Environment. May 23, 2001, Charge Number: 265A00651, Tech Law Journal, www.techlawjournal.com/internet/20010523eeocdet.asp (accessed September 25, 2007).
[2] *United States v. American Library Ass'n.*, 539 U.S. 194 (2003).
[3] *Ashcroft v. Free Speech Coal.*, 122 S.Ct. 1389 (2002). This case is included in the Cases Section on the Issues in Internet Law website (www.IssuesinInternetLaw.com).

CHAPTER TEN

QUIZ ANSWERS

ClassmateFinders.com is a website where people set up accounts entering their name, address, age, e-mail address, schools attended, occupation, employer, and other personal information about themselves, their lives and their families, hoping to reconnect with former classmates and friends. The website charges a $25 fee to open an account and while it has a form requesting certain information it also contains blank spaces for the individual to enter any additional information he chooses to add. Any member can read any other member's account profile. Hannah Hottie listed her name, address, employer, and a history of her life since graduating from school. Oliver Obsessione had a huge crush on Hannah in high school but lost track of her after graduation. Now, many years later, he joined ClassmateFinders.com and received access to her profile with her contact information. He began by sending Hannah erotic anonymous e-mails and then progressed to phoning her at home and at work. Later, he would leave disturbing notes on her doorstep describing the clothes she had worn and the places she had visited that day. Realizing that Oliver was a cyberstalker, Hannah sought a restraining order against him and filed a civil lawsuit against ClassmateFinders.com, the source of the information he had used to stalk her. What will be her arguments for finding ClassmateFinders.com liable and is she likely to prevail?

Hannah might argue that the threats posed by stalking and identity theft meant that the risk of criminal misconduct was sufficiently foreseeable so that ClassmateFinders.com had a duty to exercise reasonable care in disclosing a third person's personal information to a client.[1] However, in this case, unlike *Remsburg*,[2] Hannah freely supplied all of her profile information, knowing that it would be available on the Internet to other ClassmateFinders.com members. While people are free to disclose and share such information with the world, they must realize there is also a risk of the wrong people gaining unrestricted access to such personal information.

Meanwhile, Hannah's 14-year-old daughter Holly Hottie was in a chat room when she was approached by Pete-the-Perv, a 38-year-old haberdasher. Holly reported Pete to the ISP who in turn reported Pete to the police. Detective Dick Tracy took over Holly's account and, pretending to be the 14-year-old girl, engaged in two dozen instant messages (IMs) with Pete, who made sexual advances toward "her," culminating in an arranged meeting at a local hotel for sex. Pete was arrested and transcripts of the chat room IMs were the main evidence against Pete. What are the legal arguments for and against admitting the chat room transcripts into evidence?

One argument against admitting the chat room transcripts into evidence would be that it was an illegal eavesdropping, assuming the state's wiretap statute can be construed to apply to a computer recording the chat conversation. Also, it would depend whether the state law requires all parties to a conversation to consent before the conversation can be intercepted or recorded. Some courts may also consider whether the chat software used had a default setting to make a permanent record of the conversation, thereby using a combination of imputed knowledge and implied consent to reason that the defendant should have known about the default setting and thus effectively consented to the making of the recording.

Additionally, some courts have focused on the *mens rea* or "state of mind" of the defendant, looking at whether the defendant had a guilty mind and took steps toward bringing the criminal act about, such as showing up at an agreed upon location to meet the "minor." Here Pete did arrange a meeting with Holly and he actually showed up to meet her, and the chat transcripts are evidence of Pete's state of mind and his intent.

Chapter Ten Quiz Answer Notes ▬▬▬▬▬▬▬▬▬▬▬▬▬▬▬▬▬▬▬

[1] *Remsburg v. Docusearch, Inc.*, 816 A.2d 1001 (N.H. Feb. 18, 2003).
[2] *Ibid.*

CHAPTER ELEVEN

QUIZ ANSWERS

Lovebirds.com is an online dating website. Its posted privacy policy states that Lovebirds.com respects the privacy of its members and will never rent or sell any information supplied by members. A year later, Lovebirds.com is sold to a rival dating website, MeetYourMatch.com, which sells copies of its membership list, including the Lovebirds.com members, to various marketers interested in reaching the singles market. MeetYourMatch.com in its privacy policy reserves the right to rent or sell member information.

Lovebirds.com customers might complain to the F.T.C. that by including its membership list in the sale to MeetYourMatch.com it had violated its stated privacy policy by in effect selling its membership list, something its privacy policy said it would not do. Section 5 of the F.T.C. Act prohibits unfair or deceptive acts. If Lovebirds.com was sold to MeetYourMatch.com subject to its existing contracts, then assuming that the privacy policy was a contract between the Lovebirds.com members and Lovebirds.com, then MeetYourMatch.com would be bound to adhere to the privacy policy and not release the names of the Lovebirds.com customers. The F.T.C. considers it a deceptive and unfair practice in violation of §5 of the F.T.C. Act for companies subsequently to modify their privacy policies to permit sharing previously collected customer information without first obtaining express "opt-in" consent from customers.

If Lovebirds.com was not sold to MeetYourMatch.com subject to its existing contracts, then it would appear that the Lovebirds.com members would have little recourse against MeetYourMatch.com.

CHAPTER TWELVE

QUIZ ANSWERS

Krusty the Clown has a website where children enter various contests by submitting their names, ages, addresses, and other personal information online. Krusty wants to make sure that his website does not violate COPPA. What does Krusty need to do to be in full compliance with COPPA?

COPPA defines a child as a person under the age of 13. Under COPPA, the Krusty's website must provide notice about its information collection practices — this means *what* information is collected, *how* it is used, and *to whom* it may be disclosed. The notice must be posted from a link on the home page and on each page where information is collected from children. Krusty's website must also obtain verifiable parental consent before collecting, using, or disclosing any information from a child. It must provide the parent, upon request, with the right to view information submitted by the child and the opportunity to prevent further use, maintenance or subsequent collection of the child's personal information. COPPA also requires that Krusty limit the collection of information required to participate in games or prize offers, and provide reasonable procedures to protect the confidentiality, security, and integrity of personal information that his website receives.

CHAPTER THIRTEEN

QUIZ ANSWERS

Beetle Bailey is an employee of Food Services Corp., an independent contractor for the U.S. military. Bailey travels to foreign U.S. military bases to survey the quality of the food supplied to U.S. troops by Food Services Corp. On one such trip, Bailey noticed that many of the soldiers were keeping milblogs on the Internet so he decided to start his own blog. Bailey read an entry in Private Blabbit's blog stating that the base cook, a local restaurateur who had a contract to prepare meals for the base using the food supplied by Food Services Corp., was actually selling the food shipped by Food Services Corp. on the black market and substituting cheaper, poor quality foodstuffs.

Bailey reprinted Blabbit's entire blog entry in his own blog, "Food for Thought." By publishing someone else's writing without permission Bailey may be liable for copyright infringement. However, if Blabbit had made his blog available for syndication through RSS feeds, then Bailey would have had implied consent to reprint it. It is also possible that Blabbit may have posted his blog under a Creative Commons license that would allow republication under certain conditions.

The base cook sued Bailey for defamation and tortious interference with his business. Defamation is a "published intentional false communication that injures a person or company's reputation." Each one of these elements must be present for the tort of defamation to exist. If the statement is true then Bailey will have a defense to a charge of defamation. Also, the rationale of the decision in _Barrett v. Clark_ that a newsgroup user who posts an allegedly libelous message written by someone else was immune from liability under CDA §230 because she was not the "publisher," only the poster, may provide a defense.[1] To file a cause of action for tortious interference, the cook must show the existence of a contract or business relationship, intentional interference, causation, and damage. The last three elements may be difficult for the cook to show, especially since there is no evidence that it was Bailey's intent to interfere with the cook's contract with the military.

Food Services Corp. fired Bailey for having added in his blog, "If the base chef has been substituting foodstuffs then he must be a superb chef because his meals taste better than the usual Food Services Corp. fare I've tasted in other units." Bailey countered by suing Food Services Corp. for wrongful termination. If an employee posts information about his employer in a public forum, and he had previously signed a confidentiality agreement, then the employee may have breached his fiduciary duty to the company and be in breach of contract. Here we do not know if there was a confidentiality agreement. However, Bailey is not revealing information about his employer or confidential information; he is merely offering his opinion about how the food tastes. Bailey may have a valid claim for wrongful termination; however employers in "at will" states can fire employees even if they wrote the blog on their own time on their own computer outside of the office. Ideally, Food Services Corp. should establish a written policy for employee blogs.

Upset over the controversy, the base commander ordered all milblogs shut down. While military personnel are now required to register their blogs and the content is subject to quarterly monitoring by their commanding officers to ensure they are not violating operational security and privacy restrictions, ordering all milblogs shut down merely to avoid controversy would be a violation of the soldiers' First Amendment rights. In order to order a milblog shut down it would have to violate operational security and privacy restrictions or violate the Uniform Code of Military Justice (UCMJ) by disclosing or "encouraging widespread publication" of classified or specific information about troop movement and location, military strategy and tactics, and soldiers who have been wounded or killed.

Chapter Thirteen Quiz Answer Notes

[1] *Barrett v. Clark*, 2001 WL 881259, 2001 Extra LEXIS 46 (CA Super. Ct. 1996).

CHAPTER FOURTEEN

QUIZ ANSWERS

Charlie Brown is a black student at Ecumenical High School. Each student is given 14mb of space on the school's server to use for e-mail accounts and personal websites. Charlie has used his space to set up a website promoting his theory that blacks are a superior race and that Caucasians and Asians are inferior races. His website includes links to anti-Hispanic and anti-Semitic websites. He has an online game on his website called "Honk When You Kill a Honkey," where players earn points by killing white people. Charlie also has a "hit list" page on his website where he lists "Lucy, Linus, and Patty" as white classmates he would like to see dead. Last week, Charlie used his account to send hate e-mail to every student in the school. The school's options to deal with Charlie's hate website depend on whether Ecumenical High School is a private or public school. Private schools are not agents of the government and therefore can prohibit students from publishing offensive speech using university equipment or services. However, public schools, as agents of the government, must follow the First Amendment's prohibition against speech restrictions based on content or view. But even if Ecumenical High School is a public school, it may choose to restrict student use of its computers and server to academic activities thereby preventing a student like Charlie from creating a hate website or sending hate e-mail from his student e-mail account. Charlie's mass e-mailing to his classmates would be too small to be considered spam under the CAN-SPAM Act and state anti-spam laws. But it might fall under the online harassment laws of certain states.

Charlie has also posted a nude picture of his 15-year-old girlfriend "Snoopy" on his website. Here Charlie would be liable under state and federal child pornography laws. The Supreme Court ruled in 1982, in _New York v. Ferber_, that child pornography was not entitled to First Amendment protection.[1] Also, Snoopy might be able to file an invasion of privacy lawsuit against Charlie Brown.

Chapter Fourteen Quiz Answer Notes ▰▰▰▰▰▰▰▰▰▰▰▰▰▰▰▰▰▰

[1] _New York v. Ferber_, 458 U.S. 747 (1982)

CHAPTER FIFTEEN

QUIZ ONE ANSWERS

Sixteen-year-old Joyce loves shopping online. Joyce is a minor. As long as a minor does not cancel the contract, it is binding on the other party, but a contract with a minor is unenforceable by the other party and voidable at the minor's option. Joyce could legally void the contract and Sluts-r-Us.com could not enforce it.

Before entering the website, Joyce had to click "Yes" on a click-wrap agreement. It was more than 100 pages long, so she scrolled to the bottom and clicked yes without reading it. Most click-wrap agreements are legally binding, even if the terms were not read, if they were available to be read. So had Joyce been an adult, this would have been a legally-binding contract.

Joyce ordered a spiked collar but when it arrived she did not like it and mailed it back. As a minor, Joyce was able to void the contract, as long as she did not keep the merchandise.

Sluts-r-Us.com e-mailed Joyce that they had a "No Returns, No Refunds" policy, clearly stated on page 69 of their click-wrap agreement. While most are legally binding, at least one court has indicated there may be a question of enforceability of excessively long click-wrap agreements. In _Scarcella v. America Online_, the court appeared to accept the argument that a 91-page click-wrap agreement was deceptive because it featured two "OK, I Agree" buttons midway which, when clicked, let customers to "sign" the agreement before reaching its end, but the court did not go so far as to rule it a "deceptive practice."[1]

Joyce then filed a lawsuit against Sluts-r-Us.com, who filed a motion to dismiss based on a clause in their online "Terms and Conditions Agreement" that conditioned use of their website on agreement that all disputes would be submitted to arbitration, not litigation. Joyce really had no reason to file a lawsuit; she should have waited until she was sued by Sluts-r-Us.com and then raised her minority as a defense. The "Terms and Conditions Agreement" on the Sluts-r-Us.com website is essentially a browse-wrap agreement. While some courts have found browse-wrap agreement to be enforceable contracts, most courts would probably find that it did not create a binding contract between the website and the user. As one court remarked: "It cannot be said that merely putting the terms and conditions [on the bottom of the web page] necessarily creates a contract with anyone using the website."[2]

Chapter Fifteen Quiz Answer Notes ▰▰▰▰▰▰▰▰▰▰▰▰▰▰▰▰

[1] _Scarcella v. America Online_ (New York City Civ. Ct. Sept. 2004).
[2] _Ticketmaster Corp. v. Tickets.com, Inc.,_ 2000 U.S. Dist. LEXIS 4553 (C.D. Cal. Mar. 27, 2000).

CHAPTER FIFTEEN

QUIZ TWO ANSWERS

The Skipper hired Gilligan to design a website for the island dwellers. Ginger ordered Gilligan to make the website as glamorous as possible. Mary Ann told Gilligan it had to be practical, not flashy. Mr. Howell insisted that Gilligan make the website a financial and business portal. The Professor instructed Gilligan to make the website an educational one. Whose instructions should Gilligan follow and what clause should Gilligan have included in his web development agreement to deal with this situation? The "authorized contact person" clause designates the person with the decision-making authority. This clause clearly spells out which person in the group, organization, or company has the authority to approve work and authorize changes. This prevents a situation where different members of the group, organization, or company give the web designer conflicting instructions. Therefore, Gilligan should follow the instructions of the authorized contact person designated in the contract.

The Skipper gave Gilligan detailed coordinates to post on the website so that they could be rescued but Gilligan made a mistake and transposed the numbers. Due to Gilligan's negligent error, the castaways' rescue may be delayed indefinitely. The Skipper promised to sue Gilligan if they ever get off the island. What clause should Gilligan have included in his web development agreement to deal with this situation? Gilligan should have inserted a "hold harmless" provision to protect the designer from liability for inadvertent harm caused by changes made at the client's request (*e.g.*, making a typographical error in the price of an item or the date of an event listed on the website).

The Skipper, frustrated with Gilligan's mistakes, hired Mrs. Howell to type in the correct coordinates onto the website, but while Mrs. Howell correctly added the coordinates she inadvertently deleted several lines of HTML code and now the website will not load. The Skipper insists that Gilligan repair the website but Gilligan, referring to the website development agreement, demands to be paid on an hourly rate to do so. To which contract provision is Gilligan referring? Gilligan is referring to the "maintenance" clause that provides that if the client or an agent other than the web designer attempts updating the client's web pages, then the time required to repair any damage made to those pages will be assessed at the hourly rate.

The Skipper refuses to pay Gilligan and instead asks the Professor to fix the website. The Professor not only fixes it but adds many of the features that he originally wanted included in the website. Gilligan then informs the Skipper that he plans to sue for copyright infringement. What is Gilligan talking about? Like many companies who hire web designers, the Skipper does not realize that he does not own the intellectual property rights to the website created by the designer he has hired. The creator of a copyrightable work is deemed by law to be the copyright holder, absent a "Work-Made-For-Hire" agreement or an assignment of rights. Since Gilligan did not grant an assignment of rights to the Skipper, he is the copyright holder of the website and the Skipper has only a limited license to use it, preventing him from making changes without Gilligan's permission. By retaining the Professor to change the website, the Skipper has infringed on Gilligan's copyright. It would be a good idea if Gilligan had included a "copyright to web pages" clause to advise the client that the designer, by law, is the copyright holder of the website that he creates and to provide for the assignment of various rights between the designer and the client, if need be.

The Skipper tells Gilligan he is crazy; the website clearly states "©2008 The Skipper" so Gilligan cannot sue for copyright infringement since the Skipper is clearly the copyright holder. Who is right? Gilligan is correct. The copyright notice on the website in the client's name applies only to the client content and not to the site design or designer content.

The Skipper then agrees to pay Gilligan to return the website to its original state. Gilligan says he will have to charge based on a "major structural change." The Skipper argues that this is merely a "minor cosmetic change." What contract provision would address this issue? The "definitions" clause sets out the clear meaning and intent of the phrases used in the contract. This not only avoids confusion over what may, at first glance, appear to be clear, common terminology. Therefore, phrases like "major structural change" and "minor cosmetic change" should be specifically defined in the contract in the "definitions" clause.

After the website is completed, the Skipper wants to add a picture of his boat. Gilligan is not sure if the photograph supplied by the Skipper is copyrighted by the Skipper or the photographer. What contract provisions might be of some comfort to Gilligan? The "copyright and trademarks" clause states that the client represents that he owns the copyrights and trademarks to any materials given to the designer for inclusion on the website and will hold harmless, protect, and defend the designer and its subcontractors from any lawsuit arising from use of such materials. The "client representations and warranties" clause provides that the client has obtained the rights and licenses to use the materials provided and that the client will indemnify the designer from any third-party lawsuits arising from breach of his representations and warranties.

Glossary

Adware is software in which ads are displayed while the software program is running.

AllWhoIs is a mega search engine website that searches WHO IS databases at multiple domain name registries.

Anti-cybersquatting Consumer Protection Act (ACPA) is a domain name dispute law that gives trademark owners legal remedies against defendants who obtain domain names that are identical or confusingly similar to their trademark, with a "bad faith intent to profit from the mark."

At Will Employee is one who works for a private employer and has no union contract, and can be fired for any reason not specifically prohibited by law.

Bandwidth Theft is the direct linking of images, scripts, sound files, movies, or zipped files to a website from another website's server without that website owner's knowledge or consent, resulting in costly charges for bandwidth usage to the victim's website. Also referred to as *hot-linking* or *direct linking*.

Betamax Standard states that if the technology is capable of commercially significant non-infringing uses, then it does not violate the copyright law.

Bloggers are people who write and maintain their own blogs.

Blogosphere refers to the universe of interconnected blogs, as most blogs have multiple links to other blogs, creating in effect, a network of blogs. The phrase may also refer to the collective community of bloggers.

Blogs (short for web logs) are online diaries or commentaries by individuals.

Browse-Wrap Agreement is a contract that a user may view online but need not do anything to indicate his acceptance.

Buckley Amendment to the Family Educational Rights and Privacy Act of 1974 permits the federal government to cut funding to public schools that violate the privacy of student records. It applies to state colleges, universities, and technical schools that receive federal funds.

CAN-SPAM Act of 2003 (Controlling Assault of Non-Solicited Pornography and Marketing Act) requires use of accurate headers in e-mail messages, requires procedures for recipients to opt out of future e-mails, and forbids e-mail address harvesting.

Canadian Privacy Act of 1983 protects personal information collected by the Canadian government.

Carnivore was the controversial Internet surveillance system developed by the FBI to monitor electronic transmissions of criminal suspects.

Casino-Style Gambling Websites are gambling websites where the user has access to a wide variety of games (*e.g.*, blackjack, poker, roulette, and slot machines) with colorful graphics and background music.

Cause of Action is the legal "grounds" for a lawsuit.

Chat Room is a web page using chat software that can display typed messages in real time.

Child Online Protection Act (COPA) makes it a crime to publish "any communication for commercial purposes that includes sexual material that is harmful to minors, without restricting access to such material by minors." COPA never took effect after the Supreme Court upheld a lower court's injunction of the Act.

Children's Internet Protection Act of 2000 (CIPA) denies federal funds for Internet access to public libraries and schools that refuse to put filter software on their Internet computers.

Children's Online Privacy Protection Act (COPPA) controls how websites can collect and/ or maintain personal information about children. It defines a "child" as under age 13. COPPA applies to "websites directed at children" or where the "website knows it is collecting information from children."

Click-Wrap Agreement is an agreement displayed on a website to web user, who must click a link or button indicating acceptance of the terms in order to proceed further.

Common Law is non-codified law derived from court decisions and precedence.

Consent Decree is a court sanctioned agreement by a defendant to abide by the law, without admitting guilt for previous acts.

Contributory Infringer is one who knows or has reason to know of the infringement and induces, causes, or materially contributes to infringing conduct of another.

Copyright Term Extension Act (CTEA) is the amendment to the U.S. Copyright Act sponsored by Sonny Bono that extended U.S. copyright protection.

Cookies are data stored on the user's computer to maintain information to allow websites that the user has visited to authenticate the user's identity, speed up transactions, monitor the user's behavior, and personalize presentations for the user.

Cookie Poisoning is the modification of a cookie by an attacker to gain unauthorized information about the user for purposes such as identity theft.

Copyright Act of 1976 is the federal statute that governs copyright law in the United States.

Corporate Cyberstalking involves an organization stalking an individual online.

Cyber Griper is a dissatisfied consumer who airs his gripes against a company on the Web, usually in the form of a website devoted to publicizing his gripe with the company.

Cyber Poachers grab domain names when a domain name that a company had previously registered becomes available for any reason.

Cybersquatter is one who deliberately and in bad faith registers domain names in violation of the rights of the trademark owners.

Cyberstalking is a crime where the attacker uses electronic communication (*e.g.*, e-mail, instant messaging, or posts to message boards or chat rooms) to harasses the victim.

Deep-Linking refers to a hyperlink that bypasses a website's home page and takes the user directly to an internal page.

Defamation is a published intentional false communication that injures one's reputation.

Design Patents protect the appearance of an object.

Digital Millennium Copyright Act (DMCA) is a 1998 amendment to the U.S. Copyright Act of 1976 that provides for criminal prosecution with up to 10 years imprisonment for circumventing technical measures that protect copyrighted works.

Direct Infringer is one who actually commits an infringing act, *e.g.*, one who makes and shares copies of a copyrighted work, or otherwise directly infringes on the copyright, trademark, or patent rights of another.

Discovery is the process during litigation where prior to the start of a civil trial, both plaintiff and the defendant can use civil procedural tools such as interrogatories, depositions, requests for production, and subpoenas to compel the production of evidence, in preparation for trial.

Diversity Jurisdiction occurs in civil cases between citizens from different states where amount at stake is more than $75,000, thus requiring that the case be tried in federal rather than state court.

Domain Name Registry is a database showing which domain name maps to which IP address.

Drive-by Download is a program that is automatically and invisibly downloaded to a user's computer, often without the user's knowledge or consent.

E-mail Opt-in Rule is where the recipient must have agreed in advance to receive the e-mail, *e.g.*, by signing up for an e-mail list.

E-mail Spoofing is forgery of an e-mail header so that the message appears to have originated from someone or somewhere other than the true source.

En Banc Hearing is a rehearing of a case by all the judges of a appellate court to reconsider a decision of a panel of the court, where the case concerns a matter of exceptional public importance or conflicts with an earlier decision.

Electronic Signatures in Global and National Commerce Act (the E-SIGN Act) provides legal validity to certain contracts entered into electronically.

European Union Directive on Data Protection requires European Union member nations to implement national legislation to protect the privacy of individuals. It prohibits the transfer of personal data to non-European Union countries that do not meet its "adequacy" standard for privacy protection.

Fact Situation is a description of the facts specific to the case at hand.

"Fair Use" doctrine is an affirmative defense to a copyright infringement claim that allows limited use of a copyrighted work for criticism, comment, news reporting, research, scholarship, or teaching.

Family Educational Rights and Privacy Act (FERPA) of 1974 requires all government agencies (federal, state, and local) requesting Social Security numbers provide a statement on the request form explaining if the Social Security number disclosure is mandatory or optional, how it will be used, and under what statutory authority it is being requested.

Federalism is a system of government where power is divided between a centralized government and a number of regional governments by a written constitution.

Filters are software programs that can block access to certain websites that contain inappropriate or offensive material by scanning for certain words and phrases.

Framing is the process of allowing a user to view the contents of a second website while it is framed by information from the first website.

Gramm-Leach-Bliley Act of 1999 limits when financial institutions may disclose personal information; it also applies to companies, whether or not they are financial institutions, that receive such information.

Habeas corpus (Latin for "you have the body") is a writ directed to one holding an individual in custody or detention commanding that the detained individual be brought before a court to determine the legality of his detention. Its purpose is to ensure that individuals are not unlawfully detained. The writ of habeas corpus dates back to 13th century England and was adopted by the United States.

Hate Speech is speech that denigrates or attempts to inflame public opinion against certain groups of people.

Holding is the court's actual ruling, the answer to the question raised in the Issue; *see Ruling.*

Hotlinking is the process of displaying a graphic file on one website that originates at another; *see Bandwidth Theft* and *Inline Linking.*

HTML is Hyper Text Mark-up Language, the computer language used to create web pages.

Identity Theft is a crime in which an imposter obtains key pieces of personal information (*e.g.*, Social Security number or driver's license number), to impersonate the victim to get credit, merchandise, or services in the victim's name or to provide the thief with false credentials.

Identity Theft Penalty Enhancement Act provides mandatory prison sentences for anyone possessing another's identity-related information with the intent to commit a crime.

Internet Corporation for Assigned Names and Numbers (ICANN) is the organization responsible for overseeing the registration of domain names.

In Personam is a form of jurisdiction in which the plaintiff is proceeding against a "person" as opposed to a "thing."

In Rem is a form of jurisdiction in which the plaintiff is proceeding against a "thing" as opposed to a "person."

Inline Linking, or inlining, is the process of displaying a graphic file on one website that originates at another; *see Bandwidth Theft* and *Hotlinking.*

Instant Message (IM) or **Private Message (PM)** is a chat room feature that allows private messages to be exchanged between two parties.

Intellectual Property is comprised of copyrights, trademarks, patents, and trade secrets.

Internet Service Provider (ISP) is a company that provides access to the Internet.

Issue is the question of law raised by the fact situation.

Jurisdiction is the limit or territory within which a court has the power, right, or authority to interpret and apply the law.

Jurisprudence is the philosophy or science of law.

Keyword Search Advertising is the "sponsored" areas of search engine result listings, matching ads with listings generated by relevant keywords.

Lanham Act governs trademark law in the United States.

Linking Disclaimer is a notice on a website stating that by linking to another website it does not endorse that website or its contents.

ListServs are e-mailed compilations of newsgroup or forum postings.

Madrid Protocol is a treaty for the international registration of trademarks, adopted in Madrid, Spain, on June 27, 1989. It provides for a process of international registration, not an international trademark — trademark applicants get a bundle of national rights, not a single international right.

Mail Bomb is a massive amount of e-mail sent to a specific person or computer network with the intention to disrupt service to all mail server customers.

Malware (short for "malicious software") is any software program or file developed for the purpose of doing harm.

"Marketplace of Ideas" is a metaphor first enunciated by Supreme Court Justice Oliver Wendell Holmes that ideas compete for acceptance against each other — with the underlying faith that the truth will prevail in such an open encounter.

Message Board or Forum is a web page where messages are posted on a page and maintained in static form for an indefinite period, often even permanently archived.

Meta Tags are relevant key words used by search engines to index pages, allowing web surfers to find tagged pages in searches.

Milbloggers are military bloggers.

Miller Test defines "obscene" as "Whether to the average person, applying contemporary community standards, the dominant theme of the material taken as a whole appeals to prurient interest."

Mouse-Trapping occurs when the visitor cannot leave a website without clicking on a succession of pop-up windows.

Murkogram is spam that includes a disclaimer that the message cannot be considered spam because it is in compliance with Bill S.1618 Title III, known as the Inbox Privacy Act.

National Security Letters (NSL) are letters from the FBI typically requesting information from ISPs and other communication providers about subscribers, including home addresses, phone calls that were made, e-mail subject lines, and logs of websites visited.

No Electronic Theft Act prohibits unauthorized distribution of copyrighted material with a value greater than $2,500 over a computer network.

Office Action is a non-final rejection of a patent application by the U.S.P.T.O. because of the existence of "identical or similar marks," or if it finds that the mark is "generic or descriptive."

Online Harassment occurs when the harasser uses the Internet to cause substantial emotional distress to the victim.

Pagejacking occurs where the offender steals the contents of a website by copying some of its pages, putting them on a website that appears to be the real website, and then inviting people to the fake website through deceptive means.

Paris Convention of 1883 provides that if the inventor subsequently files patent applications for the same invention in other member countries within one year after filing the first one, the later applications receive a fictional filing date equal to the filing date of the first patent application.

Parody is literary or artistic work that imitates the characteristic style of an author or work for comic effect or ridicule. A legal parody involves the conveyance of two simultaneous but contradictory messages — it must target the work but be apparent that it is not the original.

Patent is a government-issued grant that confers on the inventor the right to exclude others from making, using, offering for sale, or selling the invention for a period of 20 years, measured from the filing date of the patent application.

Patent Agent is a non-attorney who can prepare a patent application but cannot practice law (*e.g.*, litigate patent matters or write contracts related to patents).

Patent Attorney is a specialized attorney with knowledge and experience in patent law, who has passed a special examination and is registered to practice before the U.S.P.T.O.

Patent Cooperation Treaty of 1970 makes it possible to seek patent protection for an invention simultaneously in each of a large number of countries by filing an "international" patent application.

Peer-2-Peer (P2P) Networking enables direct communication or sharing of information between individual users (*i.e.*, between their computers).

Permission-Based Marketing occurs when the recipient has asked to receive the bulk e-mail.

Personal Information Protection and Electronic Documents Act of 2000 (PIPEDA) is a Canadian statute that applies to the collection, storage, and use of personal information by non-governmental organizations.

Personal Jurisdiction asks, "Does the court have authority over the parties?"

Personalized Phishing is where the victim receives an e-mail containing personalized accurate account information that the scammers have already obtained from other sources of misappropriated consumer data as part of a ruse to obtain even more sensitive information to sell to other scammers.

Pharming is a malicious web redirect that exploits the Domain Name System (DNS) used to translate a website's address into a numerical code for Internet routing.

Phishing (pronounced "fishing") is an Internet scam in which unsuspecting users receive official-looking e-mails that attempt to trick them into disclosing online passwords, user names, and personal information.

Piggy-backing is the use of a wireless Internet connection without permission.

Plant Patents protect the appearance and color of plants.

Podcasting is a method of publishing audio files online that can be downloaded and played offline on portable MP3 players.

Pod Burping refers to the use of a portable media device to inject viruses or malicious code into a corporate network.

Pod Slurping is the use of iPods or other high-capacity mp3 players as portable hard drives to steal information from corporate PCs and networks.

Precedence is the principle that prior decisions are to be followed by courts; *see Stare Decisis*.

Prior Art consists of prior published documents and activities related to a patent claim that serve as evidence of state of the art, *i.e.*, everything publicly known before the invention, as shown in earlier patents and other published material.

Prior Restraint is a government prohibition of speech in advance of publication.

Privacy Policy is a statement on a website explaining how the website collects personal information and what it does with it.

Public Domain refers to created materials that either by law do not get copyright protection, or whose protection under the law has lapsed.

"Pump and Dump" Scheme is a scam where an individual may enter a investment message board or chat room and talk up stocks he already owns and then surreptitiously sell them into the artificial demand he has created.

Rationale is the thought process used by the court in arriving at its Decision or Holding.

Reciprocal Links are mutually agreed-upon hyperlinks between two websites.

Right of Publicity is an individual's right to control and profit from commercial use of his name, likeness, and persona.

RSS (Really Simple Syndication) is a distribution system that lets publishers share web content, such as headlines and text, via XML feeds.

Ruling is a court's actual Decision, the answer to the question raised in the Issue; *see **Holding**.*

Safe Harbor Provision in regulations allows an individual or business to comply with specified standards which then provides shelter from liability under the statute.

Shrink-Wrap Agreements are agreements printed on back of, or included inside, a commercial computer software box. By breaking the shrink-wrap on the package, the purchaser agrees to be bound by the terms of the agreement.

Sock Puppet is a false online identity to deceive others or promote a product or company.

Social Engineering is the use of a variety of methods to trick or manipulate individuals into committing acts or revealing information.

Spam is unsolicited bulk e-mail.

Spim is when spam is sent as an Instant Message (IM).

Sports Gambling Websites are gambling websites that take wagers on the outcome of sporting events.

Spyware is any software that accesses and uses a user's Internet connection in the background without the user's knowledge or explicit permission.

Stare Decisis is Latin for "let the decision stand," embodying the principle that prior decisions are to be followed by the courts; *see* **Precedence**.

Statute of Frauds makes certain oral contracts unenforceable, usually those involving the sale or transfer of land or where performance cannot be completed within one year.

Strategic Lawsuit Against Public Participation (SLAPP) is a civil lawsuit without substantial merit brought by private interests to stop citizens from exercising their political rights or to punish them for having done so.

Subject Matter Jurisdiction asks, "Does the court have authority to hear the case?"

Summary Judgment is a ruling by the court that there is no material issue of fact to be tried, and therefore the cause of action should be dismissed.

Sunshine Laws are rules that allow public inquiry into government affairs, such as laws requiring that meetings of governing bodies be open to the public (*i.e.*, "open meeting laws").

Telecommunications Theft is the crime of stealing Internet access or bandwidth.

"Terms of Use" is a statement on a website stating the rules for persons who wish to use the website.

Treble Damages are a court award of three times the actual damages incurred. They are intended to penalize the guilty party and discourage others from similar behavior.

Trojan Horse is a program in which malicious or harmful code is hidden inside an apparently harmless program or data to later gain control and cause damage. The phrase comes from Homer's *Iliad*; during the Trojan War, the Greeks presented the citizens of Troy with a large wooden horse in which they had secretly hidden their warriors. At night, the warriors emerged from the wooden horse and overran and conquered Troy.

Truth in Domain Names Act is part of the PROTECT Act that makes it illegal to use a "misleading domain name" with the intent to deceive a person into viewing obscenity or to deceive a minor into viewing "material that is harmful to minors."

Typosquatter is a person who registers one or more Internet domain names based on the most common typographical errors that a user might commit when entering a company's registered trademark name

Uniform Domain Name Dispute Resolution Policy (UDRP) is a quick, cost-effective alternative to a lawsuit where there is a dispute over a registered domain name.

Uniform Electronic Transactions Act (UETA) is a model statute for states to adopt to give legal effect to electronic signatures.

URL (Uniform Resource Locator), is the global address of documents and other resources on the World Wide Web.

U.S.P.T.O. is the U.S. Patent and Trademark Office.

Utility Patent is the most common type of patent and applies to inventions that have a use and protects functionality.

Venue is the proper location for trial of a lawsuit.

Vicarious Infringement is liability for the infringing acts of another; it occurs when a party has the right and ability to control an infringer's activity and receives a direct financial benefit from the infringement.

Video Privacy Protection Act of 1988 makes it illegal to disclose what videotapes an individual has rented.

Vlog is a video blog, *i.e.*, a vlogger will sit in front of his or her webcam and film a web log which is then uploaded to a website such as YouTube.com.

Wardriving is the practice of driving with a Wi-Fi enabled laptop computer, mapping houses and businesses that have wireless access points.

Website Development Agreement is a contract between a website designer or developer and his client.

WHOIS is a domain name database maintained by domain name registrars.

Wiki is a collaborative website whose content can be edited by anyone who has access to it.

Wire Wager Act is a 1961 law prohibiting use of "wire communication facilities for transmission in interstate or foreign commerce of bets or wagers or information assisting in placing of bets or wagers on any sporting event or contest."

"Work-Made-For-Hire" is a creative work where the employer, and not the employee, is considered the author.

Worm is a self-replicating virus that does not alter files but resides in the computer's active memory and duplicates itself.

Case Index

V

W

Y

Z

Statute & Treaty Index

Topic Index

C

D

E

AUTHOR BIOGRAPHY

Having been a journalist, web designer, and attorney, Dr. Keith B. Darrell brings a unique perspective to the subject of Internet Law, as the courts and Congress struggle to adapt the 18th Century First Amendment to the 21st Century technology of the Internet.

By age 24, Dr. Darrell had earned his A.A. from Broward Community College, his B.S. in Journalism from the University of Florida, his M.B.A. from Emory University, and his J.D. from the Emory University School of Law. Dr. Darrell is a member of the State Bar of Georgia and the Florida Bar.

Other legal publications by Dr. Darrell include *"Redefining a 'Security': Is the Sale of a Business Through a Stock Transfer Subject to the Federal Securities Laws?,"* 12 **Securities Regulation Law Journal** 22 (Warren, Gorham & Lamont), Spring 1984, and *"The Sale of Business Doctrine Revisited,"* 3 **JD/MBA Journal** 21, Winter 1987. Dr. Darrell has also written **The Web Designer's Client Handbook, Putting Your Business on the Internet, The View Through Tinted Windows,** several fiction short stories, and numerous non-fiction articles.

Throughout his lifetime, Dr. Darrell has held many positions as a reporter, an advertising representative, an entrepreneur, a retail business owner, an insurance agent, a stockbroker, a real estate agent, a web designer, an attorney, and an author. His interests include his pets, photography, genealogy, art, literature, theater, old comic books, and learning about different cultures and languages.

Also Available from Amber Book Company:

The Web Designer's Client Handbook *

Everything You Always Wanted to Know About Websites But Were Afraid to Ask Your Web Designer

by Keith B. Darrell

Softcover • ISBN: 978-0-9771611-1-9
80 pages • perfect bound • 5 x 8.

Order from www.AmberBookCompany.com

Amber Book Company

Seldom has there been so great a need for a book such as **The Web Designer's Client Handbook**. Most people are expert in their own businesses but are clueless when it comes to transporting that business to the Internet. The average person knows nothing of the limitations of web technology or what constitutes good design. Often they do not even consider applying common business principles, such as branding, to their online presence. They often approach the web designer with vague ideas and unreasonable expectations.

Web designers, on the other hand, often do a poor job of communicating to their clients why something the client wants is either technologically not feasible or esthetically undesirable from a design standpoint. There are certain basic concepts that clients need to understand before engaging a web designer to build their website. Either the designer must educate the client or the client must go out on his own and educate himself. Often the designer is too busy or impatient to do so and clients have not had the resources available to them to learn. Until now.

Web designers should stock up on copies of **The Web Designer's Client Handbook** and give them out to every new or potential client!

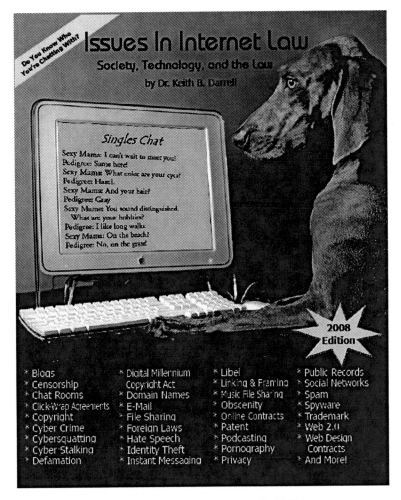

Printed in the United States
202538BV00002B/221-238/A